THE FATHERS
OF THE CHURCH

A NEW TRANSLATION

VOLUME 50

THE FATHERS
OF THE CHURCH

A NEW TRANSLATION

EDITORIAL BOARD

PAULUS OROSIUS

THE SEVEN BOOKS OF HISTORY AGAINST THE PAGANS

Translated by

ROY J. DEFERRARI

The Catholic University of America

THE CATHOLIC UNIVERSITY OF AMERICA PRESS, Inc.
Washington, D. C. 20017

NIHIL OBSTAT:

REVEREND HARRY A. ECHLE
Censor Librorum

IMPRIMATUR:

+PATRICK A. O'BOYLE
Archbishop of Washington

April 29, 1964

The *nihil obstat* and *imprimatur* are official declarations that a book or pamphlet is free of doctrinal or moral error. No implication is contained therein that those who have granted the *nihil obstat* and *imprimatur* agree with the contents, opinions, or statements expressed.

Library of Congress Catalog Card No.: 64-18670

To My Daughter-in-Law

MARY PATRICIA

CONTENTS

BOOK TWO

BOOK THREE

BOOK FOUR

BOOK FIVE

BOOK SEVEN

Chapter	Page

INTRODUCTION

AULUS OROSIUS was probably born at Bracara, now Braga, in Portugal, between 380 and 390. Although a prominent person in his time, he received scant attention in writing from his contemporaries. In fact, from the scanty material available, only a very sketchy outline of his life can be assembled. His surname, Paulus, we are told by the literary-historian Martin Schanz, was first mentioned by Jordanes (middle of sixth century) in his *Getica*. Some would put his place of birth in Tarraco in Spain, but evidence leans more heavily toward Bracara.

We are able to say very little with certitude about Orosius' early life in Hispania. He became a presbyter, that is a parish priest, and took a leading part in the controversies then raging in his region over the teachings of the Priscillianists and Origenists.

From his own writings, it is clear that Orosius was well versed in pagan and Christian culture alike. He had a thorough knowledge of the classical authors of Rome, chiefly, Vergil, Horace, and Cicero, and had undergone a thorough training in the rhetorical schools. Even while attaining all this, he acquired a thorough grounding in Christian principles and became widely known as a man of strong faith.

When Orosius was about thirty years old (413 or 414), he left his native land. The precise reason for leaving is not known. He tells us only that he departed *'sine voluntate, sine necessitate, sine consensu'*,[1] and that his ship under the guidance of divine providence was driven by a storm to the shores of Africa near Hippo, where St. Augustine was living.[2] Some

---

1 Cf. *Commonitorium* 1.
2 *Historiae* 5.2.2.

would believe that the barbarian invaders, the Alans and the Vandals, were ravaging his native land and forced him to flee. Then again, he might well have been seeking counsel and instruction elsewhere to assist him in his struggles against the Priscillianists and Origenists. At any rate, he was received with genuine enthusiasm by his fellow Romans and Christians.

Orosius at once repaired to St. Augustine at Hippo, hoping to discuss with him certain points of doctrine regarding the soul and its origin which were being attacked by the Priscillianists and Origenists. To inform St. Augustine as to the actual teachings of these heretics, Orosius in 414 wrote a *Commonitorium de errore Priscillianistarum et Origenistarum,* to which St. Augustine promptly replied with his treatise, *Ad Orosium contra Priscillianistas et Origenistas.*

But Orosius was not entirely satisfied with the information which he received, and was determined to go to Palestine, to St. Jerome for further instruction. St. Augustine heartily approved, and appeared pleased to have an opportunity to have direct correspondence with St. Jerome through a reliable messenger. He wrote a long letter (number 166) in which, among many other matters, he reveals his respect and affection for Orosius. The following passage (chapter 2) is pertinent here.

'Just now Orosius has come to me, a religious young man, a brother in the Catholic fold, in age a son, in dignity a fellow priest, alert of mind, ready of speech, burning with eagerness, longing to be a useful vessel in the house of the Lord, in order to refute the false and pernicious teachings which have been much more deadly in the souls of Spaniards than the sword of the barbarian has been to their bodies. He hastened from there, even from the shore of the ocean, moved by the report that he might be able to learn from me whatever he wished of the topics in which he was interested. And he did gain something from his coming: first, not to put too much faith in what he heard from me; then, I instructed the man as far as I could; I pointed out to him where he could learn what I could not give him, and encouraged him to go to you. Seeing that he took my advice or command willingly and obediently, I asked him to return from you by way of us when he traveled back to his own country. I have his promise, so I believe this opportunity has been granted me by the Lord to write you about the subjects on which I wish to be enlightened by you. I was looking around for someone to send to you, but it was not easy to find anyone endowed with reliability of conduct, readiness to obey, and experience in traveling; so, when I found this young man, I did not doubt that he was just the one I had been asking of the Lord.'[3]

Early in 415, Orosius traveled to Palestine by way of Egypt, paying due respect to the sacred shrines of Christianity as he went. Pelagius was then trying to spread his false teachings in Palestine, and Orosius joined St. Jerome and others in their struggle against the heresy. This involved them all in a bitter quarrel with John, the bishop of Jerusalem, who was inclined toward the teaching of Origen and influenced by Pelagius.

In 415, Bishop John called the presbyters of his church to a council at Jerusalem. At the invitation of the bishops, Orosius attended the council and set forth the views of St. Augustine and St. Jerome on Pelagianism. He sharply attacked Pelagius, and became involved in a quarrel with Bishop John who was presiding. John charged him with blasphemy. It seems that John had not heard what had actually been said, but what the interpreter thought had been said.

Since Pelagius declared that he believed it impossible for man to avoid sin and become perfect without God's assistance, he was not condemned by John. Rather Bishop John decided that Pelagius' opponents should present their arguments before Pope Innocent. But Bishop John accused Orosius of having maintained that it is not possible for man to avoid sin, even with God's grace. In answer to this charge, and at the same time to publish all the teachings of St. Augustine and

---

3 Translation by Sister Wilfrid Parsons, S.N.D., in volume 30 of this series.

St. Jerome on the disputed question, Orosius wrote his *Liber apologeticus*.[4] In this work, Orosius gives a detailed account of the Council of 415 at Jerusalem, and an accurate and clear treatment of the two chief questions against Pelagius: the capability of man's free will, and Christian perfection in doing God's will here on earth.

Early in 416, Orosius set out from Palestine on his way to St. Augustine in Africa and then home. There is some question as to whether he went directly to Africa or first to the island of Minorca and then to Africa. The probability is that, because of St. Augustine's urgent request, he went to Africa first. He had various commissions to carry out. He had a letter from St. Jerome[5] to deliver to St. Augustine, and writings of the two Gallic bishops, Hero and Lazarus, who were struggling in Palestine against Pelagianism.[6] There were some of the relics of St. Stephen, with an explanatory letter giving a Latin version of their discovery by Lucian, to be placed in the care of Palchonius, the bishop of Bracara.

After delivering his letters and messages and spending a little time with St. Augustine at Hippo, Orosius set out for home. When, however, he reached Minorca and heard of the wars and devastations of the Vandals in Spain, he returned to Africa and rejoined St. Augustine. He had left the relics of St. Stephen in a church on the island of Minorca, where they became the object of a great veneration which spread into Gaul and Spain. At St. Augustine's request, he began his treatise against the pagans. After finishing this work, Orosius disappeared completely from sight. Not even the slightest clue is at hand as to his fate.

Orosius' lasting reputation rests chiefly upon his *Seven Books of History against the Pagans*,[7] thought to be a supple-

---

4 *Liber apologeticus contra Pelagium,* in C. Zangemeister's edition of Orosius, CSEL (Vienna 1882), 5.603-604.

5 Epist. 134.

6 Cf. St. Augustine, Epist. 175.

7 *Historiarum adversus paganos libri septem* (PL 31.663-1174; ed. Zangemeister in CSEL 5, Vienna 1882; also B. T., Leipzig 1889).

ment to the *City of God,* especially the third book, where St. Augustine proves that the Roman Empire suffered as many calamities before Christianity appeared in the world as afterwards, thus combating the arguments of the pagans that the abandonment of their duties had led to disaster. Orosius himself describes the purpose of his work in its dedication. As Orosius tells us in his dedication, St. Augustine wished him to develop this proof in a special work through the whole period of human experience, reviewing the history of all the known peoples of ancient times, bearing in mind the fundamental idea that God determines the destinies of nations.

St. Augustine was not satisfied with the proofs of this thesis which he had drawn entirely from Roman history, from its origin in Troy to the birth of Christ. He asked Orosius to support his argument by bringing in examples from the entire history of the world, and to bring the story on the Roman side from the birth of Christ to his own day. St. Augustine himself had just finished eleven books of the *City of God* and was too busy bringing this work to completion to attempt the preparation of this more complete proof. A certain Julian of Carthage strongly supported St. Augustine in this request.

According to Orosius, two chief empires had governed the world: Babylon in the East, and Rome in the West. Through the intermediate empires of Macedon and Carthage, Rome received the heritage of Babylon. Accordingly, he maintained that there were four great empires in the world's history—Babylon, Macedon, Carthage, and Rome. This view was commonly accepted in the Middle Ages.

Book One gives a brief description of the globe, and outlines its history from the Deluge to the founding of Rome.

Book Two presents the history of Rome to the sack of the City by the Gauls, that of Persia to Cyrus, and that of Greece to the Battle of Cunaxa.

Book Three considers chiefly the Macedonian Empire under Alexander and his successors; also Roman history contemporary with this period.

Book Four continues with the history of Rome to the destruction of Carthage.

Books Five, Six, and Seven present Roman history exclusively, from the destruction of Carthage to Orosius' own time.

The work was completed in 418, and shows signs of haste. Although it does not give us much new historical data, it at least confirms information already available, and sometimes even adds information not at present at hand in other writers.

The Holy Scripture and the chronicle of Eusebius as revised by St. Jerome are widely used as sources; also Livy, Eutropius, Caesar, Suetonius, Florus, and Justin but to a much less extent.

Since Orosius' aim was essentially apologetic, all the calamities suffered by the various people are described. When he found material to suit his purpose, he borrowed it. In the case of two accounts of the same incident, he regularly took the stronger of the two, no matter how exaggerated, for it appeared the better to illustrate his point. The work is superficial and fragmentary, but yet valuable. It contains contemporary information on the period after A.D. 378. Much of this, however, is vitiated by the fact that Orosius was interested in writing apology rather than history.

During the dismemberment of the Empire in the West, Orosius escaped the fate of many of his fellow authors. The fact that in the popular mind he was associated with St. Augustine probably saved him from oblivion. At the end of the fifth century (494), Pope Gelasius in a bull gave his unqualified approval to the *Seven Books,* and thus established Orosius' position in the Church, and caused his work to be widely read. In more erudite circles, it had to yield place to St. Augustine's *De civitate Dei.* Nearly 200 manuscripts are still extant. Most authors quoted only a few passages, some borrowed at length from certain sections of the work, and still less made use of the entire work. Isidore of Seville and Otto of Freising are among these. Alfred the Great translated it into Anglo-Saxon.

SELECT BIBLIOGRAPHY

Texts:

Migne, J. P. *Patrologiae cursus completus, Series Latina.* Text with notes of Havercampus and Bivarius (Paris 1846), XXXI, pref. 635, 663-1174.

Raymond, I. W. *Seven Books of History Against the Pagans.* The Apology of Paulus Orosius, translated with Introduction and Notes (New York 1936).

Zangemeister, C. *Pauli Orosii historiarum adversum paganos libri VII; accedit eiusdem, Liber apologeticus* (Vienna 1882). Vol. V of *Corpus scriptorum ecclesiasticorum Latinorum.*

──────────. *Pauli Orosii historiarum adversum paganos libri VII* (Bibliotheca Teubneriana: Leipzig 1889).

Secondary Works:

Bardenhewer, O. *Geschichte der altkirchlichen Literatur* (Freiburg im Breisgau, 1913-24), 4 Vol.

Ebert, A. *Allgemeine Geschichte der Literatur des Mittelalters* (Leipzig 1889), Vol. I, Pt. 2, pp. 337-344.

Krüger, G. 'Orosius,' in *Geschichte der römischen Literatur* (ed. M. Schanz: Munich 1920), Vol. VIII, Pt. 4, Sec. 2, pp. 483 491.

Labriolle, P. *History and Literature of Christianity from Tertullian to Boethius,* Eng. tr. by H. Wilson, (New York 1925).

Manutius, M. *Geschichte der lateinischen Literatur des Mittelalters* (second edition: Munich 1914).

Teuffel, W. S. *Geschichte der römischen Literatur* (fifth edition: Leipzig 1890), pp. 1165-1168.

Special Works:

Beck, G. F. H. *Dissertatio de Orosii historici fontibus et auctoritate* (Gotha 1834).

Bosworth, J. *King Alfred's Anglo-Saxon Version of the Compendious History of the World by Orosius* (London 1859).

Davids, J. A. *De Orosio et Sancto Augustino Priscillianistarum adversariis, commentatio historica et philologica* (Rotterdam 1930).

Mejean, E. *Paul Orose et son apologetique contre les paiens* (Strassburg 1862).

Moller, D. G. *Dissertatio de Paulo Orosio* (Altorfii 1689).

Mörner, T. *De Orosii vitae eiusque historiarum libris septem adversus paganos* (Berlin 1844).

Paucker, C. 'Die Latinität des Orosius' in *Vorarbeiten zu lateinischer Sprachgeschichte, Kleine Studien,* III (Berlin 1883).

Sauvage, H. *De Orosio* (Paris 1874).

Schilling, H. *König Aelfred's angelsächische Bearbeitung der Weltchronik des Orosius* (Halle 1886).

Svennung, J. *Orosiana: syntaktische, semasiologische, und kritische Studien zu Orosius.* Inauguraldissertation Uppsala Universitets Arsskrift 1922. Filosofi Sprakvetenskap och Historika Vetenskaper, Vol. V (Uppsala 1922).

PAULUS OROSIUS

THE SEVEN BOOKS
OF HISTORY
AGAINST THE
PAGANS

BOOK ONE

Prologue

I HAVE OBEYED YOUR BIDDING, most blessed Father Augustine, and would that I have done so with as much competence as with pleasure. However, I am not completely convinced as to the result, whether I have done well or otherwise. Indeed, you have already labored at this decision, whether I was equal to this task which you bade me, yet I am content with the evidence of obedience alone, if at least I have distinguished it by my will and my effort. For, although on a great and spacious family estate many animals of different kinds are appropriate as a help on the estate, yet the care of the dogs is not the last consideration.[1] In these alone there has been placed by nature a will to press forward to that for which they are trained, and by a kind of inborn pattern of obedience to be held back only by the expectation and fear of punishment, until by a nod or a sign they are set free to do as they please. For they have special faculties, superior to those of beasts and approaching those of rational beings, that is, to distinguish, to love, and to serve. For in distinguishing between masters and strangers, they do not hate those whom they attack, but are zealous for those whom they love, and in loving their master and home they are watchful, not, as it were, because of a body naturally suited for this, but they are alert from a feeling of anxious love. Therefore, too, according to the mystic revelation in the gospels, the woman of Canaan was not ashamed to say that little dogs were

---

1 Vergil, *Georgics* 3.404.

3

eating crumbs under their master's table nor did our Lord
disdain to listen.[2] Blessed Tobias also, following an angel as
his guide, did not scorn to have a dog as his companion.[3] So
bound by a love for you, possessed by all, and by my own
special love, I willingly have obeyed your wish. Since my
humble self owes what I have done to your fatherly bidding
and it is entirely your own, what has come from you returns
to you; this work I have rendered my own, by this alone on
my part, that I did it gladly.

You bade me speak out in opposition to the empty perver-
sity of those who, aliens to the City of God, are called 'pagans'
(*pagani*) from the crossroads and villages of country places or
'heathen' (*gentiles*) because of their knowledge of earthly
things. Although they do not inquire into the future, and
either forget or do not know the past, yet defame present times
as most unusually beset, as it were, by evils because there is
belief in Christ and worship of God, and increasingly less
worship of idols—accordingly you bade me set forth from
all the records available of histories and annals whatever
instances I have found recorded from the past of the burdens
of war or ravages of disease or sorrows of famine or horrors
of earthquakes or of unusual floods or dreadful outbreaks of
fire or cruel strokes of lightning and storms of hail or even the
miseries caused by parricides and shameful deeds,[4] and unfold
them systematically and briefly in the context of this book.
Since you should not be concerned with a trifling work (such
as this), while your reverence is especially intent on finishing
the eleventh book of your work against those same pagans, the
rays of whose first ten books rising, as from a watchtower of
ecclesiastical splendor, rose high and shone over the whole
earth, and since your holy son, Julian of Carthage, servant of
God, demanded that his petition be satisfied in this matter
with the same confidence as that with which he asked for it,

---

2 Cf. Matt. 15.27.
3 Cf. Tob. 6.1.
4 *flagitiis,* crimes against oneself such as drunkenness.

I gave myself to the task and I was especially overcome with
confusion, to whom, as I repeatedly considered the matter, the
calamities of the present times seemed to boil over beyond
measure. For I found the days of the past not only equally
oppressive as these, but also the more wretched the more distant they are from the solace of true religion, so that it has
properly become clear that an avaricious bloody death prevailed, as long as the religion which forbade bloodshed was
unknown; that while the new dawned, the old grew faint;
that the old comes to an end as the new already prevails; that
the old will no longer be when the new shall reign alone. Of
course, we make an exception of those remote and very last
days at the end of the world and at the appearance of Antichrist, or even at the final judgment when Christ the Lord
predicted in Holy Scriptures[5] even by his own testimony that
distresses would occur such as never were before, when according to that very standard which is both now and ever will be,
truly by a clearer and more authoritative discrimination, approbation will come to the saints for the intolerable tribula-
tions of those times and destruction to the wicked.

(1) Since nearly all men interested in writing, among the
Greeks as among the Latins, who have perpetuated in words
the accomplishments of kings and peoples for a lasting record,
have made the beginning of their writing with Ninus, the son
of Belus, king of the Assyrians, because they wish it to be
believed in their blind opinion that the origin of the world
and the creation of mankind were without beginning; yet they
explain that kingdoms and wars began with him as if, indeed,
the human race up to that time lived in the manner of beasts,
and then for the first time, as if shaken and aroused, awoke to
a new wisdom. I have decided to trace the beginning of man's
wretchedness from the beginning of man's sin, touching on
only a few examples and these briefly. Now from Adam, the
first man, to the King Ninus, so-called the 'Great,' when Abra-

---

5 Matt. 24; Mark 13.

ham was born, 3,184 years passed, which either have been
omitted or unknown by all historians. But from Ninus or
Abraham to Caesar Augustus, that is, to the birth of Christ,
which was in the forty-second year of the Caesar's rule, when
the Gates of Janus[6] were closed, for peace had been made with
the Parthians and wars had ceased in the whole world, 2,015
years have passed, in which between the performers and the
writers the fruit of labors and occupations of all were wasted.
Therefore, the subject itself demands that I touch upon briefly
a few accounts from these books which, when speaking of the
origin of the world, have lent credence to past events by the
prediction of the future and the proof of subsequent happenings, not that we may seem to press their authority upon anyone, but because it is worthwhile to recall the general opinion
which is common to all of us. Since, in the first place, if the
world and man are directed by a divine providence, which as
it is good, so also it is just, but man, who by his changeable
nature and freedom of choice is both weak and stubborn, just
as he should be guided with devotion when in need of help,
so he must be reproved with justice for the immoderate use
of his freedom. Everyone, whoever sees the human race
through himself and in himself, perceives that from the beginning of man this world has been controlled by alternating
periods of good and evil, then we are taught that sin and the
punishment of sin began with the very first man. Furthermore,
those who begin with the middle period, although they never
recall early times, have described nothing but wars and calamities. What else should these wars be called but evils befalling
on one side or the other? Moreover, such evils which existed
then, just as they do now to a certain extent, are undoubtedly
either manifest sins or the hidden punishments of sins. What,

---

6 An old Italian deity, represented with a face on the front and another
on the back of his head. He had a small temple in the Forum, with
two doors opposite to each other, which in times of war were left open
to permit the god to accompany the troops, and in peace were closed
to keep him within the City.

then, prevents our unfolding the beginning of this story, the main body of which others have described, and demonstrating, by a very brief account, that earlier ages which were much more numerous endured similar miseries?

Therefore, I intend to speak of the period from the founding of the world to the founding of the City; then up to the principate of Caesar and the birth of Christ, from which time the control of the world has remained under the power of the City, down even to our own time. Insofar as I shall be able to recall them, I think it necessary to disclose the conflicts of the human race and the world, as it were, through its various parts, burning with evils, set afire with the torch of greed, viewing them as from a watchtower, so that first I shall describe the world itself which the human race inhabits, as it was divided by our ancestors into three parts and then established by regions and provinces, in order that when the locale of wars and the ravages of diseases are described, all interested may more easily obtain knowledge, not only of the events of their time, but also of their location.

(2) Our ancestors fixed a threefold decision of the whole world surrounded by a periphery of ocean, and its three parts they called Asia, Europe, and Africa, although some have thought that there should be two, that is, Asia and then Africa to be joined with Europe.

Asia, surrounded on three sides by the Ocean, extends across the entire region of the east. This towards the west on its right touches upon Europe, beginning at the North Pole, but on the left it leaves Africa; yet near Egypt and Syria it is bounded by Our Sea which we generally call the Great Sea.

Europe begins, as I have said, in the north at the Tanais[7] River, where the Riphaean Mountains turned away from the Sarmatian Sea, pour forth the Tanais flood. This river, flowing

---

7 Now called the *Don*, the traditional boundary between Europe and Asia. Its source is Lake Ivan Ozero rather than the Riphaean Mountains as indicated by Orosius.

past the altars[8] and boundaries of Alexander the Great located in the territory of the Rhobasci, swells the Maeotic marshes,[9] whose immense overflow spreads afar to the Euxine Sea near the city of Theodosia. Thence, near Constantinople, a long strait flows forth until the sea which we call Ours[10] receives it. The Western Ocean forms the boundary of Europe in Spain precisely where the Pillars of Hercules are viewed near the Gades Islands and where the Ocean tide empties into the mouth of the Tyrrhenian Sea.

The beginning of Africa is the territory of Egypt and the city of Alexandria, where the city of Paraetonium[11] is located above that Great Sea[12] which washes all the regions and lands in the center of the earth. From here through the places which the inhabitants call Catabathmon,[13] by no means far from the camp of Alexander the Great and above Lake Chalearzus, then passing near the lands of the Upper Avasitae across the deserts of Ethiopia, Africa reaches the Southern Ocean. The boundaries of Africa toward the west are the same as those of Europe, that is, the mouth of the Strait of Gades. The farthest boundaries are the Atlas Range and the islands which the people call Fortunatae.[14]

And since I have given briefly the general divisions of the tripartite world, I shall take care, as I promised, to point out the regions of the parts themselves.

---

8 The limits of Alexander's conquests as marked by the soldiers of Alexander. Cf. A. R. Anderson, *Alexander's Gate, Gog, and Magog, and the Inclosed Nations* (Cambridge, Mass., 1932).

9 The Sea of Azof.

10 *Mare Nostrum,* Our Sea, i.e., the Mediterranean Sea. Cf. V. Burr, *Mare Nostrum* (Stuttgart, 1932).

11 A seaport town in Northern Africa, between Egypt and Syrtes, now *Marsa Labeit.*

12 The Mediterranean.

13 A tract of land in Libya, between Egypt and Cyrenaica, now *Akabah,* with a city of the same name.

14 The fabulous islands of the Western Ocean, according to some, the Canary Islands.

Asia has at the center of its eastern boundary on the Eastern Ocean, the mouth of the Ganges River, on the left the Promontory of Caligardamana, to the southeast of which lies the island of Taprobane,[15] at which point the Ocean begins to be called the Indian Ocean. To the right of the Imavian Mountains, where the Caucasian[16] Mountains end, is the Promontory of Samara, at the base of which lies the mouth of the Ottorogorra River, at which point the Ocean is called the Serian Ocean.

In this territory is India, with the Indus River on the west which empties into the Red Sea, and the Caucasian Range on the north; the rest of India, as I have said, is bounded by the Eastern and the Indian oceans. This country has forty-four peoples, apart from the island Taprobane with its ten cities and the numerous other inhabited islands.

From the Indus River which is on the east, up to the Tigris River which is to the west, are the following regions: Arachosia, Parthia, Assyria, Persida, and Media, in a mountainous and rough territory. These have the Caucasian Mountains on the north, the Red Sea and the Persian Gulf on the south, but in between flow the principal rivers, the Hydaspes and the Arbis. In these regions there are thirty-two peoples. Moreover, this territory in general is called Parthia, although Holy Scripture often calls the entire area Media.

From the Tigris River up to the Euphrates River is Mesopotamia, beginning in the north between the Taurian and Caucasian Mountains. To the south of this, we have in order, Babylonia, then Chaldaea, and lastly Arabia Eudaemon, which, between the Persian and Arabian Gulfs, extends toward the east in a narrow tract of land. In these lands there are twenty-eight peoples.

From the Euphrates River which is on the east, up to Our Sea which is on the west, then from the north, that is, from

---

15 An island in the Indian Ocean, now *Ceylon*.
16 'Caucasus' as used by Orosius refers to the entire chain of mountains stretching from the Black Sea to the Pacific Ocean, as well as the shorter range usually associated with the name.

the city of Dagusa which is located on the boundary between
Cappadocia and Armenia, not far from the place where the
Euphrates rises, down to Egypt and to the end of the Arabian
Gulf, which extends southward in a long and narrow furrow
abounding in rocks and islands from the Red Sea, that is, from
the Ocean in a westerly direction, is the territory generally
called Syria. Its largest provinces are Commagene, Phoenicia,
and Palestine, not including the countries of the Saraceni and
the Nabathaei. There are twelve nations in this territory.

At the head of Syria is Cappadocia, which has Armenia as
its boundary on the east and Asia[17] on the west, on the northeast the Themiscyrian Plains and the Cimmerian Sea, and on
the south the Taurian Mountains. At the base of these mountains lie Cilicia and Isauria extending to the Cilician Gulf,
which faces towards the island of Cyprus.

Asia Regio or, to speak more correctly, Asia Minor,[18] except for the eastern part where it approaches Cappadocia and
Syria, is surrounded on all sides by water: on the north by the
Euxine Sea, on the west by the Propontis and the Hellespont,
to the south by Our Sea. Here stands Mount Olympus.

Lower Egypt has Syria and Palestine on the east, Libya on
the west, Our Sea on the north, and on the south a mountain
called Climax, Upper Egypt, and the Nile River. This river
seems to rise from the shore where the Red Sea begins at a
place which is called Mossylon Emporium; then flowing some
distance and forming an island in its midst called Meroe;[19]
finally, bending to the north, swollen by seasonal floods, it
waters the plains of Egypt. Some authors say that this river
has its source not far from Mount Atlas and straightway dis-
appears in the sands, and, after a short interval, gushes forth
into an enormous lake and then flows eastward through the
Ethiopian Desert to the Ocean, and again turning to the left
descends to Egypt. Indeed, it is true that there is such a great

---

17 i.e., Asia Minor.
18 The term 'Asia Minor' is probably used here for the first time.
19 Sometimes written 'Merve.'

river which has such a source and such a course, and which in truth begets all the monsters of the Nile. The barbarians near its source call it the Dara, but the other inhabitants call it the Nuhul; but here in the region of the peoples who are called Libyo-Egyptians, by no means far from that river which we have said rushes forth from the shore of the Red Sea, it is received and swallowed up in a huge lake; unless perchance, by a hidden course, it erupts into the bed of that river which descends from the east.

Upper Egypt extends far into the east. On the north, it has the Arabian Gulf; on the south, the Ocean. From the west, it begins with Lower Egypt, and on the east, it is terminated by the Red Sea. Here there are twenty-four peoples.

Since we have described the southern part of all Asia,[20] it remains for me to explain the part that is left, from the east to the north. The Caucasian Range first rises among the Colchi who dwell above the Cimmerian Sea, and among the Albani who are near the Caspian Sea. Indeed, up to its eastern end it seems to be one ridge, but it has many names. Many would wish these mountains to be considered as belonging to the Taurian Range, because in very fact the Parcohatras Mountains of Armenia between the Taurian and Caucasian is thought to make the Taurian continuous with the Caucasian; but the Euphrates River shows this not to be so, for pouring forth from the base of the Parcohatras Mountains, directing its course to the south, it keeps itself to the left and the Taurian Mountains to the right. So the Caucasus between the Colchi and the Albani, where it also has passes, are called the Caucasian Mountains; from the Caspian passes to the Armenian Gates or to the source of the Tigris River between Armenia and Iberia, they are called the Acroceraunian Mountains. From the source of the Tigris River to the city of Carrhae between the Massagetae and the Parthi, the mountains become the Ariobarzanes; from the city of Carrhae to

---

[20] Orosius has included parts of Africa in this description.

the town of Cathippus between the Hyrcani and the Bactriani, the mountains become the Memarmalian, where amomum[21] grows. The nearest range here is called the Parthau. From the town of Cathippus to the village of Saphri between Dahae, Sacaraucae, and the Parthyenae are the Oscobares Mountains, where the Ganges River rises and assafoetida[22] grows; from the source of the Ganges to the sources of the Ottorogorra River which are from the north, where the Paropamisadae Mountains lie, is the Taurian Range; from the sources of the Ottorogorra to the city of Ottorogorra between the Chuni Scythians and the Gangaridae are the Caucasian Mountains. The farthest range, between the Eoae and the Passyadrae is the Imavus, where the Chrysorhoas River and the Promontory of Samara meet the Eastern Ocean. So from the Imavus Mountains, that is, from the tip of the Caucasian Range and the right division of the East, where the Serian Ocean extends, to the Promontory of Boreum and the Boreum River, and thence to the Scythian Sea which is on the north and to the Caspian Sea which is on the west, and to the extended range of the Caucasus which is on the south, there are forty-two nations of the Hyrcanians and Scythians, who wander widely because of the widespread barrenness of the land.

The Caspian Sea rises from the Ocean in the region of the northeast, and its shores and lands in the vicinity of the Ocean are thought to be desert and uncultivated. From here toward the south, it extends through a long channel until, spread out over a wide expanse, it terminates at the base of the Caucasian Mountains. So in the territory from the Caspian Sea which is toward the east, along the edge of the Northern Ocean up to the Tanais River and the Palus Maeotis which are to the west, along the shores of the Cimmerian Sea which is from southwest, to the heights and passes of the Caucasus which are to the

---

21 An aromatic shrub, from which the Romans prepared a costly, fragrant balsam.
22 The juice of the plant *laserpitium, assafoetida,* a gum resin taken from its root.

south, there are thirty-four peoples. The nearest region is generally called Albania; the more distant region, near the sea and the Caspian Mountains, is called the land of the Amazons.

The territory of Asia has been described as briefly as possible. Now I shall wander over Europe with my pen to the degree that it is granted to the knowledge of man.

Europe begins from the Riphaean Mountains, the Tanais River, and the Palus Maeotis, which are toward the east, extends along the shore of the Northern Ocean to Gallia Belgica and the River Rhine which flows from the west, thence to the Danube. This last river is also called the Hister; it comes from the south and flowing toward the east empties in the Pontus. On the east is Alania; in the center, Dacia, where also is Gothia; then there is Germania where the Suebi possess the largest part. Among all these there are fifty-four peoples.

Now I shall explain the territory which the Danube separates from the land of the barbarians in the direction of Our Sea.

Moesia has on the east, the mouth of the Danube River; on the southeast, Thrace; on the south, Macedonia; on the southwest, Dalmatia; on the west, Histria; on the northwest, Pannonia; and on the north, the Danube.

Thrace has on the east, the Gulf of the Propontis and the city of Constantinople which was formerly called Byzantium; on the north it has part of Dalmatia and a gulf of the Euxine Sea;[23] on the west and on the southwest, Macedonia; and on the south, the Aegean Sea.

Macedonia has on the east, the Aegean Sea; on the northwest, Thrace; on the southeast, Euboea and the Macedonian Gulf; on the south, Achaia; on the west, the Acroceraunian Mountains in the narrows of the Adriatic Gulf, which mountains are opposite Apulia and Brundisium; on the west, Dalmatia; on the northwest, Dardania; and on the north, Moesia.

---

23 Dalmatia is southwest of Thrace. Orosius gives us a confused picture here.

Achaia is almost entirely surrounded by water, for it has on the east, the Myrtoan Sea; on the southeast, the Cretan Sea; on the south, the Ionian Sea; on the southwest and the west, the islands of Cephalenia and Cassiopa; on the north, the Corinthian Gulf; and on the northeast, a narrow ridge of land by which it is joined to Macedonia or rather to Attica. This place is called the Isthmus on which is Corinth, with the city of Athens not far away to the north in Attica.

Dalmatia has Macedonia on the east; Dardania on the northeast; Moesia on the north; Histria, the Liburnian Gulf, and the Liburnian Islands on the west; and on the south, the Adriatic Gulf.

Pannonia, Noricum, and Raetia have Moesia on the east, Histria on the south, the Poenean Alps on the southwest, Gallia Belgica on the west, the source of the Danube and the boundary that separates Germany from Gaul between the Danube and Gaul on the northwest, and the Danube and Germany on the north.

The territory of Italy extends from the northwest to the southeast, having on the southwest, the Tyrrhenian Sea; on the northeast, the Adriatic Gulf. That part of Italy which is common and contiguous with the continent is walled in by the barriers of the Alps. These, rising from the Gallic Sea above the Ligurian Gulf, first limit the territory of the Narbonese, then Gaul and Raetia, until they drop in the Liburnian Gulf.

Gallia Belgica has on the east, the River Rhine and Germany as its boundaries; on the southeast, the Poenean Alps; on the south, the province of Narbo; on the west, the province of Lugdunum; on the northwest, the Britannic Ocean; on the north the island of Britain.

Gallia Lugdunensis, extended very long and consistently very narrow, half surrounds the province of Aquitania. On the east, this has Belgica, and on the south, part of the province of Narbo, where the city of Arles is located and the Rhone River is received into the Gallic Sea.

The province of Narbo, a part of the Gauls, has on the east, the Cottian Alps; on the west, Spain; on the northwest, Aquitania; on the north, Lugdunum; on the northeast, Belgica Gallia; on the south, the Gallic Sea, which is between Sardinia and the Balearic Islands, with the Stoechades Islands[24] in front where the Rhone River empties into the sea.

The province of Aquitania is made into a circle by the slanting course of the Liger River,[25] which for the most part forms the boundary of the province. It has on the northwest, the ocean which is called the Aquitanian Gulf; on the west, Spain; on the north and the east, Lugdunum; and on the southeast and south, it touches the province of Narbo.

Spain, taken altogether, by its natural contour is a triangle, and is almost made an island by the surrounding Ocean and Tyrrhenian Sea. Its first corner, looking toward the east, pressed in on the right by the province of Aquitania, on the left by the Belearic Sea, is inserted within the territory of the Narbonese. The second corner extends toward the northwest, where Brigantia, a city of Gallaecia, is located and raises its towering lighthouse, one of the few memorable structures, toward the watchtower of Britain. Its third corner is where the Gades Islands, facing the southwest, look upon the Atlas Mountains with the gulf of the ocean intervening.

The Pyrenaean forest-pastures form the boundary of Hither Spain, beginning on the east and extending on the northern side to the Cantabri and Astures, and thence through the Vaccaei and the Oretani, whom it has to the west; Carthage, situated on the shore of Our Sea, fixes the boundary.

Further Spain has the Vaccaei, Celtiberi, and Oretani on the east; on the north, the Ocean; on the west, the Ocean; and on the south, the Strait of Gades; from here Our Sea, which is called the Tyrrhenian Sea, flows in.

---

24 A group of islands on the southern coast of Gaul, near Massilia, now *Isles d'Hyères*.
25 The Loire.

Since the Ocean has islands which are called Britain and
Ireland and which are located opposite the Gauls in the general direction of Spain, these will be described briefly.

Britain, an island in the Ocean, extends for a long distance
northward; to the south, it has the Gauls. A city which is
called Portus Rutupi[26] affords the nearest landing place in
this country for those who cross over; thence, by no means
far from the Morini, it looks upon the Menapi and the Batavi
in the south. This island is eight hundred miles in length and
two hundred miles in width.

Moreover, in the rear whence it lies open in a limitless
ocean, rest the Orcades Islands,[27] of which twenty are unin-
habited and thirteen inhabited.

Next we have the island of Thule,[28] which, separated from
the others by an indefinite space and situated in the middle of
the Ocean toward the northwest, is known to barely a few.

Ireland, an island located between Britain and Spain, extends at greater length from south to north. Its nearer parts
in the direction of the Cantabrian Ocean look from afar over
a broad expanse upon Brigantia, a city of Gallaecia, which
extends from the southwest to the northwest, from that promontory particularly where the mouth of the Scena River is
and the Velabri and the Luceni are established. This is rather
close to Britain and narrower in expanse of territory, but
more useful because of its favorable climate and soil. It is
inhabited by the tribes of the Scotti.

Mevania[29] also is very close to Britain and is itself not small
in extent and is rich in soil. It is, likewise, inhabited by the
tribes of the Scotti.

These are the boundaries of all Europe.

---

26 A town of the Cantii, in Britain, now *Richborough* in Kent.

27 Islands near Scotland, now the *Orkneys*.

28 An island in the extreme north of Europe, according to some, Iceland;
   according to others, Mainland, the largest of the Shetland Islands.

29 The Isle of Man. Cf. J. J. Keenan, *Place-Names of the Isle of Man*
   (Douglas, 1925).

As I have said, when our ancestors explained that Africa should be accepted as a third part of the world,[30] they did not follow measurements of space but computations of divisions. Indeed, this Great Sea, which rises from the Ocean on the west, turning more to the south, has limited and made the boundary of Africa narrower between itself and the Ocean. Therefore, some also, although believing it to be equal in length yet much narrower, think it unfitting to call it a third part but rather allot Africa to Europe, that is, they have preferred to call it a portion of the second part. Furthermore, since much more land is uncultivated and unknown in Africa because of the heat of the sun than in Europe because of severity of the cold, for almost all animals and plants become more lastingly and endurably adapted to the severest cold than to the severest heat, this evidently is the reason why Africa seems smaller in every respect as to location and people, for because of its nature, it has less space and because of its bad climate more desert. The description of Africa by provinces and nations is as follows.

Libya Cyrenaica and Pentapolis are in the first part of Africa, next to Egypt. This region begins at the city of Paraetonium and the Catabathmon Mountains and from here extends along the sea as far as the Altars of the Philaeni.[31] The territory behind it up to the Southern Ocean, the Libyo-Ethiopian and Garamantian peoples inhabit. Egypt is on the east of this region, the Libyan Sea on the north, the Greater Syrtis[32] and the land of the Troglodytes on the west, opposite which is the island of Calypso, and on the south is the Ethiopian Ocean.

The province of Tripolis, which is also called Subventana or the land of the Arzuges, where the city of Leptis Magna is located, although they are generally called Arzuges throughout

---

30 Cf. Orosius 1.2.1.
31 Altars of the Philaeni, a frontier town of Cyrene, named after two Carthaginian brothers who, out of love for their country, permitted themselves to be buried alive.
32 On the northern coast of Africa, near Cyrenaica, now the *Gulf of Sidra.*

the long limits of Africa, has on the east, the Altars of the
Philaeni between the Greater Syrtis and the Troglodytes; on
the north, the Sicilian Sea or rather the Adriatic Sea and the
Lesser Syrtis;[33] on the west, Byzacium as far as the Lake of
Salinae; on the south, the barbaric Gaetuli, Nathabres, and
Garamantes, stretching to the Ethiopian Ocean.

Byzacium, Zeugis, and Numidia. Now first we find that
Zeugis was not the name of one *conventus*, but a general name
for the whole province. So Byzacium where the city of Hadrumentum is, Zeugis with Magna Carthago, Numidia with the
cities of Hippo Regius and Rusiccada, have on the east the
Smaller Syrtis and the Lake of Salinae; on the north, Our Sea
which faces the islands of Sicily and Sardinia; on the west,
Mauretania Sitifensis; on the south, the Uzarae Mountains,
and behind these extending as far as the Ethiopian Ocean, the
nations of the Ethiopian peoples.

Mauretania Sitifensis and Mauretania Caesariensis have
Numidia on the east; on the north, Our Sea; on the west, the
river Malva;[34] on the south, Mount Astrixis which separates
the fertile soil and the sands that stretch as far as the Ocean
in which the Gangines Ethiopes roam.

Mauretania Tingitana is the last part of Africa. This region
has the Malva River on the east; Our Sea on the north as
far as the Strait of Gades which is hemmed in between the
two opposite promontories of Abyla and Calpe; on the west,
the Atlas Mountains and the Atlantic Ocean; on the southwest,
the tribes of the Autololes who are now called Galaules and
occupy the territory as far as the Western Ocean.

Here is the boundary line of the whole of Africa. I shall
now describe the locations, names, and extent of the islands
which are in Our Sea.

---

33 Near Byzacene, now the *Gulf of Cabes*. On account of shoals and rocks,
both Syrtes were very difficult to navigate.
34 A river in Africa, between Mauretania and Numidia, now called
Maluja.

The island of Cyprus is surrounded on the east by the Syrian Sea which is called the Gulf of Issus, on the west by the Sea of Pamphylia, on the north by Aulon of Cilicia, and on the south by the Syrian and Phoenician seas. Its extent is one hundred and seventy-five miles in length and one hundred and twenty-five miles in width.

The island of Crete is bounded on the east by the Carpathian Sea, on the west and north by the Cretan Sea, and on the south by the Libyan Sea which is also called the Adriatic. It is one hundred and seventy-two miles long and fifty miles wide.

The islands of Cyclades, of which the first is Rhodes on the east, Tenedos on the north, Carpathus on the south, and Cythera on the west, are bounded on the east by the shores of Asia; on the west by the Icarian Sea; on the north by the Aegean Sea; and on the south by the Carpathian Sea. Moreover, all the Cyclades amount to fifty-four in number. These islands have an extent from north to south of five hundred miles, from east to west of two hundred miles.

The island of Sicily has three promontories, one of which is called Pelorus and faces the northeast, the nearest city of which is Messana; the second, which is called Pachynum at which is the city of Syracuse, faces toward the southeast; and the third, which is called Lilybaeum where the city of the same name is located, is pointed toward the west. The distance from Pelorus to Pachynum is one hundred and fifty-nine miles, and from Pachynum to Lilybaeum one hundred and eighty-seven miles. This island is bounded on the east by the Adriatic Sea, on the south by the African Sea which is located opposite the Subventani and the Lesser Syrtis, and on the west and on the north it has the Tyrrhenian Sea, extending on the north to the eastern strait of the Adriatic Sea which divides the Tauromenitani of Sicily and the Bruttii of Italy.

Sardinia and Corsica are islands divided by a narrow strait of twenty miles in width. Of these, Sardinia has on the south opposite Numidia, the Caralitani; opposite the island of Corsica, that is, toward the north, it has the Ulbienses. It possesses in length an expanse of two hundred and thirty miles; in width, eighty. This island is bounded on the east and northeast by the Tyrrhenian Sea which faces the harbor of the City of Rome, on the west by the Sardinian Sea, on the southwest by Balearic Islands located far away, on the south the Numidian Gulf, and on the north, as I have said, Corsica.

The island of Corsica because of its many promontories is full of corners. On the east, it has the Tyrrhenian Sea and the harbor of the City; on the south, Sardinia; on the west, the Balearic Islands; and on the northwest and north, the Ligurian Gulf. Moreover, it is one hundred and sixty miles in length and twenty-six miles in width.

The Balearic Islands are two, the larger and the smaller, on each of which are two towns. The larger toward the north has the city of Tarracona facing it in Spain; the smaller, Barcelona. The island of Ebusus lies near the larger. Then on the east, these islands face Sardinia; on the northeast, the Gallic Sea; on the south and southwest, the Mauretanian Sea; and on the west, the Iberian Sea.

These are the islands situated throughout the entire Great Sea from the Hellespont to the Ocean which, from both their culture and history, are held to be the more famous.

I have, as briefly as possible, completed a survey of the provinces and islands of the whole world. I shall now cite the local misfortunes of the individual nations, just as they arose incessantly from the beginning, and how and by whom they came into being, insofar as I am equal to the task.

(3) Since, after the formation and adornment of this world, man, whom God had made upright and immaculate, and likewise the human race depraved by lusts had become sordid with sins, a just punishment followed upon unjust license. This sentence of the Creator, God and Judge, destined for sinning men and for the earth because of men, and to last forever as long as men should inhabit the earth, although we all either unwillingly prove it by denying it or uphold it by confessing it, man's own weakness imprints upon men's stub-

born minds that which it could not convince them to describe faithfully. Then, after the sea had poured back upon the whole earth and a flood was let loose, when with the whole world covered there was but a single expanse of sky and sea, the most truthful writers very clearly declare that the entire human race was destroyed, a few being saved in the Ark because of the worthiness of their faith to establish a new origin of the race. Yet those also testified that this was true, who though ignorant of the past, at least of its calamitous times, and of the Author of time Himself, yet from the indication and the evidence from stories which we are accustomed to see on distant mountains scabrous with shellfish and snails, also often hollowed out by water, have learned by conjecture. Although still other arguments worthy of mention and of definite trust can be set forth by us, nevertheless, let these two principal ones suffice concerning the transgression of the first man and the condemnation of his descendents and his life, and finally concerning the above-mentioned destruction of the whole human race, provided only that, if pagan historians in some way have touched upon our affairs, these instances be set forth more fully together with others in the very order in which they inveigh against us.

(4) One thousand three hundred years before the founding of the City, Ninus,[35] the first king of the Assyrians, as my opponents themselves wish to call him, because of his lust for power waged war abroad, and throughout all Asia for fifty years carried on a bloody life by warfare; starting from the south and the Red Sea, in the extreme north, he laid waste and dominated the shores of the Euxine Sea; and he taught barbaric Scythia, until then unwarlike and inoffensive, to stir up its dormant ferocity, to realize its strength, and to drink, not as heretofore the milk of domestic animals, but the blood of men, finally to conquer while she was being conquered.

---

35 The son of Belus, the first king of Assyria, husband of Semiramis, and builder of Nineveh. According to Berosus, he was the third king.

Then, he overcame in battle Zoroaster,[36] the king of the
Bactrians, and likewise, as they say, the inventor of magic,[37]
and slew him. Afterwards, he himself, while storming a city
in rebellion against him, was struck by an arrow and died.
His wife, Semiramis,[38] when he died succeeded to the throne,
bearing the spirit of a man and wearing the clothes of her
son,[39] and for forty-two years she kept her people, now lusting
for blood from their experience with it, busy with the
slaughter of nations. The woman, not content with the boundaries which she had inherited from her husband, who at that
time was the only warlike king and who had acquired these
lands in the course of fifty years, added Ethiopia to her empire by war and drenched it with blood. She also waged war
on the peoples of India,[40] where no one except herself and
Alexander the Great had ever entered. Such action at that
time, namely, to persecute and slaughter peoples living in
peace, was even more cruel and serious than it is today, because at that time there were neither the incentives for war
abroad, nor such great temptation to exercise cupidity at
home. This woman, burning with lust and thirsting for blood,
in the midst of unceasing adulteries and homicides, after she
had slaughtered all whom summoned by royal command she
had delighted by holding in her adulterous embrace, finally,
after shamelessly conceiving a son and impiously abandoning
him, and after later having incestuous relations with him, covered up her private disgrace by a public crime. For she decreed
that between parents and children no reverence for nature in

---

36 According to Berosus, Ninyas, the son of Ninus, killed him.

37 St. Augustine (*City of God* 21.14) says: 'The only new-born baby that
ever laughed, they say, was Zoroaster; but what woe that monstrous
laugh portended! He became, they say, the inventor of magical arts,
only to find that they failed to ward off even the enemies of the
empty felicity of his life on earth, for he was beaten in battle by King
Ninus of Assyria when he himself was the ruler of Bactria.'

38 The ancient Assyrian form Samiramis is regularly used by Orosius.

39 Since she had similar features and a like voice, she concealed her sex
and pretended to be the son of Ninus.

40 In this campaign she failed.

the conjugal act was to be observed and that each should be free to do as he pleased.

(5) Cornelius Tacitus also, among others, relates that one thousand one hundred and sixty years before the founding of the City, the region bordering on Arabia, which was then called Pentapolis, was burned completely by a fire from heaven. He speaks as follows: 'Not far from there the fields which they say were once fertile and occupied by great cities burned by a stroke of lightning; but traces remain of the disaster, and the land itself, substantial in appearance, has lost its power of fertility.'[41] And although in this place he said nothing about the cities which had been burned because of the sins of men, as if ignorant of them, a little later, as if forgetful of his plan, he adds the following, saying: 'Although I have admitted that cities, once famous, were burned by fire from heaven, yet I believe that the land was infected and corrupted by exhalations from the lake.'[42] By this statement having confessed, although unwillingly, what he knew and admitted regarding the burnt cities, which without doubt burned because of punishment due sins, he openly professed that he did not lack faith in his knowledge but lacked the will to express his faith. This will now be set forth by me more fully.

On the border of Arabia and Palestine, where the mountains sloping on both sides are received by the fields below them, were five cities: Sodom, Gomorrah, Adama, Soboim, and Segor. Of these, Segor was small but the others were large and spacious, for the soil near these was fertile and the Jordan River, spreading out through the plains and dividing them into sizeable areas, gave increases in productivity. For this entire region, which made bad use of its blessings, an abundance of riches was the cause of evils. For out of abundance came luxury, and out of luxury grew such disgraceful passions that men rushed upon men committing base acts with-

---

41 Cf. Tacitus, *Histories* 5.7.
42 *Ibid.*

out ever considering place, condition, or age. So God, becoming enraged, poured fire and brimstone down upon this land and, burning the entire region with its peoples and cities, condemned it to eternal ruin as a witness of His judgment for future generations,[43] so that even now, though the contour of the region is visible, the region itself is covered with ashes and the middle of the valley, which the Jordan had watered, is now covered over by the overflowing sea. So much divine indignation was roused over matters regarded by the people as small that, because of this, namely, that they, misusing their blessings, had made the fruits of His mercy into nourishment for their passions, the very land itself which had had these cities, first burned by fires, then covered by water, disappeared from public view into eternal damnation.

(6) So now, if it so pleases, let those who cast as much spit upon Christ whom we have shown to be the Judge of the centuries, distinguish between the cases of Sodom and Rome, and let them compare their punishments; these matters must not be discussed at length by me because they are known to all. Yet how gladly would I accept their opinions, if they would faithfully acknowledge what they really feel. And yet I do not think that it ought to be taken very seriously that they murmur occasionally about Christian times and this in out-of-the-way places, since the feelings and views of the entire Roman people may be learned from the harmonious expression of their unanimous judgment. Moreover, the Roman people have borne witness unmistakably that the brief interruption of their customary pleasures caused them little and slight concern so that they freely exclaim: 'If our circus is again restored to us, we will have suffered nothing'; that is to say that the swords of the Goths had accomplished nothing at Rome, if the Romans still be allowed to view the circus games. Unless perchance, as is the opinion of many people in our time, those who after a long period of freedom from

---

43 Cf. Gen. 19.24,25.

care consider even the slight anxiety that has arisen an intolerable burden, prefer these very mild admonitions with which we are all sometimes reproved to the punishments of others of which they have only heard and read. At any rate, I warn these of this very fate of the people of Sodom and Gomorrah, that they may be able to learn and understand how God has punished sinners, how He can punish them, and how He will punish them.

(7) One thousand and seventy years before the founding of the City, the Telchines and Caryatii fought a stubborn battle against Phoroneus,[44] king of the Argives, and against the Parrhasians,[45] hope of victory being doubtful and without decision. Shortly afterwards, these same Telchines defeated in battle fled from their native land and unaware of the real situation, believing that they were cutting themselves completely off from contact with the whole civilized world, seized the island of Rhodes, which was formerly called Ophiussa, as if it were a place of safety.

One thousand and forty years before the founding of the City, there was in Achaia a raging flood which caused widespread devastation to almost the entire province. Since this flood happened in the days of Ogygius, who was the founder and king of Eleusis at that time, he gave the name to the place and to the period.

(8) In the one thousand and eighth year before the founding of the City, Pompeius,[46] the historian, and Justin, his epitomizer, tell us there was first an unusual harvest, so rich as to cause disgust, then a continuous and intolerable famine which Joseph, a just and wise man, relieved by divine foresight.

---

44 Son of Inachus, king of Argos, and brother of Io, said to have been the first to use fire and to unite his people.

45 Poetic for Arcadians.

46 Pompeius Trogus, the Augustan historian, a Vocontian from Gallia Narbonensis, whose grandfather was enfranchised by Pompey and whose father served under Caesar, wrote zoological, and perhaps botanical, works, used by the Elder Pliny, and a Universal History in forty-four books, entitled *Historiae Philippicae*.

Among other things Justin says the following: 'Joseph was the youngest among his brothers. His brothers, fearing his superior ability, kidnapped him and sold him to foreign merchants. After he had been carried off by these men to Egypt, and when he had learned the arts of magic there through his shrewd native ability, in a short time he became very dear to the king himself. For he was very wise in interpreting prodigies and was the first to establish the science of interpreting dreams, and no branch of divine or human law seemed unknown to him; so true was this that, foreseeing even the barrenness of the fields many years before they became so, he gathered in the harvests, and so great were the proofs of this skill of his that his advice seemed to come not from man but from God. The son of Joseph was Moses who, besides inheriting his father's knowledge, was also graced by an attractive appearance. But the Egyptians, when they were suffering from scabies and tetter, warned by an oracle drove him together with other sick persons from the boundaries of Egypt, lest the disease spread to a greater number.'[47] This, then, is Justin's statement. But since this same Moses, who, according to the testimony of these historians, was a wise and well-informed man, described these events fully and more accurately, because they were carried on by himself and his followers, the lack of knowledge on the part of these men must first be supplemented by his trustworthiness and authority which even they acknowledge, and then there must be refuted the deceitful malice of the Egyptian priests, who through cunning, as is very evident, tried to remove from one's memory the manifest wrath and mercy of the true God, and gave a particularly confused story piecemeal, so as not to show that He, to the reproach of their idols, ought to be worshiped, who by His counsel had taught them to announce these disasters and by His help to avoid them; or perchance if we accept these matters more kindly, they have forgotten the truth. For through the foresight of that Joseph of ours, who

---

17 Justin, *Histories* 36.2.

was a servant of the true God and who was dutifully and seriously intent upon the welfare of his Master's people, they themselves as priests had an abundance of the fruits of the earth: yet because they were false priests, they were not pained when others went hungry. As the saying goes: 'Whoever is satisfied, forgets; he who suffers pain, remembers.'[48] Although the histories and records hold back proof, the land of Egypt itself as a witness offers proof of that period, for at that time, being brought under the power of the king and restored to its own cultivators, it has from that day down to the present time unceasingly paid a tax of a fifth part of its entire harvest. Thus this great famine occurred during the reign of Diopolita, king of Egypt, also known as Amasis, at the time when Baleus was ruling among the Assyrians and Apis among the Argives. Preceding the seven years of famine, however, there were seven other years of plenty. The abundance of these years, which would have perished through neglect in proportion to the abundance of the crops, our Joseph with his usual shrewdness collected and stored up and saved all Egypt. He amassed all the money for the Pharao and all the glory for God, rendering by his most just stewardship 'tribute to whom tribute was due and honor to whom honor,'[49] and he acquired the flocks, lands, and wealth of all; moreover, the very ones who had sold themselves with their lands in return for a fixed agreement, he released in return for a fifth of their property. This Joseph, whom God had established for the Egyptians as the author of their salvation, who would believe that this Joseph had passed out of their memory in so short a time that a little later the Egyptians condemned his sons and his entire kinship to slavery, afflicted them with hardships, and crushed them by massacres? Therefore, it is not surprising if now also some are found who, when they would remove the sword hanging over their necks by pretending to be Christians, either conceal the very

---

48 Cf. Cicero, *Pro Murena* 20.42.
49 Cf. Rom. 13.7.

name of Christ by which alone they are saved, or make accusations against Him and assert that they are oppressed in the time of those through whose merits they are liberated.

(9) Eight hundred and ten years before the founding of the City, Amphictyon,[50] the third king after Cecrops,[51] reigned at Athens. In his time, a great flood carried away the larger part of the people of Thessaly, a few being saved by taking refuge in the mountains, especially on Mount Parnassus, in whose environs Deucalion then held sway; those who then fled to him on rafts and took refuge with him upon the twin ridges of Parnassus he assisted and supported; on this account it is said that the human race was saved by him. Plato testifies that at this time, too, in Ethiopia numerous plagues and terrible diseases afflicted Ethiopia almost to the point of desolation. And lest perchance it be believed that there were intervals between God's anger and the fury of war, Father Liber[52] at this time drenched India with blood, a land already reduced to subjection, filled it with slaughters and polluted it with lusts—and this to a nation that was never offensive to anyone, being content with the quiet peace of a slave.

(10) Pompeius and Cornelius[53] testify that in the eight hundred and fifth year before the founding of the City, unspeakable disasters and intolerable plagues settled upon the Egyptians. Although, indeed, both of these authors gave out the following facts to be recorded relative to the Jews, they disturbed me somewhat by their diversity. For Pompeius or perhaps Justin speaks in this manner: 'When the Egyptians were suffering from scabies and tetter, being warned by an oracle they banished Moses and the sick from the boundaries of Egypt, so that pestilence might not make its way among more peoples. So, having become the leader of the exiles, he

---

50 An Amphictyon is said to have named the city.
51 The legendary most ancient king of Attica and founder of the citadel of Athens.
52 Later identified with Dionysus and Greek 'Bacchus.'
53 i.e., Pompeius Trogus and Cornelius Tacitus.

stealthily carried off the sacred vessels of the Egyptians; the Egyptians, seeking to regain these by force, were compelled by storms to return home.'[54] But yet Cornelius on the same subject says: 'Most authors agree that, when a wasting disease which disfigured the body had broken out throughout Egypt, the King Bocchoris, having approached the oracle of Ammon[55] in search of a remedy, was ordered to purge his kingdom and to drive into other lands this race of men as being hateful to the gods. Thus, when these peoples were sought out and gathered together, and afterwards were abandoned in the desert, while all the others were downcast with weeping, Moses alone of the exiles advised them not to look for aid from their gods nor from men, but to place their trust in themselves and in him as a God-sent leader, by whose help, first of all, they would cast off their present miseries.'[56] Thus Cornelius tells us that the Egyptians themselves forced and drove the Jews into the desert, but later he adds unwittingly that in Egypt they cast off the afflictions with the help of their leader, Moses. So it is shown that certain actions vigorously taken by Moses had been concealed. Justin, likewise, asserts that when Moses was driven out together with his people, he stole the sacred vessels of the Egyptians and that when the Egyptians strove to recover them by force, they were repulsed and forced back by storms and returned home. This particular writer set forth more data but yet does not state all that the other one concealed. So, since both have given testimony to Moses as a great leader, his deeds and his words should be set forth just as they were carried out and related by him.

When the Egyptians tortured the people of God, that is, the race of Joseph, through whose efforts they had been saved, after having oppressed them by the labor of slaves, and when furthermore by a cruel edict they had forced these people to

---

54 Justin, *Histories* 36.2.
55 Zeus Ammon, originally the god of the city of Thebes in Egypt.
56 Tacitus, *Histories* 5.3. The exact meaning of this entire passage is very much in doubt.

slay their own offspring, God through Moses as His messenger
ordered His people to be set free so as to serve Him; He inflicted very harsh punishments upon the Egyptians for their
contempt and stubbornness, and they, crushed and worn out
by ten plagues, finally forced those whom they had been unwilling to set free even to hasten their departure. After offering water turned into blood to those burning with thirst, a
remedy for their torments worse than the torments themselves;
after the horrible spreading of the filth of frogs over all clean
and unclean things; after the glowing sciniphes,[57] nowhere to
be avoided, made the entire atmosphere alive; after even the
dog-flies ran through the interior parts of their bodies with
loathsome movements and brought torments as severe as they
were filthy; after the general ruin and destruction of all the
flocks and cattle; after running sores and spreading ulcers and,
as they themselves preferred to call them, 'scabies and tetter'
erupted over their entire bodies; after hail mixed with fire
crushed men, flocks, and trees; after swarms of locusts when
they had devoured everything and had attacked even the very
roots and seeds; after a darkness had come that was terrifying
with its apparitions, so dense as to be felt, and so lasting as to
bring death; and finally, after a general slaughter of the first-
born throughout all Egypt and a common period of mourning
for everyone, those who had not yielded to God when He
commanded, yielded when He punished,[58] but soon, because
of very insincere repentance, they had the audacity to pursue
the exiles and for their impious obstinacy, paid the extreme
penalty. For their king led the entire army of Egypt equipped
with chariots and cavalry against the exiles, whose number we
can infer from this evidence, or at least, especially from this
argument alone, that once six hundred thousand men became
frightened and fled before it. But God, the protector of the
oppressed and the punisher of the stubborn, suddenly divided

---

57 Usually *cinifes* in Latin, a stinging insect.
58 Cf. Exod. 1-14.

the Red Sea and, with the boundaries of rigid water spread
apart on both sides, He held the sides erect like mountains,
so that without hindrance the good, urged on by the hope of
finding an end to their journey, entered upon the road to
safety of which they had despaired and the wicked entered
a pitfall of unexpected death. And so as the Hebrews proceeded safely over the dry passage, and the masses of stationary
water collapsed behind them, the entire Egyptian multitude
with their king[59] was overwhelmed and killed, and the entire
province, which had previously been tortured by plagues, became empty by this last slaughter. Even today there exists
most reliable evidence of these events. For the tracks of chariots and the ruts made by wheels are visible, not only on the
shore, but also in the deep, as far as sight can reach, and, if
perchance for the moment they are disturbed either accident-
ally or purposely, they are immediately restored through divine
providence by winds and waves to their original appearances,
so that whoever is not taught the fear of God by the study of
revealed religion, may be terrified by His anger through this
example of His accomplished vengeance.

In these days, too, the heat became so strong, continuous,
and intense that it is said that the sun, having passed through
the regions outside of its course, affected the whole world, not
with warmth, but burned it with fire, and neither the Ethi-
opians who were more accustomed than others to tolerate
heat, nor the Scythians who were unaccustomed to it, could
endure this heat pressing down and beating upon them. From
this instance, some people, while not attributing to God His
ineffable power, but seeking empty, petty explanations, in-
vented the ridiculous story of Phaethon.

(11) Again, in the seven hundred and seventy-fifth year before the founding of the City, in the struggle between the
children of the brothers Danaus and Aegyptus, fifty parricides

---

59 Cf. Exod. 14.

were committed in one night.[60] Later Danaus himself, the contriver of so many crimes, being driven from the kingdom which he had acquired by so many shameful deeds, withdrew to Argos, and there shamefully persuading the Argives to an outrageous act drove Sthenelas, who had received him as a fugitive and in need, from his kingdom and he himself became king. The hospitality of the blood-thirsty tyrant Busiris[61] in Egypt was barbarous and his religion at the time was more so; he drank the blood of his innocent guests to the health of the gods who were participants in his crimes, and this practice I would view as undoubtedly detestable to men or perhaps it would seem detestable even to the gods themselves. At that time, too, a parricide was added to the incest involving Tereus, Procne, and Philomela, and more horrible than either of these crimes was a meal prepared of food too horrible to mention, for because her sister (Philomela) had been deprived of her chastity and her tongue cut out, the mother (Procne) killed her little son, and his father (Tereus) ate him. In those days, too, Perseus traveled from Greece into Asia, and there, after a severe and long war, he conquered barbarian tribes and, finally, as victor he gave his own name to a conquered tribe, for they are called Persians from Perseus.

(12) But now I am forced to confess that for the purpose of anticipating the end of my book, I am passing over many de-

---

60 This legend is much confused. The following is its core. The two fathers quarrelled; to settle the dispute Aegyptus wanted his sons to marry Danaus' daughters, while Danaus and his offspring were strongly opposed. As the weaker party, Danaus and his family fled to Argos, where they claimed help and shelter from their kin. Aegyptus' sons pursued them, and Danaus consented to the marriages, secretly instructing his daughters to kill their husbands on the wedding night. They all obeyed him except Hypermestra who spared her husband Lynceus and helped him escape. The legend becomes hopelessly involved from this point on. Thus there were only forty-nine and not fifty murders.

61 According to Greek mythology, an Egyptian king, son of Poseidon, who slaughtered on the altar of Zeus all foreigners who entered Egypt. He did this on the advice of Phrasius, a soothsayer from Cyprus, in order to free the land of continued famine.

tails concerning the circumstances of the numerous evils of the age and am abbreviating everything. For in no way could I have at any time passed through so dense a forest of evils unless I were able at times to hasten my progress by frequent leaps. For inasmuch as the kingdom of the Assyrians was governed by some fifty kings through the one thousand one hundred and sixty years up to the reign of Sardanapallus, and almost never up to that time had peace from offensive and defensive wars, what end will be achieved if we try to recall them by enumerating them to say nothing of describing them? This is especially so, since the deeds of the Greeks must not be passed over and those of the Romans especially must be surveyed. Nor is there any need for me now to recount the disgraceful deeds of Tantalus and Pelops, more disgraceful when told. Among these is the story of how Tantalus, king of the Phrygians, after most disgracefully seizing Ganymede, the son of Tros, king of the Dardanians, held him firmly in his most disgusting embrace, as the poet Phanocles[62] confirms, who relates that a very great war was stirred up because of this; or perhaps because he wishes this very Tantalus to seem to be a servant of the gods, he tells that he seized the boy and prepared him in his household for the lust of Zeus—this very Tantalus who did not hesitate to use his own son, Pelops, at Zeus' banquets. One grows tired, too, of referring to the struggles of Pelops, however great they may have been, against Dardanus and the Trojans, which, since they are customarily recounted in stories, are listened to with little attention. I am also omitting those stories about Perseus, Cadmus, the Thebans, and the Spartans which are related by Palaephatus[63] as he describes them through inextricable windings of successive

---

62 A Greek elegiac poet, place and date of birth unknown, living in the period of Philip and Alexander. The six fragments from his verse seem all that has come down to us from one elegiac poem, entitled Ἔρυτες ἢ Καλοί. This was a catalogue poem which dealt with the affection of gods and heroes for beautiful boys.

63 Wrote, perhaps in the late fourth century B.C., a work, extant only in an excerpt, in which myths are rationalized.

evils. I am silent about the disgraceful acts of the Lemnian women;[64] I pass over the lamentable flight of Pandion, king of the Athenians; I keep secret the hatreds, debaucheries, and parricides of Atreus and Thyestes, hateful even to the gods. I omit Oedipus, the killer of his father, the husband of his mother, the brother of their children, and his own stepfather. I prefer not to speak of how Eteocles and Polynices labored in mutual combat that one of them might become a parricide. I do not wish to recall Medea, 'smitten with a cruel love' and joyful with the slaughter of her little children, and whatever else was committed in those times. It is to be wondered at how men endured what even the stars are said to have fled from.

(13) In the five hundred and sixtieth year before the founding of the City, a very bitter struggle arose between the Cretans and the Athenians in which, after disastrous losses on both sides, the Cretans won a bloodstained victory; they delivered the children of noble Athenians over to the Minotaur to be cruelly devoured (I do not know whether I would speak of this creature more aptly as a wild animal with the qualities of a man or as a human being with the qualities of a beast), and they fattened this hideous monster on the royal children snatched from Greece. In these same days, the Lapithae and the Thessalians struggled in conflicts no less renowned. But Palaephatus also relates in the first book of his *Concerning Incredible Tales* that the Lapithae believed and asserted that the Thessalians were themselves Centaurs, for the reason that, when their horsemen ran here and there in battle, each of them seemed to be a single body made up of horse and man.

(14) Four hundred and eighty years before the founding of the City, Vesozes,[65] king of Egypt, eager to engage in war with the South and North regions, separated by almost the whole heaven and the whole sea, or to annex them to his

---

64 All murdered their husbands in one night.
65 Justin, *Histories* 2.3, gives the name as Sesostris.

kingdom, first declared war on the Scythians after he had previously sent ambassadors to tell them as enemies to obey his
laws. In answer to this, the Scythians replied to the ambassadors that their extremely rich king had taken up a war against
poor people foolishly, and that he himself ought to fear this
war more than they because it was clear that, on account of the
uncertain results of the war, there would be losses rather than
rewards. Furthermore, they said that they would not wait
until he attacked them, but that they of their own accord
would go forward to plunder. There was no delay, for deeds
followed these words. First, they forced Vesozes to flee in
terror back into his own kingdom; then, they attacked the
army now without a leader and they seized all its war equipment, and they would likewise have ravaged all of Egypt had
they not been impeded and repelled by the marshes. Then,
returning immediately, they forced Asia, overcome by endless
slaughter, to pay tribute, and after remaining there for fifteen
years at war, they were recalled finally by the demands of their
wives who declared that unless they returned they would seek
offspring from their neighbors.

(15) Moreover, in the meantime among the Scythians, two
youths of the royal family, Plynos and Scolopetius, driven from
home by a faction of the nobility, took with them a large band
of young men and settled on the shore of Cappadocia Pontica
near the Thermodon River with the Themiscyrian Plains
nearby, where, after a long period of plundering, they were
slaughtered in ambush by the united action of their neighbors.[66] The wives of these, aroused by their exile and widowhood, took up arms and, that there might be a common incentive for all from a like condition, they killed the husbands
who had survived and, incensed against the enemy, at the cost
of their own blood exacted vengeance for the slaughter of their
husbands by destroying their neighbors. Then, after obtaining peace by force of arms, they entered marital relations with

---

66 This entire chapter is taken, almost bodily, from Justin, *Histories* 2.4.

foreigners; they killed male children as soon as they were born; but nurtured the females carefully after burning off the right breasts of the infants, that they might not be impeded in the shooting of arrows. For this reason, they have been called Amazons.[67]

These women had two queens, Marpesia and Lampeto, who divided the army into two parts and drew lots for the responsibilities of war and the defense of the homeland in turn. Then, when they had subdued Europe for the most part and had captured some cities of Asia, and furthermore, had themselves founded Ephesus and other cities,[68] they summoned home the principal part of their army, heavily laden with the richest booty; the rest of the army, which had been left to guard their empire in Asia, together with Queen Marpesia, was slaughtered in an encounter with the enemy. Sinope, the daughter of Marpesia, took her place. She achieved a unique reputation for courage by reason of her permanent virginity.

Such great admiration and fear spread by her fame through the peoples already alarmed that even Hercules, when he had been ordered by his master to bring the weapons of the queen, as if destined for inevitable danger, brought together the pick of all the noble youth of Greece and prepared nine vessels of war, and still not content with this gathering of strength, preferred to attack suddenly and to surround them unaware. At that time, two sisters, Antiope and Orithyia, were in command of the kingdom. Hercules, traveling by sea, caught them off-guard and unarmed and indolent from the inactivity of peaceful times. Among the large number of killed and captured were two sisters of Antiope. One of these, Melanippe, was taken by Hercules, and Hippolyte was taken by Theseus. Theseus married Hippolyte, but Hercules gave Melanippe back to her sister, Antiope, and received as the ransom price the weapons of the queen. After Orithyia, Penthesilea ruled

---

67 The real derivation of the work is unknown. In antiquity it was commonly associated with $á—\mu a\zeta ós$ 'without a breast.'

68 Smyrna, Cyme, and Myrine.

the kingdom, of whose courage among men in the Trojan War we have received very distinguished accounts.

(16) O tribulation! The shame of human error! Women, fugitives from their native land, entered Europe and Asia, that is, the greatest and most powerful parts of the world, wandered far and wide, destroyed, and for almost a hundred years kept control by overthrowing many cities and establishing others. Yet the affliction of the times is not to be attributed entirely to the helplessness of men. On the contrary, recently the Getae, those who today are called Goths, whom Alexander proclaimed should be avoided, whom Pyrrhus dreaded, and whom Caesar also shunned, after evacuating and abandoning their homes, with all their forces united, invaded the Roman provinces, and at the same time, having for long proved themselves a source of terror, they hoped by their requests to obtain an alliance with Rome which they could have claimed by arms. They asked only for a place for a small settlement, not of their own selection, but according to our own judgment. These people who were free to take whatever they pleased, and to whom the whole earth was subject and lay open; they, whom alone the unconquered kingdoms feared, offered themselves as a protection for the Roman Empire. And yet, since the pagans in their blindness do not see that these things took place through Roman virtue, and were won by the Christian faith of the Romans, they do not believe and are unwilling to admit, although they realize it, that it was through the blessing of the Christian religion which unites all peoples through a common faith, that those men, whose wives destroyed the greater part of the earth with boundless slaughter, became subject to them without a battle.

(17) But four hundred and thirty years before the founding of the City, the abduction of Helen, the conspiracy of the Greeks, and the gathering of a thousand ships, then the ten years' siege, and finally the renowned destruction of Troy are known generally. In that war, waged most cruelly for ten years, the very renowned poet, Homer, has made clear in his glorious

song what nations and how many peoples were caught up and destroyed in that whirlwind, and it is not our place to unfold this story in detail now, for it is both a long task and one that seems known to all. But let those who have learned of the length of that siege, the atrocious slaughter of the city's overthrow, and the bondage, see if they are rightly offended by the condition of present times, whatever this is; what enemies by the hidden mercy of God, although they could have followed over all lands with troops drawn up for war, for the sake of peace and offering hostages followed them over all seas. And lest perchance they are believed to have done these things from a love of a quiet life, they offered themselves and the risk of their lives against other nations to obtain the Roman peace.

(18) Furthermore, in the few intervening years, came Aeneas' arrival in Italy from Troy[69] as a fugitive, the strifes he aroused, the wars he stirred up over a period of three years, the many peoples he involved in hatred and afflicted with destruction, all these have been imprinted in our minds by the instruction of the elementary school. In addition, in the midst of these events, lie the exiles and shipwrecks of the Greeks, the disasters of the Peloponnesians who were crushed when Codrus died, the ignoble Thracians rising in new wars, and the general unrest at that time throughout all Asia and Greece.

(19) In the sixty-fourth year before the founding of the City, Sardanapallus, the last of the Assyrian kings, ruled, a man more corrupt than any woman. While he was wearing purple cloth in the garb of a female in the midst of a flock of harlots, he was seen by his prefect, Arbatus, who was then in command of the Medes and he was cursed by him. Soon also, when the people of the Medes rose in revolt, he was called forth to war and when conquered cast himself upon a burning pyre. Then, the kingdom of the Assyrians yielded to the Medes. Later, when many wars were breaking out on all

---

69 Cf. Vergil, *Aeneid* 1.1 ff.

Let the Latins and Sicilians now choose, if it seems good, whether they would have preferred to live in the days of Aremulus and Phalaris, who extorted the lives of the innocent by punishments, or in these Christian times when the Roman emperors, among the first to be converted to the Christian religion, did not even exact punishment for the injuries committed by the tyrants themselves after their tyrannies had been crushed to the good of the Republic.

(21) Thirty years before the founding of the City, a very great war, in which both peoples engaged their full strength and spirit, was entered upon by the Peloponnesians and the Athenians. In this war, they were forced, because of mutual slaughters to this extremity, to withdraw from conflict with each other and to give up the war, as if both had been conquered. At this time, too, a sudden invasion into Asia by a tribe of the Amazons and Cimmerians caused lengthy and very widespread devastation and destruction.

In the twentieth year before the founding of the City, the Lacedaemonians, by waging war of untiring fury for twenty years against the Messenians, because their virgin daughters had been spurned by them at a solemn sacrifice of the Messenians, involved the entire strength of Greece in its own ruin. Since they had bound themselves by great oaths and had pledged themselves by vows not to return home until Messena had been captured, being made weary by the long siege over a period of ten years, and yet obtaining nothing of the fruits of victory, and when, furthermore, being moved also by the complaints of their wives over their long widowhood and the danger of the contestants becoming sterile, after deliberating on the matter, fearing that by this perseverance the hope of offspring would be cut off for them rather than ruin be achieved for the Messenians, they sent back to Sparta men chosen from the army who, after taking the oath of allegiance, had come as reinforcements to the army. To these they gave permission to have promiscuous relations with all the women —a license infamous enough and not of much use. But they themselves persisting in their plan, captured the Messenians by fraud, and having conquered them forced them into slavery. Finally, the Messenians, after they had long endured a bloody domination midst scourgings and chains, cast off the yoke, took up arms and renewed the war. The Lacedaemonians selected Tyrtaeus, the Athenian poet, as their leader in this war. After they had been defeated in three encounters, they made up the losses of their army with a band of slaves who had been given their freedom. But just when they thought that even then, because of their threatening danger, they should give up the struggle, and their poet and leader, Tyrtaeus, composed a poem and recited it before an assembly of the people, they were aroused and rushed again into the struggle. In fact, to such an extent were they stirred up in this battle that hardly ever has a bloodier battle raged. At length victory went to the Lacedaemonians. The Messenians renewed the battle a third time, and the Lacedaemonians showed no delay. Both sides brought up many auxiliary forces. The Athenians prepared to attack the Lacedaemonians from a different direction while the latter were occupied elsewhere. And the Lacedaemonians did not abstain from action, for, although they were occupied with the Messenians, they sent Peloponnesian troops to meet the Athenians in battle. The Athenians, however, unequal to them in power, since they had sent a small fleet to Egypt, were easily overcome in a naval battle. Later, when the fleet had returned and their forces had also been strengthened by the vigor of their troops, they challenged the victors to battle. Then the Lacedaemonians, giving up their struggle against the Messenians, turned their arms against the Athenians. For a long time, varied and serious battles went on and there existed a doubtful state of victory, and finally, with the result hanging in the balance, both sides withdrew. Now, it must be very clearly understood that it was Sparta herself that was called the Lacedaemonian state, and that from this fact, the Lacedaemonians were called Spartans. So the Lacedaemonians, being recalled to war with the Messenians, so as not to leave the interim as a period of peace for

the Athenians, made an agreement with the Thebans to restore to them sovereignty over the Boeotians, which the latter
had lost at the time of the Persian War, provided they would
take up arms against the Athenians. So great was the fury of
the Spartans that, although they were involved in two wars,
they did not refuse a third, provided they could obtain enemies for their own enemies. The Athenians, alarmed by so
great a tempest of wars, selected two leaders: Pericles, a man
of outstanding courage, and Sophocles, a writer of tragedies.
These generals, after dividing the army, devastated the territory of the Spartans far and wide and added many cities of
Asia to the Athenian empire. From this time on for fifty years,
always with victory uncertain, there was fighting on land and
sea, until the Spartans, with their resources dissipated and their
confidence shattered, were a disgrace even to their allies.

But these afflictions of Greece which rested heavily on her
for so long a time, we consider of little importance. That our
pleasures are sometimes interfered with and our passions
somewhat restrained, this we cannot endure. And yet there
is this difference between men of that time and the present,
namely, that the former endured these intolerable things with
equanimity, because they were born and nurtured among them
and knew no better, whereas the men of today being per-
petually and serenely accustomed in their lives to tranquillity
and pleasure, are aroused by every even moderate cloud of
anxiety that envelops them. Yet if only they would pray to
Him who can end this unrest though it be small, and through
whose blessing they have this continued peace unknown to
other times! And since I recall that I promised, although I
defined the order of my narrative by certain divisions, as it
were, to speak of events from the creation of the world to
the founding of the City, let this be the end of this book in
which we have unfolded events from the creation of the world
so that the following book may begin with the founding of
the City, and will contain the more complex evils of those
times, inasmuch as men had become versed and skilled in
wickedness.

BOOK TWO

NOW I THINK THAT there is no one among men from whom it is possible to conceal that God made man in this world. Therefore also, when man sins the world is censured and, because of our failure to check the intemperance, this earth on which we live is punished by the disappearance of other living creatures and by the failure of our crops. So if we are the creation of God, we are properly also the object of his attention; for who loves us more than He who made us? Moreover, who regulates more orderly than He who both has made and loves us? Indeed, who can order and regulate our deeds more wisely and more firmly than He who both foresaw what had to be done and brought to accomplishment what He had foreseen? Therefore, that all power and all ordering are from God, both those who have not read feel, and those who have read recognize. But if powers are from God, how much the more are the kingdoms, from which the remaining powers proceed; but if the kingdoms are hostile to one another, how much better it is if some one be the greatest to which all the power of the other kingdoms is subject, such as the Babylonian kingdom was in the beginning and, then, the Macedonian, afterward also, the African and, finally, the Roman which remains up to this day, and by the same ineffable plan at the four cardinal points of the world, four chief kingdoms preeminent in distinct stages, namely: the Babylonian kingdom in the East, the Carthaginian in the South, the Macedonian in the North, and the Roman in the West. Between the first and last of these, that is, between the Babylonian and the Roman, as it were, between an aged father and a little son, the intervening and brief kingdoms of Africa and Macedonia came as protectors and guardians, accepted by the power of time, not by the law of inheritance. Whether this is so, I shall try to explain as clearly as possible.

(2) The first king among the Assyrians, who was able to rise above the rest, was Ninus. When Ninus was killed, Semiramis, his wife, the queen of all Asia, restored the city of Babylon and arranged for it to be the capital of the kingdom of Assyria. The kingdom of the Assyrians stood for a long time with power unshaken, but when Arbatus, whom some call Arbaces, the prefect of the Medes and himself a Mede by nationality, had killed Sardanapallus, his king, at Babylon, he transferred the name and chief power of the kingdom to the Medes. Thus, the kingdom of Ninus and Babylon was turned over to the Medes in that year in which among the Latins Procas, the father of Amulius and Numitor, furthermore the grandfather of Rhea Silvia, who was the mother of Romulus, began to rule. Moreover, to show beyond doubt that all these events were disposed by the ineffable mysteries and the most profound judgments of God and did not happen by the powers of man or by uncertain accident, all the ancient histories begin with Ninus, and all histories of Rome proceed from Procas. Then, from the first year of the reign of Ninus down to the time when Babylon began to be restored by Semiramis, sixty-four years intervened, and from the first year of Procas, when he began to reign, until the City was founded by Romulus, there was a like interval of sixty-four years. Thus, during the reign of Procas, the seed of the future Rome was sown, although its sprout was not yet evident. In the same year of the reign of this same Procas, the kingdom of Babylon came to an end, although Babylon itself still exists. But when Arbatus went over to the Medes, the Chaldaeans retained part of the kingdom among themselves and they laid claim for themselves to Babylon against the Medes. Thus, power over Babylonia rested with the Medes, actual ownership with the Chaldaeans. Moreover, on account of the ancient dignity of the royal city, the Chaldaeans preferred not to call it their own, but to call themselves a part of it. Thus, it has come

about that Nebuchadrezzar[1] and the other kings after him down to Cyrus, although they are viewed as strong because of the power of the Chaldaeans and famous because of the name of Babylonia, yet are not found among the number and line of famous kings. Thus, Babylon was dishonored when Arbatus was prefect in that year when, as I have properly said, the seeds of Rome were sown under King Procas. Babylon was finally overthrown by King Cyrus at that time when Rome was first freed from the domination of the Tarquinian kings. Indeed, at one and the same accord of time, the one fell, the other arose; the one, at the time, first endured the domination of foreigners; the other, at that time, also first rejected the haughtiness of her own princes; the one, at that time like a person at the door of death, left an inheritance; but the other, then attaining maturity recognized itself as the heir; at that time the power of the East fell, that of the West rose.

And not to delay longer with words, I commit myself to the teeth of the madmen, but to be freed by the support of truth.

(3) Ninus ruled for fifty-two years. He was succeeded, as I have said, by his wife, Semiramis. When she, too, had ruled for forty-two years, in the middle of her reign, she founded Babylon as the capital of her kingdom. Thus Babylon, almost one thousand one hundred and sixty-four years after it had been founded, was despoiled of its wealth by the Medes and their king, Arbatus, moreover their prefect, and was deprived of the kingdom and king himself; yet the city itself remained unsubdued for sometime afterwards. Similarly, Rome also after the same number of years, that is, almost one thousand one hundred and sixty-four years, was invaded by the Goths and their king, Alaric, also their count, and was despoiled of her riches, not of her sovereignty. She still remains and rules unsubdued, although between both cities by hidden decrees (of God) the order of the whole parallelism was so preserved

---

1 Properly written 'Nebuchadrezzar,' but Orosius writes 'Nabuchodnos-sor'; also frequently spelled Nebuchadnezzar.

that in the one case its prefect, Arbatus, seized the power and in the other its prefect, Attalus, tried to rule; yet in Rome alone was the impious attempt frustrated with the aid of a Christian emperor.

And so I have believed that especially for this reason should these events be related, that by a partial disclosure of the ineffable judgments of God, those who especially grumble foolishly about Christian times may understand that the one God has so disposed the times in the beginning for the Babylonians and in the end for the Romans, and that it is due to His clemency that we live, but that it is due to our intemperance that we live wretchedly. Behold, the similar beginnings of Babylonia and Rome, the similar powers, the similar greatness, the similar times, the similar blessings, and the similar evils, yet not a similar decline or similar fall. For the one lost its power, the other retains it; the one was deprived of its king by murder, the other is secure with its emperor unharmed. And why is this? Because in the one case the turpitude of the passions was punished in the king; in the other the very serene tranquility of the Christian religion was preserved in the king; in Babylon, without reverence for religion, furious license satisfied thirst for pleasure; in Rome, there were Christians who showed mercy, and Christians to whom mercy was shown, and Christians because of whose memory and in whose memory mercy was shown. Therefore, let them cease to rail at religion and exasperate the patience of God so that this also they may possess unpunished, if at some time they may desist. Let them truly reflect upon the times of their ancestors, so disturbed by wars, accursed with crimes, horrible with dissensions, most constant in miseries, at whose existence they can properly shudder, and they necessarily should ask that they not return. Indeed, they should ask that God alone who, by His inscrutable justice, both permitted that they take place in the past, and, by His manifest mercy, is responsible that they not return. These matters will now be set forth by me more fully, unfolding my history orderly.

(4) In the four hundred and fourteenth year after the overthrow of Troy, moreover in the sixth Olympiad, which precisely in the fifth year, after the intervening four years had been completed, was customarily celebrated in Elis, a city of Greece, the city of Rome was founded in Italy by Romulus and Remus, twin originators. Romulus continually stained his rule by parricide and, in a succession of like acts of cruelty, without delay seized the Sabine women, bound them in shameless wedlock, and gave them the blood of their husbands and parents as a dowry. And so Romulus, after first killing his grandfather, Numitor, then his brother, Remus, seized the power and founded the City. The kingdom of his grandfather, the walls of his brother, and the temple of his father-in-law, he dedicated with blood; and he gathered together a band of criminals promising them impunity. His first field of battle was the Forum of the City, indicating that foreign and civil wars, mingled together, would never cease. The women of the Sabines, whom he had enticed by a treaty and by games, he seized first as dishonorably as he abominably guarded them. Their leader, Titus Tatius, an old man who pursued the causes of honesty and piety, after he had been repulsed in battle, he presently killed when he had received him into a share of the power. He carried on war with the Veientes, still of little reputation, but already of great power. The town of the Caeninenses was captured and demolished. When once arms were taken up, there was never rest, for wretched poverty and repulsive hunger would be feared at home if ever they should rest peacefully. Now, henceforth, I shall touch very briefly upon the never-ending struggles, and yet always serious according to the size of the forces involved. Tullus Hostilius,[2] the founder of military tactics, with confidence in his well-trained youth, brought war on the Albans and for a long time

---

2 Traditionally the third king of Rome (673-642 B.C.), probably an historical figure. His capture of Alba Longa and his founding of the *Curia Hostilia* may be accepted as facts. The laws, reform, and public works are pure inventions.

the issue was uncertain on both sides, slaughter certain; finally, the disastrous catastrophies and doubtful events came to an end with the brief conflict of the triplets.[3] When peace was again broken, Mettus Fufetius in the war with the Fidenates, when he also planned the betrayal of his country, was prevented and paid the penalty for his double dealing by having his body divided by chariots dragging it in different directions. The Latins, usually under the leadership of Ancus Marcius, were at last defeated. Tarquinius Priscus destroyed all his neighbors, at that time the twelve peoples of Tuscany, by innumerable conflicts. The Veientes were conquered by Servius Tullius making repeated attacks, but they were not crushed. The kingdom of Tarquinius Superbus was assumed by a crime against his father-in-law who was murdered, was held on to by committing acts of cruelty against the citizens, was lost by his disgraceful defilement of Lucretia, and midst the domestic vices, there were brilliant acts of courage abroad, that is, his capture of the strong towns in Latium, namely, Ardea, Oricolum, and Suessa Pometia, and whatever he perpetrated against the Gabii, either by his own deceit or by the punishments inflicted by his son or by the power of the Romans.[4] But how many continuous evils the Romans suffered for two hundred and forty-three years in that domination of kings, not only the expulsion of one king, but also the abjuration of the name and office of king shows. For if the arrogance of one alone had been a

---

3 The Horatii, according to a popular tradition, were three Roman brothers, two of whom were killed in combat with the Curatii, three Alban brothers, while the survivor was tried, but acquitted on appeal, for the murder of his sister, Horatia.

4 The historicity of Tarquinius Superbus, the last king of Rome (traditionally 534-510 B.C.) is probably proved by the treaty between Rome and Gabii ascribed to him, which survived in the temple of Semo Seucus till the time of Augustus. According to tradition, Tarquinius deceived the people of Gabii by pretending to hold his own son, Sextus, in disfavor. Sextus fled to Gabii, presumably to escape his father's cruelty and wrath. There he worked his way into the confidence of the people and became their leader. On his father's advice, he gradually killed the leading men of the city and so facilitated its capture.

fault, he alone should have been expelled and the kingly system preserved for better men. Therefore, when the kings had been expelled from the City, the Romans, thinking that they ought to look after their own welfare rather than that anyone else should restrain their liberty, created the office of consul, by whom, as it were, the adult age of the growing Republic was directed as more difficult projects were dared.

(5) Two hundred and forty-four years after the founding of the City, the first consul[5] among the Romans, Brutus, sought not only to equal the founder and first king of Rome in parricides, but also to surpass him; for his own two young sons and likewise the two brothers of his wife, the youthful Vitellii, were charged with a plot to recall the kings to the City, and he dragged them before the assembly, had them struck with rods and beheaded. Then he himself in a war with the Veientes and the Tarquinienses, together with Arruns, the son of Superbus, who met and died with him, fell. Porsenna, the king of the Etruscans, a very strong supporter of the name of king, attempting to bring in Tarquinius by force, for three continuous years terrified, enclosed, and beseiged the fearful City; and unless Mucius[6] had moved the enemy by his heroic endurance in burning his hand or the virgin Cloelia[7] by her admirable daring in crossing the river, the Romans would surely have been forced either to endure captivity, defeated by a pressing enemy, or slavery, being forced to take back a king and become subject to him. After this, the Sabines gathered together troops from all sides and with a great army

---

5 L. Junius Brutus, 509 B.C.

6 Gaius Mucius Scaevola, according to some, first bore the cognomen Cordus, which he later changed to Scaevola. This was an amulet worn by Roman children, but popular etymology wrongly connected it with *scaeva*, the left hand. Thus arose the story of the brave Roman, who, on failing to kill Porsenna, showed his indifference to physical pain by holding his right hand in fire.

7 Cloelia, a Roman girl given as hostage to Porsenna. She escaped to Rome by swimming the Tiber, but was handed back to Porsenna, who out of admiration for her bravery set her free with other hostages. Cf. Livy, *Histories* 2.12-14.

hastened to Rome. The Romans, thrown into confusion by fear of this, elected a dictator whose authority and power exceeded that of a consul. This action at the time produced the greatest advantage in that war. There followed a secession of the plebeians from the patricians, when, while Marcus Valerius, the dictator, was carrying on a levy of troops, the people stirred up by various wrongs took up arms and settled on the Sacred Mount.[8] What could have been more dreadful than this destruction when the body, severed from its head, planned the ruin of that through which it drew its life? It would have been a matter of internal destruction of the Roman name, if a hasty reconciliation had not come forth before the secession identified itself. A hidden disease by its wretched advance presses forward and threatens more than the open slaughters of wars. For, in the consulships of T. Gesonius and P. Minucius,[9] the two greatest and most detestable of all evils, famine and pestilence, racked the tired City. For a little while, there was a cessation from battles but there was no cessation from deaths. The Veientes and the Etruscans, dangerous enemies, joined by the forces of their neighbors, rushed into battle and were met by the consuls, M. Fabius and Cn. Manlius.[10] On this occasion, after taking a solemn oath by which the Romans vowed that they would not return to camp until they were victorious, such a violent battle took place, of like nature to both conquered and conquerors, that, after most of the army had been lost and Manlius, the consul, and Quintus Fabius, of consular rank, had been killed in battle, M. Fabius, the consul, refused to accept the triumph offered him by the Senate, because a period of mourning was rather due for such great losses to the Republic. That family of the Fabii, very famous for its numbers and power, having obtained the conflict with the Veientes by lot, as to how great a loss was brought

---

8 On the right bank of the Anis and west of the Via Nomentana, three miles from Rome.

9 T. Geganius Macerinus and P. Minucius Augurinus, 492 B.C.

10 M. Fabius Vibulanus II and Cn. Manlius Cincinnatus, 480 B.C.

upon the State by their death, even to this day the river in which they were drowned and the gate which sent them forth bear witness[11] by their infamous names. For when three hundred and six Fabii, truly the brightest lights of the Roman State, petitioned that a special war against the Veientes be decreed to them, they were confirmed by their first successes in their hope for the success of the expedition rashly undertaken. Then, drawn into ambush and surrounded by the enemy, all were slaughtered on the spot, with the exception of one only who was reserved to announce the disaster, so that the fatherland might learn with greater suffering of the losses which it had experienced.[12] Not only were such events as these taking place in Rome, but every province was blazing forth with its own fires, and what a distinguished poet has described in one city, I shall express in regard to the whole world:

Cruel mourning everywhere, everywhere fear and the widespread shadow of death.[13]

(6) At the same time, then, Cyrus, king of the Persians, whom I have mentioned above in the unfolding of my history, who at that time was overrunning Asia, Scythia, and the entire Orient with his arms; when Tarquinius Superbus, either king or enemy, was oppressing the City either by slavery or war, Cyrus, as I have said, having overcome all against whom he had gone, attacked the Assyrians and Babylon, at that time a people and a city richer than all others. But the Gyndes River, second in size to the Euphrates, interrupted his attack. For one of the royal horses, outstanding for its shiny coat and beauty, convinced of his ability to cross the river at a fork

---

11 Cf. Livy, *Histories* 2.49-51, where the story is told in detail. The river near Veii is the Cremera. The gate is the *Porta Carmentalis* at Rome, near the temple of Carmentis, through which the Fabii marched to their destructive contest.

12 Livy and Dionysius of Halicarnassus tell entirely different stories about this legend, but they agree that all the Fabii were killed. One member of the family, too young to join the expedition, stayed at home.

13 Vergil, *Aeneid* 2.368-369.

where the crashing waves were raised high by the rapacious current, was snatched up, cast headlong, and drowned. The enraged king decided to take vengeance on the river, calling to witness that the river which had just devoured his magnificent horse must be left passable for women with scarcely the wetting of their knees. Rather reluctant to spend a year with all his troops in operations here, Cyrus diminished the River Gyndes by cutting large channels through it and drawing it off through four hundred and sixty streams. Having first taught the trench-diggers in this project, he also drew off the water of the Euphrates, which was by far the strongest of rivers and flowed through the middle of Babylonia. And thus by passable fords, he made a dry road, with even parts of the riverbed exposed, and he took the city, to have been able to construct which with human labor or to be able to destroy which by human courage, were both almost incredible achievements among mortals. For many have related that Babylon was established by the giant, Nebrot, and was restored by Ninus or by Semiramis. This city was conspicuous on all sides by level plains; the nature of its site was most delightful, and it was arranged like a camp with equal walls in the form of a square. The strength and size of its walls are scarcely believable in the relating, that is, fifty cubits wide and four times as high. Moreover, it was surrounded by a circumference of four hundred and eighty stades. The wall was made of burnt brick with bitumen pressed in between, and a wide waterway surrounded it in place of a river. In front of the walls were a hundred bronze gates. Moreover, the width itself, with small stations for defenders being placed at equal intervals at the consummation of the pinnacles on both sides, could receive by its intervening spaces swift, four-horse chariots. The houses within, of eight stories, were remarkable for their menacing height. Yet that great Babylon, the first city to be founded after the restoration of the human race, was now, almost with no delay, conquered, captured, and overthrown. At this time, Croesus, king of the Lydians, famous for his wealth, when he had come to the aid of the Babylonians, was defeated and fled anxiously back to his kingdom. Moreover, Cyrus, after he had attacked Babylon as an enemy, had overthrown it as a victor and organized it as a king, transferred the war against Lydia, where, with little trouble, he overcame the army already in panic from the previous battle. He even captured Croesus himself, and in his captivity granted him his life and a patrimony.

It is not necessary at this point to amplify the unstable conditions of changing events. For whatever is made by the hand and work of man collapses and is consumed by the passage of time, as the capture of Babylon confirms. As soon as its power reached its peak, then it immediately declined, so that by a kind of law of succeeding generations due inheritance was passed on to posterity, which itself was to preserve the same law of inheritance. Thus, great Babylon and vast Lydia fell at the first attacks of advancing Cyrus. The mightiest arms of the East, together with its head,[14] fell in the campaign of a single battle. And our people with unrestrained anxiety debate whether that powerful structure of the once very powerful Roman Republic is now trembling from the weakness common to old age rather than because it has been battered by foreign forces.

(7) Thus, the same Cyrus with the approach of the next season brought war upon the Scythians. Queen Thamyris, who was then ruling the people, although she could have kept him from crossing the Araxes River,[15] permitted him to cross; first, because of her confidence in herself; then, because of the opportunity of blocking off the enemy from using the river. After Cyrus had advanced into Scythia and had pitched his camp far from the river which he had crossed; furthermore, after preparing wine and food, he abandoned the camp, as if he fled because he was frightened. The queen, when she learned of this, sent a third of her troops and her young son

---

14 Babylon is the head and the members of its empire are the arms.
15 Not the large river of this name in Armenia, but a small river of the same name in eastern Scythia.

to pursue Cyrus. The barbarians, as if invited to a banquet, were overcome by drunkenness, and when Cyrus presently returned, all of them together with the young man were slaughtered. Thamyris, after the loss of her army and her son, prepared to wash away the sorrow of a mother or of a queen with the blood of the enemy rather than with her tears. She pretended diffidence because of her despair over the calamity brought upon her, and withdrawing gradually she drew the proud enemy into ambush. Then, when she had arranged the ambush between the mountains, she destroyed two hundred thousand of the Persians and her added joy over this accomplishment was, above all else, that not even a messenger survived for so great a disaster. The queen ordered Cyrus' head to be cut off and cast into a leather bottle full of human blood, rebuking him in unwomanly fashion. She said: 'Satiate yourself with the blood for which you thirsted, with which for thirty years you have continued to be unsatiated.'[16]

(8) In the two hundred and forty-fifth year after the founding of the City, after an interval of some duration following Cyrus' death among the Scythians, Darius acquired the kingdom by luck. In between these, Cambyses, the son of Cyrus, ruled. He, after conquering Egypt, abominating the entire religion of Egypt, abolished its ceremonies and temples. After this king, the magi also under the name of the king[17] whom they had killed, dared by deception to seize the kingdom, but they were detected and overcome. So Darius, one of those who had repressed the audacity of the magi by the sword, by the consent of all was created king. After he had regained by war the Assyrians and Babylon, which had defected from the kingdom of the Persians, brought war upon Idanthyrsus, king of the Scythians, for the following reason chiefly, because he had not obtained his daughter whom he had sought in marriage. Surely, a great and urgent reason, that seven hundred thousand men be exposed to the danger of death for

16 Cf. Justin, *Histories* 1.8.
17 i.e., Smerdis; cf. Justin, *Histories* 1.9.

the lust of one man! For with an incredible amount of war
material and with seven hundred thousand armed men, he
invaded Scythia against an enemy that gave no opportunity for
a fair battle; moreover, that slashed his rear guard by sudden
attacks. Fearing lest his return might be denied him by the
destruction of the bridge across the Hister river, after losing
eighty thousand of his soldiers, he fled in terror, although he
did not consider the number of the slain among his losses,[18]
and he did not consider as a loss what any king would scarcely
have dared to consider it necessary to surround. Then, he
attacked and subdued Asia and Macedonia. He also overpowered the Ionians in a naval encounter. Then, he made an
attack and directed his arms against the Athenians because
they had aided the Ionians by giving help against himself.
Furthermore, when the Athenians learned that Darius was
rapidly approaching, although they had asked the Lacedaemonians for aid, nevertheless, when they had learned that the
Persians were being detained by a religious holiday of four
days duration,[19] took hope from the occasion and drawing up
only ten thousand of their citizens and a thousand Plataean
allies rushed forth against six hundred thousand of the enemy
on the plains of Marathon. Miltiades at this time was in
command of the battle. He, relying more on speed than on
courage, with a swift attack came to close quarters with the
enemy before he could be repulsed with a swift shower of
arrows. So great was the diversity of warfare in this battle
that on the one side men were thought prepared to slay, and
on the other cattle prepared to die. Two hundred thousand
Persians fell on the plains of Marathon on that day. Darius
felt that loss; for beaten and routed, he fled back to Persia
in ships which he had seized. But when he renewed the battle
and tried to take vengeance on the victors, in the very midst
of his preparations he fell, in the seventy-fourth Olympiad,

18 A small number in comparison with the size of his army.
19 Orosius is confused here. The Lacedaemonians rather than the Persians were delayed by a religious holiday.

that is, in the two hundred and seventy-fifth year after the founding of the City, at the time when at Rome, Popilia, a Vestal Virgin, was buried alive for the sin of defilement.

(9) Xerxes, succeeding his father, Darius, on the throne, took five years to prepare for the war against Greece which he had inherited from his father. Demaratus, the Lacedaemonian, who at that time by chance was in exile in the court of Xerxes, gave this information to his countrymen by tablets first written upon and then covered with wax. Thus, Xerxes is said to have had seven hundred thousand armed men from his kingdom and three hundred thousand from his allies, also two hundred thousand beaked ships; furthermore, transports three thousand in number, so that it has been recorded, not unreasonably, that for an army and a fleet so large, scarcely did the rivers suffice for drink, the lands for invading, and the seas for traversing. To oppose this expedition, so incredible in our time, whose number it is more difficult now to be reckoned than it was then to be conquered, the king of the Spartans placed Leonidas with four thousand men in the passes of Thermopylae. Xerxes, moreover, with contempt for the small number opposing him, ordered the battle to be begun and to be fought at close quarters. Furthermore, those whose relatives and fellows-in-arms had fallen on the plains of Marathon, were both first in the struggle and in the slaughter. Then, following close upon them was a larger and more sluggish crowd, since it was neither free to rush forward nor free to fight nor prepared to flee, but was standing upon the dead alone. The battle, which lasted for three continuous days, was not one of two peoples, but the slaughter of one. On the fourth day, when Leonidas saw that the enemy was surrounded on all sides, he urged his auxiliary allies to withdraw from the battle and escape to the top of the mountain, and to save themselves for more opportune times; but for himself, together with his Spartans, another fate must be undergone; that they owed more to the fatherland than to life itself. After dismissing his allies, he warned the Spartans that a great deal was to

be hoped for from glory, nothing from life; that neither the
enemy nor daybreak were to be awaited, but when night fell
they were to break through the camp, attack at close quarters,
and throw the battle lines into confusion; that nowhere would
victors perish more honorably than in the camp of the enemy.
Therefore, persuaded to prefer to die, they armed themselves
to avenge their imminent death, as if they were both exacting
and taking vengeance for their death. Marvelous to relate,
six hundred men broke into a camp of six hundred thousand.
A tumult arose in the entire camp; the Persians themselves
also aided the Spartans by their own mutual slaughter; the
Spartans, seeking the king and not finding him, slew and
scattered everything; they overran the entire camp, and in the
midst of the dense piles of bodies, with difficulty followed
scattered men, undoubtedly victors, had they not elected to
die.[20] The battle was prolonged from the beginning of the
night into the greater part of the day, and finally, worn out
by conquering, when, with their limbs failing, each one seemed
satiated with the vengeance of his own death, there in the
midst of entanglements of dead bodies and the fields palpitat-
ing with thick and half-congealed blood, he fell exhausted
and died.

(10) Xerxes, twice overcome on land, prepared for a naval
battle. But when Themistocles, leader of the Athenians,
learned that the Ionians, for whom, while he offered aid to
them in an earlier war, he had turned the attack of the Persians against himself, were leading a fleet ready for battle to the
aid of Xerxes, decided to win them over to his side and take
them away from the enemy. Because an opportunity for a
conference was denied, in places where the Ionians seemed
about to approach with their ships, he ordered signs to be
displayed and fastened on rocks, reproaching his former allies
and sharers in dangers, but now unjustly indifferent, with
befitting rebukes, and especially persuading them by religious

---

20 Cf. Justin, *Histories* 2.11.

exhortations to return to the oaths of their ancient treaties, and especially urging that, when the battle had begun, to stop rowing instead of advancing and to withdraw from the battle. Thus, the king kept a part of the fleet back for himself and remained on shore as a spectator of the battle. On the other hand, however, Artemidora, queen of Halicarnassus, who had come to the aid of Xerxes, mingled in the battle most fiercely with the foremost, so that the reverse of the usual was seen— feminine caution in a man, manly daring in a woman. When the battle[21] was still in doubt, the Ionians, according to the request of Themistocles, began to withdraw from the conflict gradually. Their defection persuaded the Persians who were already considering flight to flee openly. In this confusion, many ships were sunk and captured, yet more fearing the rage of the king as well as the cruelty of the enemy, dispersed toward home. Mardonius approached the king who was anxious because of so many misfortunes and urged him to return to his kingdom before the adverse report should effect a revolution at home; moreover, that he, if the remaining troops were handed over to him, would wreak vengeance on the enemy and would ward off a family disgrace, or, if the misfortunes of war should persist, he would, indeed, yield to the enemy, but yet without dishonor to his king. The plan was approved and the army was handed over to Mardonius. The king set out for Abydos with a few men, where as victor on the sea he had kept a bridge. But when he found the bridge destroyed by the winter storms, in fear he crossed in a fishing skiff. It was truly a sight for the race of men to view and bemoan, as it measured the changes of events especially by this reversal of fortune; he was content to hide in a small boat, before whom the very sea had before lain concealed and had borne as a yoke of its captivity the bridge that joined its shores; he lacked the very menial services of a single slave, to whose power, while mountains were leveled, valleys were filled, and rivers were

---

21 It was fought in the Strait of Salamis, between the eastern end of the island and the coast of Attica.

drained, the very nature of things had yielded. The foot soldiers also, who had been committed to generals, were so exhausted by labor, hunger, and fear, and as disease spread, so great a pestilence and stench arose from the dying that the roads were filled with corpses and even horrible birds of prey and monstrous beasts attracted by the lure of food followed the dying army.

(11) But Mardonius, to whom Xerxes had committed the remainder of the war, at first puffed up with a little success, soon was reduced to extreme dejection. Indeed, he took Olynthus, a city of Greece, by storm. By various inducements, he tried to win over the Athenians to an agreement of peace, but when he saw their incalculable spirit of freedom, he burned part of the city and brought all his resources for war into Boeotia. There, also, a hundred thousand Greeks followed him and, going into battle[22] without delay and crushing his forces, they compelled Mardonius with a few men to flee destitute as from a shipwreck. They captured his camp full of royal treasure, but with no small loss of their former industry, for, after the division of this booty, Persian gold became the first corruption of Greek virtue. Complete ruin, therefore, followed upon these wretched beginnings. For, by chance, on the same day as that on which the troops of Mardonius were destroyed, part of the Persian army in Asia near Mount Mycale[23] engaged in a naval battle. There a fresh rumor suddenly circulated among both fleets and the people that the forces of Mardonius had been wiped out and the Greeks were victorious. A wonderful ordering of divine judgment, that a battle had been joined in Boeotia at sunrise and was announced in Asia at noon on the same day with so great an expanse of sea and land intervening! This report, indeed, agreed very well with the fact, because when the Persians heard of the destruction of the allies, seized first with grief and then with

---

22 The battle of Plataea, 479 B.C.
23 A promontory in Ionia, opposite the island of Samos. The battle was fought both on water and land.

despair, they were rendered neither ready for battle nor fit
for flight. And so the Greek army, made stronger by continuous success, attacked the enemy terrified and demoralized.
Xerxes, having become an object of contempt in the eyes of
his own because of the unsuccessful outcome of the war in
Greece, was surrounded in the royal palace and killed.

Such times, so desirable and most worthy of commemoration!
Oh those days of uninterrupted serenity which are placed
before us to be viewed, as it were, from shadows! In these
days, in a very short interval, three wars under three neighboring kings snatched away from the vitals of one kingdom
nine million men to say nothing of most unhappy Greece at
that time, which surpassed this total number of deaths, at the
thought of which we grow faint. Leonidas, that most famous
of the Lacedaemonians, in this war against Xerxes, which for
himself and the enemy was the last, when he had spoken to
his six hundred men these very famous words of encouragement: 'Eat your breakfast as if you are about to eat your
dinner among the dead,' mercifully persuaded his auxiliaries,
whom he had ordered to withdraw from the battle, to save
themselves for better times. Behold! When the one (Leonidas) promised better things to come, and our contemporaries
assert that better things were in the past, what else may be
concluded when both denounce their own times, but that
times have always been good but unappreciated, or that by no
means will they ever be better?

(12) But at Rome—to return to that time whence I have
digressed, for I am not compelled by any surcease of miseries
to go over to other peoples, but just as in former times evils
which raged everywhere brought themselves together by their
very acts, so, too, they are also reported in mingled fashion;
for it has been my purpose to compare the periods of world
history with one another, not to revile any part of it for its
troubles—at Rome, then, two hundred and ninety years after
the founding of the City, when there was a moderate cessation
of war, a severe plague, which always interrupted periods of

truce that were rarely made or were forced to be made, raged violently, so that, according to a noteworthy omen which preceded, the sky seemed to be aflame, when the chief City of the nations burned with such a fire of disease. For in that year, the plague killed both consuls, Aebutius and Servilius;[24] it destroyed the military forces for the most part; and with its horrible contagion, ended the lives of many nobles, and especially of the plebeians, although already, forty years earlier, an abortive plague had depleted them.

Then in the next year exiled citizens and fugitive slaves, under the leadership of Herbonius, a Sabine, invaded and burned the Capitol. Here, under the leadership of Valerius,[25] consul and general, the young men opposed them most bravely, but the decision in the battle was so savage and desperate that the consul, Valerius, himself was killed there and his death, furthermore, sullied the victory which was unworthy because won over slaves.

A year followed in which the consul[26] was besieged, together with his conquered army. For the Aequi and the Volsci had met and overcome him and, while he was fleeing to Algidus,[27] they surrounded him with famine and sword, and it would have resulted badly if Quintius Cincinnatus, the renowned dictator, had not dissolved the tight siege by overcoming the enemy. He was found in the country and summoned from the plough to the fasces, and after assuming command and drawing up his army, he imposed a cattle yoke upon the Aequi, and holding victory in his hand like a plough handle, he was the first to drive the subjugated enemy before him.

---

24 Lucius Aebutius Elva and Publius Servilius Priscus Structus, 463 B.C.
25 Publius Valerius Publicola, 460 B.C., second consulship.
26 Lucius Minucius Esquilinus Augurinus, 458 B.C.
27 A high snow-capped mountain with the forest upon it, southeast of Rome, between Tusculum and Velitrae, now *Monte Compatri*. The name is usually applied to the eastern section of the outer crater rim of the Alban Hills, famous for its temples of Diana and Fortune and its fashionable villas.

(13) In the two hundred and ninety-ninth year since the founding of the City, while the legates who had been sent to the Athenians to copy the laws of Solon were being awaited, famine and pestilence checked the Roman arms.

Moreover, in the three hundredth year, that is, in the ninety-fifth Olympiad, the *potestas*[28] of the consuls, being given over to the decemvirate to establish the laws of Attica, brought great destruction upon the Republic. For the first of the decemvirs, although the rest retired, Appius Claudius alone continued the *imperium* for himself, and immediately there followed a conspiracy of the others, so that, ignoring the custom whereby the honor of the *imperium* rested with one but the *potestas* was common to all, all threw everything into confusion according to their own passions. Thus, among other things which they all insolently presumed, they suddenly, one by one, marched forth with the twelve fasces and with other honors of authority. When this new evil rule had begun, and the sense of duty on the part of the consuls had been cast aside, a line of tyrants sprang up; after adding two tables of laws to the ten previous ones, acting always in a most insolent and scornful manner, on the day when it was customary to lay aside their official powers, they proceeded with the same signs of authority. The lust of Appius Claudius also increased the greatest hatred against him, who, in order that he might bring dishonor upon the virgin, Verginia, first charged her with being a slave. Therefore, Verginius, her father, driven by grief over her loss of freedom and by shame at her disgrace, dragged his daughter publicly to slavery and as a righteous parricide slew her. The people, aroused by this necessary atrocity and warned of the danger to their liberty, armed themselves and occupied Mount Aventine. And they did not

---

28 *Imperium* is the supreme authority of the community in its dealings with the individual. *Potestas* is a generic term used to indicate the power with which a magistrate was vested for the discharge of his duties. Cf. F. F. Abbott, *A History and Description of Roman Political Institutions* (Boston, 1901) 153.

cease to guard their liberty with arms, except when the conspiring plotters had also renounced their powers.

In the one hundred and third and one hundred and fifth Olympiads, so frequent and so severe earthquakes took place in Italy for almost the entire year that Rome was wearied by the constant reports of the innumerable tremors and of the destruction of villas and towns; then there was such a continuing and parching drought that it denied hope for raising the crops of the land in that year and the next year; and at the same time, when the Fidenates, terrible enemies supported by a very large band of auxiliaries, were threatening the Roman strongholds, Aemilius, dictator for the third time, with difficulty captured the city of Fidenae and so rid the Romans of a great mass of evil and restored the State to health. So great was the struggle against evils and the uneasiness within their minds that, either the wars spread far and wide abroad caused them to overlook the disasters at home, or after the losses of wars, the various plagues, which raged in heaven and on earth with unceasing malignity, caused the treaties which had been relaxed to be broken.

(14) Sicily in the earliest times was the land of the Cyclopes, and after them was always the nurse of tyrants; it was often also under the rule of slaves.[29] Of these, the first fed on the flesh of men; the next on the torture of men; and the last on the deaths of men, with this exception, that in foreign wars, it was held to be either booty or a prize. This island, to state it as briefly as possible, never knew a respite from evils until now, nay rather, that her diverse fortunes may be made more manifest, just as before it alone among all countries endured either internal or external upheavals, so now it alone of all countries never experiences them. Furthermore, to pass over the length both of the ruin by which it was oppressed and, on

---

29 Probably a reference to Micythus, a slave of Rhegium, who in 476 B.C. exercised the regency for the young sons of the king. He was a wise and vigorous ruler, who retired to private life when the sons came of age.

the contrary, of the peace which it enjoyed, Etna, which in
the past boiled over in frequent eruptions with the destruction
of cities and fields, now only smokes in an innocent manner
to give faith to its activity in the past. So, to pass over the
period of tyrants, one of whom was an avenger and presently
became the successor, in the middle period, that is, from the
three hundred and thirty-fifth year after the founding of the
City, when the people of Rhegium in Sicily were laboring in
discord, and the city through dissension was divided into two
parties, one party called the veterans from Himera, a city of
Sicily, to its aid. Furthermore, these veterans, when those were
first driven from the city against whom they were invoked to
fight, then also killed those to whose aid they had come together, and they seized the city, together with the wives and
the children of their allies, daring to commit a crime incom-
parable to that of any tyrant, for it would have been better
for the people of Rhegium to endure anything, rather than
of their own accord to invite those in to whom they themselves
as exiles would leave their fatherland, wives, children, and
household gods.

The people of Catana[30] also, when they were suffering at
the hands of the oppressive and hostile Syracusans, asked the
Athenians for help. But the Athenians, with zeal rather for
their own cause than that of their allies, equipped a fleet and
sent it to Sicily, since they were striving to extend their own
power and they feared that the Syracusan fleet, which had
recently been equipped, was advantageous to the Lacedaemonians. And since the Athenians who had been sent before
had made an auspicious beginning by cutting down the enemy,
they again sent a larger force and a stronger army into Sicily
under the leadership of Laches and Chariades. But the people
of Catana, influenced by the weariness of war, entered a truce
with the Syracusans, and spurned the aid of the Athenians;

---

30 Orosius writes 'Catina,' a town on the east coast of Sicily, at the foot
of Mount Etna, now *Catania*. As in the case of the preceding episode,
taken almost word for word from Justin, *Histories*, 4.3.

but afterwards, when the Syracusans transgressed the conditions of peace with a view to expanding their power, they again sent envoys to Athens, with hair and beard unshorn and clad in mourning, to beg for mercy and help by their dress and speech. So a large fleet was fitted out under the leadership of Nicias and Lamachus, and Sicily was visited again with so strong a force, that even the people of Catana, who had summoned them, feared their own decision. The Athenians immediately fought two infantry battles with successful results; crushing the enemy in the city and surrounding them by putting the fleet in their way, they enclosed them on land and sea. But the Syracusans, with their resources crushed and exhausted, sought help from the Lacedaemonians. They immediately sent Gylippus, alone indeed, but a man in whom the form of all kinds of assistance was presented. When he came and heard that the state of the war was adverse, with the help of auxiliaries gathered partly in Greece and partly in Sicily, he seized positions favorable for battle. Then, although defeated in two battles but not afraid, in a third encounter he killed Lamachus, put the enemy to flight, and freed the allies from the siege. Then the Athenians, having been defeated in battle on land, tried their fortune by sea and prepared to join in a naval engagement. When this was learned by Gylippus, he summoned the fleet which had been fitted out by the Lacedaemonians. In like manner, the Athenians sent Demosthenes and Eurymedon, in place of the leader who had been lost, with an auxiliary force. The Peloponnesians also, with the consent and decree of many cities, sent heavy reinforcements to the Syracusans. Thus, under the appearance of waging a war for their allies, they carried on domestic quarrels, and, as if the struggle had by agreement been transferred from Greece to Sicily, on both sides there was fighting with full strength. So the Athenians were conquered in the first encounter and lost their camp, together with all their money, both public and private, and with all their equipment gathered for a long campaign. When their resources had been lost and they were reduced to a critical position, Demosthenes urged that, while all was not entirely lost, however much they seemed hard pressed, they return home and leave Sicily. Nicias, however, rendered more desperate because of his shame at the bad management of affairs from the beginning, struggled to remain. They prepared for a naval battle and presently, through ignorance being enticed into the straits of the Syracusan sea, they were caught in a trap set by the enemy. Eurylochus,[31] their leader, was the first to be killed and eleven ships were burned. Demosthenes and Nicias abandoned the fleet as if to flee more safely by an expedition by land. Gylippus, however, first seized their ships, one hundred and thirty of them, which had been abandoned; then, proceeding to pursue the fugitives themselves, he captured and killed a very large number. Demosthenes escaped the disgrace of slavery by taking his own life, but Nicias brought his unworthy and disgraceful life to a climax by the dishonor of captivity.

(15) So the Athenians, harassed for two years in Sicily, not without inflicting losses on the Lacedaemonians, were surrounded by other evils at home.[32] For Alcibiades, who had earlier been pronounced general against the Syracusans, and had soon been summoned to trial on a certain accusation, betook himself to Lacedaemon in voluntary exile, and he urged the Spartans to center their attention again on a new war while the Athenians were in confusion, and not allow them any time to recover without being oppressed. Thus, all Greece agreed to this undertaking, as if consideration was being given to the public good by gathering their forces to extinguish a common conflagration. Darius, the king of the Persians also, mindful of his father's and grandfather's hatred for this city, made a treaty with the Lacedaemonians through Tissaphernes, the prefect of Lydia, and promised them expenses and troops to carry on the war. Strange to see, so great were the resources of the Athenians at that time that, although

---

31 The Eurymedon mentioned above.
32 Chapters 15 through 19 follow Justin closely.

there was an attack against them, that is, against one city, by the forces of Greece, Asia, and the whole Orient, by fighting and never yielding they seem to have been wasted away rather than conquered. For in the beginning Alcibiades forced all the Athenian allies to go over from them to the Lacedaemonians, but when he, too, was plotted against by these in their envy, he fled and took refuge in Media with Tissaphernes. At once, by accommodating his nature to him and by becoming more friendly for the purpose of easy communication, he persuaded Tissaphernes not to aid the Lacedaemonians with such lavish resources, saying that he should rather be the arbiter and spectator of this struggle, that forces of Lydia should be kept intact against the victor. Therefore, Tissaphernes ordered a part of the fleet with a considerable force to be dispatched to Lacedaemon, lest abounding in support they might fight safely without danger from the enemy, or completely abandoned they might give up the struggle which they had undertaken.

(16) When, however, domestic discord among the Athenians had long been agitated, on account of the imminent danger the highest power was transferred by the will of the people to the Senate, for discords are nourished by leisure, but when necessity settles upon them, they lay aside their private contentions and hatreds and take counsel together. Although this move was ruinous because of the pride and prevailing passions lodged in the race, nevertheless, Alcibiades was recalled from exile by the army and made leader of the fleet. When this was learned, the nobles first tried to give over the city to the Spartans; then, when they considered this fruitless, they voluntarily withdrew into exile. After freeing his country, Alcibiades directed the fleet against the enemy. When battle was joined, the Athenians won the victory. And furthermore, the greater part of the Spartan army was slain; almost all the leaders were killed, and eighty ships were captured, not counting those which were burned in conflict, sank, and were

destroyed.[33] Again, war was transferred to the land with
equally unfortunate results to the Spartans. Crushed by this
turn of events, the Lacedaemonians sought peace, but were
unable to obtain it. Furthermore, the Syracusan troops were
recalled to Sicily when the disturbance of a war with Carthage
was reported. So Alcibiades with his victorious fleet moved
up and down the coast of all Asia, and he ravaged and destroyed everything by war, fire, and slaughter; and the cities
which some time before had defected from the alliance, as
many as possible of them he captured and took back. Thus,
Alcibiades became very famous and entered Athens as victor
with the joy and admiration of all. A little while later, he
increased his forces, enlarged his army and fleet numerically,
and again attacked Asia. Then the Lacedaemonians put
Lysander in charge of the fleet and the war. Cyrus, the brother
of Darius, who had been put over Ionia and Lydia in place
of Tissaphernes, also strengthened the Lacedaemonians with
great supplies and reinforcements. So Lysander with a sudden
attack pressed upon the army of Alcibiades which was intent
upon booty and, for this reason, was dispersed and wandering
everywhere; he conquered and slaughtered them as they fled
without a conflict. This was a great disaster to the Athenians,[34]
and they received a much greater blow than they had ever
inflicted. When the Athenians learned this, they thought that
Alcibiades had taken care of the old pain of his exile by this
crime of betrayal, and so in his place they established Conon,
to whom they committed the remainder of the forces and the
highest command of the war. He wished to restore his depleted forces in at least numbers, and he enrolled an army by
selecting old men and boys. But a force of this kind brings
no delay to war, because this is brought about by the strength,
not the numbers, of an army. And so immediately, the unwarlike band was either captured or slaughtered, and so great
was the mass of dead which took place in that battle that, not

---

33 The battle of Cyzicus, 410 B.C.
34 i.e., the battle of Notium, 406 B.C.

only did the Athenian state seem to be destroyed, but the
Athenian name also. Moreover, because of these desperate
conditions, the Athenians decided to give the city over to
foreigners, so that those, who a little while before held domination over all Asia, now guard their walls at least from this
ragtag line of defense; and, although in their own judgment
they were not able to protect the city even behind walls, yet
they prepared to try a naval battle again. Madness without
reason considers indignation bravery, and what wrath con-
templates, rashness promises. And so of them all, some were
captured and some were killed, and there was nothing left for
the survivors.[35] Conon was the only general to survive the
war and the people, and he fearing the cruelty of the citizens
withdrew to King Cyrus.[36] But Evacoras, leader of the Lacedaemonians, deprived them of all their cities and left the
Athenians nothing but an empty city, and this did not last
long, for later he surrounded the city itself with a siege.
Within the city, famine, desolation, and disease harassed the
besieged, and when, after all the abominations of miseries
which it is a horror even to mention, no hope but death appeared, they sought peace.

(17) Then, an important conference took place between
the Spartans and their allies. When a great many proclaimed
that this most restless city should be razed to the ground and
her most troublesome people, together with its very name, be
blotted out, the Spartans said that they would not permit one
of the two eyes of Greece to be torn out. Furthermore, they
also promised peace, if the fortifications of the harbor of
Piraeus which led into the city be overturned and they give
over voluntarily the remaining ships, and then, if they would
accept the thirty rulers selected for them. When the Athenians
had agreed and submitted to this condition, the Lacedaemonians appointed Lysander to establish the laws to be obeyed

---

35 The battle of Aegospotami, 405 B.C.
36 Conon withdrew to enter the service of Evacoras in Cyprus. He an-
    nihilated the Spartan fleet at Cnidos (394). The text appears to be
    in error here.

in the city. This year was distinguished for the capture of Athens, for the death of Darius, king of the Persians, and for the exile of Dionysius, tyrant of Sicily. So the thirty rulers arranged for the Athenians turned out to be thirty tyrants, who at first encompassed themselves with three thousand attendants, and soon also surrounded themselves on all sides with seven hundred soldiers from their victorious army. They began a slaughter of all, which was to be indiscriminate, after killing Alcibiades who as he fled was caught en route in a bedroom and burned alive. When he had been killed, without concern, as if their possible avenger had been put out of the way, they exhausted the wretched remains of the city by slaughter and plundering. Theramenes, also, one of their own number, to whom they felt these acts were displeasing, they killed as an example to inspire fear among the rest. And so all fled from the city in every direction, but when by an interdict of the Lacedaemonians hospitality throughout all Greece was denied the exiles, all betook themselves to Argos and Thebes,[37] where they were so favored with willing hospitality that, not only did they mitigate the grief of a lost fatherland, but even nourished the hope of recovering it. There was among the exiles a Thrasybulus, a vigorous man famous among his own for nobility of birth, and he was the author of a daring plan in behalf of his fatherland. Thus the exiles came together and captured the fortress of Phyle on Attica territory, and assisted by the resources of many states, they gathered strength. To these also Lysias, a Syracusan orator, as if for the aid of the city which was the common fatherland of eloquence, sent five hundred soldiers together with money to pay them. This was a fierce battle, but to those who were fighting for fatherland and liberty, and to the others who fought for the rule of a foreign power, the battle brought a judgment as to spirit and causes, for the tyrants were overcome and fled back into the city, and all whom they had selected before from the Athenians as their guards, they then suspected of treachery and

---

37 Cities which had refused to obey the edict.

removed them from the guardianship of the city. They also
dared to tempt Thrasybulus with bribery. When this was
hoped for in vain, they summoned aid from Lacedaemonia and
again rushed into battle, in which the two by far most cruel
of all tyrants were killed. When Thrasybulus perceived that
the others who had been conquered and turned into flight
were chiefly Athenians, he followed them with a shout, and
halted them with a speech, and bound them with entreaties,
placing before their eyes the people whom they wished to flee
and with whom they wished to take refuge; that the war had
been taken up by themselves against the thirty tyrants, not
against the wretched citizens; indeed, all rather who remembered that they were Athenians should follow those who were
exacting vengeance for the liberty of the Athenians. So this
exhortation had such force among them that presently they
turned back into the city and forced the tyrants to withdraw
from the citadel and to emigrate to Eleusis. After they had
received their own fellow citizens, hitherto exiles, back into
the community of the city, they stirred the tyrants through
jealousy into strife, to whom the freedom of others seemed
to be their own slavery. Then, when war had been declared,
after they had first come together as if for a conference,[38] they
were surrounded by ambuscades and slaughtered like sacrificial victims in peace time. Being thus recalled into unity,
and after insatiable tears of great joy, they established these
first foundations of their newly acquired liberty, set forth
with the attestation of a binding oath that the discords and
animosities of the past be assigned to perpetual oblivion and
unending silence. This kind of a pact they formed as a new
arrangement of life and a new happiness for their civil status
and they called it an amnesty, that is, an abolition of their
misfortunes. A most wise provision on the part of the Athenians, especially after so many instances of wretchedness; if
according to this pact with the abiding harmony among men,

---

38 They expected to enter into agreements whereby they would be able
to recover their power.

human affairs had remained as they were originally arranged, they would have prospered, but this same decree was corrupted almost in the midst of the very words of the decree so that scarcely two years had passed when Socrates, that most famous of philosophers, driven by contemporary evils deprived himself of life by drinking poison; then, scarcely forty years had passed, to be silent about other events, when these same Athenians, being deprived completely of their liberty became slaves under Philip, king of the Macedonians. Nevertheless, the Athenians, the wisest of all peoples, being well taught even by their own misfortunes that the smallest affairs prosper by concord and the greatest collapse by discord, and that all things either good or even evil which are carried on abroad have their roots and sprout in internal beginnings, wiped out their hatreds at home and pressed wars abroad, and they left to their descendents an example of their own ruin and a plan for recovery, if, however, because of the extremely weak vacillation of the human mind, what is given heed in ruinous circumstances is preserved in prosperity.

(18) Almost at this same time a civil war, rather even more than a civil war since it barely ended with fratricide, was carried on among the Persians. For when king Darius died, and Artaxerxes and Cyrus, his sons, wrangled over the kingdom, finally, after great preparations on both sides, a struggle arose which brought disaster to the provinces and the people. In this conflict, when fortune set both brothers against each other as they charged from opposite directions, Artaxerxes[39] was the first to be wounded by his brother, but he escaped death when he was carried away by the swiftness of his horse. But Cyrus being hard pressed by the royal cohort soon put an end to the struggle. Artaxerxes, therefore, gaining possession of the army and the booty of his brother's expedition, strengthened his power over the kingdom by fratricide. Thus, all Asia and Europe, partly one against the other, partly among

39 Artaxerxes II. The battle of Cunaxa, 401 B.C.

themselves, were intermingled with murders and shameful deeds.

Behold, how many actions involving so many provinces, peoples, and cities I have set forth in the smallest book and in the fewest words; how I have involved masses of misfortunes. For who will unfold the slaughter of that time, who the deaths in words, or who can equal the grief with tears?[40] Yet these very misfortunes, because they have grown dim by the passing of many centuries, have become exercises for our talents and delightful topics for stories. And yet if anyone applies himself completely with the entire force of his mind to wars and their causes, and furthermore, as if placed in a watchtower, measures both ages as to their conditions, I would easily say that he would judge that these affairs could not be so unfortunately confused and mixed up except by a God angry and estranged, and that present times cannot be composed without a gracious and merciful God.

Later in those times Sicily was shaken by a very severe earthquake; moreover, was laid waste by erupting fires and hot ashes from Mount Etna to the very great damage of the fields and villages.

Then, too, the city of Atalante, bordering closely on the territory of Locris, was cut off by a sudden rush of the sea and was left an island. Also a plague invaded the wretched remnants of the Athenians and long ravaged them.

(19) In the three hundred and fifty-fifth year after the founding of the City, the seige of Veii in ten continuous years wore out the besiegers rather than the besieged. For the Romans were weakened by frequent and sudden sorties on the part of the enemy, besides they were forced to hazard war while in winter quarters, and to spend the winter under furs, and, finally, to endure famine and cold in the sight of the enemy. Finally, they captured the city without any worthy display of Roman courage by mines and a secret attack. Exile for the dictator, Camillus, who captured this city from the

---

40 Cf. Vergil, *Aeneid* 2.361 ff.

Veientes, at first followed this useful rather than famous victory, then an invasion by the Gauls and the burning of the City. Let anyone, if he can, compare some of the disturbances of this age with this disaster, although he does not weigh equally the story of a past disaster with a calamity in the present. Now when the Senonian Gauls under the leadership of Brennus with a very large and strong army were besieging the city of Clusium, which is now called Tuscia, they saw the Roman legates, who had come at that time to conclude a peace between them, fighting in the battle line against them. Roused by this affront they abandoned the siege of the city of Clusium and rushed with all their forces to Rome. Fabius,[41] consul, with his army received them as they so rushed on, yet he did not halt them; rather that hostile attack cut them down, laid them low, and passed over them like a withered harvest. The Allia River[42] testifies to this disaster of Fabius as the Cremera did to that of the Fabii. Not easily would one recall a similar downfall of a Roman army, even if in addition Rome had not been burned. The Gauls entered the City which lay open to them, slew the senators who sat rigid as statues in their chairs, and after burning them by the fire of their homes, buried them under the collapsing roofs. All the remaining youth, whom it is established amounted at that time to barely a thousand men, they shut in with a siege as they lay concealed in the citadel of Capitoline Hill and there they wore down those unfortunate survivors by famine, disease, desperation, and fear; then they subdued them and sold them into slavery. The Gauls set as a price for their departure a thousand pounds of gold, not because Rome was of little repute with the Gauls, but because they had already so worn it down that it could not pay more at that time. As the Gauls departed there had remained within the circuit of the former City a repulsive mass of shapeless ruins, and on all sides the echo of the unfortunate

---

41 Quintus Fabius Ambustus, Military Tribune, 390 B.C.
42 A little river eleven miles north of Rome, near Crustumerium, in the country of the Sabines, passing through a wide plain.

voices of those wandering over obstructions and not knowing that they were among their own possessions resounded and kept ears alarmed. Horror shook men's minds; the very silence terrified, for the material of fear is loneliness in open spaces. Hence, the Romans considered, voted, and attempted to change their homes to inhabit another town, and even to be called by another name.

Behold the times in comparison with which the present is weighed; behold the times for which our memory sighs; behold the times which strike us with penitence because of our *elected* religion or rather because of our *rejected* religion. Truly, these two captivities are similar and comparable to each other, the one raging for six months and the other running its course in three days; the Gauls, after wiping out the population and destroying the City, persecuting also the very name of Rome in the last ashes; and the Goths, giving up their intention of plundering, driving the unknown hoards into refuges of safety, that is, sacred places; there, scarcely any senator was found who by flight had escaped; here, scarcely anyone was sought who by chance perished while hiding. I could, indeed, rightly make the comparison that the number of senators in the one case was the same as that of the lost in the other. Clearly, as is set forth in fact and must be confessed, in this present disaster God was more angry and men less so, since by Himself performing what they would not have fulfilled, He demonstrated why He sent them. For since it was beyond human strength to burn bronze beams and to overthrow large massive structures, the Forum, together with its empty images, was struck by a bolt of lightning which by a wretched superstition made a mockery of both God and man, and of all these abominations, that which the fire let loose by the enemy did not reach, fire sent from heaven cast down.

And since material for discussion is rich, which by no means can be confined to this book, let this be the end of the present volume, so that we may pursue the remaining matters in subsequent books.

BOOK THREE

Preface

IN AN EARLIER BOOK, I called to witness and, now of necessity, according to your instructions, I take up again the story of the conflicts of past ages; neither can all things be unfolded nor through all things what were accomplished and just as they were accomplished, because important and innumerable matters were described by a great many writers at very great length; moreover, the writers, although they did not have the same motives, yet they did have at their disposal the same materials, for whereas they unfold wars, we unfold the miseries of wars. Besides, from this very abundance about which I complain, there arises a difficulty and a rather knotty problem restricts me. For if I omit some things in my zeal for brevity, they will be thought either to have been lacking to me now or never to have taken place then; but if being anxious to point all things out, but not to describe them, I summarize them in a brief compendium, I shall make them obscure and so with many they will have been said in such a way that they seem not to have been said, especially since we, on the contrary, are anxious to set forth the essence of things not their description; but brevity and obscurity, rather brevity inasmuch as it is always obscure, although it sets forth the appearance of understanding, yet takes away the vigor of comprehension. Although I know that both ought to be avoided, I shall do both in order that in some way one may be tempered by the other, if much seems not to be omitted and events seem not to be greatly compressed.

(1) In the three hundred and sixty-fourth year after the founding of the City, which year Rome felt to be most severe on account of the captivity not before experienced by her, just as Greece held it to be glorious because of the unaccustomed peace; indeed, at this time when the Gauls, after capturing and burning Rome, held it and sold it, Artaxerxes, king of the Persians, gave orders through legates for Greece to lay aside arms and remain at peace, announcing that any breaker of the peace would be assailed by war. Surely, the Greeks could have disdained him who ordered just as firmly as they often bravely conquered him, but they gladly seized the opportunity offered them from whatever source for the peace which they so eagerly desired, for they showed with what difficulty and how wretchedly they hitherto had carried on those wars which they so easily laid aside on even unworthy terms; for what is so intolerable for free and brave men as to lay aside their arms to the power of one who is far away, often conquered, still an enemy, and still threatening, and to serve his peace? The Greeks would not have acted in this way had not the bitter intention of war melted in the hearts of all at only the very sound of a proclaimed peace, and had not the unexpected quiet of peace relaxed them as they became listless and bewildered after long and laborious vigils, before their desires had been stipulated and had arranged the respite itself. But I shall show as briefly as possible how such great lassitude oppressed the hearts and bodies of all the peoples throughout all Greece, which persuaded these fierce spirits so easily to rest in a leisure hitherto unknown to them.

The Lacedaemonians, in the manner of men and in particular Greek men, as they possessed more, desired more, and, after they overpowered the Athenians, clung to all Asia in the hope of domination. And so stirring up war in the entire East, they selected Dercyllidas as leader for this campaign. When he saw that he would have to fight against the two most powerful satraps of Artaxerxes, the king of the Persians, namely, Pharnabazus and Tissaphernes, taking counsel for the

moment on how to avoid the consequences of a double encounter, declared war and sought the one; he postponed the
other by making a treaty. Pharnabazus brought Tissaphernes
before Artaxerxes, at that time their common king, accusing
him of being a traitor, particularly since he had concluded
a treaty with the enemy in time of war, and he urged the king
to put in his place Conon, a man from Athens, in charge of
naval operations, who at that time happened to be an exile in
Cyprus. So Conon was summoned by Pharnabazus, and, after
giving him five hundred silver talents, placed him in charge
of the fleet. When these matters were learned, the Lacedaemonians themselves also through legates sought aid for a naval
war from the king of Egypt, Hercynio,[1] from whom they received one hundred fully equipped triremes and six hundred
thousand *modii*[2] of grain; from the allies also on all sides,
they brought together large auxiliary forces. Over this military
operation with the consent of all they appointed Agesilaus as
general, a lame man, but in a very difficult condition of affairs,
they preferred that their king rather than their kingdom limp.
Rarely, if ever, have generals come together in war so equal
in every activity, who, exhausted in turn by the severest battles
and smeared with much blood, withdrew from each other as
if unconquered. So Conon, after receiving a second payment
for himself from the Great King, returned to the fleet and invaded hostile lands, took citadels, fortresses, and other defenses
by storm, and like a bursting storm laid low everything that
stood in his way. But the Lacedaemonians surrounded by
troubles at home ceased to be interested in foreign affairs and
with the imminent danger of becoming enslaved, they abandoned hope of unrestricted power and recalled Agesilaus,
whom they had sent with an army into Asia, to the defense of
the fatherland. In the meantime, Pisander, left as leader at

---

1 Diodorus Siculus, 14.35, calls him Psammiticus.
2 *modius* or *modium*, the Roman corn-measure, a measure, a peck; one-
  sixth of the Greek *medimnus* or one-third of a *amphora;* about equal
  to two English gallons.

Sparta by Agesilaus, had equipped a very large and at that time strong fleet, moved by emulation of the courage of Agesilaus in order that as he carried on an infantry expedition, he himself might also harass the sea coast with naval encounters. But Conon, who had assumed responsibility, weighed a twofold anxiety, a debt of concern to his allies and of loyalty to his fatherland, to show a natural feeling to the one and to exhibit an example of industry to the other. In the latter case, he leaned more toward his fellow citizens, because the imperiling of foreign blood weighed more in the direction of their peace and liberty and militated against most arrogant enemies at the risk of the king and to the reward of his fatherland.³ So they came together in a naval battle, the Persians under Conon and the Spartans under Pisander; soldiers, rowers, and the generals themselves were seized alike with a single desire to slaughter one another. The position of the Lacedaemonians ever growing weaker henceforth indicates the magnitude and fierceness of this war; for from this time on the hope of the Spartans seemed to ebb and collapsing to recede,⁴ until by rising with difficulty and falling back wretchedly, it became exhausted and lost both its power and its name. But for the Athenians, this same battle was the beginning of the recuperation of their power, just as for the Lacedaemonians, it was the beginning of its loss. So the Thebans, relying on the support of the Athenians, were the first to attack them, wounded and fearful because of the earlier defeat, filled with great courage on account of the bravery and energy of their general, Epaminondas, with whom they seemed able easily to obtain power over all Greece. So a battle by land took place, the Thebans conquering with very little difficulty. For Lysander also was conquered and slain in this conflict;⁵ Pau-

---

3 i.e., by helping the Persians to conquer, the Lacedaemonians would be weakened and Athens would have a better opportunity to reestablish herself.

4 Cf. Vergil, *Aeneid* 2.169,170.

5 This battle was fought in 395 B.C. near Haliartus, a city of Boeotia, near the modern village of *Mazi*.

sanias, the other general of the Lacedaemonians, also was accused of treason and driven into exile; but the Thebans after gaining the victory, gathered their entire army and hastened to Sparta thinking that they would easily enter the city void of defenders, nearly all of whose troops, including the king himself, they had destroyed and which they saw deserted by all its allies. The Lacedaemonians alarmed by the danger to the city, holding a levy of untrained troops from whatever source, went out to meet the enemy. When these recruits had once been conquered, there was no courage or spirit on the part of the Spartans to go out and meet the victors. When, then, the slaughter was being carried on almost entirely on one side, King Agesilaus, being summoned from Asia, suddenly and unexpectedly appeared in the battle. He then attacked the Thebans who were rather overconfident and careless because of their twofold victory and overcame them without difficulty, especially since his forces up to that time were maintained almost intact. However, Agesilaus himself was gravely wounded. And when the Athenians learned that the Lacedaemonians were elated by their unexpected victory, becoming alarmed by fear of their former slavery from which they were then beginning with difficulty to recover, they gathered their army and added it as an auxiliary force to that of the Boeotians, committing it to the Iphicrates as general. He was a very young man, barely twenty years of age, whose tenderness of age was compensated for by maturity of mind. Conon also, indeed an Athenian, although the leader of the Persian army, when he heard of the return of Agesilaus, returned to plunder the fields of the Lacedaemonians. Thus, the Spartans, enclosed and terrified by the din of the enemy resounding on all sides, declined almost to the ultimate in desperation. But Conon, after he had satisfied himself with the vast devastation of the enemy's soil, proceeded to Athens, midst the greatest joy on the part of his fellow citizens but himself sad on seeing the city, once most famous for her people and her culture, now crushed with the wretched squalor of ruin and desolation.

Thus, as a great memorial to his patriotism and compassion,
he devoted himself to its reparation. For with the booty of
the Lacedaemonians, he replenished the city which had been
burned by Persian incendiaries. Meanwhile, Artarxerxes, the
king of the Persians, as was said in the beginning, sent word
through legates to all the peoples of Greece to depart from
their arms and to remain at peace, not because he was consulting their own good in their exhaustion, but for fear that,
while he was occupied with wars in Egypt, an attack might
be attempted against his own kingdom.

(2) Thus, when all the Greeks had been enfeebled by the
quiet which had been especially desired and became sluggish
by the leisure at home, the Lacedaemonians, restless rather
than energetic, unbearable by reason of their fury rather than
their bravery after laying aside wars, attempted the trickeries
of wars. For having observed the absence of the Arcadians,
by a sudden attack broke into their citadel. But the Arcadians,
aroused by the injustice, joining forces with the Thebans,
sought to regain what they had lost by the sneak attack. In this
battle,[6] Archidamus, the leader of the Lacedaemonians, was
wounded, and when he saw that his men were now being slaughtered as if conquered, through a herald asked for the bodies of
the dead for burial, which among the Greeks is customarily held
to be an acknowledgment of defeat. The Thebans, moreover,
satisfied with this confession gave the signal to cease and put
an end to the struggle. Then, while a few days of truce intervened, and the Lacedaemonians had turned to other wars,
the Thebans with Epaminondas as leader, took confidence in
invading Lacedaemon since it was off-guard and deserted.
Silently, in the dead of night, they came to the city of Lacedaemon; but they did not find it as off-guard or undefended as
they expected, for the old men, together with the remaining
throng unfit for war, being informed of the coming of the
enemy, had stationed themselves at the very entrance of the

---

6 Fought near Cromnus, to which Archidamus was advancing to raise
the siege, 365 B.C.

gates and scarcely a hundred men, enfeebled by age, rushed forth against fifteen thousand soldiers. Thus, while these were bearing such a weighty attack, the young men arrived and decided without delay to come to close quarters with the Thebans in open combat. After the battle had been joined, when the Lacedaemonians were being conquered, suddenly Epaminondas, the leader of the Thebans, fought rather recklessly and was wounded.[7] So, while with the one, fear arose from grief, and with the others amazement from joy, as it were, by tacit consent there was a withdrawal on both sides. But Epaminondas, gravely wounded, on learning of the victory of his men and kissing his shield, removed his hand with which he had closed up the wound, made clear an egress of blood and an entrance of death. Thus, the destruction of the Thebans followed on his death so that they seemed not to have lost a leader, but themselves to have then perished with him.

I have woven together an inextricable wicker-work of confused history and I have worked in with words the uncertain cycles of war carried on here and there with frantic fury, following the evidence closely, for the more I kept to the order of events, the more, as I see it, I wrote in a disorderly fashion. To how many people, to what cities, to what provinces the wicked lust for conquest on the part of the Lacedaemonians stirred up emotions of all kinds of hatred, and how many causes of strife it caused, who could arrange these either by number, or order, or reason? Yet, the Lacedaemonians themselves also are reported to have been afflicted no more by the wars than by the confusion caused by wars, for when this war had been carried on continuously for several years, the Athenians, Lacedaemonians, Arcadians, Boeotians, Thebans, and finally, Greece, Asia, Persia, and Egypt, together with Libya and the largest islands, carried on simultaneously battles by land and sea in indiscriminate movements. Even if I were to

---

7 There is some confusion here. Epaminondas was wounded at Mantinea in 362 B.C.

enumerate the wars, I could not record the thousands of men slaughtered.

But let him rant at these times and praise those of the past who does not know that all the peoples of those cities and provinces are today so growing old at games and theaters alone just as in those days they wasted away chiefly in camps and battles. That very flourishing state of the Lacedaemonians, then seeking power even over the entire East, was able then to possess barely a hundred old men; so surrounded by unceasing evils it wretchedly wasted the lives of her youth; and now complaints arise from men, whose cities, filled with children and old men, grow rich as their young men travel safely and acquire from peaceful pursuits funds for pleasures at home! Unless perchance—as present things are customarily held of no account by fickle human nature—life itself also is a bore to those who itch for new things to do and hear.

(3) In the three hundred and seventy-sixth year after the founding of the City, all Achaia was shaken by a most violent earthquake, and two cities, that is, Ebora and Helice, were then swallowed up by precipitous openings in the ground.

But now, on the other hand, I could tell of similar happenings in our days at Constantinople, now as before the center of the world, predicted and being brought about but not accomplished, when after a terrible intimation and consciousness of its own disaster, the earth below was shaken to its depths and trembled, and a flame spreading from above hung from heaven until God, implored by the prayers of the emperor, Arcadius, and the Christian people, averted the imminent destruction, proving Himself alone to be the preserver of the humble and the punisher of the wicked. But that these have been mentioned rather than set forth in detail, I would concede to modesty, so that both he who knows them may refresh his memory and he who does not may inquire about them.

Meanwhile, the Romans, for seventy years held in subjection by the city of the Volsci and also by the cities of the Falisci, Aequi, and Sutrini, worn out by continuous wars be-

came exhausted, but in the days mentioned above, under the
leadership of Camillus,[8] they finally captured those same cities
and put an end to the renewed struggle. Also at the same
time, under the leadership of Titus Quintius at the River
Allia, they overcame the Praenestini who had come fighting
and slaughtering up to the gates of Rome.

(4) In the three hundred and eighty-fourth year after the
founding of the City, in the consulship of Lucius Genucius
and Quintus Servilius,[9] a great pestilence seized all Rome; not
as usual a more or less than customary disturbed temperature
of the seasons, that is, either untimely dryness in winter or
sudden heat in spring or unseasonable moisture in summer or
the confused allurement of a fruitful autumn, over and above
all this, a devastating breeze blown in from the pasture land
of Calabria brought in sudden flashes of violent epidemics;
moreover, it was severe and long-lasting, without regard for
sex and age for two continuous years it crushed all with
wasting disease, so that even those whom it did not drive to
death, it left wasted and afflicted with horrible emaciation.
The detractors of the Christian period would complain at this
point, as I think, if by chance I passed over in silence the
ceremonies with which at that time the Romans tried to
placate the gods and to allay the diseases. When the pestilence
increased day by day, the pontifices persuaded the writers to
put on dramatic performances for the gods who coveted them.
Thus, to dispel a temporal plague of their bodies, an eternal
disease of the souls was summoned. Rich, indeed, now is this
opportunity for grief and reproach, but where already your
reverence[10] has exercised the zeal for wisdom and truth, it is
not right for me to venture beyond this. Let it suffice that I

---

8 M. Furius Camillus, the most distinguished member of the *gens Furia*.
He conquered Veii and freed Rome from the Gauls. He was consular
tribune several times, interrex, and dictator. These events took place
from 401 to 381 B.C.

9 Lucius Genucius Aventinensis and Quintus Servilius Ahala, 365 B.C.

10 St. Augustine.

have reminded the reader and have turned him from any other intention to the fullness of that text of yours.

(5) In the next year, a very sad prodigy followed this wretched pestilence and its more wretched expiation. For suddenly in the middle of the City, the earth burst asunder, and immediately by a vast open chasm the gaping vitals of the earth were exposed. The impudent cavern with its open abyss for long remained a spectacle and an object of terror to all and, according to interpreters of the gods, required the burial of a man alive, a nefarious act. M. Curtius, an armored knight, gave satisfaction to those wicked jaws by casting himself into them and injected the sorry satiety into the cruel earth, to which it was not enough to receive those who died from the pestilence through burial without also swallowing the living in its open chasm.

(6) In the three hundred and eighty-eighth year after the founding of the City, there was again a terrible influx of Gauls who encamped along the Anio River at the fourth milestone from the City, and without doubt would easily have occupied the City, which was in confusion by reason of their overwhelming numbers and the ardor of their courage, had they not became torpid through ease and slothfulness. When Manlius Torquatus[11] began the very fierce battle by single combat, T. Quintius, the dictator, ended the battle after a very bloody encounter.[12] A great many Gauls were put to flight in this battle and when, after they had rested, they renewed the battle they were overcome by the dictator, Sulpicius.[13] A little later, under C. Marcius,[14] there followed also the battle against the Tuscans, where one may conjecture how many men were killed, when eight thousand of the Tuscans were captured.

---

11 Titus Manlius Torquatus engaged in combat with a Gallic champion and, after he slew him, put on the neckchain of the Gaul and so obtained the name Torquatus.

12 This battle was fought not far from the Colline Gate. The dictator was Titus Quintius Pennus.

13 The dictator, Gaius Sulpicius Peticus, after much delay finally conquered the Gauls near Pedum in Latium.

14 Gaius Marcius Rutilius.

Moreover, for the third time in the same days, the Gauls in pursuit of booty overran the maritime regions and the fields at the foot of the Alban Mountains, against whom the Romans proceeded after a new levy of troops was held and ten legions, sixty thousand Romans, had been enrolled, since the aid of the Latins had been refused them. M. Valerius brought this battle to a close with the help of a crow, as a result of which he was thereafter called Corvinus.[15] For when the Gallic challenger was killed, the enemy, frightened and fleeing dispersedly, were slaughtered in great numbers.

(7) Among these evils also I think should be numbered that first treaty which was struck with the Carthaginians, which took place at the same time, after which especially such serious troubles arose that they seem to have had their origin in it. Indeed, in the four hundred and second year after the founding of the City, legates were sent by Carthage to Rome and concluded a treaty. The trustworthiness of histories, the ill-omened character of the places, and the horror of the days in which these affairs happened, testify that a hailstorm of evils and a perpetual night of continued miseries would follow the coming of the Carthaginians into Italy.

Then, also, night seemed to extend into the greatest part of the day, and stone-like hail descending from the clouds lashed the earth with veritable stones.

In these days also Alexander the Great, truly that whirlpool of evils and most horrible hurricane sweeping the entire East, was born.

Then, too, Ochus,[16] who was also called Artaxerxes, after having carried on a very extensive and long-lasting war in Egypt, forced a great many Jews to migrate and ordered them to live in Hyrcania near the Caspian Sea, and it is common belief that these have lived there up to the present day with

---

15 As told by Livy (*Histories*, 7.26), when M. Valerius advanced to meet the Gallic challenger, a crow lighted on his helmet. During the combat, the crow attacked the Gaul with its beak and talons. This prodigy so affected the Gaul that he succumbed to the Roman soldier's attack.
16 Artaxerxes III who ruled from 362 to 339 B.C.

very ample increases in their race, and that some day they
will break forth from this location. Also, at the time of this
war, Ochus, while passing through the land, destroyed Sidon,
the richest city of the province of Phoenicia, and brought
Egypt under his power, although it had been previously subjected and crushed by the sword of the Persians.

(8) Immediately after this, wars were undertaken by the
Romans against the Samnites, strong in resources and arms,
in behalf of the Campanians and Sidicinians. The Samnite
War, which had been carried on with indecisive results, was
assumed by Pyrrhus, truly the greatest enemy of the Roman
name; the Punic War soon followed the war against Pyrrhus;
and although the ever-open gates of Janus indicate that never,
after the death of Numa, was there a cessation from the slaughters of wars, yet from that time on, the heat of misfortunes
glowed as if pressed down at noon from the entire sky. Furthermore, when the Punic War had once begun, let anyone
who thinks that Christian times should be branded with infamy inquire, discover, and proclaim whether at any time
wars, slaughters, destruction, and all manner of infamous
deaths ever ceased except when Caesar Augustus ruled. Except for that period of a year between the Punic wars, like a
bird flying by, the Romans, because the gates of Janus were
closed in the midst of fevers and diseases in the Republic, were
deluded by a very brief sign of peace; moreover, as by a very
slight draught of cold water, so that becoming more feverish,
they were afflicted much more seriously and violently.

But, indeed, if it is established beyond dispute that under
Augustus Caesar for the first time, after the peace with the
Parthians, the whole world having laid down its arms and
abandoned its discords, composed in a general peace and
new quiet, obeyed the laws of the Romans, preferred the laws
of the Romans to their own arms, and, spurning their own
leaders, elected Roman judges, finally (if it is established)
that there was a single will with a free and honest zeal to
serve the peace and consult the common good of all nations,

entire provinces, innumerable cities, countless peoples, and
the whole world, which formerly not even one city nor one
group of citizens nor, what is worse, one household of brothers
had been able to possess continually, moreover, if also when
under the rule of Caesar these things came to pass, it is manifest that the birth of our Lord Jesus Christ had begun to
illuminate this world with the brightest approbation. Although unwillingly, those whom ill-will urged to blasphemy
will be forced to recognize and confess that this peace and most
tranquil serenity of the whole world existed, not by the greatness of Caesar, but by the power of the Son of God who appeared in the days of Caesar, and that the world itself, according to general knowledge obeyed, not the ruler of one city,
but the Creator of the whole world, who like the rising sun
pervades the day with light, and thus by His coming mercifully
clothed the world with prolonged peace. This will be set
forth more fully when we have come to it, when the Lord
Himself wills it.

(9) So in the four hundred and ninth year after the founding of the City, the Romans in the consulship of Manlius
Torquatus and Decius Mus[17] brought war upon the rebelling
Latins. In this war, one consul was killed, the other survived
as a parricide. For Manlius Torquatus killed his own son, a
young man, victorious in war, and the slayer of Maecius
Tusculanus, a noble knight, and at that time a provoking
and abusive enemy. Now the other consul, when, as the conflict was renewed, he saw that the wing over which he was in
command was being hard pressed and slaughtered, of his own
accord slipped forth into the most crowded ranks of the
enemy and was killed. Manlius, although victorious, yet tri-
umphing as a parricide, did not receive the reception from
the noble youths of Rome which is customarily given under
the law.

---

17 Titus Manlius Imperiosus Torquatus III and Publius Decius Mus,
340 B.C.

Moreover, in the year after this, Minucia, a Vestal Virgin, having admitted incest, was condemned and buried alive in a field which is now called 'Polluted.'

(10) But I truly shudder to relate what took place a short time after this. For in the consulship of Claudius Marcellus and Valerius Flaccus,[18] Roman matrons were inflamed with an incredible madness and love of crime. It was, indeed, that horrible pestilential year when on all sides corpses of the dead were heaped up in piles and carried away, and still there prevailed among all the simple the belief that this came from the contaminated air, when, as a certain maidservant became an informer and convinced them, they learned that, first, many matrons were compelled to drink the poisons which they had concocted, then, as soon as they had drained them they died. Moreover, so great a number of the matrons were involved in these crimes that three hundred and seventy of them are reported to have been condemned at one time.

(11) In the four hundred and twenty-second year after the founding of the City, when Alexander, king of the Epirots, the maternal uncle of the famous Alexander the Great, transported his troops to Italy and prepared for war against the Romans, and in his eagerness for war tried around the cities in the vicinity of Rome to strengthen the forces of his own army and his auxiliaries, either by bringing them over to his own side or by detaching them from the enemy, he was conquered in a very great battle in Lucania by the Samnites, who were bringing aid to a Lucanian tribe, and killed.

But since I have progressed somewhat in enumerating the disasters of the Romans, and being moved by the mention of this Alexander, insofar as I can, going back a very few years, I shall gather briefly important things about Philip, king of Macedon, who had as a wife, Olympias, sister of Alexander of Epirus, from whom he begot Alexander the Great.

(12) In the four hundredth year after the founding of the City, Philip, the son of Amyntas and the father of Alexander,

---

18 Marcus Claudius Marcellus and Gaius Valerius Potitus Flaccus, 331 B.C.

obtained the kingdom of the Macedonians and held it for twenty-five years, during which he accumulated all the following masses of afflictions and all multitudes of evils. In the first place, he was given as a hostage to the Thebans by his brother, Alexander, and for three years he was educated in the company of Epaminondas, a most vigorous general and a very distinguished philosopher. Moreover, when Alexander himself had been killed through the wickedness of his mother, Eurydice, although, after she had already committed adultery and had first killed one son and had made her daughter a widow, she had contracted marriage with her cousin on the death of her husband, Philip, being forced to do so by the people, took over the kingdom which he was guarding for the son of his murdered brother. He, since he was harassed on the outside by the attack of the enemy arising on all sides and at home by fear of plots which he often detected, waged war first with the Athenians.[19] When these had been conquered, he transferred his arms against the Illyrians and, after many thousands of the enemy had been killed, captured the very famous city of Larissa. Then, he invaded Thessaly not so much through love of victory as for the sake of possessing the Thessalian cavalry, that he might mingle their strength with his own army. Thus, after taking the Thessalians by surprise and reducing them under his power, by joining the strongest divisions and forces of their cavalry and infantry, he formed an unsurpassable army. So after conquering the Athenians and bringing the Thessalians under subjection he married Olympias, the sister of Arubas,[20] the king of the Molossians. This Arubas, although he thought that by this action, namely, by making an alliance with the Macedonians by his marital relationship with the king he would extend his own empire, was deceived and failed in this, and spent his old age as a private citizen in exile.[21] Then,

---

19 The Athenians had tried to help in establishing a rival of Philip on the Macedonian throne by sending a fleet to the scene.
20 The usual Greek form is 'Αρύββας. Its Latin form varies greatly.
21 Philip unthroned him.

Philip when he was besieging the city of Methone,[22] was hit by an arrow and lost an eye. But he soon stormed the city itself and captured it.

Then, with his forces he subdued almost all Greece, although it had foreknowledge of his plans. For while the Greek states desired to rule individually, all lost their power, and while they rushed at random to mutual destruction, after they had been overcome and were in slavery, they learned at last that what they had lost individually had perished for them all. While Philip, as from a watchtower, observed their foolish associations and always, as a skillful contriver of trickery, favored the weaker by fostering disputes, the kindling wood of war, he subjected to himself both the conquered and the conquerers alike. Moreover, the unbridled despotism of the Thebans gave Philip the opportunity to obtain power over all Greece, for after conquering the Lacedaemonians and the Phoceans, who were already crushed by slaughter and rapine, when in addition, in the common council of Greece, they had burdened them with such a great pecuniary fine as they were in no wise able to pay, they forced them to take refuge in arms. So the Phoceans, under the leadership of Philomelus and supported by the auxiliaries of the Lacedaemonians and Athenians, joined battle and after putting the enemy to flight captured the camp of the Thebans. In a following battle, in the midst of great slaughter on both sides, Philomelus was killed, and in his place the Phoceans appointed Onomarchus as their leader.

Furthermore, moreover, the Thebans and Thessalians, overlooking any election by the citizens, of their own accord sought Philip, king of the Macedonians, as their leader, whom they had previously struggled to repel as an enemy. When battle was joined and the Phoceans were slaughtered almost to a man, victory came to Philip. But the Athenians, when they heard of the outcome of the war, lest Philip might pass over into

---

22 Methone, a town of Pieria in Macedonia, on the Thermaic Gulf.

Greece, occupied the passes of Thermopylae for the same reason as they did in the past when the Persians were approaching.[23]

So Philip, when he saw that he was prevented from entering Greece by the previous occupation of Thermopylae, turned the war, which had been prepared against the enemy, against his allies; for the states, of which a little before he had been the leader, and which were ready to receive him and congratulate him, he invaded as an enemy, cruelly tore to pieces, and completely abolishing all feeling of being an ally, sold their wives and children into slavery, also destroyed and despoiled all their temples, and yet never in twenty-five years, as if the gods were offended, was he defeated. After these accomplishments, Philip passed over into Cappadocia and there carried on war with equal perfidy. Through trickery, he captured the neighboring kings and killed them, and brought Cappadocia under the rule of Macedonia. Then, after carrying on slaughters, conflagrations, and plunderings in the cities of the allies, he turned murder upon his brothers whom, since he feared them as co-heirs of his kingdom, being born to his father from his stepmother, he attempted to kill. But when he had killed one of these, two fled to Olynthus, which Philip at once approached with hostile intent, and after felling this most ancient and flourishing city with slaughter and blood, he emptied it of its resources and population; and he also carried off his brothers and gave them over to torture and death. Then when, elated by the overthrow of his allies and the murder of his brothers, he thought that all that he had planned was permitted him, he seized the gold mines in Thessaly and the silver mines in Thrace, and lest he leave any human or divine law inviolate, he took possession of the sea, and dispersing his fleet he began also to practice piracy. Furthermore, when two brothers, kings of Thrace, arguing over the boundaries of their kingdom, by common consent chose him as judge, Philip

---

23 Cf. Justin, *Histories* 8.2, where other reasons are presented for this course of action.

in the manner of his genius approached the judgment with an army drawn up as if for war and deprived the unsuspecting youths of their lives and kingdom.

Now the Athenians, who previously had repelled the advance of Philip by fortifying Thermopylae, seeking peace with him of their own volition, advised the most deceitful enemy of their careless watch over the pass. The other Greek states also, that they might pay greater attention to civil wars, under the appearance of a peace and an alliance, of their own accord subjected themselves to a foreign power, especially since the Thessalians and Boeotians asked Philip to present and acknowledge himself as their leader against the Phoceans and to carry on the war which had been undertaken, the Athenians and Lacedaemonians having joined with them against the Phoceans either to work for a delay of the war or to avert it by bribery and entreaties. Philip secretly made different promises to both, confirming under oath that he would grant peace and forgiveness to the Phoceans, but to the Thessalians he promised that he would soon be on hand with an army, yet he forbade both to prepare for war. So Philip drew up his troops and entered the passes of Thermopylae without fear, and after occupying them, fortified them by placing garrisons here and there. Then, for the first time, not only the Phoceans, but all Greece perceived that they had been captured, since Philip, breaking his pledge and scorning his oath, gave over the foremost Phoceans to a terrible massacre; then, ravaging the cities and territories of all, he made his bloody presence so felt that he was feared even when absent. When he returned to his kingdom, in the manner of shepherds who lead their flocks about, now through summer and now through winter pastures, according to his pleasure he transferred peoples and cities according as certain localities seemed to him to need to be replenished or to be abandoned. Everywhere the pitiful sights and the most atrocious kinds of wretchedness were visible—the endurance of destruction without invasion, captivity without war, exile without accusation, domination without a victor. The fear which was spread about in the midst of the torments of injuries pressed them in their wretchedness and the pain by its very concealment increased the more as it descended upon them, and they could not express their fear lest the very tears be also taken as obstinate disobedience. Some peoples Philip tore from their settlements and placed them opposite the territory of the enemy; others he located on the extreme borders of his kingdom; certain of them out of jealousy of their strength, that they might not have the power which they were believed to possess, he distributed to supplement cities already exhausted. Thus, that most glorious body of once flourishing Greece fell into many mutilated pieces as soon as their liberty was destroyed.

(13) When he had carried on these operations in a goodly number of Greek cities and yet was pressing them all with fear, conjecturing the wealth of all from the booty of a few, and thinking that a maritime city of profitable wealth was necessary to carry out a like devastation in all the cities, judged Byzantium, that noble and endowed city, to be the base for his operations by land and sea, and when it resisted he immediately surrounded it with a siege. Moreover, this Byzantium was first founded by Pausanias, king of the Spartans, but later it was enlarged by Constantine, the Christian emperor, and called Constantinople, and now it is the seat of our most glorious empire and the chief city of the entire East. Now, after a long and fruitless siege, to recover by plundering the wealth which he had exhausted in the siege, Philip took up piracy. Thus he sold one hundred and seventy ships loaded with merchandise and came to the assistance of his distressed poverty with a little relief. Then, so as to take in booty and to carry on a siege, he divided his army. Moreover, he himself going forth with his bravest soldiers captured many cities of the Chersonese[24] and, after overcoming the people, took away

---

24 Cherronesus, or Chersonesus, Thracica or *absol.* Cherronesus, the Thracian peninsula at the west of the Hellespont, the Chersonese.

their wealth. He also passed over to Scythia with his son, Alexander, with the intention of plundering. Atheas then was ruling over the Scythians. When he was hard-pressed in his war with the Istriani, he sought aid of Philip through the people of Apollonia, but immediately, when the king of the Histriani died and he was freed of the fear of war and the necessity of aid, he broke the treaty of alliance which he had with Philip. Philip, abandoning the siege of Byzantium, entered the war against the Scythians with all his forces, and when after joining battle the Scythians were superior in number and bravery, they were overcome by the treachery of Philip. In this battle, twenty thousand children and women of the Scythian people were captured, a great supply of cattle was taken away, but no gold and silver were discovered, for this fact gave proof, first of all, to the want of the Scythians. Twenty thousand fine mares were sent to Macedonia to improve the breed.

But Triballi blocked Philip in battle as he returned, in which Philip was so wounded in the thigh that his horse was killed by the weapon which passed through his body. Since all thought that he had been killed, they turned to flight and abandoned the booty. Then, after some delay, while Philip convalesced from his wound, he rested in peace; but as soon as he regained his strength, he made war on the Athenians, who being placed in such great danger, then accepted the Lacedaemonians as their allies who were formerly enemies, and they wearied the states of all Greece with legations to seek the common enemy with common forces. Thus some cities joined with the Athenians, but fear of war brought certain ones over to Philip. When battle was joined,[25] although the Athenians were far superior in the number of soldiers, nevertheless, they were conquered by the courage of the Macedonians which had been steeled in constant warfare. That this battle was by far more severe than any previous battle,

---

25 At Chaeronea in Boeotia, 338 B.C.

the very result of events has shown. For this day brought to an end in all Greece the glory of their acquired rule and the existence of their most ancient freedom.

(14) Later, Philip carried out a most bloody victory against the Thebans and Lacedaemonians; for he beheaded some leaders of these people, others he drove into exile; he deprived all of their goods. Those who a short time ago had been banished by the citizens, he restored to the fatherland, of whom he made three hundred exiles judges and officials. These, in order to cure their old grief with their new power, did not allow these unhappily oppressed people to breath in any hope of freedom. Furthermore, after holding a great levy of soldiers from all Greece in support of his royal plan, he drew up to send on his Persian expedition into Asia two hundred thousand infantry and fifteen thousand cavalry, without the army of Macedonians, and a limitless number of barbarian tribes. He selected three leaders to be sent on ahead, among the Persians, Parmenio, Amyntas, and Attalus. While the troops mentioned above were coming together from Greece, he decided to bring his daughter, Cleopatra, together in marriage with Alexander,[26] who was the brother of his wife, Olympias, and later was overthrown by the Sabines in Lucania,[27] and whom he had established as king of Epirus as a reward for the debauchery which he had committed upon him.[28] When on the day before he was killed he had been asked what end was most to be desired by man, he is said to have replied that he was more fortunate who, when reigning as a brave man in peace after the glories of his virtues, was able without damage to body and without dishonor on his soul to fall suddenly and swiftly by an unexpected stroke of the sword. This soon happened to him. Nor could he be

---

26 Alexander I, king of Epirus.
27 Warned by an oracle to avoid Pandosia, he became mindful of Pandosia in Epirus on the Acheron, but was unaware of the Italian town of that name near which he was defeated.
28 As a youth, this Alexander, on going to the court of Philip, was used by Philip to gratify his lust.

prevented by the irate gods, whom he always had held as of little importance and whose altars, temples, and images he had destroyed, from obtaining the most desired death as it seemed to him. For on the day of the wedding, when he was walking between the two Alexanders, son and son-in-law, to the games which had been elaborately prepared, he was surrounded without bodyguards in a narrow passage and killed by Pausanias, a young Macedonian nobleman.

Let people now declare and set forth with a multitude of voices these events as the praiseworthy and fortunate deeds of brave men; for them the bitterest calamities of others become pleasant stories, if, however, they themselves never deplore with a rather sad report the injuries by which they are sometimes distressed. But if they wish others, when they hear them, to be affected by their complaints as much as they themselves felt them on suffering them, first let them not compare past deeds, and let the judges decide both according to the evidence of strangers. For twenty-five years, the fraud, ferocity, and tyranny of one king brought about the burning of cities, the slaughter of men, plundering of wealth, the pillaging of flocks, robbery of the dead, and the enslavement of men.

(15) These deeds accomplished by Philip, which have been impressed upon our memory, would suffice as examples of calamaties, even if Alexander had not succeeded him on the throne. I shall interrupt for a little while the calamities of the world during his wars, rather those which followed, in order that I may add in this place, according to the proper sequence of events, the Roman wars.

In the four hundred and twenty-sixth year after the founding of the City, a notorious infamy on the part of the Romans made the Caudine Forks[29] quite celebrated and scandalous. For when in a previous war the Romans had killed twenty thousand Samnites, Fabius, master of the horse, joining in

---

29 The narrow defile where a Roman army was trapped by, and surrendered to, Gavius Pontius, 321 B.C. It lay between Capua and Beneventum. Cf. Livy 9.2-6.

the battle, the Samnites more cautiously and with better organized equipment took their position at Caudine Forks,
where, when they had cut off the consuls, Veturius and Postumius,[30] and all the Roman troops by the narrow location
and by arms, Pontius, their leader, was so confident in the
security of victory that he thought he should consult his father,
Herennius, as to whether he should kill those who were entrapped or spare them when subjugated. He elected to spare
them, but for dishonor. For it was well established that the
Romans in previous years were very often conquered and
killed, but never captured or forced to surrender. So the Samnites, obtaining their victory, ordered the entire Roman army,
which had been dishonorably captured and even stripped of
its arms and clothing, bare coverings only being granted to
each to be placed over the nakedness of their bodies, to be
sent under the yoke and subjected to slavery, and to take their
places at the head of a long line in public procession. Moreover, after taking six hundred Roman knights as hostages,
they sent the consuls back burdened with disgrace and bereft
of all possessions.

Why should I, who would have preferred to remain silent,
struggle to enlarge with words upon the blemish of this most
disgraceful treaty? For the Romans today would not exist at
all, or would be slaves under Samnite domination, if they
themselves, made subject to the Samnites, had preserved the
sanctity of the treaty which they wished to be preserved by
those subject to themselves.

In the following year, the Romans broke the treaty which
had been made with the Samnites and forced them into war
which, entered upon on the insistence of the consul, Papirius,[31]
caused great disasters to both peoples. Although on the one
hand, anger over their recent disgrace, and on the other the
glory of their last victory, spurred the fighters on, the Romans

---

30 Titus Veturius Calvinus II and Spurius Postumius Albinus II, 321 B.C.
31 Lucius Papirius Mugillanus Cursor, consul in 326, 320, 319, 315, 313
    B.C.; dictator in 325, 309. Cf. Livy 9.15.

by fighting to the death,[32] finally conquered. They did not cease alike to slaughter and be slaughtered until, after conquering the Samnites and capturing their leader, they laid aside their yoke. Then Papirius stormed and captured Satricum,[33] and drove out its Samnite garrison. Now this Papirius at that time was held among the Romans to be most warlike and energetic, so that when Alexander the Great was reported to be arranging to come down upon Africa from the East, to take it by force, and then to pass over into Italy, the Romans considered that this general, among all the other very excellent leaders then in the Republic, was best fitted to sustain the attack of Alexander.

(16) So Alexander, in the four hundred and twenty-sixth year after the founding of the City, succeeded Philip on the throne. He gave the first proof of his spirit and courage by quickly suppressing the revolts of the Greeks, the author of which, to remove themselves from Macedonian rule, was the orator, Demosthenes, bribed by Persian gold. So at the intercessions of the Athenians, he gave up the war, which also relieved them of fear of penalty. When he destroyed the Thebans, after demolishing the city, he sold the survivors into slavery. He made the other cities of Achaia and Thessaly subject to paying tribute. Soon he transferred the war from here and conquered the Illyrians and the Thracians. Then, as he was about to set forth on the Persian War, he killed all his relatives and next of kin. In his army, there were thirty-two thousand infantry, four thousand five hundred cavalry, and one hundred and eighty ships. With so small a force it is uncertain whether Alexander is more to be admired for having conquered the whole world or for having dared to undertake it. In his first encounter with King Darius,[34] there were six

---

32 Fought at Luceria in Apulia.
33 Situated on the frontier of the Volscian territory between the Alban Hills and the sea. After the Roman defeat at Caudine Forks, the people of Satricum went over to the Samnites.
34 Usually known as the battle of Granicus, 334 B.C.

hundred thousand Persians in battle formation who were overcome and turned into flight no less by the strategy of Alexander than by the bravery of the Macedonians. Thus, a great
slaughter of Persians took place. In the army of Alexander,
one hundred and twenty cavalrymen and only nine infantrymen were lost. Then he besieged, stormed, captured, and gave
over to pillage Gordie, a city of Phrygia, which is now called
Sardis.[35] Then, when he was informed of the approach of
Darius with a large number of troops, fearing the narrow
defiles of the terrain in which he was, he crossed over the
Taurus Range with remarkable speed and, covering five hundred stades in a day's march,[36] he came to Tarsus, and there,
when he descended into the very cold waters of the Cydnus
while overheated, he suffered cramps and very nearly died.
Meanwhile, Darius with three hundred thousand infantry and
one hundred thousand cavalry proceeded into battle. This
multitude of the enemy disturbed even Alexander, especially
in the light of his own small numbers, although some time
before, after he had overcome six hundred thousand of the
enemy with the same small numbers, he had learned, not
only not to fear battle, but even to hope for victory. So, when
both armies took their stand within spear range and the two
generals running up and down were rousing their men, intently waiting for the signal for battle by various incentives,
battle was joined with high spirits on both sides. In this
battle,[37] the two kings, Alexander and Darius, were wounded,
and for a long time, the struggle was uncertain until Darius
fled. Then followed a slaughter of the Persians. Eighty thousand of the infantry and ten thousand of the cavalry were
killed; moreover, sixty thousand were captured. Now of the
Macedonians, one hundred of the infantry fell, one hundred
and fifty of the cavalry. Much gold and other wealth was

---

35 Usually identified as Gordium, although its association with Sardis is
probably an error.
36 About fifty-seven and one-half miles.
37 Fought at Issus, 333 B.C.

found in the camp of the Persians. Among the captives taken
in the camp were the mother and wife, who was also his sister,
and two daughters of Darius. When Darius, although he
offered even a half part of his kingdom, did not obtain their
ransom, he brought together all the forces of the Persians and
the auxiliaries of his allies and renewed the war for a third
time. Now, while Darius was accomplishing these things, Alexander sent Parmenio with troops to attack the Persian fleet
and he himself proceeded into Syria, and there of the many
kings who, with fillets, came to meet him of their own accord
he made allies of some, others he removed from their thrones
and others he destroyed, and the most ancient and flourishing
city of Tyre, which opposed him because of their trust in its
kinsmen, the Carthaginians, he overwhelmed and captured.
Then he overran Cilicia, Rhodes, and Egypt with unyielding
fury. From here, he went on to the Temple of Jupiter Ammon, in order that by fabricating a lie for the occasion he
might destroy the ignominy of his uncertain paternity and the
infamy of his adulterous mother. For he summoned to his
presence the priest of the temple itself and secretly advised
him what answers he wished to be made when he consulted
him, as the historians of these events tell us. Thus Alexander
was certain and has so handed down to us, although the gods
themselves are both deaf and dumb, that it was either in the
power of the priest to fashion what he wished or in the will
of the petitioners to hear what he preferred. Returning from
Ammon to the Third Persian War, Alexander founded Alexandria in Egypt.

(17) Now Darius, having lost hope of peace, drew up in
battle array at Tarsus against Alexander as he returned from
Egypt four hundred thousand infantry and one hundred thousand cavalry. There was no delay in the battle. All rushed
with blind madness to the sword,[38] the Macedonians roused
against the enemy who had been defeated so often by them,

---

38 Fought in 331 B.C. near Gaugamela, a village eighteen miles northeast
of Mosul.

the Persians preferring to die rather than be conquered. Rarely has so much blood been spilled in any battle. But Darius, when he saw that his men were being conquered, although prepared to die in battle, was compelled by the persuasiveness of his men to flee. By this battle, the strength and the kingdoms of Asia fell and the entire East submitted to the power of Macedon and all the confidence of the Persians was so shattered in this war that after this no one dared to rebel and following so many years of power accepted the yoke of slavery patiently. For thirty-four continuous days Alexander counted the booty of the camp. He then attacked Persepolis, the capital of the Persian kingdom, the most renowned and the richest city in the whole world. But when he learned that Darius was being held bound in golden fetters by his own relatives, he decided to hasten to him. So giving orders for his army to follow, he himself with six thousand cavalry set forth and found Darius abandoned alone on the road, pierced with many wounds and, as a result of these wounds, breathing his very last. Alexander ordered this dead man with an empty sort of pity to be brought back to the burial place of his ancestors and laid to rest there; not to mention his mother and wife, his little daughter also he held in cruel captivity.

In the midst of such a multitude of evils, the truth is most difficult to express. In three battles and in as many years, five million infantry and cavalry were annihilated, and these, indeed, from that kingdom and those peoples from whom already not many years before more than one million, nine hundred thousand are reported to have been destroyed; and yet in addition to these slaughters, over the same three years a great many states of Asia were overcome and all Syria was laid waste, Tyre was demolished, Cilicia was made desolate, Cappadocia was subdued, Egypt was enslaved, the island of Rhodes also fearful of slavery of its own accord submitted, and a great many provinces near the Taurus and the Taurus Range itself, after being subdued and conquered, accepted the yoke which had long been refused.

(18) And lest anyone think that at this time by chance either the East alone had succumbed to the forces of Alexander or that just Italy had been made weary by Roman restlessness, at that time also war was being carried on in Greece with Agis, king of the Spartans, in Lucania with Alexander, king of Epirus, and in Scythia with Zopyrion, the prefect. Of these, Agis, the Lacedaemonian, after he had stirred up all Greece and persuaded it to join him in rebellion, met with the bravest troops of Antipater and in the midst of great slaughter on both sides he, too, fell.[39] Moreover, in Italy, Alexander who was striving for power over the West and emulating Alexander the Great, after numerous and serious battles had been carried on in that region, was overcome by the Bruttians and Lucanians, and his body was bought for burial. Now Zopyrion, prefect of Pontus, assembling an army of thirty thousand, and daring to carry on war with the Scythians, even to annihilation, was killed and completely wiped out together with all his troops.

So Alexander the Great after the death of Darius subjugated the Hyrcani and the Mardi, where, too, the shameless Amazon, Thalestris, or Minothea, with three hundred women met him, still intent on war, she being stirred with the desire to conceive offspring from him. After this, he entered upon a battle with the Parthians, whom he destroyed, although they resisted for a long time, almost before he conquered them; then he subjugated the Drangae, Evergetae, Parimae, Paropamisadae, Adaspii, and other peoples who resided at the base of the Caucasus, and there on the Tanais River he established the city of Alexandria. But his cruelty toward his own was no less than his frenzy against his enemies. His slaying of his cousin, Amyntas, shows this; also his killing of his stepmother and her brothers, and the murder of Parmenio and Philotas, and the wiping out of Attalus, Eurylochus, Pausanias, and many of the leading men of Macedonia, not to mention the nefarious

---

39 In 331 B.C. at Megalopolis, the capital of Arcadia.

destruction of Clitus, heavy with years and old in friendship
who, when at a banquet trusting in his friendship with the
king he defended the memory of Alexander's father against
the king who was placing his accomplishments ahead of those
of his father, Philip, was pierced with a hunting spear by the
unreasonably offended king, and as he died stained the entire
banquet hall with his blood. But Alexander, insatiable for
human blood, whether of enemies or even allies, was always
thirsting for fresh bloodshed. So with a stubborn attack rushing forward into battle, he received in surrender the Chorasmi
and Dahae, a tribe which had not been conquered. He killed
Callisthenes, the philosopher, a fellow disciple of his under
Aristotle, together with many other prominent men, because
he would not adore him as a god in the customary manner
of salutation.

(19) After this, he sought India, in order that his empire
might be bounded by the Ocean and the farthest East. He
attacked the city of Nysa. He captured the Daedalian mountains and the dominions of Queen Cleophidis who, after
giving herself up, redeemed her kingdom by concubinage.
India being very docile and thoroughly conquered, when
Alexander had come to a rock of remarkable roughness and
height to which many peoples had taken refuge, he learned
that Hercules had been prevented from capturing this same
rock by an earthquake. Roused by the spirit of rivalry to
surpass the deeds of Hercules, with the greatest labor and
danger he took possession of the rock and received in surrender
all the peoples of this locality. He carried on a very bloody
battle with Porus, the most powerful king of the Indians, in
which Alexander, when he met Porus himself in single combat
and fell from his horse which had been killed, escaped on-
coming death by the gathering of his bodyguards. Porus was
pierced by many wounds and captured. After Alexander had
restored Porus to his kingdom as a testimonial to his courage,
he founded two cities there, Nicaea and Bucephale, which he
ordered to be so called after the name of his horse. Then the

Macedonians captured the Adrestae,[40] Catheni, Praesidae, and Gangaridae after cutting their armies to pieces. When they came to Cofides,[41] there they joined battle with two hundred thousand of the enemy's cavalry, and when now exhausted by the heat, depressed in spirit, with strength weakened, they conquered with difficulty, they established a camp of more than ordinary magnificence as a memorial. From there, Alexander proceeded to the Acesines River.[42] Through this he descended to the Ocean. There he captured the Gesonae and the Sibi whom Hercules established. Thence he sailed to the Mandri and Subagrae, which nations received him with eighty thousand armed infantrymen and sixty thousand cavalry. After battle had been joined, the fighting, long doubtful and bloody, at last gave almost a disastrous victory to the Macedonians. For when the troops of the enemy had been dispersed, Alexander led his army against the city, and when he was the first to scale the wall, thinking that the city was deserted, he jumped down inside alone. When the dangerous enemy had surrounded him from all sides, it is incredible to relate that the multitude of the enemy, the great force of weapons, such a great clamor on the part of the excited assailants did not frighten him, that he alone killed and put to flight so many thousands. But when he perceived that he was being overwhelmed by the surrounding multitude, protecting his rear by placing it against the wall, he more easily held off those who faced him until through a breach in the wall the entire army rushed in to his danger and the clamor of the enemy. In this battle, an arrow was hurled at his breast and resting on one knee he fought until he killed the man by whom he was wounded. Then, when he came to the shores of the Ocean, embarking on his vessels he came to a certain city over which Ambira ruled as king. But in the storming of the city he lost a large part of his army, because the arrows of the enemy had

---

40 The battle of the Hydaspes, a tributary of the Indus, 326 B.C.
41 A corruption of 'Sopithis' or 'Sopithes.'
42 A river in India, which flows into the Indus; now the *Chenaub*.

been smeared with poison, and after herbs, revealed to him in a dream and applied to the wounded in drink, cured him and the others, he stormed and captured the city.

(20) Afterwards, driving around the turning post, as it were, he entered upon the Indus River from the Ocean, and quickly returned to Babylon.[43] There legates from terrified provinces of the whole world awaited him, that is, of the Carthaginians and of all Africa, and also of the Spanish provinces, the Gallic provinces, Sicily, Sardinia, besides the greater part of Italy. Such great fear of the leader in the most distant East had penetrated the peoples of the farthest West that you would perceive foreign legations from all over the world, whither you would scarcely believe that a rumor of Alexander had reached. But Alexander died in Babylon, when, still thirsting for blood, he drank poison, his wicked appetite being punished by the trickery of a servant.

O wicked soul of man and heart always inhuman. Did I not fill my eyes with tears as I reviewed these events to prove the recurring in cycles of the misfortunes of all ages, in the relating of so much evil, because of which the whole world on learning of death itself or because of the fear of death trembled? Did I not grieve at heart? As I turned these things over in my mind, did I not make the miseries of my ancestors my own, viewing them as the common lot of man? And yet, if I at times speak about myself, how for the first time I saw barbarians previously unknown to me, how I avoided enemies, how I flattered those in authority, how I guarded against pagans, how I fled from those lying in wait for me; finally, how suddenly enveloped in a mist I evaded those pursuing me on sea and seeking me with stones and spears, even almost seizing me with their hands, I would wish that all who hear me be moved to tears and I would grieve in silence for those who do not grieve, reflecting upon the insensibility of those who do not believe what they have not experienced. The Spaniards

---

43 Alexander returned by land from Barce, a city built by him on the Indus River.

and the Morini came to Babylon to implore Alexander, and throughout Assyria and India voluntarily begged the bloody lord not to regard them as enemies, going around the ends of the earth and, unfortunately, becoming acquainted with both oceans, and yet the memory of so strong a necessity has failed in oblivion or become dim with age. Do we think that a fleeing thief will achieve everlasting remembrance because, while leaving most of the world safe, he despoiled a small corner of it? Indeed, it would be as if an Indian or an Assyrian sought peace of the Goths and the Suebi, not to mention the reverse, or even the Spaniard himself who is sustaining the enemy. But yet whether those times of Alexander are judged to be praiseworthy because of the bravery with which the whole world was seized rather than to be abhorred on account of the ruin by which the whole world was overturned, many, indeed, will be found who judge these times praiseworthy because they themselves have overcome many obstacles and regard the miseries of others their own good fortune. But let someone say: 'Those Goths are the enemies of the Roman world'; the reply will be: 'This, too, seemed true to the whole East about Alexander in those days,' and such also did the Romans seem to others, when they sought unknown and peaceful peoples in war. But the former were eager to acquire kingdoms, the latter to overturn them. The destructions committed by an enemy are one thing, the judgments passed on to the victor another. If, indeed, the former (i.e., the Romans and Alexander) in earlier times afflicted with wars those whom later they ordered under their own laws, and the latter (i.e., the Goths) are now in hostile fashion throwing into disorder those whom, if they should overcome and hold (which may God not permit), they would strive to control in their own way, they are to be called great kings who are now judged by us to be most cruel enemies. By whatever name such deeds as these are called, that is, whether they are spoken of as sufferings or acts of bravery, when compared with those of former times both are fewer in this age, and so in comparison with the times of Alexander and the Persians work to our advantage. If 'bravery' is the word to be used now, it is less on the part of the enemy; if suffering, it is less on the part of the Romans.

(21) In the four hundred and fiftieth year after the founding of the City, in the consulship of Fabius Maximus for the fifth time and Decius Mus for the fourth time,[44] four very strong and most flourishing peoples of Italy made a treaty and formed a single army. For the Etruscans, Umbrians, Samnites, and Gauls, conspiring with a single army, tried to destroy the Romans. The minds of the Romans were shaken by this war and their self-confidence destroyed; nor did they dare rely completely on their forces. They divided the enemy by strategy, thinking it safer to implicate themselves in several wars than in serious ones. Thus, when, after sending some of their troops ahead into Umbria and Etruria to ravage hostile lands, they had forced the army of the Umbrians and the Etruscans to return to the protection of their own territories, they hastened to enter upon war with the Samnites and Gauls. When in this war,[45] the Romans were hard pressed, the consul, Decius, was killed; Fabius, however, after the slaughter of a great portion of the Decian army, finally conquered. In that battle, forty thousand Samnites and Gauls were killed, but only seven thousand Romans are reported to have been destroyed from the division of Decius who was killed. Livy, however, reports that, excluding the Etruscans and Umbrians whom the Romans by trickery diverted from the war, the losses of the Gauls and Samnites were one hundred forty thousand three hundred thirty infantry and forty-seven thousand cavalry, and that one thousand chariots in armor opposed the Roman battle line.

But, as it has often been said that the domestic peace of the Romans was always interrupted by foreign wars or that

---

44 Quintus Fabius Maximus Rullianus V and Publius Decius Mus IV, 295 B.C.
45 Battle of Sentinum, 295 B.C.

their outside ventures were aggravated by internal disorders, to such extent was this true that their excessive arrogance was kept in every way on all sides. A pestilence in the City overwhelmed this bloody and sad victory and funeral corteges of the dead met and polluted the triumphal processions. Nor was there anyone who was convinced of the joy of the triumph, since the entire City was sighing over either the sick or the dead.

(22) A year followed in which the Romans, in a war renewed by the Samnites, were conquered and fled into their camp. Later, however, the Samnites, taking on a new garb and a new spirit, that is, covering their arms and clothing with silver, and with their minds prepared to die if they did not conquer, gave themselves over to war. Against these Papirius,[46] the consul, was sent with an army, although the *Augures Pullarii,* predicting fruitless results, prohibited the advance. Laughing at them, he carried out the war as successfully as he had firmly undertaken it. For in this battle,[47] twelve thousand of the enemy are reported to have been killed and three thousand captured. But diseases suddenly broke out and ruined this truly praiseworthy victory of his which the empty auspices were unable to hinder. For so great and such an intolerable pestilence then gripped the City that, to allay it in some manner, they thought that the Sibylline Books[48] should be consulted and they brought in that horrible Epidaurian snake[49] with the statue itself of Aesculapius, as if,

---

46 Lucius Papirius Cursor, 293 B.C.

47 In the heart of Samnium.

48 The Sibylla, a female soothsayer, appears in various places. In Roman mythology, the most celebrated is the Sibyl at Cumae, in the service of Apollo, in the time of Aeneas. A later Sibyl was in the time of Tarquinius Superbus, whose predictions were deposited in the Capitol, and in time of danger were consulted by a college of priests, appointed for that special purpose.

49 Aesculapius was brought to Rome from Epidaurus at the instance of Sibylline Books after a plague in 293 B.C. Legend told how the sacred snake, incarnating the god, itself chose the Insula Tiberina for its abode, and there on January 1, 281, a temple was dedicated to Aesculapius.

indeed, the pestilence either had never before been stayed or would not arise in the future.

Later, in the next year, Fabius Gurges[50] fought unsuccessfully against the Samnites. For, after losing his army and being conquered, he took refuge in the City. So, when the Senate deliberated about removing him from office, his father, Fabius Maximus, although deprecating his son's disgrace, offered of his own accord to go as his son's delegate, if the opportunity were given him of dispelling the disgrace and of making war a second time. This opportunity being obtained and the battle being joined, when suddenly he saw the consul, his son, fighting with Pontius, the leader of the Samnites, who was pressing the attack, and surrounded by the hostile weapons of the enemy, the dutiful old man riding on his horse drove into the middle of the battle line. The Romans, roused by this deed, held fast there along the entire battle line, until they destroyed the enemy's army and captured the leader, Pontius himself, after overcoming and crushing him. In this battle, twenty thousand Samnites were killed and four thousand, together with their king, were captured; and, finally, the Samnite war, which was carried on for forty-nine years with a great slaughter of the Romans, was ended with the failure of the leader.

In the following year, while Curius[51] was consul, war was carried on with the Sabines, in which the number of thousands of men killed and the number captured the consul himself disclosed. When, in the Senate, he wished to record the extent of the Sabine territory which was acquired and the great number of people captured, he was unable to give the figures in detail.

In the four hundred and sixty-third year after the founding of the City, in the consulship of Dolabella and Domitius,[52]

---

50 Quintus Fabius Maximus Gurges, 292 B.C.
51 Marcus Curius Dentatus, 290 B.C.
52 Publius Cornelius Dolabella Maximus and Gnaius Domitius Calvinus Maximus, 283 B.C.

when the Lucanians, Bruttians, and Samnites, after making
an alliance with the Etruscans and the Senonian Gauls, tried
to renew the war against the Romans, the Romans sent legates
to dissuade the Gauls. When the Gauls killed these legates,
Caecilius, the praetor, being sent with an army to obtain
vengeance for the killing of the legates and to crush the insurrection of the enemy, was overcome by the Etruscans and
the Gauls and perished. Furthermore, seven tribunes of the
soldiers were killed in this battle;[53] many nobles were slain,
thirteen thousand Roman soldiers also were destroyed in that
war.

But thus, as often as the Gauls flared up, the resources of
Rome were diminished, so that in the present trouble with the
Goths, we should rather recall the Gauls.

(23) But I now turn back to relate the wars over these same
periods, in which the Romans endured those events (mentioned above) which the Macedonian leaders carried on with
one another; who on Alexander's death obtained the different
provinces by lot and met their death by mutual warfare. Thus,
I seem to see the tumultuous period of these wars; viewing,
as it were, some immense camp through the night from the
watchtower of a mountain, I perceive nothing in the great
expanse of the field but innumerable camp fires. Thus,
throughout the entire kingdom of Macedonia, that is, through
all Asia and the greater part of Europe, and even the most
of Libya, the terrible fires of war burst forth; and when these
fires laid waste especially the places where they had broken
out, they disturbed all other lands by the terror of rumor as
by a cloud of smoke. But I shall by no means unfold the wars
and destructions of so many kings and kingdoms, until I have
first set forth the kingdoms themselves together with their
kings.

Thus, Alexander for twelve years oppressed by the sword
a world trembling beneath him, but his generals for fourteen

---

53 At Lake Vadimo in Etruria, near Ameria, now *Laghetto de Bassano.*

years tore it to pieces and, as eager whelps tear apart a rich prize brought to earth by a great lion, they, roused to strife by their eagerness for the prize, attacked one another. Thus, by the first lot, Egypt and part of Africa and Arabia fell to Ptolemy. Laomedon of Mytilene received Syria bordering on this province; Philotas, Cilicia; Philo, the Illyrians. Atropatus was placed over Greater Media; the father-in-law of Perdiccas over Lesser Media. The people of Susiana were assigned to Scynus; Greater Phrygia to Antigonus, the son of Philip. Nearchus drew Lycia and Pamphylia by lot; Cassander, Caria; Menander, Lydia. Leonnatus received Lesser Phrygia. Thrace and the regions of the Pontic Sea were given to Lysimachus; Cappadocia with Paphlagonia to Eumenes. The highest command of the camp went to Seleucus, the son of Antiochus; Cassander was placed over the bodyguard and attendants of the king. In Further Bactriana and the regions of India, the former prefects, who came into existence under Alexander, continued in office. Taxiles had the Seres who were established between the two rivers, Hydaspes and Indus. To the colonies in India, Python, the son of Agenor, was sent. Oxyarches received the Paropamisadae at the foot of the Caucasus Mountains. The Arachossi and Cedrosi were decided for Sibyrtius; Statanor was allotted the Dranchei and the Arei; Amyntas, the Bactriani; Scythaeus obtained the Sogdiani; Stacanor, the Parthi; Philip, the Hyrcanii; Phratafernes, the Armenii; Tleptolemus, the Persians; Peucestes, the Babylonians; Archon, the Pelassi; and Archelaus, Mesopotamia.

Now the cause and origin of the wars was the letter of King Alexander in which he ordered that all exiles be restored to their fatherland and to freedom. So the powerful cities of Greece, fearing lest the exiles on receiving their freedom would plan revenge, seceded from the rule of the Macedonians. The leading Athenians, after bringing together an army of thirty thousand and two hundred ships, made war on Antipater to whom Greece had fallen by lot; and through Demosthenes, also an orator, joined to themselves as allies Sicyon, Argos,

Corinth, and other states, and surrounded Antipater by siege. There, their leader, Leosthénes, was pierced by a spear thrown from the walls and killed. The Athenians met Leonnatus as he was bringing aid to Antipater, and, after crushing his troops, killed Antipater himself.

Perdiccas, however, brought war upon Ariaratus, king of the Cappadocians,[54] and conquered him. In this victory, he gained nothing but wounds and dangers; for all the people, before the attack on the city, set fire to their homes and consumed themselves and all their possessions.[55]

After this, war arose between Antigonus and Perdiccas; many provinces and islands being torn apart whether they refused aid or furnished it. Long counsel was taken whether to transfer the war into Macedonia or to carry it on in Asia. Finally, Perdiccas himself sought Egypt with a large army. Thus Macedonia, its leaders separating into parts, was armed against its own vitals. Ptolemy, provided with the forces of Egypt and with Cyrenean troops, prepared to meet Perdiccas in war. While all this was going on, Neoptolemus and Eumenes contended fiercely in a most bloody battle. Neoptolemus was conquered and fled to Antipater, whom he urged to attack Eumenes by surprise. Eumenes thought that this would take place and caught the plotters by a stratagem. In this battle Polypercon was killed; Neoptolemus and Eumenes inflicted wounds on each other, but Neoptolemus died and Eumenes escaped as victor. Perdiccas met with Ptolemy in a very bitter war, and after losing his forces he himself was killed. Eumenes, Peithon, Illyrius, and Alcetas, the brother of Perdiccas, were pronounced enemies by the Macedonians, and the war against them was decided for Antigonus.

---

54 Ariarathes, the satrap of Cappadocia, refused to submit to Alexander and remained virtually independent.

55 This battle took place in the spring of 322 B.C. Perdiccas invaded Pisidia and attacked the city of Isaura, whose inhabitants died as described here by Orosius. Orosius has apparently confused two separate incidents.

Thus Eumenes and Antigonus, after gathering a very large number of troops, met in conflict.[56] Eumenes was conquered and fled to a certain very well fortified citadel,[57] from which through legates he asked for the aid of Antipater, who was then very powerful. Antigonus terrified by this report departed from the siege. But not even so was the hope of Eumenes firm or his safety certain. Therefore, as a measure of desperation, he summoned to his aid the Silver Shields,[58] so called because their arms were covered with silver, that is, the soldiers who had waged war under Alexander. These, listening with disdain to their leader as he laid plans for the battle, were conquered by Antigonus[59] and deprived of their camp; and they lost their wives and children, and at the same time, all that they had acquired under Alexander. Later, they shamefully asked the victor through legates that what they had lost be returned to them. Now Antigonus promised that he would make the restitution, if they would turn over to him Eumenes bound. Thus, allured by the hope of recovering their property, in a most disgraceful betrayal they themselves led captive their leader, whose standards they had followed a little while before, captured and in chains, and presently they were distributed with the most disgraceful ignominy in the army of Antigonus.[60] Meanwhile, Eurydice, the wife of Arridaeus,[61] the king of the Macedonians, carried on many disgraceful deeds in the name of her husband through Cassander, whom she knew in a shameful manner and had advanced to the highest dignity through all the grades of honor, and who out of lust for the woman struck down many cities of Greece. Then Olympias, the mother of King Alexander, on the urging of Polypercon, when she came into Macedonia from Epirus

56 On the plains of Orcynium in Cappadocia.

57 A hill-fort between Lycaonia and Cappadocia.

58 The Argyraspids, who were regarded as invincible.

59 The engagement was indecisive. The camp of the Silver Shields was plundered during the battle.

60 An old familiar ruse was employed. They were sent to frontier districts where constant fighting would kill them off.

61 Philip Arridaeus, the feeble-minded, half-brother of Alexander.

accompanied by Aeacides, king of the Molossians,[62] and was barred by Eurydice from the territory, with the support of the Macedonians, ordered King Arridaeus and Eurydice to be killed. Nevertheless, Olympias herself also immediately suffered just punishment for her cruelty; for when, with the recklessness of a woman she was carrying on the slaughter of many nobles, on hearing of the coming of Cassander and distrusting the Macedonians, she, together with her daughter-in-law, Roxana, and her grandson, Hercules, withdrew to the city of Pydna; and here she was immediately captured by Cassander and killed. The son of Alexander the Great with his mother was sent to the citadel of Amphipolis in protective custody. When Perdiccas, Alcetas, Polypercon, and other generals, too numerous to mention, of the opposite party had been killed, the wars among the successors of Alexander seem to have ended, when Antigonus, burning with a desire to dominate, pretended that it was necessary by war to free Hercules, the son of the king, from captivity. When these actions became known, Ptolemy and Cassander, entering into an alliance with Lysimachus and Seleucus, strenuously prepared for war on land and sea. In this war, Antigonus with his son, Demetrius, were defeated. Cassander, who was made a partner with Ptolemy in the victory, when returning to Apollonia, came upon the Avieniatae, who, on account of the intolerable number of frogs and mice, had left their native soil and had emigrated from their ancestral land, and were seeking new homes during the interval of an extended peace. But Cassander, knowing both the courage and the great numbers of these people, lest driven by necessity they might agitate Macedonia with war and invade it, received them into an alliance and placed them on the farthest borders of Macedonia. Then, since Hercules, the son of Alexander, had reached his fourteenth year, fearing lest all might prefer him as the lawful king, he had him and his mother secretly killed.

---

62 The Molossians, a people in the eastern part of Epirus; so-called from Molossus, the son of Pyrrhus, king of Epirus and Andromache.

Ptolemy a second time entered upon a naval battle with Demetrius, and when he was conquered and lost almost all his fleet and army,[63] he took refuge in Egypt. Elated by this victory, Antigonus ordered that he himself and his son, Demetrius, be called king, which all followed as an example and assumed for themselves the name and power of king. So Ptolemy and Cassander and the rest of the leaders of the other faction, on seeing that they were being deceived one by one by Antigonus, communicated with one another by letter, agreed on a time and place of meeting, and planned on war against Antigonus with a common force. Cassander, being involved in wars with his neighbors, sent Lysimachus, the most famous of all his generals, with a large force to aid his allies in his place. Seleucus, coming down from Greater Asia, approached Antigonus as a new enemy. This Seleucus, indeed, took part in most of the wars throughout the East among the allies of the kingdom of Macedonia. In the beginning of the war, he stormed and captured Babylon. He subdued the Bactriani who were rising up in new revolts. Then, he made a journey into India, which, after the death of Alexander, as it were, removing and casting the yoke from its neck, had killed his prefects under the leadership of a certain Androcottus[64] to win their freedom. This Androcottus afterwards acted cruelly toward the citizens whom he had defended against outside domination, and himself oppressed these with servitude. So Seleucus, although he had carried on many serious wars with this Androcottus, finally confirmed the terms for his retaining the kingdom and, after arranging a peace pact, departed. And, so, after the troops of Ptolemy and his allies had been united, battle was joined. In this battle the more powerful the equipment, the more serious was the ruin, for in this struggle the forces of almost the entire Macedonian kingdom fell.[65] In the

---

63 Occurred in 306 B.C. off the harbor of Salamis, a city on the east coast of Cyprus.
64 Chandragupta was his Indian name.
65 Fought in 301 B.C. on the plains of Ipsus, a small town of Phrygia.

battle Antigonus was killed. But the end of this battle was the beginning of another. For since there was no agreement on the part of the victors with respect to the booty, they again split into two factions. Seleucus joined with Demetrius; Ptolemy with Lysimachus. When Cassander died, his son, Philip, succeeded him. Thus, all over again, as it were, wars arose for Macedonia.

Antipater with his own hand transfixed Thessalonice, his mother and wife of Cassander, although she pleaded pitifully for her life. Alexander, his brother, while he was preparing war against Antipater to avenge his mother, was surrounded by Demetrius, whose help he had sought, and killed. Since Lysimachus was hard-pressed in a most dangerous war with Dromichaetes, king of the Thracians, he was unable to fight against Demetrius. Demetrius, elated by the addition of Greece and of all Macedonia to his kingdom, arranged to cross over into Asia. But Ptolemy, Seleucus, and Lysimachus, having learned from the earlier struggle how much strength there was in union, again formed an alliance, united their armies, and transferred their war against Demetrius into Europe. Pyrrhus, the king of Epirus, joined with them as a comrade and ally in war, hoping that Demetrius could be driven out of Macedonia. And the hope was not in vain. For after his army had been destroyed and he himself was driven into flight, Pyrrhus invaded the kingdom of Macedonia. Then, Lysimachus killed his son-in-law, Antipater, who was plotting against him, and he slew his son, Agathocles, whom he hated contrary to the feelings of human nature. Indeed, in those days, the city of Lysimachus was unrooted by a most terrible earthquake and became a cruel tomb to its people who had been crushed. All the allies, however, deserted Lysimachus, who was covering himself with blood through constant murders; and deserting to Seleucus, already a king so inclined by his rivalry for the kingdom, urged him to bring war upon Lysimachus. This was a most abominable spectacle; two kings, of whom Lysimachus was seventy-four years old and Seleucus seventy-seven, engaging in combat to deprive each other of the kingdom, standing in battle line and bearing arms. This, indeed, was the last war among the fellow-soldiers of Alexander, but one which has been reserved as an example of human misery; for when they alone possessed the world, after thirty-four of Alexander's generals had already been killed, and failing to see the very narrow limits of their old age and life, they thought that the limits of the whole world were narrow for their own empire. In this war, Lysimachus was the last to be killed,[66] after his fourteen children before the battle had already been either sent away or killed. Thus, Lysimachus was the dissolution of the Macedonian War. But not even Seleucus rejoiced over so great a victory with impunity, for he himself after seventy-seven years did not experience the peace of a natural death, but ended his life which had been wrested from him unhappily by an immature death, as it were, inasmuch as while Ptolemy, whose sister Lysimachus had taken in marriage, was making an attack, he was surrounded in ambush and killed.[67]

These are the relationships of blood and society between parents, children, and friends. Of such value were human and divine obligations weighed among them. Let those, indeed, blush on recalling past events who now know that by the intervention of the Christian faith alone, and only by means of the sworn oath do they live with enemies and do not suffer hostile acts. By these events it is proven beyond all doubt that, not as before 'they made treaties with the sacrifice of a sow,'[68] but that now among barbarians and Romans, they preserve as much faith by calling to witness their Creator and Lord by oaths taken on the Gospels as in the past nature was unable to preserve between fathers and sons.

But let the end of the Macedonian War now also be the end of this book; especially because, from this point, now the wars with Pyrrhus begin and the Punic wars immediately follow.

---

66 This battle was fought on the plains of Corus in 281 B.C.
67 He was stabbed by Ptolemy Ceraunus, the eldest son of Ptolemy Lagus.
68 Vergil, *Aeneid* 8.641.

BOOK FOUR

Preface

ERGIL REPORTS THAT Aeneas said, when he was with difficulty consoling his remaining companions after their common dangers and their shipwrecks: 'Perhaps some day it will be pleasing to recall even these events.'[1] This sentiment, aptly expressed once, always carries with it by its very different effects a threefold force: when past events are held the more pleasing as they are the more serious when carried out; and future events, while they are made desirable by an aversion for the present are always believed to be better; but with present events, no just comparison can be made with miseries on this account, because they afflict us with much greater annoyance, however trifling those are which are ours, than those which have either transpired or are to come; although they are called great, nevertheless, they do not exist at all at the moment. For example, if one irritated by fleas at night, and on this account is kept awake, may by chance recall the other vigils which he at some time sustained for a long time as the result of very burning fevers, undoubtedly he will endure the unrest of the latter with more impatience than the recollection of the former. But although in the feelings of all there can thus seem to be a consideration of time, yet does anyone exist who, in his every anxiety, will declare fleas to be more serious than fevers? Or will anyone admit it to be more grievous to be awake while healthy than not to have been able to sleep when about to die? Since this is so,

---

1 Vergil, *Aeneid,* 1.203.

in whatever way, I agree with these dandies and our other critics that these evils, with which we are sometimes admonished because it so befits, they consider serious; yet I do not overlook the fact that they also assert them by comparison to be more serious than they really are. Just as if someone going forth from his very soft bed and comfortable chamber early in the morning should see that the surfaces of the ponds had frozen from the cold of the night and the grass had become white with frost and warned by the unexpected sight should say: 'It is cold today,' this person would seem to be by no means blameworthy, because he had spoken in language either according to its general usage or its proper sense. But if in fear, running back into his bedchamber and covering himself with blankets or rather hiding himself in them, he should cry out that never was it as cold as this, not even as it was once in the Appennines, when Hannibal, covered and overcome with snow, lost elephants, horses, and the greater part of his army, this man I would not endure uttering such childish nonsense and talking in such a way, but I would drag him forth from his blankets, witnesses of his soft living, before the people publicly, and, when he was taken out of doors, I would show him the children playing in this cold and delighting in it and perspiring, so that he would be taught that his verbose nonsense vitiated by soft living was not due to the severity of the weather, but to the sluggishness in himself; and by making a comparison of situations, it would be proven that his ancestors had endured no small hardships, but that they themselves were not able to endure even small ones.

I shall prove this more clearly as I turn over in my mind the disasters of the past, setting them forth according to order, the war with Pyrrhus among the first. The cause and origin of this war were the following.

(1) In the four hundred and sixty-fourth year after the founding of the City, the Tarentines attending a theatrical performance saw a Roman fleet by chance passing by and viciously attacked it, only five vessels barely escaping by flight;

the rest of the fleet was dragged into the harbor and destroyed; the prefects of the ships were slaughtered, all men useful for war were killed, and the remainder sold for a price. Immediately, legates were sent to Tarentum by the Romans to complain about the injuries which had been brought upon them, but they were beaten and brought back additional injuries from the same people. For these reasons, a great war arose. The Romans, surveying who and how many of the enemy were raising a clamor about them, were forced by ultimate necessity to force the proletariat also into arms, that is, to enroll for military service those who always had time to give to children, for care of children is in vain, unless consideration is given to present emergencies. So a Roman army, under Aemilius[2] as consul, rushed into the entire territory of the Tarentines, laid waste all with fire and sword, took most of the towns by storm, and exacted in cruel fashion vengeance for the injury which had been insolently received. Pyrrhus at once especially increased the number of the Tarentini, who were supported by the numerous auxiliaries of their neighbors. Pyrrhus, also on account of the magnitude of his forces, took over the leadership in the planning and gave his name to the war. For to liberate Tarentum, inasmuch as it was founded by the Lacedaemonians and was a city related to Greece, he brought all the forces of Epirus, Thessaly, and Macedonia, and was also the first to bring elephants, up to that time unseen by the Romans, into Italy, twenty in number. A man to inspire terror by land and by sea, by his men and horses, by his arms and beasts, and especially by his own power and trickery, except for the fact that he was deceived by the ambiguous response of that most deceptive Delphic spirit and most lying scoundrel, whom they themselves called a great prophet, he met the fate of him who had not consulted the

---

2 Quintus Aemilius Papus, 282 B.C., consul for the second time in 278 B.C. when, with the other consul, Gaius Fabricius Luscinus, he forced Pyrrhus to leave Italy. He was granted a triumph for his victories.

oracle. And so at Heraclea, a city of Campania, and the Liris River,[3] the first battle was joined between King Pyrrhus and the consul, Laevinus.[4] A day was spent in a most severe struggle, all on both sides waiting to die, ignorant of flight. But when the Romans saw the elephants, fierce in appearance, offensive in odor, and terrifying in size, led in between the clashing battle lines, surrounded and terrified by this new kind of fighting, with their horses especially trembling with fear, they fled in different directions. But after Minucius, a first *hastatus* of the fourth legion, cut off the trunk of an elephant and forced it, distracted by the pain of the wound, to turn aside from the battle and vent its anger on its own, by this wild rushing the soldiers of Pyrrhus began to be thrown into confusion and disorder. An end was brought to the battle by the benefit of the night. The disgraceful flight disclosed that the Romans had been conquered, of whom it is reported that, at that time, fourteen thousand eight hundred and eighty of the infantry fell; one thousand three hundred and ten were captured; two hundred and forty-six horsemen were slain; and eight hundred and two were captured. Twenty-two standards were lost. How great a number of Pyrrhus' allies on the opposite side were destroyed, tradition has not handed down, especially because it is the custom of ancient writers not to preserve the number of the slain on the side of those who were victorious, lest the losses of the victor tarnish the glory of the victor, unless perchance when so few fall that the small number of the losses increases the admiration and fear of the victor's courage, as was the case with Alexander the Great in the battle of the Persian War. It is reported that, as compared to the nearly four hundred thousand of the enemy who were killed, only nine infantrymen in his army were lost. But Pyrrhus bore witness before his gods and men to the savage slaughter which he had suffered in this battle by affixing an

---

3 Rather the Siris River in Lucania, on which Heraclea is located.
4 Publius Valerius Laevinus, 280 B.C.

inscription in the temple of Jove at Tarentum, in which he
wrote the following words:

> Those men who formerly were unconquered, O
>   highest father of Olympus,
> These I have conquered in battle and have been
>   conquered by them.

And when he was chided by his allies for saying that he who
had conquered was conquered, he is said to have replied:
'Surely, if I shall conquer again in the same manner, I shall
return to Epirus without a soldier.' Meanwhile, the Roman
army, after it was conquered and fled secretly from the camp,
perceived the wretched slaughter of battle increased and accumulated by more serious portents. For a storm arising with
a terrific crash from the heavens, as if an enemy force, seized
and with dreadful lightning bolts burned foragers who had
gone forth from the camp. Indeed, this same hurricane laid
low thirty-four of these men; twenty-two were left half alive;
baggage animals were driven mad and died; so that rightly
is this said to have happened, not as a sign of future devastation, but as a devastation in itself.

A second battle took place between Pyrrhus and the Roman
consuls on the borders of Apulia.[5] In this, the losses of war
went to both, but especially to Pyrrhus; victory went to the
Romans. For when all rushed together with all their strength
for mutual slaughter, and for a long time the result of the
battle hung in the balance, Pyrrhus was wounded by a thrust
in the arm and was the first to withdraw from the battle. But
Fabricius, the legate, was also wounded at that time. In the
first battle, it was discovered that the elephants could be
wounded and forced to flee; then, roused by fire brands im-
bedded in their hind quarters and sensitive parts, carrying
scaffolding on their backs with fierce fury, they became a source
of destruction to their own. In this battle, five thousand
Romans were killed, but of Pyrrhus' army, twenty thousand

---

5 Near Asculum, the capital of Picenum, now *Ascoli*.

were laid low. Fifty-three of the king's standards were lost, eleven of the Romans'.

Pyrrhus was crushed by this battle, and he withdrew to Syracuse, having been summoned there on the death of Agathocles, the Syracusan king, to the rule of Sicily.

(2) But the wretchedness of the Romans did not cease with the truce; the period between wars was taken with the evils of diseases and, when there was a cessation of fighting abroad, the wrath of heaven was raging at home. For, when Fabius Gurges, for the second time, and Gaius Genucius Clepsina[6] were consuls, a severe pestilence assailed the City and its surroundings. When it seized all, but especially the women and the flocks, killing the young in the womb, it took away hope of future off-spring. And when miscarriages were taking place with danger to mothers by the premature births, this became so widespread that it was believed that the continuation of the human race would fail and that the life of living things would cease, since birth in the natural manner was brought to a close.

Meanwhile, Curius,[7] the consul, intercepted Pyrrhus as he returned from Sicily, and this battle, the third against the Epirots, was fought at Lucania in the Arusinian Plains.[8] And so when in the first meeting the soldiers of Pyrrhus became frightened by the attack of the Romans and, considering flight, were trying to withdraw from the battle, Pyrrhus ordered the elephants to be brought in from the reserve. When the Romans, now accustomed to fight with the beasts, had prepared fire-darts wound with tow, smeared with pitch, and capped with barbed spurs, and hurled them flaming upon the backs of the beast and towers thereon, without difficulty they turned back the beasts, raging and burning, to the destruction of those whose reserve they had been. It is said that the king had eighty thousand infantry in that battle and six thousand cavalry. Of

6 Quintus Fabius Gurges II and Gaius Genucius Clepsina, 276 B.C.

7 Marcus Curius Dentatus II, 275 B.C.

8 274 B.C., near Beneventum.

these, thirty-three thousand are reported to have been slain, but a thousand three hundred captured. Finally, in the fifth year after he had come, Pyrrhus fled from Italy conquered. After the many very serious wars which he had fought, carried away by his desire for the kingdom of Sparta, he was struck with a rock in Greece at Argos, a very flourishing city of Achaia, and died.

At that time also among the Romans, Sextilia, a Vestal Virgin, being convicted of unchastity and condemned to death, was buried alive at the Colline Gate.

(3) In the four hundred and seventy-fifth year after the founding of the City, the Tarentines, having learned of the death of Pyrrhus, again stirred up hostilities against the Romans, and through legates asked for and received assistance from the Carthaginians. When the battle was fought, the Romans were victorious, whereupon the Carthaginians, although not yet judged to be enemies, nevertheless realized that they could be conquered by the Romans.

In the following year, Roman severity destroyed a large part of their own vitals. For shortly before Pyrrhus arrived, the eighth legion,[9] despairing of any hope for the Romans, dared a strange crime: it killed all the inhabitants of Rhegium over whose protection they were in charge, and claimed for itself all the plunder and the very town. An order was given to Genucius,[10] the consul, to wreak punishment for this crime on such nefarious rebels. After he had besieged the city of Rhegium and had captured all within it, he exacted worthy punishments of the surviving fugitives and brigands, but he sent the Roman soldiers of the legion unharmed to Rome. These, by order of the people, were beaten with switches in the middle of the Forum and beheaded.

At that time, Rome seemed to itself to be the conqueror, when it killed its own full legion which would, undoubtedly,

9 The Campanian legion.
10 Lucius Genucius Clepsina, 271 B.C.

have been conquered if she had lost it in a battle with the enemy.

(4) In the four hundred and seventy-eighth year after the founding of the City, ill-boding and terrible omens were seen or reported at Rome. The temple of Salus was destroyed by a stroke of lightning; part of the wall at the same place, as it is said, was struck. Before daybreak, three wolves entering the City brought in a half-eaten corpse and, after dispersing it member by member in the Forum, departed in fright at the din raised by the populace. At Formiae[11] the walls on all sides were burned by many strokes of lightning and destroyed. In Calenian[12] territory, a flame, bursting forth suddenly from an opening torn in the ground and blazing terribly for three days and three nights, drained completely five jugera of land of its moisture and fertility and burned it to ashes, so that the flame is reported to have consumed, not only plants, but also trees to their lowest roots.

In the year following, Sempronius,[13] the consul, led an army against the Picentes. And when both lines took their stand directly within spear range, the earth suddenly shook with such a horrible roar that both lines were stunned by the miracle and grew faint. For a long time, the people on both sides hesitated in amazement with a feeling that their undertaking had been prejudged. Finally, renewing the attack they entered upon the conflict. So sorrowful was this battle that rightly is it said that the earth, which was then about to receive so much human blood, also shook with a dreadful groan. The few Romans, surely, who escaped alive from this battle were victorious.

(5) In the four hundred and eightieth year after the founding of the City, among the many prodigies blood seemed to come up from the ground and milk down from the heavens.

---

11 An ancient city of Latium on the borders of Campania, now *Mola di Gaeta*.
12 Cales, a town in Southern Campania, noted for its good wine.
13 Publius Sempronius Sophus, 268 B.C.

For gushing forth in many places blood flowed from springs, and milk, let down drop by drop from the clouds like rain, flooded the land, as it seemed to the people, in terrible showers. At that time, when the Carthaginians, who had given aid to the Tarentines against the Romans, were censured by the Senate through legates, they added to the most shameful disgrace of a broken treaty by assuming a perjury.

Then, too, the Volsinians, the most flourishing people of the Etruscans, almost perished in riotous living. For when, after license was extended to a habit, they made their slaves free at random, invited them to banquets, and honored them with marriages, the freedmen, being received into a share of the power, plotted through trickery to usurp complete rule, and once freed from the yoke of slavery burned with the desire to be masters, and those whom they as slaves loved with devotion, now as free men, because they remembered that they had been their masters, they cursed. And so these, who had been made free, plotting a conspiracy (their band was so great that they gained possession of what they attempted without contention), seized the city and claimed it for their class alone, and criminally took possession of the property and wives of their masters. Their masters they drove into distant exile, and these wretched and impoverished exiles betook themselves to Rome, where displaying their wretchedness and bemoaning their complaint, they were avenged by Roman sternness and restored to their rightful places.

In the four hundred and eighty-first year after the founding of the City, a great pestilence blazed forth in Rome, whose horror I am content to point out, since I cannot do it justice with words. For if inquiry is made as to the extent of time that it lasted, its ravages were prolonged for more than two years; if as to the waste which it caused, the census has been published which examines, not how many persons perished, but how many survived; if the violence with which it afflicted the people, the Sibylline Books are witnesses, which have responded that this was sent by the wrath of heaven. But lest the temptation to scoff, as it were, offend anyone, because, whereas the Sibyl said that the gods were angry, we seem to have said that it was the wrath of heaven, let him hear and understand that, although these things for the most part take place through the powers above, yet they do not by any means take place without the will of Omnipotent God.

At the same time, Caparronia, a Vestal Virgin, convicted of unchastity, perished by hanging; her seducer and the slaves conspiring with her were dealt the same punishment.

Behold the events and their great number which I have enumerated as having taken place continuously year by year, during which surely rarely, or almost never, did nothing tragic occur, and this, when these same writers, being more concerned with the business of giving praise, shied away from great numbers of miseries, lest they offend those for whom, and likewise about whom, they described these events, and lest they seem to terrify their hearers by examples from the past rather than to instruct them. Furthermore, we who are placed at the end of these times are not able to know the calamities of the Romans except through those who have praised the Romans. Thence, it may be understood how numerous those happenings were which were purposely suppressed because of their horror when so many are discovered which were able to come forth so faintly amidst praises.

(6) Now since from this point on the Punic wars follow, this very fact demands that at least a few words be reported about Carthage, which is found to have been established by Elissa[14] seventy-two years before the founding of the City of Rome, and about its disasters and domestic misfortunes as Pompeius Trogus and Justin describe them. The Carthaginians have always domestic and internal trouble among them; a discord by whose constant agitation, unfortunately, they have never had periods of prosperity abroad or quiet at home. But when among other misfortunes they labored also

---

14 Another name, occurring usually in poetry, for Dido.

with pestilence, they made use of homicides as medicines, for they immolated human beings as sacrificial victims and they brought young children to their altars, which aroused the pity even of the enemy. Regarding this kind of sacrifice, nay, rather sacrilege, I do not find anything which should especially be discussed. For if some demons have had the temerity to order rites of this kind, to satisfy the deaths of men by the slaughter of men, it must have been understood that they were employed as workers and helpers of the pestilence, that they themselves might kill those whom the pestilence had not seized, for it is the custom to offer sound and undefiled victims, so that they might not allay the pestilences but prevent them.

So the Carthaginians, when the gods had been turned aside because of sacrifices of this kind, as Pompeius Trogus and Justin confess, but as it is established by us, because God had been angered by their presumption and impiety, after fighting for a long time disastrously in Sicily, transferred the war to Sardinia and were again defeated more disastrously. On account of this, they ordered their leader, Malcus, and the few soldiers who survived to go into exile. When the exiles through legates asked for pardon and were refused, they surrounded their native city with a war and a siege. There then Malcus, the leader of the exiles, had his son, Carthalo, a priest of Hercules, because he came to meet him arrayed in purple as if to insult him, hung up on a cross under the eyes of his fatherland just as he was, with purple garments and sacred fillets. After a few days, he captured the city. And when, after a great many of the senators had been killed, the city was ruled with cruelty, he himself was killed. These events took place in the times of Cyrus, king of the Persians.

But after this, Himilco, king of the Carthaginians, when he was waging war in Sicily, suddenly lost his army by a horrible plague. The plague did not delay. The people fell in groups with the diseases; everyone was seized quickly and presently died, and there was no burial. When the news of this misfortune filled astonished Carthage with sudden lamentation, the city was in as great confusion as it would have been if it had been captured. All places in the city resounded with wailings, everywhere gates were closed, and all public and private services were forbidden. All ran down to the harbor and questioned the few who had survived the disaster and were disembarking from ships about their relatives. After the unfortunate people learned about the disaster to their own people, remaining silent or groaning, along the entire shore sometimes the voices of those mourning, at other times the groans and doleful lamentations of unfortunate mothers, were heard. In the midst of all this, the commander himself, ungirt in the soiled tunic of a slave, disembarked. At this sight, mourning bands came together. He himself also, raising his hands to heaven, reproached and bemoaned now his own and now the public misfortune. At last, crying aloud as he passed through the city, and finally entering his home, he dismissed all who followed him as they wept with a last word of consolation, and then, bolting the doors and excluding even his sons, he put an end to his grief and his life with the sword. These matters took place in the time of Darius.

After this, Hanno, surpassing the resources of the state with his private fortune, took to himself a passion for seizing the government. For this scheme he thought it a useful plan to kill all the senators, whose rank he felt would stand in the way of his plans, by poisoning their cups at a pretended marriage of his only daughter. This scheme was betrayed by the servants and was frustrated without any act of vengeance, lest, in the case of a powerful man, the affair on becoming known might cause more trouble than when it was planned. Hanno, being foiled in this plan, prepared to advance his crime by another stratagem. He roused the slaves with whom he suddenly attacked the city when off her guard. But when, before the stated day for the slaughter, he learned that he had been betrayed and foiled, arming twenty thousand of his slaves, he seized a certain fort. There, while he was inciting the

Africans and the king of the Moors, he was captured, and being first beaten with rods, then having his eyes gouged and his hands and legs broken, as if punishment were being exacted from each member, he was killed in the view of all the people. His body torn by lashes was nailed to a cross; all his children and relatives were given over to a like punishment, lest anyone of the same family might plan to imitate or avenge him. These things took place in the time of Philip.

After this, when the Carthaginians learned that Tyre, their parent city, had been captured and destroyed by Alexander the Great, fearing lest his crossing into Africa would now take place, sent a certain Hamilcar, with the surname Rhodanus, pre-eminent in eloquence and shrewdness, to examine thoroughly the activities of Alexander. He was received as a deserter by Parmenio, and then being admitted into the military service of the king, informed his fellow citizens of everything by writing on tablets and then covering the writing with wax. This man, on the death of Alexander, returned to Carthage and was killed, not only by reason of an ungrateful spirit, but also because of a cruel envy, as if he had betrayed his city to the king. Later, when they were waging constant and never sufficiently prosperous wars against the Sicilians and had surrounded by siege the city of Syracuse, then the most flourishing city of Sicily, they were circumvented by Agathocles, the king of Sicily, a man of extraordinary genius, and reduced to extreme desperation. For when Agathocles was being besieged at Syracuse by the Carthaginians and he saw himself unequal in battle with respect to the preparation of his troops and without sufficient supplies to withstand a siege, planning well and concealing it even better, he crossed into Africa with his army. There, he disclosed to his men what he was attempting; then, explained what had to be done. Immediately with one mind, they, first, set fire to the ships in which they came, lest there might be some hope of escape by flight; then, when he was laying low everything with which he came in contact, and was burning towns and fortresses, he met a certain Hanno with thirty thousand Carthaginians, and he killed him with two thousand of his men, but he himself lost only two men in this battle.[15] The spirits of the Africans being unbelievably crushed by this battle, and those of his own men greatly raised, he stormed cities and fortresses, took much booty, and slaughtered many thousands of the enemy. Then, he pitched camp at the fifth milestone from Carthage, that the Carthaginians might see the damage to their very rich possessions and the laying waste of their fields and the burning of their villas from the walls of the city itself. Added to these existing evils was a still gloomier report. For it was reported that in Sicily an army of Africans with its general had been destroyed, which army, indeed, Antander, the brother of Agathocles, had caught off its guard and almost at ease. When this rumor had spread through all Africa, not only the tributary cities, but also the allied kings, revolted from the Carthaginians. Among the latter, the king of Cyrene, Ophellas, entered an alliance of war with Agathocles while he was eagerly seeking the rule of Africa. But after they joined armies and camps, tricked by the blandishments and wiles of Agathocles, he was killed. The Carthaginians, gathering together troops from all sides, were eager for battle. Agathocles, having with him the troops of Ophellas, met them, and with great loss of blood on the part of both armies in a severe battle overcame them. At the decisive point in the struggle, so great a feeling of desperation came upon the Carthaginians that, if a revolt had not arisen in the army of Agathocles, the general of the Carthaginians, Hamilcar, with his army would have deserted to him. For this offense, by order of the Carthaginians, he was fastened to the *patibulum*[16] in the middle of the Forum and furnished a cruel spectacle to his fellows. Then, after the death of Agathocles when the Carthaginians fitted

---

15 According to report, fought within sight of Carthage.
16 *A fork-shaped yoke or gibbet,* placed on the necks of criminals, to which their hands were tied. The Carthaginian general here in question was Bomilcar and not Hamilcar.

out a fleet and laid waste Sicily, and were often defeated in struggles on land and sea by Pyrrhus, king of Epirus, who had been summoned from Italy, they finally turned to wars against the Romans.

Such affliction! Do those who complain about recent affairs read about those of the past? Yes, they read about them and they make comparisons, not with justice, but with jealousy. For with that very great and ineffable spur which they themselves do not discern, they are goaded on, not because the times are evil, but because the times are Christian, and there arises an invidious ulcer, so that whatever is done under detestable circumstances seems more atrocious than it really is, just as also among ourselves it is often customary to view with the eyes of enemies those whom we detest; we think that they do nothing that is not vicious, nothing that is not in excess, and nothing by word or deed that is not to their own harm; and yet this is plainly and simply seen, for the heart so captured by envy is so twisted that it by nature does not see the right. In this number are those objectors because as enemies of God, they are consequently enemies of truth. Of these we speak thus with tears and, if they suffer, we reprove them that we may make them sound. These people see these things with a defective eye and so what they see seems to them to be double, and being confused by a cloud of wickedness, they fall into such a condition that by seeing less they see more, since they cannot see that which is just as it is. They think that the whipping by a father is more serious than fires set by an enemy. They call God, who caresses, admonishes, and redeems, harsher than the devil who persecutes, domineers, and destroys them. And yet, if they understood the Father, they would rejoice in His chastising and, if the fruits of this experience were foreseen, the discipline would be bearable, and on account of the hope which was now given to the people and which, indeed, had not existed before, they would consider the experiences lighter although they suffered more. And yet they can also learn to contemn their miseries from their own people with whom the highest evils were regarded as the highest blessings, provided they attained the celebrated and illustrious glory of high renown. Through these, it may be gathered how much must be endured for life by us, to whom a blessed eternity is promised, when they were able to endure so much for the glory of renown.

(7) In the four hundred and eighty-third year after the founding of the City, that is, in the consulship of Appius Claudius[17] and Q. Fabius, the Romans sent auxiliaries to the Mamertines, who controlled Messana, a renowned city of Sicily, and Appius Claudius, the consul, with an army against Hiero, the king of the Syracusans, and the forces of the Carthaginians allied with him. Appius Claudius so quickly overcame the Syracusans and the Carthaginians that Hiero, the king, became terrified by the magnitude of the operations and admitted that he had been conquered before he had joined battle. Then he, with his forces crushed and his confidence lost, on asking for peace as suppliant was granted it after paying a fine of two hundred silver talents by order of the consuls. The consuls surrounded Agrigentum, a city of Sicily, and the garrison of Carthaginians with earthworks and a wall. And when the elder Hannibal,[18] the general of the Carthaginians, shut in by this siege was reduced to extreme want, Hanno, the new commander of the Carthaginians, intervened suddenly with one thousand five hundred cavalry, thirty thousand infantry, and thirty elephants, and in a short time dispersed the siege. But immediately the city was captured; the Carthaginians were conquered and overcome in a very great battle; eleven elephants were brought under control; the inhabitants of Agrigentum were all sold into slavery; but the elder Hannibal with a few men made a sally and escaped.

---

17 Appius Claudius Caudex, 264 B.C. Marcus Fulvius Flaccus is usually given as his colleague.
18 Not the famous general.

In the consulship of Cn. Cornelius Asina and C. Duilius,[19]
when the elder Hannibal, after fitting out a fleet of seventy
vessels, was laying waste the seacoast of Italy, the Romans and
the consuls ordered a fleet to be built and fitted out. Duilius,
the consul, carried this out quickly, for within sixty days after
the trees were cut, a fleet of one hundred and thirty ships was
brought down to the water and stood at anchor. Cornelius
Asina, one consul, with sixteen ships set out for the island of
Lipara, where invited by Hannibal, as it were, to a conference
on peace, with Punic trickery he was captured and killed
while in chains. When the other consul, Duilius, heard this,
he proceeded with thirty ships against Hannibal. When the
naval battle was joined and the ship in which Hannibal was
sailing was lost, he escaped by pulling away in a skiff. Thirty-
one of his ships are reported as having been captured, three
thousand men killed, and seven thousand captured.

Afterwards, in the consulship of C. Aquillius Florus and
L. Cornelius Scipio,[20] the Carthaginians substituted Hanno
for Hannibal and put him in command of naval operations
for the defense of Sardis and Corsica; and when he was conquered by Scipio, the consul, and had lost his army, he mingled
in the very dense ranks of the enemy and there was killed. In
the same year, three thousand slaves and four thousand naval
allies conspired to destroyed the City of Rome, and, unless
the hastened betrayal had anticipated the plan, the City, deprived of its garrison, would have perished at the hands of
slaves.

(8) In the year following this, the consul, Calatinus,[21] attacking Camarina,[22] a city of Sicily, rashly led his army into
a ravine which Carthaginian troops had fortified shortly before.
When there was no opportunity at all open to him, either for

---

19 Gaius Cornelius Scipio Asina and Gaius Duilius, 260 B.C.
20 Gaius Aquillius Florus and Lucius Cornelius Scipio, 259 B.C.
21 Aulua Atilius Calatinus, 258 B.C.
22 A city on the southwest coast of Sicily, a colony from Syracuse, now
   Camarana, located at the mouth of the Hipparis River.

resisting or escaping, he was freed by the courage and action of Calpurnius Flamma, who with a picked band of three hundred men seized the mound occupied by the enemy and by fighting turned all the Carthaginians against himself, until the Roman army, with no enemy pressing upon the besieged ravine, had passed through. In this battle, all three hundred were killed; Calpurnius, pierced by many wounds and concealed among the corpses, alone escaped. The elder Hannibal, being placed in command of a fleet by the Carthaginians for a second time, having unfortunately met with the Romans in a naval battle and been conquered, was stoned to death by his own army which had rebelled. Atilius,[23] the consul, passed through Lipara and Melita, famous cities of Sicily, and destroyed them. The consuls, having been ordered to transfer the war into Africa, attacked Sicily with three hundred and thirty ships. Hamilcar, the general of the Carthaginians, and Hanno, who was in charge of the fleet, met these. A naval battle was joined, and the Carthaginians being routed lost sixty-four vessels. The victorious consuls sailed over to Africa, and received in surrender, first of all, the city of Clybea.[24] Then, attacking Carthage, they devastated three hundred or more forts and surrounded Carthage with their hostile standards. Manlius,[25] the consul, withdrawing from Africa with his victorious fleet, brought back to Rome twenty-seven thousand captives together with large quantities of booty. Regulus,[26] having been chosen by lot for the Carthaginian War, marched with his army and pitched his camp not far from the Bagrada River.[27] Here, when a reptile of extraordinary size devoured many of the soldiers who had gone down to the river to fetch water, Regulus set out with his army to attack

---

23 The consul Atilius mentioned above.
24 A strongly fortified city in Africa, now *Kalibia* or *Clybea,* also called *Aspis.*
25 Lucius Manlius Vulso Longus, 256 B.C.
26 Marcus Atilius Regulus II, 256 B.C.
27 A river in Zeugitana in Africa near Utica, now *Mejerdah;* although very large, fordable in many places.

the beast. But as the javelins and every ineffective stroke of the weapons proceeded, nothing stayed on the animal's back. They slid over the horrible wickerwork of scales as if over a slanting testudo of shields, and in some marvelous fashion were pushed off the body, lest they might damage the body. Moreover, when Regulus saw that a great multitude were being crushed by its teeth, were being trampled down by its attack, and also being deprived of life by its poisonous breath, he ordered the *ballistae* to be brought up, by which a stone from the wall was dashed against its back and the structure of its whole body was loosened. For such is the nature of the reptile that, although it seems to be lacking feet, it is so fitted out with ribs and scales, which it had arranged evenly from the top of its throat to the lowest part of its belly, that it rested on its scales as if upon claws, and upon its ribs as if upon legs. For it was not like a worm, which does not have a stiff spine and unfolds its motion by stretching its contracted parts gradually in the direction of its small body and by contracting its parts when stretched out, but it moved its extended sides by a sinuous movement, first right and then left, so that it might keep the lines of its ribs rigid along the external curvature of the spine. Moreover, nature fastened the claws of its scales to its ribs straight to their highest points. By doing this alternately and quickly, it not only glided over level spaces, but it also ascended inclines, equipped with as many footsteps as ribs. Thus, the effect of this arrangement is that, if the animal is struck by any blow in any part of the body from the belly up to the head, rendered weak, it cannot hold its course, because wherever the blow falls it resolves the spine through which the feet of the ribs and the motion of the body are propelled. Therefore, this reptile, which for so long stood invulnerable against so many javelins, from the stroke of one stone relaxed in weakness, and being quickly encompassed by spears was easily destroyed. Moreover, its hide was conveyed to Rome—the hide they say was one hundred and twenty feet in length—and for some time was a marvel to all.

Regulus carried on a very severe war against three emperors, that is, the two Hasdrubals and Hamilcar, who had been summoned from Sicily, in which seventeen thousand Carthaginians were killed and five thousand captured; eighteen elephants were led away and eighty-two towns gave up to the Romans in surrender.

(9) The Carthaginians, crushed in battles and exhausted by slaughters, asked for peace from Regulus. But when they heard the intolerable and harsh conditions of peace, thinking it more prudent to die armed than to live in wretchedness, decided not only to hire Spanish and Gallic auxiliaries, which they had had for a long time in great numbers, but also Greek troops. And so they summoned Xanthippus, the king of the Lacedaemonians, and placed him in charge of the war. Xanthippus, after inspecting the troops of the Carthaginians and leading them down into a plain,[28] his forces being greatly changed for the better, he joined battle with the Romans. There a great destruction of Roman forces took place, for thirty thousand of their soldiers were laid low in the meeting at that time. Regulus, the renowned leader, together with fifty men were captured and cast into chains, and, finally, in the tenth year of the Punic War, he gave the Carthaginians a renowned triumph. Xanthippus, conscious of a deed so daring and fearing a change in an unstable situation, immediately moved from Africa into Greece.

Thus, Aemilius Paulus and Fulvius Nobilior,[29] consuls, when the captivity of Regulus and the slaughter of the Roman army were reported, being ordered to cross over into Africa with a fleet of three hundred ships, attacked Clybea. On this account, the Carthaginians arrived immediately with a similar fleet, and the naval struggle could not have been put off.[30] One hundred and four ships of the Carthaginians were sunk; thirty with their soldiers were captured; and in addition thirty-five

28 The plains of the Bagrada River.
29 Marcus Aemilius Paulus and Ser. Fulvius Paetinus Nobilior, 255 B.C.
30 Fought off the Hermean Promontory not far from Clybea.

thousand soldiers were slain; but nine of the ships of the Romans were sunk and one thousand one hundred soldiers perished. The consuls pitched camp at Clybea. The two Hannos, the Punic generals, again came together there with a large army and, after joining battle, lost nine thousand soldiers. But, inasmuch as there never was at that time a long period of good fortune among the Romans and whatever were their successes, these were overwhelmed immediately by heavy misfortunes, when the Roman fleet loaded with booty was returning to Italy, it was crushed by an unspeakable wreckage,[31] for, of the three hundred ships, two hundred and twenty were destroyed, eight barely escaped by throwing their cargoes overboard. Hamilcar, the Punic general, was sent with an army into Numidia and Mauretania, and after acting as an enemy and in a bloody manner against all, because they were said to have received Regulus kindly, he fined the people a thousand silver talents and twenty thousand cattle, and had the leaders of all the peoples fastened to the *patibulum*.

In the third year, when as always an uncontrolled fury quickly causes forgetfulness of dangers, Servilius Caepio and Sempronius Blaesus,[32] the consuls, crossing over to Africa, ravaged the entire maritime coast which lies about the Syrtes, and proceeding inland, after capturing and overthrowing many cities, brought large quantities of booty back to the fleet. Then, when they were returning to Italy, around the Promontory of Palinurus, which runs out from the Lucanian Mountains into the deep, being dashed upon the rocks they lost one hundred and fifty transports and, unfortunately, the splendid booty which had been cruelly acquired. Sometimes among the Romans, the enormity of misfortunes overcame their very shameless greed; for the fathers, who were now disgusted with their naval affairs, decreed that a fleet of no more than sixty ships should be maintained for the protection of Italy. This

31 Off the city of Camarina, as the fleet was about to round Pachynus, the southeastern promontory of Sicily, now *Capo Passaro*.
32 Gnaeus Servilius Caepio and Gaius Sempronius Blaesus, 253 B.C.

decree, indeed, they broke immediately, driven on by their ungovernable greed. Furthermore, the consul, Cotta, crossing over into Sicily, fought against the Carthaginians and Sicilians in many battles on land and sea, and throughout all Sicily, he left unburied masses of the dead; partly of the enemy, partly also of the allies.

When L. Caecilius and C. Furius Pacilus[33] were consuls, Hasdrubal, the new general of the Carthaginians, with one hundred and thirty elephants and more than thirty thousand horsemen and infantrymen, went from Africa to Lilybaeum[34] and immediately joined battle with the consul, Metellus, at Panormus.[35] Now Metellus, previously fearing the great strength of the elephants, by making use of a great strategem drove them either into flight or to their death, and, thus, easily overcame the force of the enemy, however great. Twenty thousand Carthaginians were killed in this battle; also twenty-six elephants were slain, and one hundred and four were captured, and when led through Italy furnished a great spectacle to the Italian peoples. Hasdrubal with a few followers fled to Lilybaeum, and while absent was condemned to death by the Carthaginians.

(10) After these events, the Carthaginians, exhausted by so many evils, decided that peace should be sought from the Romans. For this purpose, they thought that Atilius Regulus, formerly a Roman general whom they had held prisoner for five years, should especially be sent among others, and when he returned from Italy without having obtained a peace, they killed him by cutting off his eyelids and by binding him to a machine to keep him awake. Then, the other Atilius Regulus and Manlius Vulso,[36] both consuls for the second time, set

---

33 Lucius Caecilius Metellus and Gaius Furius Pacilus, 251 B.C. The text has Placidus rather than Pacilus.

34 A promontory on the southern coast of Sicily, with a town of the same name, now *Capo Boeo*.

35 Situated on the northwest coast of Sicily, modern *Palermo*.

36 Gaius Atilius Regulus Serranus, son of Marcus, and Lucius Manlius Vulso Longus, 250 B.C.

out for Lilybaeum with a fleet of two hundred ships and four legions. This town located on a promontory they attempted to besiege. When Hannibal, who was the son of Hamilcar, arrived, they were conquered, and when the greater part of their army was lost, they themselves escaped with difficulty. After this, Claudius,[37] the consul, with a fleet of one hundred and twenty ships proceeded against the enemy at the harbor of Drepanum,[38] where presently he was intercepted by a Punic fleet and defeated. He himself, indeed, with thirty ships took refuge in the camp at Lilybaeum; all the rest, that is, ninety, were either captured or sunk. Eight thousand soldiers are reported to have been killed; twenty thousand to have been captured. Gaius Junius,[39] a colleague of Claudius, also lost all his fleet by shipwreck.

In the following year also, a Punic fleet crossed into Italy and lay waste to a great many parts of it, far and wide. In the meantime, Lutatius[40] with a fleet of three hundred ships sailed over to Sicily. While he was in the front ranks stirring up a battle at the city of Drepana, he was very seriously wounded in the thigh and, when he was now being overcome, he was snatched away. But in addition, the Carthaginians, with forty ships and many troops, gathered at Sicily under the leadership of Hanno. Nor was Lutatius more dilatory; rather, with amazing speed, he anticipated the plans of the Carthaginians. After the fleets of both lay very close to each other all night long at the Aegates Islands[41] with their anchors almost intermeshed, at daybreak Lutatius was the first to give the signal for battle. As the battle grew more violent, Hanno, being defeated, abandoned ship and was the first leader to

---

37 Publius Claudius Pulcher, 249 B.C.
38 Drepanum or Drepana, fifteen miles from Lilybaeum. The battle was fought in 249 B.C.
39 Lucius Junius Pullus, 249 B.C.
40 Gaius Lutatius Catulus, 242 B.C.
41 Three islands in the Mediterranean, west of Sicily, nearly opposite to Drepanum and Lilybaeum. The battle took place in 241 B.C.

flee. With him a considerable part of his army sought Africa, the others took refuge in Lilybaeum. Sixty-three Punic ships were captured; one hundred and twenty-five were sunk; thirty-two thousand men were captured; fourteen thousand were slain; but twelve ships of the Romans were sunk. Then, Lutatius went to the city of Eryx,[42] which was in the possession of the Carthaginians, and there joining in battle, he killed two thousand Carthaginians.

(11) Then, the Carthaginians with headlong speed sent legates to the consul, Lutatius,[43] and then to Rome. They begged for peace which they obtained immediately on the terms previously proposed. Moreover, the conditions were: that they should withdraw from Sicily and Sardinia and should pay for the expenses of the war with a sum of three thousand Euboic talents of pure silver in equal installments over a period of twenty years. The terms of this peace were maintained beyond the twenty-third year after the First Punic War had begun.

Who, I ask, will unfold in words the one war of these two cities which was waged for twenty-three years; how many kings of the Carthaginians; how many consuls of the Romans; how many army battle lines; how great a number of ships it brought together, dispersed, and crushed? And then, at last, these seem to have been examined carefully, let judgment be passed on present events.

In the five hundred and seventh year after the founding of the City, a sudden disaster which befell Rome herself prevented the celebration of a triumph by the Romans, for I would not speak rashly in saying that a very serious affliction, coming up suddenly, crushed the immoderate joy of Rome itself. Indeed, in the consulship of Q. Lutatius Catulus and A.

---

42 The name of a high mountain, now called *S. Giuliano,* in the northwestern angle of Sicily, and of a city near it famous for its temple of Venus, six miles from Drepanum.
43 Quintus Lutatius Cerco, 241 B.C.

Manlius[44] diverse disasters of fire and water almost destroyed the City. The Tiber, swollen by unaccustomed rains and overflowing beyond belief by the length and magnitude of the storms, destroyed all the buildings in Rome situated in the plain. The different natures of the locations combined for one destruction, since the buildings where a sluggish flood prevailed became thoroughly soaked and crumbled and those which a raging torrent reached were struck down and leveled. The very serious destruction of the waters was followed by a more serious devastation by fire. This fire, whence it started is uncertain, swept through many parts of the City and not only caused a deplorable destruction of human lives and homes, but also in one conflagration consumed as much wealth as many foreign victories could not have brought together. Thus, as the temporary fire lay waste everything around the Forum, it swept the temple of Vesta and overcame that fire, without even the gods coming to its assistance, which was regarded as eternal. Also in this conflagration Metellus, while he was snatching away the gods on the point of being burned, barely escaped with a half-burnt arm.

(12) When T. Sempronius Gracchus and C. Valerius Falto[45] were consuls, the Romans went to war with the Falisci, and in that conflict fifteen thousand Falisci were killed. In the same year, the Cisalpine Gauls arose as new enemies.[46] War was carried on against these with varying fortune; for in the first conflict, when Valerius was consul, three thousand five hundred Romans fell; in the second, fourteen thousand Gauls fell, two thousand were captured, but on account of the prior disaster, a triumph was denied the consul.

---

44 This is an error. The consuls were Quintus Lutatius Cerco and Aulus Manlius Torquatus Atticus II, 241 B.C.

45 Titus Sempronius Gracchus and Gaius Valerius Falto, 238 B.C.

46 The Boii, a people in Gallia Lugdunensis, now the *Bourbonnais*. They made an alliance with kindred tribes on the Po and with the Ligurians. Valerius attacked the enemy with a defeated army before reinforcements, which were on the way, had arrived, and so was denied a triumph.

When T. Manlius Torquatus and C. Atilius Bulbus[47] were consuls, the island of Sardinia rebelled against its Carthaginian rulers. Soon thereafter the Sardinians were subjected and crushed. But it was decided to carry on war against the Carthaginians as violators of the peace which they themselves had requested. The Carthaginians on their part humbly requested peace and when, after twice sending legates, they had accomplished nothing, and later also, when ten of their leading men twice made supplication and failed in their demands, at last by the eloquence of Hanno, the least important man among the legates, they were successful. In this year, the gates of Janus Geminus were closed, because nowhere in that year was there war, which had happened before only under the king, Numa Pompilius.

At this point, at least, we must hold our peace and pass over in silence those times with which ours can by no means be compared, lest by this commotion we arouse the detractors of our times to revile their age rather than themselves. Behold, the gates of Janus have been closed; the Romans had no war abroad; Rome, holding all her progeny quietly at rest within its bosom, did not heave a sigh. And when did this take place? After the First Punic War. After how long a time? After four hundred and forty years. How long did it continue? For one year. And what followed in the next year? Not to mention other events, the Gallic War and Hannibal in the Second Punic War. Alas, how ashamed I am to have learned these things and laid them bare! Was that peace, or rather shadow of a peace, an alleviation of miseries or an incentive to evils? Did that drop of oil falling in the midst of a great flame extinguish the blaze of so great a fire or nourish it? Did a small drink of cold water swallowed by those burning with fever cure the sick or rather set the fever ablaze? For almost seven hundred years, that is, from Hostilius Tullus until Caesar Augustus, in only one year did the Roman viscera not sweat

---

47 The text reads 'Bubulcus.' Titus Manlius Torquatus and Gaius Atilius Bulbus II, 235 B.C.

blood, and in the midst of the many periods of long centuries
the wretched City, truly a wretched mother, has enjoyed rest
scarcely at any time from the fear of sorrows, not to say sorrows themselves. If any man had had so little rest in his life,
would he be said to have lived? Or, if anyone through a whole
year should be driven by sorrows and torments, yet in the
middle space of the year itself pass one day only in peace and
without conflicts, will he receive from this an alleviation of
his troubles and not assign the whole year to a period of
miseries? But those critics, he says, have set up this year as
a glorious example of indefatigable courage. Would that they
might have passed over it in return for a forgetfulness of the
continuous misery. For just as at last leprosy is so diagnosed
in the body or a person if in various places in the sound parts
of the skin a different color appears, but if it spreads everywhere so that it makes all of one color, however foreign, this
method of distinguishing has no value, so if continuous labor
should flow on with calm tolerance and with a desire for a
breathing spell, this would be called the intent of the will
and a customary choice. But when for a brief moment of
quiet either the joys of greater things or the concern for lesser
matters are released, it is immediately observed both how much
pleasure this brief period possessed and how much bitterness
that long period offered; that is, they now realize both how
pleasing that rest would have been if it had lasted a long time,
and how this incessant wretchedness was also to be avoided if
in any way it could have been avoided.

(13) In the five hundred and seventeenth year after the
founding of the City, Hamilcar, the leader of the Carthaginians, while secretly preparing another war against the
Romans, was killed by the Spaniards in battle.[48]

In the following year, legates of the Romans were killed by
the Illyrians. Later, a most savage war was carried on with
the Illyrians, in which after many towns and peoples had

---

48 Hamilcar Barca was drowned in the Vinalapó River while withdrawing
from the siege of Helice in the winter of 229-228 B.C.

been destroyed, the survivors gave themselves up to the consuls, Fulvius and Postumius.[49]

In the third year thereafter, the pontiffs, powerful by means of their sacrilegious sacrifices, wickedly polluted the wretched City; for the decemviri, surpassing a custom of ancient superstition, buried alive a Gallic man and a Gallic woman, together also with a Greek woman in the cattle market at Rome. But this obligation of magic was immediately turned contrariwise, for they expiated those terrible deaths of foreigners which they had committed by the most loathsome slaughter of their own. Indeed, when L. Aemilius Catulus and C. Atilius Regulus[50] were consuls, the Senate was overwhelmed with great terror by the rebellion of Cisalpine Gaul, when also it was announced that a huge army was approaching from Further Gaul, made up chiefly of Gaesati, a name not of a tribe but of Gallic mercenaries. So the consuls being thoroughly roused gathered up their forces for the defense of the state. When this was done, it was reported that in the army of each consul there were eight hundred thousand armed men, just as Fabius, the historian who took part in that war, wrote. Of these, there were 299,200 Roman and Campanian foot-soldiers and 26,600 horsemen; the rest of the multitude was made up of allies. When the battle was joined at Arretium,[51] the consul, Atilius, was killed. When a part of their army had been killed, not at all so great as ought to have caused them terror, eight hundred thousand fled; for the historians hand down that at that time three thousand of them were killed, which is, therefore, more ignominious and disgraceful, that so many battle lines fled when so few had been lost, since they betrayed that in other victories they had prevailed, not by the strength of their courage, but by the fortunate issue of the battles. For who, I ask, would believe that there was that number just in the

---

49 Gnaeus Fulvius Centumalus and Lucius Postumius Albinus II, 229 B.C.
50 Lucius Aemilius Papus (not Catulus) and Gaius Atilius Regulus, 225 B.C.
51 A large town in Etruria, now *Arezzo*.

army of the Romans; I do not mean the number that fled? After this, a second battle was fought with the Gauls, in which at least forty thousand Gauls were slaughtered.[52]

In the following year, Manlius Torquatus and Fulvius Flaccus[53] were the first consuls to lead Roman legions across the Po. There was a battle there with the Insubrian Gauls, of whom twenty-three thousand were killed and five thousand captured.

Later in that year which was next to this one, dire portents terrified the wretched City, wretched indeed, which was terrified by the clamor of the enemy on one side, and by villainy of demons on the other. For in Picenum[54] a river flowed with blood, and among the Tuscans the sky seemed to be ablaze, and at Ariminum[55] late at night a bright light seemed to shine and three moons arising in the distant regions of the sky seemed to have appeared. Then, also, the islands of Caria and Rhodes were so shaken by a great earthquake that buildings in general collapsed and also the great Colossus fell. In the same year, Flaminius,[56] the consul, defying the auspices by which he was prohibited to fight, fought against the Gauls and conquered them. In this war, nine thousand Gauls were killed and seventeen thousand were captured.[57]

After this Claudius,[58] the consul, killed thirty thousand of the Gaesati, when also, advancing into the first line, he himself killed their king, Virdomarus,[59] and among the many

---

52 This occurred at Telamon, a city on the coast of Etruria, 225 B.C.
53 Titus Manlius Torquatus II and Quintus Fulvius Flaccus II, 224 B.C.
54 A district in the eastern part of Italy, famous for its fruits and oil.
55 A town in Umbria, on the shore of the Adriatic, at the mouth of a river of the same name.
56 Gaius Flaminius, 223 B.C.
57 Somewhere near Bergomum (modern *Bergamo*), a town in Gallia Transpadana, about thirty-five miles northeast of Milan.
58 Marcus Claudius Marcellus, 222 B.C.
59 The Roman consul advanced to the relief of Clastidium, now *Chiasteggio*, near the Po, 222 B.C. He killed the leader of the Insubres in single combat.

towns of the Insubres, whom he had forced to surrender, he also captured Milan, a very flourishing city.

Then the Histri, new enemies, were aroused, whom the consuls, Cornelius and Minucius,[60] subjugated, indeed, with the shedding of much Roman blood. At this time, there arose for a short time that ancient passion of the Romans for fame, shameless since it involved parricide. For Fabius Censorius killed his son, Fabius Buteo, who had been accused of theft; surely a crime which not even the laws considered worthy except of a fine or at most of exile in the case of any man, but which the father thought should be punished by death.

(14) In the five hundred and thirty-fourth year after the founding of the City, Hannibal, the commander of the Carthaginians, after he first attacked Saguntum, a very flourishing city of Spain and a friend[61] of the Roman people, and surrounded it by a siege and tortured it with famine, all of which it endured bravely, whether deserved or not, by reason of the promise which the inhabitants had made to the Romans, finally, in the eighth month, destroyed it. The legates of the Romans who had been sent to him he very unlawfully also kept from his presence. Then, because of his hatred of the Roman name, which, when he was nine years of age, he had very faithfully, although very faithless in other matters, sworn before altars to his father, Hamilcar, Hannibal, in the consulship of P. Cornelius Scipio and P. Sempronius Longus,[62] crossed the Pyrenees Mountains in the midst of very fierce Gallic tribes, opening a path with the sword and, at last on the ninth day, came from the Pyrenees to the Alps. Here, after he overcame the Gallic mountaineers in battle, who tried to

---

60 Publius Scipio Asina and Marcus Minucius Rufus, 221 B.C.
61 The term *amicus* embraces both general and different specific obligations, and is to be distinguished from *socius*. Hannibal claimed that Saguntum, with which Rome had previously entered into a defensive alliance, had made an unprovoked war upon some of his Spanish allies.
62 Publius Cornelius Scipio (a cousin of the consul of 221 B.C., Publius Cornelius Scipio Asina), and Tiberius Sempronius Longus, 218 B.C.

prevent his ascent, and cut through the pathless cliffs with fire and sword, he was delayed for four days, and finally on the fifth day, with a supreme effort, he arrived at the plains. At that time, they explain that his army consisted of about one hundred thousand foot-soldiers and twenty thousand horsemen. Scipio, the consul, was the first to meet Hannibal and, on joining battle at the Ticinus,[63] he was seriously wounded and he escaped by being freed from death by Scipio, his son,[64] who was still wearing the *toga praetextata* and was afterwards called Africanus. There almost the entire Roman army was killed. Then, there was a battle under the same consul at the river Trebia[65] and again the Romans were overcome with a like slaughter. Sempronius, the consul, when he learned of the misfortune of his colleague, returned from Sicily with his army. In a similar manner, he joined forces at the same river, and, after losing his army, was almost the only one to escape. But in this battle, Hannibal also was wounded. He, afterwards, in the early spring when he was passing over into Etruria, was caught by a storm high on the Appennines and for two continuous days he, together with his army, was rendered immobile[66] by snow, and loaded down with snow became numb with cold. Here, a great number of the men, many beasts of burden, and almost all the elephants perished from the severity of the cold. But at this time, the other Scipio,[67] brother of the consul, Scipio, carried on many battles in Spain; he also conquered and captured Mago,[68] the leader of the Carthaginians.

(15) Then, too, the Romans were terrified by dire prodigies. For the sun's orbit seemed to be contracted, and at Arpi[69]

---

63 In Gallia Cisalpina, a tributary of the Po, now *Ticino*. The battle was fought in 218 B.C.
64 Publius Cornelius Scipio Africanus Major.
65 A river in Upper Italy, which joins the Po about two miles west of Placentia.
66 Cf. Livy, *Histories*, 21.38.
67 Gnaius Scipio Calvus.
68 Mago escaped; Hanno was captured.
69 A city in Apulia, formerly called Argyripa, now *Arpa*,

parmae[70] were seen in the sky; the sun also seemed to have fought with the moon; at Capena[71] during the daytime two moons seemed to have risen; in Sardinia two shields seemed to have sweated blood; among the Faliscans[72] the sky seemed to be split, as it were, by a great fissure; at Antium,[73] as men were harvesting, bloody ears of corn seemed to have fallen into the basket. So Hannibal, knowing that Flaminius,[74] the consul, was alone in the camp, that he might more quickly crush him when unprepared, advancing in the early spring took the shorter but marshy road, and when the Sarnus[75] happened to have overflowed its banks far and wide and had left the fields about it uncertain and loose, about which it has been said:

'And the plains which Sarnus floods.'

When Hannibal proceeded into these fields with his army, with the mist especially as it rose from the marsh cutting off his view, he lost a large part of his allies and beasts of burden. He himself, moreover, seated upon an elephant which alone had survived, barely escaped the hardship of the journey; but he lost one eye, with which he had long been afflicted, because of the rigor of the cold, lack of sleep, and hardships. But when he was near the camp of Flaminius, the consul, he roused Flaminius to battle by devastating the surrounding country. This battle took place at Lake Trasimene.[76] Here, the Roman army was most unfortunately deceived by the trickery of Hannibal and was completely massacred; the consul himself also was killed; twenty-five thousand Romans are reported to have been slain in this battle and six thousand captured. Of

---

70 *parmae* are small round shields.
71 A city of Etruria, eight miles from the foot of Mount Soracte.
72 A people of Etruria.
73 An ancient town in Latium, not far from the seacoast, now *Porto d'Anzio*.
74 Gaius Flaminius II, 217 B.C.
75 A river in Campania, near Pompeii, now the *Sarno*.
76 One of the largest lakes in Etruria, between Cortona and Perusia, ten miles long and eight wide, now *Lago Trasimene* or *Lago di Perugia*.

Hannibal's army, two thousand fell. This battle at Lake
Trasimene was renowned because of so great a slaughter of
the Romans, especially since the eagerness of the fighters was
so tense that these fighters did not at all perceive the very
severe earthquake which then, by chance, became so powerful
that it is reported to have ruined cities, moved mountains,
cut rocks asunder, and forced rivers backward. The battle of
Cannae[77] followed the disaster which took place at Trasimene,
although the intervening period was the time of the dictator,
Fabius Maximus, who retarded Hannibal's attack by his delaying tactics.

(16) In the five hundred and fortieth year after the founding of the City, L. Aemilius Paulus and P. Terentius Varro,[78]
consuls who had been sent against Hannibal, most unfortunately because of the impatience of Varro, the consul, at
Cannae, a village of Apulia, lost almost all of the forces of
the Romans, the source of their hopes. For in this battle,
forty-four thousand Romans were killed, although of Hannibal's army also a large part was slain. Yet, in no war with the
Carthaginians were the Romans brought so close to annihilation. For in that battle the consul, Aemilius Paulus, perished,
twenty men of consular and praetorian rank were killed, and
thirty senators were either captured or slain; also three hundred men of noble rank, forty thousand infantrymen, and
three thousand five hundred horsemen lost their lives. Varro,
the consul, with five hundred cavalry fled to Venusia.[79] There
is no doubt that that day would have been the last day of the
Roman state, if Hannibal, immediately after his victory, had
hastened to penetrate the City. As proof of his victory, Hannibal sent to Carthage three pecks of gold rings which he had
taken from the hands of the slain Roman knights and senators. To such a degree was the despair among the remaining

---

77 A village in Apulia, north of Canusium. The battle took place in
    216 B.C.
78 Lucius Aemilius II and Gaius Terentius Varro, 216 B.C.
79 A town on the borders of Apulia and Lucania, about ten miles from
    Cannae, now *Venosa*.

Romans that the senators thought a plan should be entered upon for abandoning Italy and seeking another home. This would have been confirmed on the motion of Caecilius Metellus, unless Cornelius Scipio, then military tribune and the same man who later was called Africanus, had drawn his sword and prevented it, but rather had forced him to swear in his own words to defend his native land. The Romans, daring to breath again, brought back from the lowest depths to hope of life, created Decimus Junius dictator. He, holding a levy of those of seventeen years of age and over, gathered fourteen legions of immature and untrained soldiery. Then, also, he induced the slaves of proven strength and good will, either volunteers or, if it was so necessary, bought with public money, to take the oath with a promise of freedom. The arms, which were lacking, they took from the temples; the impoverished treasury was restored by private wealth. Thus the equestrian order and the frightened plebeians, forgetful of their private interests, had regard for the common good. Junius, the dictator, also recalling an ancient practice in the days of Roman misery, to supplement the Roman army, by an edict opening up an asylum, as it were, obtained for military service by a promise of impunity whatever men had been found punishable for crimes and debts. The number of these was about six thousand men. But Campania, or rather all Italy, in utter despair over the restoration of the Roman position, went over to Hannibal. After this, L. Postumius, the praetor, who was sent to fight against the Gauls, was cut down together with his army.

Then, when Sempronius Gracchus and Q. Fabius Maximus[80] were consuls, Claudius Marcellus, the ex-praetor elected proconsul, dispersed the army of Hannibal in battle[81] and was the first person, after the great disasters to the Republic, to create hope that Hannibal could be overcome. Moreover, in

---

80 Tiberius Sempronius Gracchus and Quintus Fabius Maximus Verrocosus III, 215 B.C.
81 In an engagement near Nola.

Spain the Scipios[82] overcame Hasdrubal, the Carthaginian general, in a very difficult battle as he was preparing an army against Italy; for by killing or capturing them, they diminished his army by thirty-five thousand soldiers. The Celtiberian soldiers, whom as a foreign group the Romans had begun to accept in their camp for the first time, the Romans took over through bribery into their own camp away from an alliance with the enemy. Sempronius Gracchus was led into a trap by a certain Lucanian,[83] his host and a proconsul, and killed. Centenius Paenula, a centurion, of his own accord asked that the war against Hannibal be turned over to him. He, together with eight thousand soldiers whom he had led forth into battle, was killed by Hannibal. After him the praetor, Cn. Fulvius, was overcome by Hannibal and, after losing his army, barely escaped.

I am ashamed of these recollections. For what shall I rather speak of: the shamelessness or the wretchedness of the Romans? Rather and more truly, of the shameless wretchedness or the wretched shamelessness? Who would believe that at that time, when the public treasury of the Roman people was asking for niggardly donations by way of private contributions, when there was no one in the camp who was not a boy or a slave or a criminal or a debtor, and not even so was the army sufficient in number, and when the Senate in the Curia seemed composed almost entirely of new members, and finally, when they were in such despair with all their losses and disasters that they resorted to a plan for abandoning Italy—that at this time, when, as we have said, one war could in no wise be carried on at home, three more wars had been undertaken abroad: one in Macedonia against Philip, the very powerful king of Macedonia; another in Spain against Hasdrubal, the

---

82 Publius Cornelius Scipio and Gnaeus Cornelius Scipio Calvus. The identity of this battle is not clear. A series of battles is concerned here, from Nova Carthago in 209 B.C. until Hasdrubal left for Italy after his defeat near Baecula.

83 Flavius, the leader of the Roman party among the Lucanians, betrayed Sempronius Gracchus into the hands of Mago, the brother of Hannibal.

brother of Hannibal; a third in Sardinia against the Sardinians and the other Hasdrubal, a general of the Carthaginians; and in addition to these, a fourth against Hannibal by whom they were hard pressed in Italy? And yet strong desperation toward one another led to better things, for in all these wars because of despair they fought, and by fighting they conquered. From this it is clearly shown that those times were not more tranquil for leisurely pursuits, but men were braver because of their miseries.

(17) In the year five hundred and forty-third year after the founding of the City, Claudius Marcellus with difficulty captured Syracuse, the richest city in Sicily, by a second assault, which, although he had previously besieged it, he was not able to take, being repulsed by the machine of the Syracusan Archimedes, a citizen endowed with a remarkable genius. In the tenth year after Hannibal had come into Italy, in the consulship of Cn. Fulvius and P. Sulpicius,[84] Hannibal moved his army from Campania, and with great slaughter of all, proceeding through the territory of the Sidicini and Suessani by way of the Via Latina to the Anio River, pitched camp three miles from the City to the incredible fear of the entire City, when, as the Senate and the people became frightened by their various anxieties, the matrons, also frantic with fear, ran along the defenses and brought stones to the walls and desired passionately to fight in the front line in defense of the walls. Hannibal himself with light-armed cavalry advanced in a hostile manner up to the Colline Gate[85] and then arranged all his troops for battle. But the consuls and the proconsul, Fulvius, refused battle. And when the battle lines stood drawn up on both sides in the sight of Rome, which was to be the prize of the victor, so great a storm mingled with hail suddenly burst forth that the disorganized lines, with difficulty retaining their arms, withdrew to their own camps. Then, when, as fair weather returned, the troops had returned

---

84 Gnaeus Fulvius Centumalus and Publius Sulpicius Galba Maximus, 211 B.C.
85 The gate in Rome near the Quirinal Hill.

to the battle field and battle array, again a storm, even more violent, burst out causing greater fear to mortal man and checking his presumption, and it forced the terrified armies to take refuge in their tents. Then Hannibal, turning toward religion, is reported to have said that the will to take possession of Rome was given him but not the power.

Let the detractors of the true God now tell me at this point, whether Roman bravery prevented Hannibal from seizing and overthrowing Rome or Divine compassion. Or perhaps those who were left unharmed refuse to confess that Hannibal, even as the victor, became frightened and by withdrawing proved it and, if it is manifest that the Divine protection came from heaven through rain; moreover, that the rain itself was not provided at the opportune and necessary moments except through Christ who is the true God, I think that it can be learned sufficiently from evidence of this kind and cannot be denied. This is especially proven true now when as a proof of His power, it happened during a damaging period of drought that there was constant petitioning for rain, and, in turn, now the pagans and now the Christians asked and never, as they themselves testify, did it happen that the desired rainfall took place except on the day when it was permitted that Christ be asked and that the Christians ask. It is established beyond doubt that the City of Rome through this same true God, who is Christ Jesus, ordaining according to the decision of His ineffable judgment, was both preserved then for its belief in the future faith and was punished now in part for its unbelief.

But in Spain, both Scipios[86] were killed by the brother of Hasdrubal.[87] In Campania, Capua was captured by Q.

---

86 Publius Scipio, consul with Titus Sempronius Longus in 218 B.C. and Gnaeus Cornelius Scipio Calvus, consul with Marcus Claudius Marcellus in 222 B.C.

87 Publius Scipio was overcome by Mago and Hasdrubal, son of Gisco. Gnaeus Scipio was defeated later by these same generals with the added strength of Hasdrubal, son of Barca.

Fulvius, the proconsul; the leaders of the Campanians committed suicide with poison; and Fulvius punished by death the entire senate of Capua, even though the Roman Senate prohibited it. After the Scipios had been killed in Spain and all action was being delayed because of the fear which had been roused, when Scipio,[88] still a young man, offered his services and the shameful scarcity of money in the treasury existed, at the suggestion of Claudius Marcellus and Valerius Laevinus,[89] who were then consuls, all the senators brought gold and silver coins to the quaestors at the treasury so that they left nothing except individual rings and bullae[90] for themselves and their sons and, then, for their daughters and wives only a single ounce of gold and not more than a single pound of silver.

(18) Scipio, at the age of twenty-four years, obtaining proconsular power for Spain, being intent especially on avenging his father and uncle, crossed the Pyrenees, and on the first attack captured New Carthage,[91] where very extensive tribute, strong defenses, and great supplies of gold and silver were kept by the Carthaginians. There also he captured Mago, the brother of Hannibal, and sent him with others to Rome. The consul, Laevinus, returning from Macedonia, took by storm Agrigentum, a city of Sicily, and there he captured Hanno, the general of the Africans. He received forty cities in surrender and took twenty-six by storm. Hannibal in Italy killed Cn. Fulvius, the proconsul, and in addition eleven tribunes and seventeen thousand soldiers. Marcellus, the consul, fought with Hannibal continuously for three days.[92] On the first day,

---

88 Publius Cornelius Scipio Africanus Major (236–184 B.C.), sent to Spain to command the army, on the death of his father and uncle.

89 Marcus Valerius Laevinus and Marcus Claudius Marcellus IV, 210 B.C.

90 A kind of amulet, mostly of gold, worn upon the neck.

91 A town in Hispania Tarraconensis, now *Cartagena*. It was located on one of the best harbors of the Mediterranean. It was originally named Mastia, and later refounded as New Carthage by Hasdrubal in 228 B.C. as a base for the Carthaginian conquest of Spain.

92 The battle was fought in 210 B.C. at Herdonea in Apulia.

there was a stalemate in the fighting; on the following day, the consul was conquered; on the third day, as victor he killed eight thousand of the enemy, and forced Hannibal himself with others to flee to their own camp. Fabius Maximus,[93] the consul, stormed Tarentum a second time, which had revolted from the Romans, and captured it, and there he destroyed large numbers of Hannibal's troops together with their general himself, Carthalo; he sold thirty thousand of the captured men, and turned the proceeds over to the State treasury.

In the following year in Italy, Claudius Marcellus,[94] the consul, together with his army, was destroyed by Hannibal.[95] Scipio in Spain conquered Hasdrubal, the Carthaginian general, and stripped his camp;[96] in addition, he brought eighty cities under his power either by surrender or by battle. Although he sold the Africans into slavery, he dismissed the Spaniards without a price. Hannibal beset both consuls, Marcellus and Crispinus, by ambush and killed them.

In the consulship of Claudius Nero and M. Livius Salinator,[97] when Hasdrubal, Hannibal's brother, was going from Spain through the Gauls to Italy, and, having been ordered by the Carthaginians to join his brother with his troops, he was taking with him large groups of Spanish and Gallic auxiliaries, and when he was reported to the consuls as having already descended from the Alps by a forced march, unbeknown to Hannibal, his plans were anticipated and together with his whole army he was killed.[98] Indeed, for a long time the outcome of the battle was in doubt for the elephants especially troubled the Roman battle line. These elephants

---

93 Quintus Fabius Maximus Verrocosus V, 209 B.C.
94 Marcus Claudius Marcellus in his fifth consulship, 208 B.C.
95 In a battle fought in 208 B.C. near Venusia in Apulia.
96 At Ilipa, a city of Hispania Baetica, upon the right bank of the Boetis, near Seville, 207 B.C.
97 Gaius Claudius Nero and Marcus Livius Salinator II, 207 B.C.
98 The battle of the Metaurus River, 207 B.C., in Umbria, now known as *Meturo*.

were driven back by Roman soldiers whom they called *velites*
because they rushed here and there. This kind of warfare
had been discovered shortly before; for example, young men,
selected for their agility, would with their weapons mount
behind horsemen, and presently, when contact was made with
the enemy, would dismount and immediately they themselves
as infantrymen would harass the enemy, while the horsemen
in another place would fight those against whom they had
been carried. So when these elephants were driven back by
these *velites* and could not now be controlled by their masters,
they were killed by driving an artificer's knife between their
ears. This method of killing the beast when need arose was
first discovered by this same general, Hasdrubal. By this
battle the Metaurus River, where Hasdrubal was conquered,
was to the Carthaginians as Lake Trasimene, the city of
Cesena in Picenum and that famous village of Cannae were
to the Romans; for fifty-eight thousand of Hasdrubal's army
were slaughtered there, five thousand four hundred were captured, but among these, four thousand were found to be
Roman citizens and were restored to citizenship, which was
a consolation to the victorious consuls, for they had lost eight
hundred of their own army. The head of his brother, Hasdrubal, was cast in front of Hannibal's camp. When he saw
it and at once was aware of the disaster of the Carthaginians,
in the thirteenth year after he had come into Italy he took
refuge among the Bruttii. Following these events, for a whole
year a respite from the tumult of wars between Hannibal and
the Romans seemed to have intervened, because there was the
restlessness of diseases in the camps and a very serious pestilence broke out in both armies. Meanwhile, Scipio, after all
Spain from the Pyrenees to the Ocean had been reduced to a
province, went to Rome. When he was made consul, together
with Licinius Crassus,[99] he passed over into Africa and killed
Hanno, the son of Hamilcar, general of the Carthaginians,

---

99 Publius Licinius Crassus Dives, 205 B.C.

and destroyed his army partly by slaughter and partly by captivity; for he killed eleven thousand Carthaginians in that battle.[100] Sempronius,[101] the consul, met with Hannibal and when conquered fled to Rome. Scipio, in Africa, attacked the winter quarters of the Carthaginians and those of the Numidians, both of which were not far from Utica, and early in the night set fire to them. The Carthaginians, since they thought that the fire had started by accident, rushed unarmed to extinguish it. Thus, they were easily overcome by those who were armed. In both camps, forty thousand men were killed by fire and sword; five thousand were captured; and the leaders themselves being wretchedly burned escaped with difficulty. Hasdrubal, the commander, went to Carthage as a fugitive. Thus, Syphax and Hasdrubal soon recruited a very large army and again met with Scipio, and when conquered fled.[102] Laelius and Masinissa captured Syphax as he fled; the rest of the multitude took refuge in Cirta,[103] which Masinissa stormed and took in surrender; he took Syphax, bound by chains, to Scipio. Scipio handed him over, together with a great deal of booty and many captives, to Laelius to take away.

(19) Hannibal was ordered to return to Africa, that he might give aid to the tired Carthaginians. After killing all the soldiers of Italian stock who were unwilling to follow him, he left Italy weeping. As he was approaching the shore of Africa, one of the sailors was ordered to climb a mast and from there observe the region which they were approaching, and he replied that he saw a ruined sepulchre. Hannibal, deprecating these words as an ill omen, changed his course toward Leptis and disembarked his troops there. While his men were being refreshed, he went to Carthage immediately

---

100 A cavalry engagement near Utica, 204 B.C.
101 Publius Sempronius Tuditanus, 204 B.C.
102 Fought on the plains of the Bagrada River, 203 B.C., a river in Zeugitana in Africa near Utica, now *Mejerdah*.
103 Cirta, an important city in Numidia forty-eight miles from the sea, now *Constantine*.

and then asked for a conference with Scipio. There, when the two very famous generals had surveyed each other for a long time with mutual admiration, and after the negotiations for peace had failed, battle was joined. This battle,[104] arranged long in advance with the great skill of the generals, carried on with great masses of troops, and consummated with great forces of soldiers, brought victory to the Romans. Eighty elephants were either captured or killed here; twenty thousand five hundred Carthaginians fell. Hannibal, having tried everything both before and in the battle, with a few men, that is, with barely four horsemen, slipped away in the din of the battle and fled to Hadrumentum. Later, he came to Carthage, which he had left thirty-six years earlier as a small boy with his father, and he persuaded the senate, then in session, that there was no hope left except in seeking peace.

In the consulship of C. Cornelius Lentulus and P. Aelius Paetus,[105] by the will of the Senate and the people, peace was granted the Carthaginians through Scipio. But more than fifty ships were brought out into the deep and, in sight of the City, were burned. Scipio, already at that time with the surname Africanus, entered the City in a triumph. Terence,[106] who afterwards became a comic poet, one of the noble Carthaginian captives, wearing the *pilleus*—which was a sign of the liberty granted him—followed him behind his chariot as he triumphed.

(20) In the five hundred and forty-sixth year after the founding of the City, the Second Punic War, which had been carried on for seventeen years, was ended. The Macedonian War immediately followed it, which the consul, Quintius Flamininus,[107] took over, and, after many very serious battles in which the Macedonians were conquered, granted peace to Philip. Then, he fought with the Lacedaemonians, and

---

104 The battle of Zama, 202 B.C.
105 Gnaeus Cornelius Lentulus and Publius Aelius Paetus, 201 B.C.
106 Terentius Afer, born in 195 B.C. at Carthage, the famous writer of comedies.
107 Titus Quintius Flamininus, 198 B.C.

after conquering their leader, Nabis,[108] he led Demetrius, the son of Philip, and Armenes, the son of Nabis, who were the most noble of the captives, before his chariot. The Roman captives, who had been sold under Hannibal throughout Greece, were all returned to freedom, and with their heads shaven as a sign of being cleansed of slavery followed the chariot of the conqueror. At the same time, the Insubres, the Boii, and the Cenomani, bringing their forces together under the Carthaginian general, Hamilcar, who had remained in Italy, and were laying waste to Cremona and Placentia,[109] were overcome in a very difficult battle[110] by the praetor, L. Furius.[111] Afterwards, Flamininus, the proconsul, overcame in war[112] Philip, the king, and with him the Thracians, Macedonians, and Illyrians, and many tribes besides who had come to his aid. The Macedonians were conquered and lost their camp; Polybius writes that eight thousand of the enemy were killed on that day and five thousand were captured; Valerius says that forty thousand were massacred; but Claudius relates that thirty-two thousand were destroyed.

This inconsistency among the writers is surely a falsehood, but the cause of the falsehood is certainly flattery, for they are eager to pile up the praises of the victor and to extol the courage of the fatherland for present and future generations. Otherwise, if the number had not been investigated, whatever it had been would not have been expressed. But if it is glorious for a general and the fatherland to have killed a large number of the enemy, how much more joyful can it seem to the fatherland and happier to the commander to have lost none or very few of his men. Thus, it is very clear that this takes place with the like shamelessness of lying, by which an

---

108 Not Navid as the text reads, but rather Nabis.
109 All these cities were on the left and right banks of the Po River in Cisalpine Gaul.
110 200 B.C. In the shadow of Cremona.
111 Lucius Furius, not Fulvius as the text reads.
112 The battle of Cynoscephalae, 197 B.C. The exact location of the field of battle is in doubt.

addition is made to the number of the enemy killed, and also the loss suffered by the allies are diminished or even completely overlooked.

Thus, Sempronius Tuditanus in Hither Spain was overcome with his entire army and was killed. The consul, Marcellus,[113] in Etruria was overwhelmed by the Boii and lost a large part of his army. Later Furius, the other consul, came to his aid, and thus ravaging the entire nation of the Boii with fire and sword, they almost completely annihilated it.

In the consulship of L. Valerius Flaccus and M. Porcius Cato,[114] Antiochus, the king of Syria, arranging for war against the Roman people, crossed over into Europe from Asia. Then, also, Hannibal, because of the rumors of his stirring up war which were being spread about him among the Romans, being ordered by the Senate to present himself at Rome, set out secretly from Africa and went to Antiochus. When he found him lingering in Ephesus, he urged him to war immediately. At that time also, the law which had been proposed by Oppius, a tribune of the people, that no women should have more than a half ounce of gold and should not make use of a garment of divers colors nor of a carriage in the City, was repealed after twenty years.

In the second consulship of P. Scipio Africanus and T. Sempronius Longus,[115] ten thousand Gauls were slain in Milan, but in a following battle eleven thousand Gauls and five thousand Romans were killed. Publius Digitius, praetor in Hither Spain, lost almost his entire army. M. Fulvius, the praetor, conquered the Celtiberi, together with neighboring peoples, and captured their king. Minucius was drawn into extreme danger by the Ligurians and, when entrapped by the ambuscades of the enemy, was with difficulty freed by the

---

113 Marcus Claudius Marcellus, son of the great Marcellus, and Furius Purpurio, 196 B.C.
114 Marcus Porcius Cato and Lucius Valerius Flaccus, 195 B.C.
115 Publius Cornelius Scipio Africanus II and Tiberius Sempronius Longus, 194 B.C.

activity of the Numidian cavalry. Scipio Africanus, together with other legates, was sent to Antiochus, and also had a private talk with Hannibal. But when the negotiations for peace failed, he departed from Antiochus. In both Spains, very terrible and bloody wars for both peoples were carried on by the praetors, Flaminius and Fulvius.

In the consulship of P. Cornelius Scipio and M. Acilius Glabrio,[116] Antiochus, although he had occupied Thermopylae, by whose defense on account of the uncertain outcomes of battle he was more secure, nevertheless, when battle[117] was joined, was overcome by the consul, Glabrio, and with difficulty escaped with a few men and arrived at Ephesus. He is said to have had sixty thousand armed men, of whom forty thousand are reported to have been killed, more than five thousand to have been captured. The other consul, Scipio, entered into conflict with the nation of the Boii, in which battle he killed twenty thousand of the enemy.

The following year, Scipio Africanus, with Eumenes, the son of Attalus, as an ally, carried on a naval battle against Hannibal, who was then in command of the fleet of Antiochus. After Hannibal was defeated and put to flight and at the same time lost almost his entire army, Antiochus sought peace, and of his own accord sent back the son of Africanus. It is uncertain whether he had captured him while on a scouting expedition or in battle. In Further Spain, L. Aemilius, the proconsul, with his whole army was cut down by the Lusitani and perished. L. Baebius, while advancing into Spain, with his entire army was surrounded by the Ligurians and killed. Since it was established that not even a messenger survived, the result was that the Massilians took care to announce the massacre to Rome. Fulvius,[118] the consul, passed from Greece into Gallo-Greece, which is now Galatia, as far as Mount

---

116 Publius Cornelius Scipio Nasica and Marcus Acilius Glabrio, 191 B.C.

117 The battle of Magnesia, 190 B.C.

118 Marcus Fulvius Nobilior, 189 B.C.

Olympus,[119] at which all the Gallo-Greeks with their wives and children had taken refuge, and there he waged a very bitter battle; for, although the Romans suffered seriously from arrows, leaden balls, stones, and other missiles thrown from higher positions, they pushed through to make contact with the enemy. Forty thousand Gallo-Greeks are reported to have lost their lives in that battle. Marcius,[120] the consul, who had proceeded against the Ligurians and was defeated, lost four thousand soldiers and if, after being overcome he had not taken speedy refuge in his camp, he would have suffered the same destructive slaughter which Baebius had received from the same enemy a little while before.

When M. Claudius Marcellus and Q. Fabius Labeo[121] were consuls, King Philip, who had killed the legates of the Roman people, merited pardon for this act through the very revered prayers of his son, Demetrius, whom he had sent as a legate, and he immediately, with the help of the boy's brother in the father's parricide, killed this same Demetrius by poisoning, on the ground that he was a friend of the Romans and a traitor of his own, although the poor wretch suspected no evil from either. In the same year, Scipio Africanus, long in exile from a city ungrateful to him, died of disease in the town of Liternum.[122] Also at the same time, Hannibal, at the court of Prusias,[123] the king of Bithynia, when he was demanded by the Romans, committed suicide by taking poison, and Philopoemen,[124] the leader of the Achaeans, was captured

---

119 Several mountains bear this name. The most celebrated of these is the one on the borders of Macedonia and Thessaly (now *Lacha*), of great height and so regarded as the seat of the gods; a part of the Mysian chain.

120 Quintus Marcius Philippus, 186 B.C.

121 Marcus Claudius Marcellus and Quintus Fabius Labeo, 183 B.C.

122 Liternum, a city of Campania, situated to the north of the mouth of the river Liternus, now the village of *Patria*.

123 Prusias, a king of Bithynia, who received Hannibal hospitably, but afterwards betrayed him to the Romans.

124 Philopoemen, a celebrated general of the Achaean League, called 'the last of the Greeks.'

and killed by the Messenians. At that time, near Sicily, the island of Vulcan, which had not existed before, suddenly to the amazement of all, came forth from the sea and remains there to this day. Q. Fulvius Flaccus, praetor in Hither Spain, in a tremendous battle routed twenty-three thousand men and captured four thousand. Tiberius Sempronius Gracchus, in Further Spain, after sacking and shattering one hundred and five towns in battles, forced them to surrender. In the same summer also, L. Postumius, in Hither Spain, killed forty thousand of the enemy in battle. In the same place, Gracchus, the praetor, in a second attack stormed and captured two hundred towns.

In the consulship of Lepidus and Mucius,[125] the very fierce nation of the Basternae, on the advice of Perseus, the son of Philip, induced by the hope of plunder and by the opportunity of crossing the Hister River without battle or any hostilities, was destroyed. For at that time, the Danube, which is also known as the Ister, was covered with a thick layer of ice and easily permitted a crossing on foot. And so when improvidently an inestimable number of men and horses attempted to cross in a single long column, because of the tremendous weight and the steady beat of the moving army, the icy, frozen surface broke up, and the entire column, which had been sustained for a long time, finally was overcome in midstream as the surface, broken into small pieces, gave way. And this ice, in turn, carried over the soldiers in obstructing pieces, caused them to drown. Few out of all these people with difficulty escaped by either bank after being seriously cut up.

In the consulship of P. Licinius Crassus and C. Cassius Longinus,[126] the Macedonian War was carried on, and is rightly to be considered among the greatest wars. For among the auxiliaries of the Romans were, first of all, entire Italy; then, Ptolemy, the king of Egypt; and Ariarathes of Cappadocia, Eumenes of Asia, and Masinissa of Numidia. The

---

125 Marcus Aemilius Lepidus II and Publius Mucius Scaevula, 175 B.C.
126 Publius Licinius Crassus and Gaius Cassius Longinus, 171 B.C.

Thracians, with King Cotys and all the Illyrians under King Gentius, followed Perseus and the Macedonians. And so Perseus went to meet the consul, Crassus, as he approached, and when battle was joined, the Romans were wretchedly defeated and fled. After a following battle, with almost equal slaughter on both sides, there was a dispersal into winter quarters. Then Perseus, after defeating the Roman army in many battles, passed over into Illyricum and with an attack captured Uscana, a town defended by a Roman garrison. Here, he killed a large part of the Roman garrison, a large part he sold into slavery, and a large part he took with him into Macedonia.

Afterwards, L. Aemilius Paulus, the consul, fought with him and conquered. For example, he killed twenty thousand foot-soldiers in this battle;[127] the king fled with his cavalry, but was immediately captured and, together with his sons, was led in triumph before the chariot; afterwards at Alba, he died in prison. His younger son, to sustain dire poverty, learned the art of working in brass in Rome and died there. Furthermore, everywhere among many people a great many wars with quite different results were waged which, for the sake of brevity, I have passed over.

(21) In the six hundredth year after the founding of the City, in the consulship of L. Licinius Lucullus and A. Postumius Albinus,[128] when a great fear of the Celtiberi overcame all the Romans and there was no one among all the Romans who dared go into Spain, as tribune or legate, P. Scipio,[129] who later was known as Africanus, volunteered to make war in Spain, although he had already been assigned by lot to do so in Macedonia. And so he set out for Spain and caused great slaughter among the people, making use more

---

127 The battle of Pydna (a city in Macedonia on the Thermaic Gulf), 168 B.C., in which Perseus was defeated by Lucius Aemilius Paulus.
128 Licinius Lucullus and Aulus Postumius Albinus, 151 B.C.
129 Publius Cornelius Scipio Aemilianus Africanus Minor, son of Paulus and grandson, by adoption, of the elder Africanus.

often of the office even of a soldier than a general, for he met a barbarian who had challenged him to single combat and killed him. But Sergius Galba, the praetor, was overcome in a great battle by the Lusitani and, after losing all his army, he himself with a few men slipped away and barely escaped. At the same time, the censors voted to build a stone theatre in the City. Scipio Nasica,[130] in a very serious speech, opposed its being done at this time, saying that this would be most inimical to a warlike people and a device to foster slothfulness and wantonness, and he so moved the Senate that it not only ordered everything prepared for the theatre to be sold, but it even prohibited the seats for the games from being put into place.

So let our people understand, to whom whatever occurs outside the pleasure of lust is an aversion, that on this account, because they themselves feel and confess that they are weaker than their enemies, the theaters, not the times, are to be blamed, that the true God is not to be blasphemed who has always prohibited these things, but their gods and demons should be abominated who demanded them, indeed, with a very clear proof of their malignity demanding such a sacrifice, since they fed no more on the spilt blood of cattle than on the abandoned virtue of men. For, surely, at that time, neither enemies nor famines nor diseases nor prodigies were lacking, nay, rather they were very numerous; but there were no theaters in which, incredible to relate, victims of virtues were slaughtered at the altar of voluptuousness. At one time, it seemed good to the Carthaginians to sacrifice human beings, but this wickedly conceived belief was soon passed over. Yet it was demanded by the Romans that they apply themselves to their own perdition. It has been done; it is being done; it is loved and the cry is raised that it should be done. Those who perhaps might be offended at the sacrifice of cattle from their herds rejoice at the slaughter of the virtue of their hearts.

---

130 Scipio Nasica Corculum, *curule sedile* in 169 B.C.

Yea, rather, let them, indeed, blush in the presence of Nasica who think that Christians should be reproached, and let them not complain to us about enemies whom they have always had with them, but to him (Nasica) about the theater which he kept them from having.

So in Spain, Sergius Galba, the praetor, when he had received in voluntary surrender the Lusitani who lived on this side of the Tagus River,[131] killed them through trickery. For pretending that he would act to their advantage, he surrounded them with his soldiers and killed them all unarmed and off their guard. This affair afterwards became the cause of the greatest commotion in all Spain because of the Roman's treachery.

(22) Six hundred and two years after the founding of the City, in the consulship of L. Censorinus and M. Manilius,[132] the Third Punic War broke out. And so when the Senate voted that Carthage must be destroyed, the consuls and Scipio, then tribune of the soldiers, set out for Africa and reached the camp of the elder Africanus near Utica. There, when they had summoned the Carthaginians and ordered them to hand over their arms and ships and not to delay about it, so great a quantity of arms was handed over that all Africa could have been armed with them. But the Carthaginians, after they had given over their arms and had been ordered to abandon their city and to withdraw ten miles from the sea, brought their grief to the despair either of defending the city or of being buried with it and for it, and they appointed the two Hasdrubals[133] as their leaders. First, they set out to make arms and supplemented the lack of bronze and iron with gold and silver metals. The consuls decided to storm Carthage

---

131 A river in Lusitania, which empties into the Atlantic Ocean, famous for its golden sands, now *Tajo* or *Tagus*.
132 Lucius Marcius Censorinus and Marcus Manilius, 149 B.C.
133 Although in exile, because of the desperate situation at Carthage, one Hasdrubal was asked in the name of patriotism to take the leadership of the forces outside the city; the other Hasdrubal took charge of the forces within the city.

whose location is said to have been as follows:[134] For twenty-
two miles it was surrounded by a wall; it was almost entirely
enclosed by the sea except for a neck of land which was open
for a space of three miles. This had a wall thirty feet wide and
made of hewn rock forty cubits in height. The citadel, the
name of which was Byrsa, was a little more than two miles
long. On one side, the wall was continuous with the city and
Byrsa, overhanging the sea, which sea they call Stagnum because it was made calm by the projection of a strip of land.
So the consuls, although they had battered and destroyed a
good part of the wall by machines, were beaten and driven
back by the Carthaginians. As the Romans fled, Scipio protected them by driving the enemy back behind the walls.[135]
Censorinus returned to the City. Manilius passed by Carthage
and turned his forces against Hasdrubal. On the death of
Masinissa, Scipio divided the kingdom of Numidia between
the three sons of Masinissa.[136] When Scipio had returned to
the region of Carthage, Manilius stormed the city of Tezaga
and plundered it. Twelve thousand Africans were killed here
and six thousand were captured. Hasdrubal,[137] the Punic
general and the grandson of Masinissa, on account of a suspicion of treachery, was killed by his own who made use of
pieces of the benches in the Senate House. Juventius, the
praetor, in Macedonia joined arms with Pseudo-Philip and
was killed with very heavy losses to the entire Roman army.

(23) In the six hundred and sixth year after the founding
of the City, that is, in the fiftieth year after the Second Punic
War, in the consulship of Cn. Cornelius Lentulus and L. Mummius,[138] P. Scipio,[139] consul of the previous year, as a final

---

134 Cf. Appian, *Punic Wars* 16.95.
135 Scipio covered the retreat of some soldiers, who had impulsively
    rushed through a break in the wall, by stationing soldiers on the wall.
136 Scipio had the complete confidence of Masinissa. The three sons
    were Micipsa, Gulussa, and Mastanabal.
137 The Hasdrubal directing operations from within the city.
138 Gnaeus Cornelius Lentulus and Lucius Mummius Achaicus.
139 Publius Cornelius Scipio Africanus Aemilianus, 146 **B.C.**

resort attempting to destroy Carthage, attacked Gothon.[140]
As the fighting here lasted six continuous days and nights,
final desperation brought the Carthaginians to surrender,
begging that those whom the slaughter of war had allowed to
remain be permitted at least to live in slavery. First, a line
of women, quite wretched, came down;[141] afterwards, a line
of men, more unsightly. Indeed, it has been handed down in
memory that there were twenty-five thousand women and
thirty thousand men. Hasdrubal, the king, gave himself up
voluntarily. The (Roman) deserters, who had occupied the
temple of Aesculapius, voluntarily cast themselves down headlong and were consumed by fire. The wife of Hasdrubal, with
the grief of a man and the fury of a woman, cast herself and
her two sons into the midst of the fire; she, the last queen
of Carthage, now bringing about the same end in death as in
the past the first had done. Now the city itself burned for
seventeen consecutive days and furnished a pitiful spectacle
of the changeableness of human fortune. Now Carthage was
demolished, its entire stone wall being reduced to dust, in the
seven hundredth year after it was founded. The entire multitude of captives, with the exception of a few leading persons,
were sold into slavery. So in the fourth year after the Third
Punic War was began, it was terminated.

But to me, a rather zealous inquirer but a man of rather
slow mind, the cause of the Third Punic War has never appeared clear, to the extent that Carthage was so much the
cause of it that it was justly decided that she be destroyed;
this especially moved me, the fact that, if, as in previous wars,
an evident cause and grievance roused them against a rising
power, there was no necessity for deliberation. But, since
some Romans proposed that Carthage must be destroyed for
the sake of the permanent security of Rome, and others, on
the other hand, because of their constant anxiety for Roman

---

140 Gothon, the war harbor of Carthage.
141 They came down from Byrsa, the citadel of Carthage, where they
had taken refuge.

courage which they always applied to themselves out of suspicion of a rival city, lest the Roman energy always exercised in war should be relaxed by freedom from anxiety and leisure into a sluggish indolence, moved that Carthage be left to itself in safety, I do not find that the cause of the war arose from injury by the harassing Carthaginians, but from the inconstancy of the phlegmatic Romans. Since this is so, why do they impute to Christian times their dullness and ruse with which they are outwardly solid but inwardly corroded? Furthermore, these men, almost six hundred years before, as their wise and cautious citizens had predicted, lost that great whetstone of their brilliance and sharpness—Carthage.

So I shall bring this book to an end, lest perchance by rubbing rather strongly and having temporarily removed the rust where I cannot elicit the necessary sharpness, I discover superfluous harshness. And yet by no means would I fear any harshness opposing me, if I discovered hope of an interior sharpness.

BOOK FIVE

I REALIZE THAT some people in the light of these events can be moved by the fact that Roman victories, with the overthrow of many peoples and cities, multiplied. And yet, if they weigh the facts carefully, they will discover that more harm than good resulted. For so many wars, against slaves, allies, citizens, and fugitives, surely bringing no gains but great miseries, are not to be weighed lightly. But I pass over this situation in order that it may seem to have been as they wish. So I think that they will say: 'Has there ever been a happier period than those times in which were continuous triumphs, famous victories, rich booty, celebrated processions, and when great kings and conquered peoples were driven in a long line before the chariot?' To these it shall be answered briefly that they are accustomd to plead for certain times and we to have instituted discussion in behalf of the same times, which times it is established are attributed, not only to one city, but are common to the whole world. Behold, then, how happily Rome conquers, to the extent that whatever is outside Rome is unhappily conquered. Therefore, at what value is this drop of happiness obtained with great labor to be weighed, to which the felicity of one city ascribed in the midst of so great a mass of unhappiness through which the upheaval of the whole world is brought about? Or if, on this account, these times are thought happy because the wealth of one city has been increased, why are they not rather judged most unhappy in which, by the wretched devastation of many well established peoples, very mighty realms have fallen? Or perchance it seemed different at that time to Carthage, when after a hundred and twenty years, in which, shuddering at the

173

slaughters of wars and the conditions of peace, now with a
rebellious purpose and now humbly it exchanges peace
for war and war for peace, finally, as its wretched citizens
cast themselves at random with a final desperation into the
fire, the whole city became a single funeral pyre? It is also
now a part of the wretchedness of this city, small in com-
pass, destitute in walls, to hear what she was. Let Spain
present her own opinion. When for two hundred years everywhere it watered its fields with its own blood and was unable
to drive back or to endure the troublesome enemy constantly
attacking on every frontier, when with their cities and towns
dislodged, crushed by the slaughter of wars, exhausted by the
famine of sieges, with their wives and children killed, as a
remedy for their miseries they killed one another by pitiful
conflict and mutual slaughter, what did Spain, then, think
about its times? Finally, let Italy itself speak. Why did Italy
for four hundred years, indeed, oppose, stand in the way of,
and resist its own Romans, if their happiness was not their
own unhappiness and did not the Romans, becoming the
masters of the world, stand in the way of the common good?
I do not ask about the innumerable peoples of different nations, long free, then conquered in war, led away from their
fatherland, sold for a price, dispersed in slavery, what they,
then, preferred for themselves, what they thought about the
Romans, and what judgment they made about the times. I
pass over the kings of great wealth, of great power, of great
glory, for long the most powerful, sometimes captured, chained
in slavery, sent under the yoke, driven before the chariot,
slaughtered in prison, of whom to ask an opinion is as foolish
as it is difficult not to bemoan their wretchedness. Let us, as
I say, consult ourselves about our choice of a way of life to
which we have become accustomed. Our forefathers carried on
wars; worn out by wars and seeking peace, they offered tribute;
tribute is the price of peace. We pay tribute, lest we suffer
war, and by this means we have taken a position and remain in
the harbor at which our forefathers finally took refuge to avoid

the storms of evils. So I would view our times, whether they are happy. Indeed, we who continually possess what they finally chose, think them happier than those. For the unrest of wars, by which they were worn out, is unknown to us. Moreover, we are born and grow old in the peace which they tasted slightly after the rule of Caesar and the birth of Christ; what was for them the due payment of slavery is for us a free contribution for our defense, and so great is the difference between past and present times that what Rome extorted from our people by the sword to implement their luxurious living, she herself now contributes with us for the general use of the state. Or if it is said by someone that the Romans as enemies were much more tolerable to our forefathers than the Goths are to us, let him hear and understand how differently this seems to be the case from what is actually taking place in his regard.

Long ago, when wars raged throughout the whole world, every province enjoyed its own kings, its own laws, and its own customs, and there was no alliance of mutual good feelings where a divergence of powers divided. Finally, what brought into an alliance the unfathered and barbarous tribes which, established by different sacred rites, religious practices also kept apart? If anyone then, at that time, overcome by the severity of evils deserted his native land to the enemy, to what unknown place did he, an unknown, finally go? What people, in general an enemy, did he, an enemy, supplicate? To whom did he at a first meeting entrust himself, not having been invited by reason of an alliance by name, nor induced by a common law, nor secure by a oneness in religion? Did Busiris in Egypt, the most wicked sacrificer of foreigners who unfortunately ran into him;[1] the shores of Taurian Diana, most cruel

---

1 According to Greek mythology, an Egyptian king, son of Poseidon. A soothsayer from Cyprus told him that a famine, which had lasted for nine years, would end if he would sacrifice one foreigner to Zeus each year. Busiris then sacrificed all foreigners who entered Egypt until Heracles came there and killed him with all his followers.

toward strangers but with rites more cruel;[2] and Thrace, together with its Polymestor, abominable toward relatives and guests give a few examples?[3] Not to seem to dally with events of antiquity, Rome is a witness to the murder of Pompey, and Egypt a witness to Ptolemy, his murderer.

(2) But for me, when I flee at the first disturbance of whatever commotion, since it is a question of a secure place of refuge, everywhere there is native land, everywhere my law and my religion. Now Africa has received me as kindly as I confidently approached her; now, I say, this Africa has received me to her open peace, to her bosom, and to her common law, about whom at one time it was said and truly said:

We are kept away from the hospitality of her sands,
They stir up wars and forbid us to step on the very
edge of their land.[4]

Africa, of her own free will, spreads out wide her kindly bosom to receive allies of her religion and peace,[5] and of her own free will invites the weary ones whom she cherishes. The breadth of the East, the vastness of the North, the extensiveness of the South, and the very large and secure seats of the great islands are of my law and name because I, as a Roman and a Christian, approach Christians and Romans. I do not fear the gods of my host; I do not fear his religion as my death; nor do I have such a place that I fear, where it is permitted the possessor to do what he wishes and it is not permitted a stranger to devote attention to whatever is proper, where the law of my host is that which is not mine; the one God, who in the days when He Himself willed to become known established this unity of his kingdom, is both loved and feared by all; the same laws, which are subject to one

---

2 Tauri, a wild and savage people of Crimea.
3 The Greek tragedians made Polydorus the son of Priam and Hecuba. When Troy was about to fall, they gave a rich treasure to Polydorus to take to their guest-friend, the Thracian king, Polymestor, who in turn slew Polydorus to gain the treasure.
4 Vergil, *Aeneid*, 1.540-541.
5 The Christian religion and Roman peace.

God, prevail everywhere; and wherever I shall go unknown, I do not fear sudden violence as if I be unprotected. Among Romans, as I have said, I am a Roman; among Christians, a Christian; among men, a man; I implore the state through its laws, the conscience through religion, nature through its universality. I enjoy every land temporarily as my fatherland, because what is truly my fatherland and that which I love, is not completely on this earth. I have lost nothing, where I have loved nothing, and I have everything when He whom I love is with me, especially because He is the same among all, who makes me known to all and very near to all; nor does He desert me when I am in need, because the earth is His and its plenitude His, out of which He has ordered that all things be common to all. These are the blessings of our times, which our ancestors did not have in their entirety either in the quiet of the present or in the hope of the future or in a place of common refuge; they carried on ceaseless wars on this account, because not feeling free as a group to change their abodes and so remaining in their abodes, they were either unfortunately killed or shamefully became slaves. This will be revealed more clearly and openly as the accomplishments themselves of our ancestors are unfolded systematically.

(3) In the six hundredth and sixth year after the founding of the City, that is, in the same year as that in which Carthage was destroyed, in the consulship of Cn. Cornelius Lentulus and L. Mummius,[6] the overthrow of Corinth followed upon the destruction of Carthage, and within a short interval of a single period over different parts of the world, the pitiful burning of two very powerful cities blazed forth. Now when Metellus, the praetor, had conquered the Achaeans and Boeotians, who had joined them, in two battles, that is, first at Thermopylae, then in Phocis, in the prior battle of which Claudius,[7] the historian, relates that twenty thousand were slain, in the second that seven thousand were killed, Valerius

---

6 Gnaeus Cornelius Lentulus and Lucius Mummius Achaicus, 146 B.C.
7 Claudius Cornelius Tacitus.

Antias[8] confirms that there was a battle in Achaia and twenty thousand Achaeans with their leader Diaeus fell. Polybius,[9] the Achaean, although at that time he was with Scipio in Africa, nevertheless, since he could not ignore a disaster at home, asserts that one battle was fought in Achaia under the leadership of Critolaus, and he tells us that Diaeus, while leading his soldiers out of Arcadia, was overcome together with his army by the same praetor, Metellus; but we have already spoken somewhat about the different opinions of disagreeing historians, and let it suffice that these have been detected and that what is falsely known is the knowledge of lies, because they clearly show that they must receive little credence in other matters, who, in those things which they themselves have seen, are contrary. So after the annihilation of the garrisons in all Achaia and the destruction of cities without defense, according to the design of the praetor, Metellus, the consul, Mummius, with a few men suddenly went into camp. After Metellus had been immediately dismissed, he stormed Corinth without delay, at that time by far the richest city in the whole world, and for many generations back had been, as it were, the workshop of all craftsmen and crafts and the common market of Asia and Europe. Freedom for plundering was cruelly granted even to captives; thus all was filled with slaughter and fire, so that from the circumference of the walls, as from a chimney, the fire broke forth pressed together into a single point. Thus, after most of the people had been destroyed by sword and fire, the rest were sold into slavery; when the city had been burned, the walls were destroyed to their very foundations; the stones of the walls

---

8 The text reads Valerius and Antias which is clearly an error for Valerius Antias, the Sullan annalist who wrote a history of Rome in at least seventy-five books, from the origins to his own times. He was very unreliable, although his style was vigorous and rhetorical, if without grace, bringing annalistic history to its highest literary form before Livy.

9 The celebrated Greek historian from Megalopolis in Arcadia, the son of Lycortas and friend of the younger Scipio Africanus. He wrote a history covering the years 220-146 B.C.

were reduced to dust; large quantities of booty were carried away. Indeed, when, on account of the many and varied statues and images, gold, silver, and copper metals were mixed into one and flowed together in the burning of the city, a new kind of metal was formed, wherefore, even to the present day, either because of itself or because of its imitation of that metal, it is called Corinthian bronze according to tradition, and they speak also of Corinthian vases.

(4) In the same consulship,[10] Viriathus in Spain, a Lusitanian by origin, a shepherd and a robber, at first, by infesting the highways and, then, by laying waste the provinces, and, finally, by overcoming, routing, and subjugating the armies of praetors and Roman consuls, became a source of very great terror to all Romans. Now C. Vetilius, the praetor, met Viriathus as he was crossing the great expanse of the Ebro and Tagus, very large and very widely separated rivers. When he and his entire army were killed almost to a man, the praetor himself with a few men barely slipped away in flight and escaped.[11] Then, the same Viriathus crushed the praetor, C. Plautius, in many battles and put him to flight. Afterwards, also Claudius Unimammus with great preparation for war, on being sent against Viriathus for the purpose of wiping out the earlier stain, himself increased the infamy. For when he met Viriathus, he lost all the supplies which he had brought with him, and the greatest forces of the Roman army. Viriathus fixed upon his mountains as trophies, robes, fasces, and other Roman insignia.[12]

At the same time, three hundred Lusitani joined battle with a thousand Romans in a mountain-valley in which, moreover, Claudius reports that seventy Lusitani and three hundred and twenty Romans fell; and when the victorious Lusitani departed in scattered array and untroubled, one of these be-

---

10 Gnaeus Cornelius Lentulus and Lucius Mummius.

11 As a matter of fact, Vetilius was killed. The battle was fought near Tribola, to the south of the Tagus in Lusitania.

12 Cf. Florus, *History*, 1.33.

came widely separated from the rest and when he himself a foot-soldier, being surrounded by cavalry, was caught, he pierced the horse of one of them with his spear and decapitated the horseman himself at one stroke of his sword, and he so struck all with fear that, as they all looked on, he himself withdrew leisurely and with an air of contempt.

In the consulship of Appius Claudius and Quintus Caecilius Metellus,[13] Appius Claudius met with the Salassian Gauls and when he was conquered, he lost five thousand soldiers. When the battle was renewed, he killed five thousand of the enemy. But since, according to a law by which it was established that whoever had destroyed five thousand of the enemy might have the privilege of holding a triumph, he, too, demanded a triumph, and on account of his earlier losses he did not obtain it, he resorted to infamous impudence and ostentation and held a triumph at his own expense.

In the consulship of L. Caecilius Metellus and Q. Fabius Maximus Servilianus,[14] among other prodigies a hermaphrodite was seen in Rome and, by order of the haruspices, was thrown into the sea. But the carrying out of this impious act of expiation proved of no avail. For instantly, so great a pestilence broke out that, at first, those in charge of conducting funerals did not suffice and, then, did not exist, and presently, also the large dwellings remained free of the living and full of the dead; very large inheritances were within and no heirs at all. Finally, not only was the opportunity of living in the City denied, but also of approaching it, so violent were the odors being sent forth throughout the entire City from the bodies decaying in the houses and on the streets.

That cruel expiation, strewing the roads with dead men by reason of the death of one man, finally made known to the Romans, overcome with shame in the midst of their miseries,

---

13 Appius Claudius Pulcher and Quintus Caecilius Metellus Macedonicus, 143 B.C.

14 Lucius Caecilius Metellus Calvus and Quintus Fabius Maximus Servilianus, 142 B.C.

how wretched and useless it was. For it had been held first
to ward off impending disaster, and yet a pestilence followed,
which, however, without the reparation of any sacrifices, only
when the reproach had been fulfilled according to the measure
of an inscrutable judgment, subsided. If those haruspices,
master craftsmen in deceit, had by chance solemnized it as
they are accustomed to do when diseases are abating, without
a doubt they would have claimed for themselves, their gods,
and their rites, the glory of a return to normalcy. Thus, the
wretched City, evilly religious even to the point of sacrilege,
was deceived by falsehoods from which it was unable to free
itself.

So Fabius, the consul, as he fought against the Lusitani and
Viriathus, drove off the enemy and liberated the town of
Buccia, which Viriathus was beseiging, and he received it in
surrender together with many other strongholds. He also
committed a crime abominable even to the barbarians of
farthest Scythia, not to mention Roman good faith and moderation. He cut off the hands of five hundred leaders of the
Lusitani, whom he had lured by the promise of an alliance and
had received according to the law of surrender.

Pompey,[15] the consul for the following year, invaded the
territory of the Numantines and, after suffering very heavy
losses, departed. Not only was almost his entire army overthrown, but also a great many nobles who were serving with
him were slain.

Viriathus, however, when for fourteen years he had crushed
Roman generals and armies, was killed by the treachery of
his own men. In this case alone, the Romans acted like men
toward him, for they judged his murderers unworthy of a
reward.

But I, not only now but also repeatedly, have been able to
interweave those complicated wars of the East which rarely

---

15 Quintus Pompeius, a *homo novus* and friend of Scipio Aemilianus,
   was consul with Gnaius Servilius Caepio in 141 B.C. He tried to
   storm and blockade Numantia, but without success.

ever began or were terminated except by crimes, but those of the Romans, with whom we are now concerned, are so great that those of others are rightly scorned.

At that time, Mithridates, the sixth king of the Parthians after Arsaces, conquered the prefect, Demetrius,[16] and as victor attacked the city of Babylon and all its territories. In addition, he subjugated all the nations that dwelt between the Hydaspes and Indus rivers. He also extended his bloody rule to India. He conquered and captured Demetrius himself who met him in a second war, and, after he was captured, a certain Diodotus, with his son, Alexander, took possession of the kingdom of Demetrius and the royal name. Later Diodotus killed Alexander, whom he had taken as partner in the dangers of winning the kingdom, that he might not have a colleague in obtaining it.

In the consulship of M. Aemilius Lepidus and C. Hostilius Mancinus,[17] different prodigies appeared, and, insofar as it was in their power, were cared for in the customary way. But opportune happenings did not always come to the aid of the haruspices, those watchers of events and contrivers of deceptions. For Mancinus, the consul, after he took over the army from Popilius at Numantia, was so unsuccessful in all his wars that, in final desperation he was reduced to this: he was forced to make a most disgraceful treaty with the Numantines. Although Pompey also had concluded an equally infamous treaty with the same Numantines, the Senate ordered the treaty to be abrogated and Mancinus to be handed over to the Numantines. With his body laid bare and his hands tied behind his back, he was exposed before the gates of the Numantines, and remaining there well into the night, deserted by his own and rejected by the enemy, he offered a lamentable spectacle to both.

---

16 Demetrius Nicator of Syria, 161-126 B.C.
17 Marcus Aemilius Lepidus Porcina and Gauis Hostilius Mancinus, 137 B.C.

(5) At this point, grief forces me to cry out. Why, O Romans, do you falsely claim for yourselves those great qualities of justice, good faith, courage, and mercy? Learn these more truly from the Numantines. Was there need of courage? They conquered by fighting. Was good faith required? Trusting others to act as they themselves would have acted, after concluding a treaty they dismissed those whom they could have killed. Was justice to be proven? Surely, the Senate by its silence proved this, when the same Numantines through their legates demanded either an inviolable peace alone or the return of all whom, according to the pledge of peace which had been accepted, they had released alive. Did it seem necessary to examine mercy? The Numantines have given sufficient proof of this either by sending forth a hostile army to live or by not receiving Mancinus for punishment. Was Mancinus, I ask, to have been given over, who put off the impending slaughter of a conquered army by extending the covering of a peace treaty, who reserved the imperiled forces of the fatherland until better times? Or if the treaty which was made was displeasing, why was the army redeemed by this pledge, or, when it returned, why was it received, or, when its return was demanded, why was it not given back? Or if whatever provision for saving the army was pleasing, why was Mancinus, who made this treaty, alone given over?

Varro, that a battle might be entered upon immediately, overcame his colleague, Paulus, who objected, and pushed forward his fearful army, and he did not arrange his unfortunate troops at that Cannae, notorious for a Roman disaster, for a battle, but exposed them to death. There he lost more than forty thousand Roman soldiers by his impatience alone, a trait on which Hannibal had long counted for victory for himself. When, too, his colleague, Paulus, was lost (and what a man he was!), Varro, finally, most impudently dared to return to the City almost alone and earned the reward of his impudence. For thanks was given to him publicly in the

Senate because he had not despaired of the Republic which,
however, he himself had caused to be in desperation.

Afterwards, moreover, Mancinus, who labored not to lose
his army which had been surrounded by the fortunes of war,
was condemned by the same Senate to be given over to the
enemy. I realize, O Romans, that the case of Varro was displeasing, but you yielded to the emergency, and the case of
Mancinus was pleasing, but the decision was made according to
the emergency, and you have so acted from the beginning, that
no citizen would consistently have any regard for such ingrates
nor would an enemy confidently trust people so unworthy
of trust.

Meanwhile, Brutus[18] in Further Spain had overcome sixty
thousand of the Gallaeci, who had come to the aid of the
Lusitani; this he accomplished in a very severe and difficult
war, although he had surrounded them unawares. Of these,
fifty thousand were killed in this battle, six thousand are
reported to have been captured, and few escaped in flight.
In Nearer Spain, Lepidus, the proconsul, although the Senate
forbade it, tried to overcome the Vaccaei, a harmless and
humble tribe. But presently, he suffered a most serious defeat[19] and paid the penalty for his wicked stubbornness, for
six thousand Romans were most justly killed in this most
unjust war; the remainder escaped by stripping their camp
and even throwing away their arms.

This slaughter under Lepidus was no less disgraceful than
that under Mancinus. So let them now ascribe these times to
a period of happiness, not to mention the Spaniards who were
beaten and worn out by wars, but, indeed, the very Romans
themselves who at the least were overcome by such continuous
and frequent slaughters. Not to reproach them for the many
praetors, legates, consuls, legions, and the size of the armies
that were destroyed, I repeat this alone: with what great mad-

---

18 Decius Junius Brutus. The battle occurred in 136 B.C.
19 Lack of provisions forced a retreat, during which the Romans
   suffered great losses. This occurred in 136 B.C.

ness from fear the Roman soldier was dulled so that he could not restrain his feet and strengthen his courage for a trial of battle, but immediately on the sight of a Spaniard, his special enemy, fled and believed that he was conquered almost before he was seen. From this evidence it is clear that those times were judged wretched by both parties, since the Spaniards, although they were able to conquer, yet unwillingly gave up their pleasant leisure and endured foreign wars; the Romans, the more impudently they pressed upon the peace of foreign peoples, the more disgracefully they were conquered.

(6) In the consulship of Servius Fulvius Flaccus and Q. Calpurnius Piso,[20] there was born at Rome of a maid servant a boy with four feet, four eyes, a like number of ears, twice as many as in the nature of man. In Sicily, Mount Etna cast forth and spread vast fires which, like torrents flowing precipitously down the neighboring slopes, burned up everything with their consuming fire and scorched more distant places with glowing ashes which flew far and wide with a heavy vapor. This kind of portent, ever native to Sicily, customarily does not foretell evil, but brings it on. In the land of Bononia,[21] the products of the field came forth on trees. And in Sicily, the slave war broke out, which was so serious and fierce, because of the number of the slaves, the equipment of the troops, and the strength of its forces, that, not to mention the Roman praetors whom it thoroughly routed, it terrified even consuls. For seventy thousand slaves are reported to have been among the conspirators at that time, not including the city of Messana which kept its slaves in peace by treating them kindly. But Sicily was more wretched also in this respect, in that it was an island and never with respect to its own status had a law of its own and thus, at one time, was subject to tyrants and, at another, to slaves, or when the former exacted slavery by their wicked domination or the latter effected an inter-

---

20 Servius Fulvius Flaccus and Quintus Calpurnius Piso, 135 B.C.
21 A town in Gallia Cisalpina, in the neighborhood of Mutina, a Roman colony founded in A.U.C. 563.

change of liberty by a perverse presumption, especially because it was hemmed in on all sides by sea, its internal evils could not easily pass out. Indeed, Sicily nourished a viperous growth to its own destruction, increased by its own lust and destined to live with its death. But in this respect, the emotions of a slave tumult, insofar as it is of rarer occurrence among others, to this extent is more ferocious, because a mob of free men is moved by the urge to advance the fatherland; a mob of slaves to ruin it.

(7) In the six hundred and twentieth year after the founding of the City, when the almost greater infamy of the treaty concluded at Numantia than that formerly made at Caudine Forks burdened the Roman brow with shame, Scipio Africanus, with the consent of all the tribes, was elected consul[22] and was sent with an army to storm Numantia. Numantia, moreover, was in Hither Spain, situated not far from the Vaccaei and Cantabri on a high point of Gallaecia, the farthest city of the Celtiberi. This Numantia for fourteen years with only four thousand of its own men, not only held off forty thousand Romans, but also conquered them and afflicted them with shameful treaties. So Scipio Africanus, after entering Spain, did not immediately attack the enemy so as to overthrow them when unawares, knowing that this kind of men was never so relaxed in leisure of body and mind that in the very quality of its condition it did not excel the preparations of others, but he drilled his soldiers for some time in camp as if in a training school. When Scipio had passed part of the summer and the whole winter without even attempting a battle, even so he accomplished very little by his diligence, for when an opportunity for fighting came, the Roman army was overcome by the attack of the Numantines and fled; but finally, becoming indignant at the rebukes and threats of the consul who cast himself in its way and held it back, it returned against the enemy and compelled the enemy which it was

---

22 Publius Cornelius Scipio Africanus Aemilianus II, 134 B.C.

fleeing to flee. Trustworthiness is difficult at this point in the narrative; the Romans put the Numantines to flight and saw them as they fled. So, although Scipio rejoiced and boasted that the outcome was beyond his hope, yet he openly confessed that he should not hazard anything further in war against them. Thus Scipio felt that he should press his unexpected successes, and surrounded the city itself with a siege, and even enclosed it with a trench whose width was ten feet and whose depth was twenty feet. Then he fortified the rampart itself which had been constructed with stakes by means of frequent towers, so that if any sally should be attempted against it by an onrushing enemy, he would then not fight as a besieger with the besieged, but vice versa, as the besieged with the besieger. Now Numantia, located on a hill not far from the Durius River, was surrounded by a wall three miles in circumference, although some assert that its site was small and without a wall. Yet it is credible that they enclosed this much space for the sake of feeding and protecting their flocks or even to till the soil seasonably when they were pressed with war, while they themselves held a small citadel naturally fortified. Otherwise, it would seem that so extensive a space for the city did not protect so small a number of men rather than betray them. So when the Numantines had been besieged for a long time and were demolished by famine, they offered to surrender if tolerable conditions should be proposed, at the same time begging again and again for an opportunity to do regular battle that it might be permitted them to die like men. Finally, they all suddenly erupted from two gates, having first partaken of much drink, not of wine, for the cultivation of which the place is not fertile, but of a juice artfully concocted from wheat, which juice they called *caelia* because it caused heat. For the power of the moistened fruit bud is aroused by heat, and then it is dried and, when reduced to a powder, is mixed with a pleasant juice by which through fermentation a sour taste and the glow of drunkenness are added. So growing

warm from this drink after a long fast, they offered themselves
for battle. The struggle was fierce and long, even to the point
of endangering the Romans, and again the Romans would
have proven by fleeing that they were fighting against the
Numantines had they not been fighting under Scipio. The
Numantines, after their bravest men had been killed, withdrew from battle, but they returned to their city with ordered
ranks and not in flight, and they were unwilling to accept the
bodies of their dead which were offered for burial. All destined for death, with the last hope of desperation, of their
own accord they set fire from within to their besieged city
and all in like manner met their death by the sword, by poison,
and by fire. The Romans gained absolutely nothing from
conquering these people except their own security; for they
did not think that by the overthrow of Numantia they had
conquered the Numantines rather than that they had escaped
them. The chains of the victor did not hold a single Numantine. Rome did not see any reason for granting a triumph.
There was neither gold nor silver which could have survived
the fire among the poor Numantines. The fire consumed their
arms and clothing.

(8) So at this time when these events took place in Numantia, in Rome the seditions of the Gracchi[23] were being
stirred up. But when, after the destruction of Numantia,
Scipio had arranged a peace with the other tribes of Spain,
he inquired of a certain Thyresus, a Celtic chieftain, for what
reason the Numantine state had previously remained unconquered and later had been overthrown. Thyresus replied:
'With harmony Numantia was unconquerable; without harmony it was destroyed.' The Romans accepted this as said to
themselves and about themselves in the nature of a warning
for they presently received news about the seditions which
were throwing their City into complete discord. When Carthage and Numantia were destroyed, there died among the

---

23 Tiberius Sempronius Gracchus and Gaius Sempronius Gracchus.

Romans useful cooperation about the future, and there arose
over their ambition infamous contention. Gracchus, the
tribune of the people, becoming angry at the nobles because
he had been listed among the authors of the Numantine
treaty, decided that the land which thus far had been held
by private interests should be divided among the people. He
took away the imperium from Octavius, the tribune of the
people who opposed him, and appointed Minucius as his
successor. For these reasons anger siezed the Senate and arrogance the people. And at this time by chance, Attalus, the son
of Eumenes, on his deathbed ordered in his will that the
Roman people should succeed as heir to the rule of Asia.
Gracchus, seeking the favor of the people for a price, passed
a law that the money which had belonged to Attalus should be
distributed among the people. When Nasica[24] objected, Pompey also promised that he would bring charges against
Gracchus as soon as the latter had left his magistracy.

(9) When Gracchus was striving to continue as tribune
of the people in the following year, and when on the day of
the elections he stirred up riots among the people, the nobles,
under the prodding of Nasica, became greatly enraged and
with fragments of the benches put the plebeians to flight.
When Gracchus, with his cloak torn off, was fleeing along the
steps which were above the Calpurnian Arch, he was struck
by a fragment of a bench and fell, and as he rose again he
was struck by a blow from a cudgel which penetrated his brain
and he was killed. Furthermore, two hundred were killed in
this riot and their bodies thrown into the Tiber; also the
unburied body of Gracchus vanished. In addition, the contagion of the Slave War in Sicily infected many provinces far
and wide. For at Minturnae,[25] four hundred and fifty slaves

---

24 Publius Scipio Nasica.
25 A city of Latium, on the border of Campania, at the mouth of the
Liris, in the neighborhood of which Marius concealed himself from
Sulla in a swamp.

were crucified, and at Sinuessa,[26] four thousand slaves were crushed by Q. Metellus and Cn. Servilius Caepio; in the mines of the Athenians also, a like uprising of the slaves was dispersed by Heraclitus; at Delos also, the slaves, rising in another revolt, were crushed by the citizens who anticipated the movement without that first fire of the evil in Sicily, from which the sparks flaring forth fostered these various fires. For in Sicily, after Fulvius, the consul, Piso,[27] the consul, captured the town of Mamertium,[28] where he killed eight thousand fugitives, but those whom he was able to capture he fastened to the *patibulum*. When Rupilius,[29] the consul, succeeded him, he regained by war Tauromenium[30] and Henna,[31] the strongest places of refuge for fugitive slaves; more than twenty thousand slaves are reported to have been slaughtered at that time.

Surely, the cause of such an inextricable war was pitiable. Undoubtedly, the masters would have had to perish had they not met the haughty slaves with the sword. But yet in the very losses of battle, which were most unfortunate, and in the more unfortunate gains of victory, the victors lost as many as perished among the conquered.

(10) In the six hundred and twenty-second year after the founding of the City, P. Licinius Crassus,[32] consul and pontifex maximus, was sent with a very well equipped army against Aristonicus, the brother of Attalus, who had invaded Asia which had been willed to the Romans; furthermore, although assisted by great kings, that is, Nicomedes of Bithynia, Mithridates of Pontus and Armenia, Ariarathes of Cappadocia, and

---

26 A colony of the Latins, formerly called Smope, in Campania, now ruins near Monte Dragone, founded about 296 B.C.
27 Lucius Calpurnius Piso Frugi, 133 B.C.
28 In the interior of the Bruttian peninsula.
29 Publius Rupilius, 132 B.C.
30 Tauromenium on the east coast.
31 Henna, less correctly Enna, a city of great antiquity in the center of Sicily with a famous temple of Ceres.
32 Publius Licinius Crassus Macianus, 131 B.C.

Pylaemenes of Paphlagonia, and by their very large forces, yet when battle was joined he was conquered;[33] and when, after his army had been driven into flight following a great slaughter, he himself had been surrounded by the enemy and almost captured, he thrust the whip which he had used on his horse in the eye of a Thracian; but when the barbarian grew hot with rage and pain, he pierced the side of Crassus with his sword. Thus, Crassus, in the manner of death devised by him, escaped both dishonor and slavery. Perperna,[34] the consul, who had succeeded Crassus, on hearing of the death of Crassus and the slaughter of the Roman army, immediately rushed into Asia, and he engaged Aristonicus in an unexpected battle as he was resting from his recent victory and drove him into flight, stripped of all his troops. And when he surrounded Stratoniceia, to which Aristonicus had fled, by a siege he forced him, now emaciated by hunger, to surrender. Perperna, the consul, was siezed by a disease at Pergamum and died; Aristonicus at Rome, by order of Senate, was strangled in prison.

In the same year, the wretched life of Ptolemy, the king of the Alexandrians, came to an end still more wretchedly. For after seducing his sister and then receiving her in marriage, he finally cast her aside, a more disgraceful act than the marriage. Then, he took as his wife his own step-daughter, that is, the daughter of his sister and wife, and he killed his own son whom he begot of his sister in addition to a son of his brother. Thus, because of such incests and parricides, he became detestable and was driven from the kingdom by the Alexandrians.

At this same time, Antiochus,[35] not content with Babylon, Ecbatana, and the entire Median Empire, engaged in battle

---

33 Near Lencae, a town of Ionia near Phocaea, 131 B.C.
34 Marcus Perperna and Gaius Claudius Pulcher Lentulus were consuls in 130 B.C.
35 Antiochus VII (Sidetes), c. 159-129 B.C., second son of Demetrius I of Syria.

with Phraates,[36] king of the Parthians, and was conquered. Although he seemed to have a hundred thousand armed men in his army, he brought along in addition two hundred thousand servants and camp followers including prostitutes and actors. And so he, together with his entire army, was overcome by the forces of the Parthians and perished.[37]

In the consulship of C. Sempronius Tuditanus and M. Acilius,[38] that P. Scipio Africanus, who bore witness before the assembly about the danger to his safety because he knew that accusations were being made against him by wicked and ungrateful men as he labored for the fatherland, was found dead on the next morning in his own bedroom. I would not hesitate to reckon this among the greatest evils of the Romans, especially because his strength and moderation were so strong that it was believed that had he lived there could not have been either a social or a civil war. Indeed, the report was that he had been killed by the treachery of his wife, Sempronia, a sister moreover of the Gracchi, in order that, as I believe, a family already defiled and born to bring destruction on its own fatherland in the midst of the wicked seditions of its men might also be more monstrous by the crimes of its women.

In the consulship of M. Aemilius and L. Orestes,[39] Etna was shaken by a tremendous tremor and poured forth masses of fire, and again, on another day, the island of Lipara and the sea nearby around it boiled over so much that it burned and also dissolved the rocks, scorched the planks of the ships after melting the binding wax, killed and boiled the fish as they swam near the surface, and also suffocated human beings, except for those who were able to flee some distance, who, by constantly breathing hot air, burned their inner organs.

(11) In the consulship of M. Plautius Hypsaeus and M. Fulvius Flaccus,[40] scarcely had Africa quieted down from the

---

36 Phraetes II, known also as Arsaces VII.
37 In 128 B.C.
38 Gaius Sempronius Tuditanus and Marcus Aquillius, 129 B.C.
39 Marcus Aemilius Lepidus and Lucius Aurelius Orestes, 126 B.C.
40 Marcus Plautius Hypsaeus and Marcus Fulvius Flaccus, 125 B.C.

ravages of war when a horrible and unusual destruction came upon it. For when great numbers of locusts had gathered over all Africa and had not only destroyed all hope of crops, but had consumed all plants with parts of their roots, and the foliage of trees with their tender branches, and had even gnawed the bitter bark and dry wood, being swept away by a sudden wind and driven into masses and carried through the air for a long time, they were, finally, plunged into the African Sea. When, as the waters forced large masses of these a long distance and drove them far and wide along a wide expanse of the shore, the decaying and putrifying masses gave forth a foul and noxious odor beyond belief, from which followed so great a pestilence of all living beings alike that the putrifying bodies of birds, cattle, and wild beasts everywhere destroyed by the contaminated air increased the destruction of the pestilence. Moreover, as I relate these things, I shudder with my whole body at the great destruction of human beings that took place. Indeed, in Numidia, where at that time Micipsa was king it is handed down that eight hundred thousand men perished, and along the maritime coast which lies especially close to Carthage and Utica, more than two hundred thousand, and at the city of Utica itself thirty thousand soldiers, who had been stationed there for the protection of all Africa, were destroyed and wiped out. This calamity was so sudden and so violent that at Utica at that time, in one day through one gate, more than one thousand five hundred bodies of the youth are said to have been carried out for burial. Nevertheless, by the amity and grace of the omnipotent God, I should say, by whose mercy and in whose trust I speak these words: Although even in our time locusts have sprung up on occasions in different places, and for the most part with tolerable damage, yet never in Christian times has so great a force of inextricable evil taken place that the calamity of the locusts, which could not have been endured when alive, did more harm when dead, and while they lived all was destined to perish, and when they were destroyed all on the point of death would have preferred that the locusts had not perished.

(12) In the six hundred and twenty-seventh year after the founding of the City, in the consulship of L. Caecilius Metellus and Q. Titius Flamininus,[41] Carthage in Africa, having been ordered to be restored in the twenty-second year after it had been overthrown, by bringing families of Roman citizens to inhabit it, was restored and repopulated, after a great prodigy had previously taken place. For when the surveyors, sent to determine the territory of Carthage, found that the posts erected to mark the boundaries had been pulled up by wolves and gnawed to pieces, there was some hesitation as to whether it was expedient for the Roman peace that Carthage be restored.

In the same year, C. Gracchus, the brother of that famous Gracchus[42] who had previously been killed in a civil insurrection, was elected tribune of the people with the help of a riot and was destructful to the state. For when he had again and again stirred up the Roman people into very bitter seditions by his briberies and excessive promises, especially in the interest of the agrarian law, in behalf of which his brother, Tiberius Gracchus, had been killed, he at last withdrew from the tribuneship and was succeeded by Minucius. When Minucius, tribune of the people, tore up the statutes of Gracchus, his predecessor, for the most part and repealed his laws, C. Gracchus, together with Fulvius Flaccus and surrounded by a large crowd, went up to the Capitol where an assembly was in session. There, when a great tumult was stirred up, a certain herald was killed by followers of Gracchus as a signal for battle. Flaccus, surrounded by his two sons who were armed, and accompanied by Gracchus who was wearing a toga and concealing a short sword under his left arm, although to no avail he had sent a herald in advance

---

41 Lucius Caecilius Metellus and Titius Quintus (not Quintus Titius) Flamininus, 123 B.C.
42 Tiberius Gracchus.

to call the slaves to freedom, occupied the temple of Diana as
a citadel. On the other hand, D. Brutus, a man of consular
rank, rushed down the Publican Road with a great attack.
There Flaccus fought long and most stubbornly. When
Gracchus had withdrawn to the temple of Minerva, wishing
to fall upon his sword, he was restrained from doing so by
the intervention of Laetorius. So when the battle was waged
for a long time with uncertain issue, finally, the bowmen
sent by Opimius broke up the multitude engaged in hand-to-
hand fighting. The two Flacci, father and son, when, fleeing
through the temple of Luna, they leaped down into a private
house and bolted the doors, were stabbed to death, the wall
of wickerwork being torn down. Gracchus, while his friends
fought long for him and died, with difficulty reached the Sub-
lician Bridge and there, lest he be captured alive, offered his
neck to his slave. The severed head of Gracchus was brought
to the consul, and his body conveyed to his mother, Cornelia,
in the town of Misenum.[43] Now this Cornelia, the daughter
of the greater Africanus, had withdrawn to Misenum, as I
have said, on the death of her elder son. The goods of
Gracchus were confiscated; the youthful Flaccus was killed in
prison; and of the faction of Gracchus, two hundred and fifty
are reported to have been killed on the Aventine Hill.
Opimius,[44] the consul, just as he was brave in battle, so was
he cruel in a judicial investigation. For he killed more than
three thousand men, most of whom were put to death innocent without even a trial.

(13) At the same time, Metellus[45] overran the Balearic
Islands and overcame them, and he checked a disturbance of
piracy which had broken out here at this time by a wholesale
slaughter of the inhabitants. Gnaeus Domitius, the proconsul,
also conquered the Allobrogian Gauls in a very severe battle

---

43 A promontory and town with harbor in Campania, now *Punta di
  Miseno*, situated on one extremity of the Bay of Naples.
44 Lucius Opimius, consul in 121 B.C.
45 Quintus Caecilius Metellus, consul in 123 B.C.

near the town of Vindalium,[46] especially because the horses of
the enemy and the enemy, frightened by the strange appearance of the elephants, had fled in different directions. Twenty
thousand of the Allobroges are reported to have been killed
there and three thousand were captured.

At this same time, Mount Etna erupted more than usual
and, as the fiery torrents overflowed and spread far and wide,
it overwhelmed the city of Catana and its territory to such an
extent that the roofs of the buildings, being burnt and weighed
down by the hot ashes, crumbled to the ground. For the sake
of relieving the disaster, the Senate freed the people of Catana
from paying tribute for ten years.

(14) In the six hundred and twenty-eighth year after the
founding of the City, Fabius,[47] the consul, met Bituitus, the
king of the Arverni of the Gallic state who was making extensive preparations for war, with such a small army that
Bituitus boasted that the small number of Romans could
scarcely suffice to feed the dogs which he had in his army.
Since Bituitus realized that one bridge across the Rhone River
could not suffice for him to lead his troops across, he constructed another by putting small boats together and joining
them with chains, spreading boards over them and fastening
them down. Battle was joined[48] and carried on fiercely for a
long time. The Gauls were conquered and turned into flight.
While everyone feared for himself, the columns being formed
thoughtlessly and with precipitous haste for the crossing, they
broke the chains of the bridge and presently sank with the
boats. One hundred and eighty thousand armed men are
reported to have been in the army of Bituitus, of which one
hundred and fifty thousand were either killed or drowned.

Q. Marcius,[49] the consul, made an attack on a people of
the Gauls settled at the foot of the Alps. When they saw that

---

46 In Gallia Narbonensis.
47 Quintus Fabius Maximus, later called Allobrogicus, 121 B.C.
48 121 B.C., where the Isara empties into the Rhone.
49 Quintus Marcius Rex, 118 B.C.

they were surrounded by Roman troops and realized that they
would be unequal to the Romans in combat, after killing their
wives and children, they hurled themselves into blazing fire.
Those who had not had an opportunity of taking their lives
by reason of the Romans first seizing them and had been captured, some destroyed themselves by the sword, others by
hanging, and others by denying themselves food, and no one
survived, not even a little child, by his love of life to endure
slavery.

(15) In the six hundred and thirty-fifth year after the found-
ing of the City, when P. Scipio Nasica and L. Calpurnius
Bestia[50] were consuls, the Senate, with the consent of the
Roman people, declared war on Jugurtha, the king of the
Numidians.

But I shall touch on Jugurtha briefly, only in his proper
place and only to mention him, because all people, by reason
of the fine work of the historians, are sufficiently well acquainted with his fickle and unbearable character and with
his deeds carried on as craftily as they were strenuously.

Now Jugurtha, when he was made the adopted son of
Micipsa, the Numidian king, and heir with his natural sons,
first killed one of his coheirs, that is Hiempsal, and, after
overcoming Adherbal in battle, drove him out of Africa. Then
he bribed Calpurnius, the consul who had been sent against
him, and induced him to accept the most disgraceful conditions of peace. Furthermore, when he himself went to Rome,
by bribing or attempting to bribe everyone, he involved them
in seditions and dissensions, and when he departed, he marked
the City with a very shameful utterance: 'O city for sale and
soon to perish, if it should find a buyer!'[51]

In the following year, he overcame in battle A. Postumius,[52]
the brother of Postumius,[53] the consul, through whom he had

---

50 Publius Cornelius Scipio Nasica and Lucius Calpurnius Bestia, 111
   B.C.
51 Cf. Sallust, *Jugurthine War* 35.10.
52 Aulus Postumius.
53 Spurius Postumius Albinus, 110 B.C.

been placed in charge of an army of forty thousand armed
men. This took place at the city of Calama,[54] which was
replete with royal treasure, and, after conquering him, Jugurtha exacted a most humiliating treaty. He annexed to his
own kingdom almost all Africa which was withdrawing from
the Romans. Later, however, he was checked by the integrity
and the military discipline of the consul, Metellus, and being
defeated in two battles, he saw before his very eyes his Numidia
being laid waste and himself unable to defend it. Being forced
by Metellus to surrender, he gave three hundred hostages,
promised that he would turn over grain and other supplies,
and gave back more than three thousand deserters. Then,
since he was unreliable in peace and did not check his outrageous attacks, he was crushed by the cunning of C. Marius,[55]
the consul, with which he was endowed almost no less than
Jugurtha himself, and by the forces of the Romans, especially
after Marius by craft surrounded and captured the city of
Capsa, which, they say, was founded by the Phoenician Hercules and was then quite full of royal treasure. Then Jugurtha,
having lost confidence in his own resources and forces, made
an alliance with Bocchus, the king of the Moors, supported by
whose cavalry he made frequent raids on the immense army of
Marius and exhausted it. Finally, at Cirta, an ancient city,
the capital of Masinissa, equipped with sixty thousand horsemen, he met the Romans who were preparing an attack.
Never has there been a battle more tumultuous and more terrible for a Roman soldier, so much so that, by the circling
around and the rushing of the horsemen, a cloud was stirred
up which covered the sky; it took away the light and brought
on the darkness. Moreover, so great a shower of missiles fell
upon the Romans that no part of the body was safe from a
blow because visibility was lacking from the density of the
atmosphere for looking any distance ahead, and because ma-

---

54 Not Calama but Suthul, a fortress in Numidia.
55 Gaius Marius and Lucius Cassius Longinus, 107 B.C.

neuverability for self-protection was difficult from the pressure
of the multitude. The Moorish and Numidian cavalry did
not exert themselves greatly to dislodge, with a well-timed
attack of missiles, the enemy who had a favorable position,
but rather they hurled javelins blindly, certain that the re-
sultant wounds would not be uncertain. Thus the Roman
infantrymen, being forced into one place, were pressed close
together. Intervening night gave a pause to the great danger.
On the next day, the same condition of war and danger existed.
The soldiers were not able to rush forth against the enemy
although with drawn swords, for they were driven back by
javelins thrown from a distance. They were unable to escape,
for the cavalry had hemmed them in on all sides and were
swifter in the pursuit. Now it was the third day and there
was no help from any source, and on all sides the dreadful
appearance of death faced them. Finally, the consul, Marius,
in great desperation supplied a way of hope. With his entire
battle line, all at once from valley and plain, he rushed forth
and offered battle. And when the enemy, surrounding them
a second time, not only lacerated the flanks of the line, but
also cut down the middle by missiles thrown from a distance,
and the heat of the sun, the intolerable thirst, and presence of
death all around brought them to an extreme state of desperation, suddenly that form of aid well known to the Romans,
being sent from heaven against the Africans in the form of
wind and rain, became an unexpected deliverance. For the
sudden rain furnished coolness and drink to the Romans who
were hot and thirsty, and furthermore, for the Numidians,
rendered the shafts of their missiles, which they were accustomed to hurl with their hands and without ammenta,[56]
slippery and so useless. Also the shields, made of stretched
and toughened elephant hide, which being easy to handle
and good protection they were accustomed to carry, and whose

---

56 *ammenta* (or *amenta*), straps or thongs, especially upon missile
weapons, by means of which they were thrown with greater force.

nature was such that when they received the shower they drank it in like sponges, became difficult to manipulate due to the sudden weight; and because they could not be moved around, they could not be of any defense. So when the Moors and the Numidians were thrown into unexpected confusion and helplessness, Bocchus and Jugurtha fled. Later, ninety thousand armed men were thrown into a final battle by these same kings. These also are reported to have been utterly destroyed by the conquering Romans. As a result of this, Bocchus, abandoning hope of victory in battle, asked for peace and, as a price for peace, sent Jugurtha, who had been captured by trickery and weighed down by chains, to Marius through Sulla as a legate. Jugurtha with his two sons was driven before the chariot in triumph and afterwards was strangled in prison.

In these same days, an ominous and sad prodigy was seen. L. Helvius, a Roman knight, while returning from Rome into Apulia with his wife and daughter, was overtaken by a storm. When he saw that his daughter was terrified, abandoning the carriages and taking to horse in order to reach nearby protection more quickly, he took his unmarried daughter who was riding on a horse into the middle of his cavalcade. The girl was immediately knocked senseless by a bolt of lightning, but, although all her clothes were stripped off without any tearing, and the bands at her breast and feet unloosened, and her necklaces and rings broken, yet her body was unharmed and lay there in an unseemly manner, bare with her tongue protruding a little. The horse also, which she had been riding, lay lifeless some distance away with its trappings, reins, and girth loosened and scattered about.

A little while after this, L. Veturius, a Roman knight, secretly defiled Aemilia, a Vestal Virgin. Besides, this same Aemilia induced two Vestal Virgins to participate in the incest by exposing them and handing them over to the companions of her own betrayer. When evidence was presented by a slave, punishment was exacted of all.

Furthermore, in the same period of the Jugurthine War, L. Cassius,[57] the consul, who was in Gaul, pursued the Tigurini as far as the Ocean, and, in turn, was surrounded by the same ambush and was killed.[58] Lucius Piso, a man of consular rank and a legate of the consul, Cassius, was also killed. C. Publius, the other legate, that the remaining part of the army which had taken refuge in camp might not be destroyed, in a most disgraceful truce gave over hostages and half of all their property to the Tigurini. When he returned to Rome, C. Publius was summoned to court by the tribune of the people, Caelius, on the charge of having given hostages to the Tigurini, and he fled into exile. Caepio,[59] the proconsul, after capturing a city of the Gauls by the name of Tolosa, took away from the temple of Apollo one hundred thousand pounds of gold and one hundred and ten thousand pounds of silver. When he sent this under guard to Massilia, a city friendly to the Roman people, he secretly killed those to whom he had committed it for transportation and safe keeping, as some testify, and he is said to have criminally made away with all of it. As a result of this, a great investigation was afterwards carried on at Rome.

(16) In the six hundred and forty-second year after the founding of the City, C. Manlius,[60] the consul, and Q. Caepio, the proconsul, being sent against the Cimbri, Teutones, Tigurini, and Ambrones, Gallic and German tribes, which at that time had conspired to blot out the Roman Empire, divided the provinces among themselves, making the Rhone River the boundary. While they, then, disputed among themselves with most serious bitterness and contention, they were conquered to the great disgrace and danger of the Roman name. For in this battle,[61] M. Aemilius, a man of consular rank, was

57 Lucius Cassius Longinus and Marius, 107 B.C.
58 Probably fought southeast of Bordeaux.
59 Quintus Servilius Caepio, consul in 106 B.C. He triumphed in 108 B.C. for achievements as propraetor in Lusitania.
60 Gnaeus Mallius Maximus, consul in 105 B.C.
61 Fought north of Arles, near Arausio, on the sixth of October, 105 B.C.

captured and killed, and the two sons of the consul were slain. Antias writes that eighty thousand Romans and allies were slaughtered at this time and that forty thousand servants and camp followers were killed. Thus, of the entire army, only ten persons are said to have survived to bring back the wretched news to increase the miseries of the people. The enemy, after gaining possession of both camps and great booty, by a certain strange and unusual bitterness completely destroyed all that they had captured; clothing was cut to pieces and thrown about, gold and silver were thrown into the river, corselets of men were cut up, trappings of horses were destroyed, and the horses themselves were drowned in whirlpools, and men with fetters tied around their necks were hung from trees, so that the victor laid claim to no booty, and the conquered to no mercy. At that time, there not only was very great grief at Rome, but also fear lest the Cimbri would immediately cross the Alps and destroy Italy.

At the same time, Q. Fabius Maximus sent his youthful son to the country and, with two slaves as accomplices in parricide, killed him; he immediately freed the slaves themselves as a reward for the crime. Being brought to court and accused by Cn. Pompey, he was condemned.

When Marius, then consul for the fourth time, pitched his camp near the rivers Isère and Rhone where they flow into each other, after the Teutones, Cimbri, Tigurini, and Ambrones had fought continuously for three days around the Roman camp to see if, in any way, they might drive them from their ramparts and into the open, they decided to invade Italy in three columns. Marius, after the departure of the enemy, moved his camp and occupied a hill which overlooked the plain and the river where the enemy had spread out. When his army lacked drinking water and there were querulous arguments on the part of all, he replied that water was, indeed, in sight, but that it had to be claimed by the sword. So when the camp servants, first of all, rushed with a shout into battle, the army followed; presently, with the battle lines formed for regular combat,[62] battle was carried on and the Romans were victorious. On the fourth day, battle lines were drawn up again on both sides in the plain, and they fought on almost equal terms until midday. Afterwards, when, as the sun grew hot, the flabby bodies of the Gauls melted like snow, a slaughter rather than a battle was prolonged into the night. Two hundred thousand armed men were killed in this battle; eighty thousand are reported to have been captured; hardly three thousand are reported to have escaped; their leader, Teutobodus, was also killed. Their women, with a more steadfast spirit than they would have exhibited if they had conquered, advised the consul that if their chastity should be inviolate and they would have to serve the Vestal Virgins and the gods, they would not take their own lives. And so, when they did not obtain what they asked for, after dashing their little ones against rocks, they destroyed themselves by the sword and hanging. These things were carried on regarding the Tigurini and Ambrones. The Teutones and the Cimbri, however, with their forces intact, passed over the snow of the Alps and swept over the plains of Italy, and there, when the hardy race became softened after a while by the milder climate, drink, food, and baths, Marius, consul for the fifth time, and Catulus were sent against them, and following Hannibal's genius, granted the day and place for the battle, they arranged the battle in a mist, but fought it in the sun. The first confusion, indeed, arose among the Gauls because they realized that the Roman line of battle was ready for action, having been drawn up before they put in an appearance. And when, suddenly, horsemen were wounded and forced back against their own men and threw into confusion the whole multitude which was still advancing in disarray, and when the sun which arose with the wind was shining in their faces, their eyes were filled with dust and the brightness of the sun dimmed their sight.

---

62 In 102 B.C., near Aquae Sextiae, now *Aix*, about eighteen Roman miles north of Massilia.

So it happened that so great and so terrible a number were killed with slight losses to the Romans, but with the ultimate slaughter of their own. One hundred and forty thousand of their men are reported to have been killed in battle[63] at that time and sixty thousand captured. The women stirred up an almost more serious battle, for arranging the wagons in the form of a camp, they, by fighting from a higher position, repelled the Romans for a long time. But when they were frightened by the Romans with a new kind of slaughter, for their scalps were cut off together with the hair and they were left unsightly with a very disgraceful wound, they turned the sword, which they had taken up against the enemy, against themselves and their own children. Some killed each other by mutual consent, others were strangled by grabbing each other's throat, others by tying ropes around the legs of the horses and, suddenly driving the horses forward after they had placed their own necks in the very ropes with which they had bound the horses' legs, were dragged along and choked to death, and others hung themselves by a halter from wagon poles raised on high. A certain woman also was found who, after slipping a noose over the necks of her two sons, then bound them to her own feet and, when she released herself to meet death by hanging, dragged them with her to be killed. Among these many deplorable kinds of death, two chieftains also are reported to have rushed against each other with drawn swords. The kings, Lugius and Boiorix, fell in battle; Claodicus and Caesorix were captured. Thus, in these two battles, three hundred and forty thousand Gauls were killed and one hundred and forty thousand captured, not to mention the innumerable number of women who, with feminine fury but masculine force, killed themselves and their little ones. Thus, this incredible crime, such as was never known before to the Romans, being suddenly perpetrated at Rome, turned the triumph of Marius and the Roman victory into

---

63 In 101 B.C., at Campi Raudii, west of Milan.

a horror and sorrow, and cast a cloud over the whole City.
Indeed, Publicius Malleolus, with his slaves helping, killed
his own mother. Being condemned for parricide and sewed
up in a sack, he was thrown into the sea, and so the Romans
satisfied the crime and the punishment, for which even Solon
had not presumed to prescribe because he did not believe that
it could take place, but the Romans who knew that they were
sprung from Romulus and also understood that it could take
place, sanctioned the special punishment.

(17) In the six hundred and forty-fifth year after the founding of the City, after the Cimbrian and Teutonic War and
the fifth consulship of Marius, in which the status of the
Roman Empire was judged to have been preserved by law,
in the sixth consulship of this same C. Marius,[64] the state was
so shaken that it fell almost to the last extreme through internal conflict. It seems to be troublesome as well as tedious
to unravel and run over the ambiguities of the dissensions
and the inextricable causes of the seditions. Indeed, let it
suffice to have touched upon them briefly, that L. Apuleius
Saturninus was the first to be responsible for the disturbance
which broke out, a most bitter enemy of Q. Metellus Numidicus, a man, indeed, of the first rank. When Metellus was
elected censor, Saturninus dragged him from his home and,
on taking refuge in the Capitol, besieged him with an armed
mob, and then, because of the indignation which he had caused
the Roman knights, Metellus was thrown out after much
bloodshed had taken place before the Capitol. Then Saturninus and Glaucia, with the help of the trickery of C. Marius,
the consul, killed A. Nunius,[65] their rival. In the following
year, Marius, consul for the sixth time, Glaucia, the praetor,
and Saturninus, tribune of the people, conspired in every way
to drive Metellus Numidicus into exile. On the day set for
the trial, Metellus, though innocent, was condemned to exile

---

64 100 B.C.
65 Aulus Nunius (Nonius), a candidate for the tribuneship of the
   people in 100 B.C.

by judges of the same faction who had been treacherously substituted, and he departed to the great grief of the entire City. The same Saturninus, fearing that Memmius,[66] a shrewd man and one of integrity, would be made consul, when a riot suddenly broke out through one of his followers, P. Mettius crushed him with a shapeless club and killed him. When the Senate and the Roman people complained loudly about the great evils afflicting the state, Marius, the consul, adapting his mind to the times, joined the common feeling of the good citizens and calmed the aroused plebeians with soft words. Saturninus, after daring such infamous deeds, held a meeting at his own home and there was called 'king' by some, and 'general' by others. Marius, after dividing the plebeians into maniples, placed the other consul[67] with a garrison on the hill, and he himself fortified the gates. In the Forum, battle was joined; Saturninus was driven from the Forum by the followers of Marius and took refuge in the Capitol; Marius cut the pipes by which water was conducted there. A terrific battle was then carried on in the entrance to the Capitol, and many about Saufeius[68] and Saturninus were killed. Saturninus, crying out aloud, bore witness that Marius was the cause of all their troubles, but when Saturninus himself and Saufeius and and Labienus were forced by Marius to take refuge in the Senate house, they were killed by Roman knights who had broken down the doors. C. Glaucia was dragged from the house of Claudius and killed. Furius, the tribune of the people, decreed that the property of all these men was to be confiscated. Cn. Dolabella, the brother of Saturninus, while fleeing through the Forum Holitorium, was killed together with L. Giganius. And so, when the authors of this great sedition had been killed, quiet came to the people. Then

---

66 Gaius Memmius, a prominent democrat, who as tribune (111 B.C.) led the agitation against the Optimate leaders. He was praetor during the period of coalition of *Equites* and *populares* (104), and as candidate for the consulship of 99 was a rival of the extremist Glaucia.
67 Lucius Valerius Flaccus.
68 Gaius Saufeius, quaestor in 100 B.C.

Cato and Pompey, to the great joy of the entire City, promul-
gated a decree for the return of Metellus Numidicus. The
factions of Marius, the consul, and of Furius, a tribune of the
people, interceded and prevented its being passed. Rutilius[69]
also, a man of highest integrity, so maintained the constancy
of his good faith and innocence that on the day set for his
trial by the accusers, up to the time for his examination, he
did not let his hair or beard grow nor did he attempt to con-
ciliate his supporters by shabby clothing or humble mien,
nor to flatter his enemies nor to moderate the judges, but with
the permission of the praetor, he gave a speech no more sub-
missive than his spirit. Although he was opposed by evident
calumny and was thought in the opinion of all good men
rightly worthy of acquital, he was condemned by perjured
judges. He emigrated to Smyrna where he lived to an old age,
devoted to literary studies.

(18) In the six hundred and fifty-ninth year after the founding of the City, and in the consulship of Sextus Julius Caesar
and L. Marcius Philippus,[70] a war against the allies, due to
domestic quarrels, disturbed all Italy. For Livius Drusus, a
tribune of the people, since he could not appease the Latins
by a decree, all of whom had been deceived in a hope for
liberty, stirred them up to arms. In addition to this, terrible
prodigies terrified the afflicted City. For at sunrise, a ball of
fire flashed forth in the north with a tremendous clap of
thunder. Among the Arretini,[71] when bread was broken at
banquets, blood flowed from the middle of the loaves as if
from bodily wounds. Furthermore, for seven continuous days,
a shower of stones intermingled also with pieces of brick lashed
the country far and wide. Among the Samnites, a flame broke
out from a very vast gap in the ground and it seemed to extend up into the heavens. Moreover, some Romans, while

---

69 Publius Rutilius Rufus, *legatus* in Asia under Quintus Mucius
Scaevola in 95 B.C.
70 Sextus Julius Caesar and Lucius Marcius Philippus, 91 B.C.
71 Inhabitants of Arretium (Aretium), a large town in Etruria, modern
Arezzo.

traveling saw a ball of golden color roll from the heavens to
the earth, and becoming larger again was carried from the
earth toward the rising sun and by its magnitude covered
the sun itself. Drusus, disturbed by such great portents, was
killed in his own house by an unknown assassin.

So the Picentes, Vestini, Marsi, Paeligni, Marrucini, Samnites, and Lucani, since they were still planning a secret
rebellion, killed C. Servius, the praetor, at Asculum,[72] who had
been sent to them as a legate, and immediately closing the
city, proclaimed a slaughter and cut the throats of all Roman
citizens. Notorious prodigies immediately preceded the most
frightful destruction. For animals of all kinds who were accustomed to endure the hands of men kindly and to live among
men, left their stables and pastures with bleating, neighing,
and pitiful bellowing, and fled to the forests and mountains.
The dogs, also, whose nature is such that they cannot exist
apart from men, with pitiful howls wandered about at random in the manner of wolves. Now Cn. Pompey, the praetor,
on orders from the Senate, waged war with the Picentes and
was conquered. Afterwards, the Samnites placed Papius Mutilus
in command of themselves, but the Marsi preferred Agamem-
non, a leader of pirates. Julius Caesar, being conquered in a
battle with the Samnites when his army was slaughtered, fled.
Rutilius,[73] the consul, selected Marius, a kinsman, as his lieutenant, and thinking that he, since he was constantly suggest-
ing that a delay would be useful for the war and that the
untrained soldiery should receive a little training in camp,
was doing this with a crafty motive, made light of the advice
and recklessly cast himself and an entire battle line of his
army into an ambush set by the Marsi, where both he himself,
the consul, and many nobles were killed and eight thousand of
the Roman soldiers were cut down. The Tolenus River[74]
carried the arms and the bodies of the dead within view of the

---

72 A city situated in the interior of Apulia.
73 Publius Rutilius Lupus, 90 B.C.
74 In central Italy.

legate, Marius, and brought them as proof of the slaughter. Marius, quickly taking hold of the troops, unexpectedly pressed upon the victors, and he on his part killed eight thousand of the Marsi. Caepio, moreover, was lured into an ambush by the Vestini and the Marsi, and together with his army was massacred. But L. Julius Caesar, after he had fled on being defeated at Aesernia,[75] bringing troops together from all sides, fought against the Samnites and Lucani and killed many thousands of the enemy. When he had been hailed as imperator by the army and had sent messengers about the victory to Rome, the senators, while this hope was smiling upon them, laid aside the sagas, that is, the dress of mourning which they had assumed at the outbreak of the Social War,[76] and resumed the elegance of the toga of old. Then Marius killed six thousand Marsi and stripped seven thousand of their arms. Sulla[77] was sent with twenty-four cohorts to Aesernia, where Roman citizens and soldiers were being hard pressed by a very tight siege, and, after a tremendous battle and inflicting great slaughter upon the enemy, saved the city and its allies. Cn. Pompey dispersed the Picentes after a severe battle, because of which victory the Senate took on the broad purple stripes and other marks of dignity, since by Caesar's victory in a moment of relief it had assumed their togas only. Porcius Cato, the praetor, conquered the Etruscans; the lieutenant, Plotius, the Umbri, with the expenditure of a great deal of blood and most difficult hardships.

In the consulship of Cn. Pompey and L. Porcius Cato,[78] Pompey besieged the city of Asculum[79] for a long time, but he would not have captured it had he not overcome with very

---

75 A town in Samnium on the river Vulturnus, modern *Isernia*.

76 Sometimes called the Marsic War.

77 Lucius Cornelius Sulla Felix.

78 Gnaeus Pompeius Strabo and Lucius Porcius Cato, 89 B.C.

79 The capital of Picenum, strongly placed amid imposing mountains near the Adriatic on the Truentus River, modern *Ascoli Piceno*. Should be distinguished from Asculum in Apulia, modern *Ascoli Satriano*, where Pyrrhus defeated the Romans in 279 B.C.

severe violence, the people who had rushed out upon an open plain. Eighteen thousand Marsi together with their general, Fraucus, were killed and three thousand were captured. Moreover, four thousand Italians, fleeing from this slaughter, by chance ascended a mountain ridge with their line pressed close together, and there, overcome and exhausted by snow, they became stiff in a wretched death. For they had taken a posture as if astounded by fear of the enemy, some reclining on stumps and stones, others resting on their weapons; all with their eyes open and teeth bared seemed like the living, and there was no indication of death to one viewing them from a distance except the continuing immobility which the liveliness of human life can in no wise endure for long. On the same day, the Picentes joined battle and were conquered, whose leader, Vidacilius, bringing together his chiefs, after a magnificent banquet and heavy drinking, calling upon all to follow his example, drank poison and died, while all praised his deed, but no one followed it.

In the six hundred and sixty-first year of the City, when a Roman army went to besiege the Pompeys, Postumius Albinus, a man of consular rank and at that time a lieutenant of L. Sulla, by his insufferable arrogance stirred up the hatred of all the soldiers against himself and was stoned to death. Sulla, the consul, declared the civil bloodshed could be atoned for only by the blood of the enemy. Roused by the knowledge of this fact, the army so entered the battle that each one realized that he must die unless he conquered. Eighteen thousand Samnites were killed in that battle. Sulla also pursued and killed L. Cluentius, an Italian leader, and a large number of his people. Porcius Cato, the consul, with the help of the Marian forces, after he had fought a number of strenuous battles, boasted that C. Marius had not accomplished greater deeds, and so, when he was urging war against the Marsi at Lake Fucinus, he was laid low by the son of C. Marius in the tumult of battle as if by an unknown person. C. Gabinius, the lieutenant, was killed in the storming of the enemy's camp.

The Marrucini and Vestini, being pursued by Sulpicius, Pompey's lieutenant, were devastated. Popaedius and Obsidius, Italian generals, were overcome and killed in a terrible battle by the same Sulpicius at the Teanus River. When Pompey entered Asculum, he beat with rods the prefect, centurions, and all their leading men and beheaded them. He sold at auction the slaves and all the booty; the rest he ordered to go away, free, indeed, but stripped and destitute; and, although the Senate hoped that some help from this booty would be forthcoming for the use of the public income, yet Pompey contributed nothing from it to the needy treasury. For since at that very time the treasury was completely exhausted and money was lacking to pay for grain, the public places which around the Capitol had been given over into possession of the pontifices, augurs, decemvirs, and flamines, under the pressure of want were sold and a sufficient amount of money was realized to relieve the need temporarily. Indeed, at that time the wealth of all the conquered cities and of the lands stripped bare was gathered from all sides and placed in the lap of the state, when Rome itself, compelled by a disgraceful need, was auctioning off its most important possessions. Therefore, let Rome dwell upon its own times of that period, when, like an insatiable stomach consuming all and always remaining hungry, itself more wretched than all the cities which it was making wretched, while leaving nothing it possessed nothing, by the pangs of hunger at home it was impelled to continue in the unrest by war.

In these same days, King Sothimus, with large auxiliary forces of Thracians, invaded Greece and plundered all the territory of Macedonia, and finally, being conquered by C. Sentius was forced to return to his kingdom.

(19) In the six hundred and sixty-second year after the founding of the City, when the Social War had not yet been ended, the First Civil War broke out at Rome, and in the same year, the Mithridatic War, although less infamous yet not less serious, began. Indeed, a varied tradition exists as to

the length of the Mithridatic War, especially since some say that it was waged for thirty years, and others say forty, according as one begins the count from the very beginning or from that time when it burst forth. But although the events of those times flared up crowded with complex evils, nevertheless they will be presented by me one by one according to kind but briefly. Marius, when Sulla, the consul, was on the point of setting out for Asia with an army against Mithridates, yet was in Campania on account of the remnants of the Social War, strove to take over the consulship for the seventh time and the Mithridatic War. When this was learned, Sulla, indeed an impatient youth and of an ungovernable temper, becoming greatly roused, first encamped in front of the City with four legions, where he killed Gratidius, the legate of Marius, the first victim, as it were, of the Civil War; then, he broke into the City with his army and thereupon demanded firebrands with which to set the City on fire. Since all through fear had concealed themselves, he went quickly over the Sacred Way with his battle line into the Forum. When Marius had tried to stir up the nobility, then to inflame the people, and then to arm the equestrian order against Sulla, all in vain, finally, after trying to arouse the slaves to arms by hope of freedom and booty, and having dared to fight back to no avail, he finally withdrew into the Capitol. But when cohorts of Sulla rushed in there, he fled with a great loss of his own men. Then in that place, Sulpicius, a colleague of Marius, being betrayed by his own slave, was laid low; now the consuls decreed that the slave, because he had given information about the enemy, be freed; but, because he had betrayed his master, that he be cast down from the Tarpeian Rock. When Marius in his flight was surrounded by persistent pursuers, he hid himself in the swamps of Minturnae,[80] out of which, unfortunately for him, he was dragged ignominiously covered

---

80 A city of Latium on the border of Campania, at the mouth of the Liris, about three miles from the sea.

with mud; moreover, being brought to Minturnae an ugly sight and on being thrust into prison, by his forsaken looks he frightened the executioner sent to dispatch him. Then, slipping from his chains, he fled to Africa, and enticing his son from Utica where he was being held under guard, he immediately returned to Rome and joined with the consul, Cinna,[81] in an alliance of crime. There, to overthrow the whole Republic, they divided their army into four parts. Indeed, three legions were given to Marius; Cn. Carbo was placed over part of the troops; Sertorius received part, that Sertorius, namely, already an inciter here and participant in civil war, who, even when this war was ended, stirred up another war in Spain which dragged on for many years with very great losses to the Romans. Now the remaining part of the army followed Cinna. Furthermore, Cn. Pompey, who had been summoned with his army by the Senate to bring aid to the Republic and who for a long time had kept aloof from the revolution, being slighted by Marius and Cinna, joined forces with Octavius, the other consul, and soon entered battle with Sertorius. The intervention of night broke up the unfortunate battle. Six hundred soldiers on each side were slaughtered. On the following day, when the bodies, all piled together, were arranged for burial, a Pompeian soldier recognized the body of his brother whom he himself had killed; for in the conflict, the helmets had prevented each other from recognizing their faces, and fury had prevented any scrutiny of them; although there is little ground for blame, in that he seems not to have known his brother whom he undoubtedly knew was a citizen. Thus, the conqueror, more unfortunate than the conquered, when he recognized his brother's body and his own parricide, cursed civil wars, and immediately piercing his own breast with a sword and at the same time pouring forth tears and blood, threw himself upon his brother's body.

---

81 Lucius Cornelius Cinna, 87 B.C. In 86 B.C. was consul with Gaius Marius, with whom he formed an alliance against Sulla.

Of what profit was this for putting an end to the confusion of the cruel undertaking that, at the very beginning of the civil wars, a disgraceful report spread about that brothers, unwittingly, indeed, fought against each other, but wittingly did so as citizens; that a brother, as victor, had sought the armour of a brother who had been killed and, presently, being responsible for such an enormity, by the same sword and the same hand atoned for the parricide which he had committed by his own death? Did an example, so sad, affect the animosities of the parties under a strain? Did the fear of such an error restrain anyone in danger of committing such a crime? Did piety and reverence for nature, which is common even with wild animals,[82] have any influence in these matters? What one person committed by destroying and being destroyed, did this cause anyone to fear because it might happen to him, and, overcome by his conscience, did it restrain him from an undertaking of this kind? Rather, over the following period of nearly forty years, civil wars continued to such an extent that the magnitude of praise was thought to be dependent on the magnitude of the crime. For all, after such an example in war, would have fled the dangers of parricides had they not wished these very parricides.

So Marius entered the colony of Ostia[83] by force and committed all kinds of lust, avarice, and cruelty. Pompey, being struck by lightning, perished. Indeed, his army, seized by a pestilence, perished almost entirely. For eleven thousand men from Pompey's camp died, and six thousand from the force of Octavius, the consul, were driven mad. Marius, as an enemy, broke into the cities of Antium[84] and Aricia,[85] and he killed

---

82 There is a gap in the text here.

83 A seaport town in Latium at the mouth of the Tiber, still called *Ostia*.

84 Antium, an ancient town in Latium famous for its temple of fortune, not far from the seacoast, modern *Porto d'Anzio*, thirty-two miles from Rome.

85 Aricia, an ancient town of Latium, in the neighborhood of Alba Longa on the Appian Way, modern *La Riccia*, about sixteen miles from Rome.

all in these places except the traitors, and he allowed his soldiers to plunder property. Later, Cinna, the consul, with his legions and Marius, with the fugitives, entered the City and killed all the most noble men of the Senate and many men of consular rank.

But what a small part of the evident wretchedness is this?[86] Would it have been possible for me to have described the killing of good men in a word, the number of which was so great, whose duration was so long, whose cruelty was so intense and diverse? However, it is more just that I have subtracted something of the advantage of my case than to have brought to notice so much horror, whether these matters be brought before persons of experience or inexperience. For we are telling these things about our native land, our fellow citizens, and our ancestors, who, disturbed by these evils, did so much that must be abhorred; at which also when heard, our ancestors shudder, who surely do not wish these to be exaggerated too much, either with the moderation of sufficient knowledge if they knew the facts, or with the consideration of pity and reverence if they did not know them.

So Marius exhibited at banquets the heads of the citizens whom he had killed and exposed them before the Capitoline temples, collecting them at the Rostra.[87] After he brought them together for a spectacle and ornamentation and had won the consulship for the seventh time together with Cinna, consul for the third time, at the beginning of his consular power he was finally at old age carried away by death. Cinna completed his killings of the good by a slaughter of the wicked. For when the band of fugitives which had been brought in by Marius became insatiable for plunder and handed over no part of the plunder to the consuls who had sanctioned it, they were invited into the Forum as if to be paid and, when they were surrounded by soldiers, they were annihilated though

---

86 There is another gap in the text here.
87 Note the play on words in Latin: *capita inlata conviviis, oblata Capitoliis conlata Rostris.*

unarmed. On that day in the Forum of the City, eight thousand fugitives were killed, and this same Cinna, consul for the fourth time, was put to death by his own army.

(20) In the meantime, the remainder of the senators, who by flight had escaped the power of Cinna, the cruelty of Marius, the madness of Fimbria,[88] and the audacity of Sertorious, crossed over to Greece, and by their entreaties prevailed upon Sulla to bring help to his native land which was in utmost danger and almost ruined. So Sulla presently, after he had reached the shore of Campania, overcame the consul, Norbanus,[89] in battle. Seven thousand of the Romans were then killed by the Romans (i.e., Sulla's men); six thousand were captured by the same; and one hundred and twenty-four of Sulla's faction fell. But Fabius Hadrianus, who had the power of a propraetor, seeking control over Africa with a band of slaves, was burned alive together with his whole family on a pyre of fagots by the masters of these slaves at Utica. Damasippus, the praetor, at the instigation of the consul, Marius, very cruelly killed Q. Scaevola, C. Carbo, L. Domitius, and P. Antistius, after calling them to the Curia as if for a conference. The bodies of the dead were dragged away by the executioners with hooks and thrown into the Tiber. At the same time, Sulla's generals fought a great many battles with most unfortunate good fortune (*infelicissima felicitate*) against the Marian party. For Q. Metellus cut down the troops of Carrinas and overran his camp, and Cn. Pompey seriously cut up Carbo's cavalry. The greatest battle at that time was between Sulla and youthful Marius at Sacriportus,[90] in which, as Claudius describes, twenty-five thousand of Marius' army were cut down. Pompey, too, forced Carbo out of his camp and, pursuing him as he fled, now by killing and now by forcing to surrender, deprived him of the largest part of his

---

88 Gaius Flavius Fimbria, a violent supporter of the Marian party. He wrought terrible destruction throughout the province of Asia.

89 Gaius Norbanus Bulbus, 83 B.C.

90 A place in Latium near Praeneste, 82 B.C.

army. Metellus overcame the army of Norbanus, in which
operation nine thousand of the Marian group were killed.
When Lucullus was being besieged by Quintius, he broke out
and, by a sudden attack, destroyed the besieging army. For
more than ten thousand are reported to have been killed there
at that time. Then Sulla, together with Camponius, the general of the Samnites, and the remaining troops of Carrinas, at
the ninth hour of the day, brought his standards together
before the very city of Rome and the Colline Gate, and
finally, after a most severe battle, won a victory. Eighty thousand men are reported to have been routed there. Twelve
thousand of these surrendered and the insatiable anger of the
victorious citizens destroyed the remaining multitude as they
turned to flight.

(21) Sulla, as soon as he had entered the City as victor,
contrary to divine law and the pledge which had been given
them, killed three thousand men who had given themselves
up through envoys, although they were unarmed and felt per-
fectly safe. At that time, also, a great many, not to mention the
fact that they were innocent but were also of Sulla's own
party, were killed; the number is reported to have been more
than nine thousand. Thus, unrestrained slaughter was carried
on throughout the City, as assassins roamed at random according as anger and booty urged them on. So, then, as all openly
bewailed what each one feared, Q. Catulus openly said to
Sulla: 'With whom at last are we going to conquer, if we
kill the armed in war and the unarmed in peace?' At that
time, Sulla, at the suggestion of L. Fursidius, centurion of the
first maniple, became the first to introduce the infamous proscription list. The first proscription list consisted of eighty
names, among whom were four of consular rank, Carbo,
Marius, Norbanus, and Scipio; and among these especially to
be feared at this time was Sertorius. Likewise, another list
with five hundred names was posted, and when Lollius was
reading this, inasmuch as he felt secure and not at all conscious of any wrong-doing, and when suddenly he found his

name, as in fear with his head covered he was withdrawing from the Forum, he was killed. But not even in these lists was confidence and an end to evils found. For some who were proscribed were strangled, and others, after they had been strangled, were proscribed. The way of death itself was not simple nor was there one stipulation in death: that in the killing of citizens the law of the enemy at least be preserved, who exact from the conquered nothing more than life. For Sulla ordered that M. Marius[91] be dragged from the hut where goats are kept and led across the Tiber to the tomb of the Lutatii, and, after gouging out his eyes and cutting his limbs into small pieces or even breaking them, be killed. After him, P. Laetorius, the senator, and Venuleius, the triumvir, were killed. The head of M. Marius was sent to Praeneste, where C. Marius was being besieged by Lucretius, and when he saw it he was siezed with the utmost desperation and, lest he fall into the hands of the enemy, tried to commit mutual suicide with Telesinus.[92] While he himself thrust his hands against the onrushing Telesinus, he weakened the hand of Telesinus striking for his wound. Thus, although Telesinus was killed, he himself being slightly wounded offered his neck to his slave. Sulla had the praetor, Carrinas, murdered. Then, proceeding to Praeneste, he ordered all the leaders of the army of Marius killed, that is, legates, quaestors, prefects, and tribunes. Pompey killed Carbo as he was trying to flee from the island of Cossura[93] into Egypt, and, when brought before him in Sicily killed many of his companions with him. Sulla was made dictator in order that his uncontrollable desire for domination and cruelty might be both armed and cloaked with the reverence due an especially honored name. Pompey, after crossing into Africa, when a sortie was made near Utica, killed eighteen thousand men. In this battle, Domitius, the Marian leader, was killed while fighting in the front ranks. Pompey, likewise,

---

91 A relative of the great Gaius Marius.
92 The brother of the Samnite general.
93 In the Mediterranean halfway between Sicily and the coast of Africa.

pursued Hiarbas, the king of Numidia, and caused him to be deprived of all his troops by Bogudes, the son of Bocchus, king of the Moors, and he put Hiarbas to death as soon as he returned to Bulla and after he had given the town over to himself.

(22) Thus, when P. Servilius and Appius Claudius became consuls,[94] Sulla finally became a private citizen. With this conclusion, two most destructive wars were brought to an end —the Italian Social War and the Civil War of Sulla. These wars, carried on for ten years, took the lives of more than one hundred and fifty thousand Romans, and in this civil war Rome lost as many of her best men and youthful soldiers as there were in Rome in the earlier period, when she was surveying her resources against Alexander the Great, and found in the various classifications by age in the census. Besides, the census shows that twenty-four men of consular rank, six of praetorian rank, sixty with the rank of aediles, and almost two hundred senators were killed, not to mention the innumerable people of all Italy who were killed at random without consideration. Let anyone deny, if he can, that Rome conquered with the same loss on its part as Italy suffered on losing these people.

For shame! Do these times need here any ambiguous comparison? Yes, most assuredly, they say, for what comparison is so aptly made as with civil wars and civil wars? Or perchance it will be said that in these times civil wars have not taken place? To these we will reply that they should more justly, indeed, be called wars against the allies, but that it is advantageous for us if they be called civil wars. For since all these wars are shown to be alike with respect to causes, names, and purposes, then reverence for the Christian religion in these wars claims as much more for itself as the irate power of the victor assumed less vengeance. For since for the most part wicked tyrants, rashly attacking the state and usurping the royal power, tore apart the body of the Roman Empire, and

---

94 Publius Servilius Vatia and Appius Claudius Pulcher, 79 B.C.

as a result of this have either brought in wars unjust in themselves or have stirred up just wars against themselves, having been brought into existence and made ready for the people of Britain and the Gauls, inasmuch as these wars are as much like wars against the allies as they are removed from civil wars, why are they not rightly called wars against the allies, since the Romans themselves to this day have not called the wars of Sertorius, or Perpenna, or Crixus, or Spartacus civil wars? Therefore, in such a case, whether it be called a defection or treason on the part of allies, surely we would be laboring with less ill-will if, perchance, either a serious battle or bloody victory had taken place. However, since in these times of ours all events produce more of necessity and less of shame, that is, cause, battle, and victory for the purpose of wiping out the insolence of tyrants, or of checking the defection of allies, or of impressing an example of vengeance, who now has any doubt as to how much more mildly civil wars are waged today, or rather are repressed rather than carried on? For who has ever heard of a single civil war in these times which has been waged for ten years? Who could recall that in one war one hundred and fifty thousand men have been killed, of the enemy by the enemy, not to mention of citizens by citizens? Who would believe that the long list of distinguished and famous men, to mention whom one by one is a long task, were slaughtered in times of peace? Finally, who would fear, would read, and would understand those infamous lists of the proscribed? Rather let it be known to all that the conquered and conquerors, composed by one peace and secure in the same safety, rejoiced alike in common gladness, and, moreover, in so many provinces, cities, and peoples of the Roman Empire, there have been scarcely a few at any time whom a just vengeance condemned even though a victor wished otherwise? And not to pile words upon words, I would say conservatively that the number of the common soldiers who were wiped out, at least in the war, was as great as the number of nobles killed at that time during peace.

So, when Sulla died, Lepidus, a follower of Marius' party, rising up against Catulus, a Sullan leader, stirred up and revived the embers of civil wars. Two battles were then fought. A great many Romans, already wretched by their lack of numbers and still raging with the fury of the struggle, were killed. The city of the Albans,[95] beset by siege and plagued by extreme hunger, was saved by the surrender of its wretched survivors, when Scipio, the son of Lepidus, was captured and killed. Brutus, when fleeing into Cisalpine Gaul with Pompey pursuing him, was killed at Rhegium. Thus, the civil war died away, no more by the clemency shown by Catulus than because of disgust at Sulla's cruelty, like fire in straw, with the same speed with which it burst forth.

(23) In the six hundred and seventy-third year after the founding of the City, with the rumbles of wars resounding on all sides, one of which was in Spain, another in Pamphylia, a third in Macedonia, and a fourth in Dalmatia, the Roman state, still feeble and exhausted by internal disaster as if by fevers, was forced to drive back with arms the strongest peoples of the West and North. For Sertorius, a man powerful in trickery and daring, since he had been of the party of Marius, fleeing Sulla, slipped from Africa into the Spains and stirred up the most warlike peoples to arms. Against this man, to explain briefly, two generals were sent, Metellus and Domitius. Of these, Domitius with his army was overcome by Hirtuleius, a general of Sertorius. Manlius, the proconsul of Gaul, crossed over into Spain with three legions and one thousand five hundred horsemen and joined in an unequal battle with Hirtuleius. Being deprived of his camp and troops by Hirtuleius, he fled, almost alone, to the town of Ilerda. Metellus, exhausted by many battles, wandering through out-of-the-way places, wearied the enemy by delaying tactics until he joined with the camp of Pompey. Pompey gathered his army at Pallantia, trying in vain to defend the city of Lauron[96] which

---

95 The city of Alba Longa.
96 A city in Hispania Tarraconensis near Sucro and the sea.

Sertorius was then attacking, but he was conquered and fled. Sertorius, after overcoming Pompey and driving him to flight, captured Lauron and ravaged it in a most bloody fashion. The remaining body of the Lauronians which had survived the slaughter, he led away to Lusitania in wretched captivity. Moreover, he boasted that Pompey, that is, that famous general of the Romans, had been conquered by him: Pompey whom Rome had dispatched to this war full of confidence, not as a consul, but as consuls. Galba writes that at that time Pompey had thirty thousand infantry and a thousand cavalry, but reminds us that Sertorius had sixty thousand infantry and eight thousand cavalry. But later, Hirtuleius met Metellus in battle at the city of Italica Baetica[97] and lost twenty thousand soldiers, and on being defeated fled with a few men into Lusitania. Pompey captured Belgida, a famous city of Celtiberia. Then Sertorius, joining in battle with Pompey, killed ten thousand of his soldiers. While Pompey was conquering on another wing, Sertorius himself lost almost a like number. Many other battles besides were fought between them. Memmius, Pompey's quaestor and, likewise, the husband of his sister, was killed. The brothers of Hirtuleius were killed. Perpenna, who had joined Sertorius, was crushed. Finally, precisely in the tenth year after the beginning of the war, Sertorius himself being killed by the same wiles on the part of his men as those by which Viriathus also was killed, made an end of the war and gave the Romans victory without glory, although a part of his army afterwards followed Perpenna who was conquered by Pompey and was destroyed with his entire army. But when all the cities were received in surrender of their own accord and without delay, two only resisted, namely, Uxama[98] and Calagurris.[99] Of these, Pompey overthrew

---

97 Modern *Santiponce* near Hispalis, now *Seville.*
98 Uxama, a town also in Hispania Tarraconensis, fifty miles north of Numantia.
99 Calagurris or Calaguris, a town in Hispania Tarraconensis, on the right bank of the Iberus, in the region of the Ilergetes, north of Osca, now *Loarre.*

Uxama, and Afranius, with final slaughter and burning, destroyed Calagurris, which had been worn out by continuous siege and forced by its pitiable want to eat horrifying food.[100] The assassins of Sertorius did not think that any reward should be sought from the Romans, inasmuch as they remembered that it had been denied before to the murderers of Viriathus.

And although these assassins at the time had brought about security for the Romans with no reward for themselves, nevertheless Spain, ever strong in faith and power, although she has given the best and most invincible rulers to the state, never, from the beginning to the present day, has sent out a usurper, nor sent away anyone still alive and powerful who attacked her from without.

Meanwhile, Claudius[101] obtained the Macedonian War by lot, and the various tribes which had spread about the Rhodopaean Mountains and at that time were laying waste most cruelly to Macedonia. For among other things horrible to mention and to hear which were committed against the captives, when there was need of a cup, they made use of the bones of the human head, still bloody and covered with hair and with the brain badly scooped out through the inner caverns and poorly bedaubed; they eagerly and without any feeling of horror made use of these as real cups. Of these tribes, the most bloody and most inhuman were the Scordisci, and so, as I have said, Claudius tried to drive these tribes from the boundaries of Macedonia by war, and laid himself open to many great evils. So when he became sick in mind and overwhelmed with worries, and finally was overcome by disease, he died. His successor, Scribonius,[102] avoiding a test of strength

---

100 Women and children were slaughtered and their flesh eaten.
101 Appius Claudius Pulcher was expelled from the Senate in 86. With Publius Servilius, was consul in 79 B.C., and proconsul in Macedonia, where he won some victories over neighboring tribes. He died in 76 B.C.
102 Gaius Scribonius Curio, a friend of Cicero.

with the tribes who had been tried in an earlier war, turned his arms against Dardania[103] and conquered it. Now Publius Servilius, the ex-consul, most cruelly attacked Cilicia and Pamphylia, which he was anxious to bring under his control, and almost destroyed them. He captured Lycia and its cities, which had been besieged and hard pressed. He also wandered about Mount Olympus[104] and overturned Phaselis;[105] he demolished Corycus;[106] and after searching through the slopes of the Taurian Range which descend into Cilicia, he broke the Isaurians in battle and reduced them to surrender. He was the first of the Romans to lead an army over the Taurus and to make it the end of his march. Three years having passed in which this war had been carried on, he assumed the name of Isauricus. Cosconius, the proconsul, was assigned Illyricum, and after crushing and subduing Dalmatia, he finally, after two years, stormed and captured Salonae,[107] a most flourishing city.

(24) In the six hundred and seventy-ninth year after the founding of the City, in the consulship of Lucullus and Cassius,[108] seventy-four gladiators at Capua escaped from the training school of Cn. Lentulus. These immediately, under the leadership of Crixus and Oenomaus who were Gauls, and Spartacus, a Thracian, occupied Mount Vesuvius. Rushing down from there, they captured the camp of Clodius, the praetor, who had encircled them in a siege, and when he had been driven into flight, they turned their complete attention to plundering. Then, going about through Consentia[109] and Metapontum,[110] they gathered together huge forces in a short

---

103 In upper Moesia.
104 A mountain range located in Mysia.
105 A town in Lycia on the Pamphylian Gulf.
106 On the coast of Lycia.
107 Salonae or Salona, a maritime town in Dalmatia, still called *Salona*.
108 Marcus Terentius Varo Lucullus and Gaius Cassius Varus, 73 B.C.
109 The capital of the Bruttii, now *Cosenza*.
110 A town of Lucania, twenty-four miles from Tarentum, now *Torre a Mare*.

time. For Crixus was reported to have had a multitude of ten thousand, and Spartacus three times as many; Oenomaus had already been killed in an earlier battle. And so when the fugitives were confusing everything with slaughters, conflagrations, plunderings, and defilements, at the funeral of a captive woman who had killed herself out of grief for her outraged honor, they presented a gladiatorial performance with four hundred captives, that is, those who had been the ones to be viewed, were to view, namely, as trainers of gladiators rather than as commanders of troops. The consuls, Gellius and Lentulus, were sent against them with their army. Of these, Gellius overcame Crixus who fought very bravely, and Lentulus, when overcome by Spartacus, fled. Later also, both consuls, after having joined forces in vain, fled, suffering heavy losses. Then the same Spartacus, after defeating C. Cassius, the proconsul, in battle, killed him. And so, with the City terrified with almost no less fear than when Hannibal was raging at the gates, they became alarmed and sent Crassus with the legions of the consuls and a new complement of soldiers. He presently, after entering battle with the fugitives, killed six thousand of them, but captured only nine hundred. Then, before he approached Spartacus himself in battle, who was laying out a camp at the head of the Silarus River,[111] he overcame the Gallic and German auxiliaries of Spartacus, of whom he killed thirty thousand men with their leaders. After he had organized his battle line, he met Spartacus himself and killed him with most of the forces of the fugitives. For sixty thousand of them are reported to have been killed and six thousand captured, and three thousand Roman citizens were recovered. The remaining gladiators, who had slipped away from this battle and wandered off, were killed by many generals in persistent pursuit.

But I repeat again and again: Do the times at this point in my narrative require any comparison? Who, I ask, would not shudder to hear, I shall not say such wars, but so many names

---

111 A river forming the boundary between Lucania and Campania, now *Sala*, flowing into the gulf of Posidonia.

of wars—foreign, servile, wars against the allies, civil, and with
fugitives? These wars at all events do not follow one another
stirred up like waves of the sea with force however great, but
they dash upon one another from all sides, stirred up and
heaped together by various causes, appellations, forms, and
evils. To take up the discussion from the last point discussed,
and to pass over that notorious Slave War, the Jugurthine War
had not yet thundered forth from Africa, and already from the
northwest the Cimbrian War was flashing forth. From those
Cimbrian clouds horrible and vast torrents of spilled blood
were being sent forth, while already Italy in her wretchedness
was breathing forth the clouds of the Social War destined to
come together immediately into clouds of evils. Furthermore,
after the endless and frequent turmoils of the Italian War, it
was not at all possible to travel in safety throughout Italy.
Thus, all, except those most dangerous whirlpools of hostile
cities, were tottering with their careless and uncertain peace.
Rome was now giving birth to the destruction of Marius and
Cinna, and another, that is, the Mithridatic, from a different
direction, the east and north, was threatening. Indeed, this
Mithridatic War began from conditions of an earlier period
and extended into later times. From the torch of Marius, the
funeral pyre of Sullan slaughter was set ablaze and, from this
most dismal funeral pyre of the Sullan and Civil War, burning
sparks were scattered through a great many parts of the earth
and many conflagrations were spread from the one torch. For
Lepidus and Scipio in Italy, Brutus in Gaul, Domitius, the
son-in-law of Cinna, in Africa, Carbo in Cossura and Italy,
Perperna in Liguria and afterwards with Sertorius in Spain,
and Sertorius, the most atrocious of all, in that same Spain,
then caused those civil wars, or by whatever other name they
are to be called, causing many wars from one and great wars
from a great one. Apart from those three very vast wars,
that is, the Pamphylian, the Macedonian, and the Dalmatian,
although, too, that great Mithridatic War, by far the longest
of all, the most dangerous, and the most dreadful, was concealed

as to its true character; still, while the Sertorian War in Spain was not yet ended, rather while Sertorius himself was still living, that war against the fugitive slaves, to describe it more accurately, that war against the gladiators, caused great horrors which were to be seen by few, but everywhere to be feared. Because this war is called the war against the fugitive slaves, let it not be held of little consequence because of the name. Often in that war, individual consuls and sometimes both consuls with their battle lines joined in vain were overcome and a great many nobles were slain. Moreover, there were more than one hundred fugitives who were slain. Therefore, we suggest that Italy console herself for the distress of the present foreign wars with a recollection of past wars begun by herself and directed against herself and of her wars which tore her to pieces incomparably more cruelly.

Accordingly, I shall now make an end to this fifth book, so that civil wars everywhere intermingled with foreign wars, both those which have been mentioned and also those which follow, since they are closely related by successive periods and by related evils, may be separated at least by the end of the book.

BOOK SIX

ALL MEN, OF WHATEVER principles or mode of life or country, are always so roused by a natural blessing to a regard for good sense that they prefer the reasoning power of the mind to the enjoyment of the body, although they prefer it not by action, but realize by their judgment that it ought to be preferred. This mind, enlightened by reason as its guide, in the midst of virtues to which it is inclined by nature although it is turned back by vices, beholds the knowledge of God like a citadel. For any man can look down upon God temporarily, but cannot be ignorant of Him entirely. Therefore, some people, since they believe in God in many forms, fashioned many gods with undivided apprehension. But now especially, not only through the operation of authoritative truth, but also by the strong arguments of reason, there has been a departure from this position. For since their philosophers, not to mention our saints, as they investigate with deep solicitude of the mind and examine everything, have discovered that God is the one author of all things, to whom alone all things should be referred, so also now the pagans, whom now revealed truth convicts of stubbornness rather than ignorance when they dispute with us, confess that they do not follow many gods, but under one great god worship many ministers of religion. There remains, therefore, regarding the understanding of the true God, a confused disagreement because of the many notions of understanding Him, because regarding the one God, there is almost one opinion. Thus far, human investigation has been possible, although with difficulty. But where reason fails, faith comes to our aid. For unless we believe, we will not understand; hear from God himself and believe in God

228

himself what truth you wish to know about God. And this same one and true God, on whom, as we have said, all sects agree, although according to different notions, changing kingdoms and ordering the times, also punishing sins, has chosen the weak elements of the world to confound the strong and has laid the foundation of the Roman Empire by selecting a shepherd of the most lowly station. After this empire had long prospered under kings and consuls, and after it had gained possession of Asia, Africa, and Europe, He conferred by His arrangement all things upon one and the same emperor, who was most powerful and merciful. Under this emperor, whom all peoples with mingled love and fear justly honored, the true God, who was worshiped with scrupulous observances by those who did not know Him, opened the great fountainhead of His knowledge and, to teach men more quickly through a man, He sent His Son, performing miracles that surpassed the powers of man, refuting demons whom some thought to be gods, that those who did not believe in Him as a man might believe in His works as of a God; also that the glory of the new name and the swift report of the announced salvation might spread in the midst of the great silence and widespread peace quickly and without hindrance, and also that His disciples, as they went through different nations and voluntarily offered to all the gifts of salvation, might have safety and liberty among Roman citizens in speaking and conversing as Roman citizens. So I have thought it necessary to recall this, because this sixth book extends to the period of Caesar Augustus, regarding whom these remarks are made. But if some think that this very clear reasoning is not valid, and rather give credit to their own gods whom they first chose out of prudence and then won over by their special devotion so that this very extensive and magnificent Empire was founded for them through these gods—for they boast in this fashion, that they themselves merited the special favor of the gods by the best kind of sacrifices, and, when these were abandoned or overlooked, all the gods departed 'from sanctuaries and abandoned altars, gods, by whose help this Empire had stood firm'[1]—therefore, although your holy reverence[2] has discussed many subjects most forthrightly and very truthfully, nevertheless, the situation demands that I add a few observations. If the Romans by worshiping the gods merited the favor of the gods, and by not worshiping them lost it, who by worshiping the gods merited that Romulus himself, the parent of Rome, was safe in the midst of so many evils that attacked him from his very birth? Was it his grandfather, Amulius, who exposed him to death? Or his father, who was unknown? Or his mother, Rhea, convicted of defilement? Or his Alban ancestors who persecuted the rising power of the Roman name from the beginning? Or all of Italy, which for four hundred years, as long as it was able to dare, longed for Rome's destruction? No, they say, but the gods themselves, because they knew that they were destined to be worshiped, protected their future worshipers. So the gods are prescient. If they are prescient, why did they bring this Empire during all those centuries to the topmost pinnacle of power at the very time when He wished to be born among men and to be acknowledged as a man, after whose coming, the gods themselves were held as nothing and departed with their whole world, even those whom they themselves had exalted. He crept into this world humbly, they say, and entered secretly. Whence such far-flung fame, such undoubted honor, and such manifest power on the part of one obscure and lowly born? It was by certain signs and powers that He captured men's minds disturbed by superstitions and held them. But if a human being was able to do this, the gods should have been more able to do it. Or because He declared that this power was given Him by His Father, has one at any time come to an understanding of that known and unknown God, which knowledge no one, as I have said, can attain except through Him? No one can do this except him who, after examining himself completely

---

1 Vergil, *Aeneid*, 2.351-352.
2 St. Augustine.

and humbling himself, is converted to the wisdom of God and has transferred all the reasoning of the seeker for truth to the faith of the believer. However, I shall discuss the subject briefly. Those gods, who the Romans say are so great that they seem to exalt the Roman state when propitious and to afflict it when estranged, surely it is well established that at that time when Christ willed to be born and to be announced to the nations, were worshiped most devotedly and most eagerly. So were they, consulting their own good and that of their worshipers, not able to repress or repel His religious rite on account of which they saw that they themselves must be rejected and their worshipers abandoned? And yet, if the people acted unwillingly, they should have been pardoned and not abandoned; if willingly, by preserving their foreknowledge, the gods should have aided them early. This is what was done, they say: we roused nations, we inflamed kings, we established laws, we set up judges, we prepared punishments by torture and crucifixion, we examined the whole earth to see if in any way the Christian name and worship could be wiped off the whole universe. This went on for a long time until the constantly renewing cruelty in the midst of tortures and through tortures reached such a point that it finally occupied the imperial throne itself by which alone it might have been kept off. And what followed thereafter? The Christian emperors ordered the sacrifices to cease and the temples to be closed, and so 'all the gods went forth, abandoning sanctuaries and altars, by whom this Empire had stood firm.'[3]

Oh, how great and how unobstructed is the light of truth, if weak eyes were not unhappily closed to it, which offers itself of its own accord! If the Christian religion over many generations in the past, although on all sides nations, kings, laws, slaughters, crucifixions, and deaths raged against it, could in no way be repressed, but rather, as I have said, in the midst

---

3 Vergil, *loc. cit.*

and because of these things, grew, yet the worship of idols, already somehow failing of itself and being ashamed of itself, came to an end at a single, most gentle order without any fear of punishment. Who will doubt that by this demonstration of wisdom those created finally learned about their Creator those things which up to then they had been seeking, however intently, through various forms of the mind's reasonings, though beclouded by other matters, and through this clung immediately to their love for Him whom they loved even in ignorance? So it is not to be wondered at if, in a large household, some servants are found who, having become accustomed to the loose society of their seducers, abuse the patience of their master to the point of being contemptuous of him. Therefore, even rightly does God reprove the ungrateful, the unbelieving, and even the contumacious with various kinds of reproofs. Surely, this must be confessed to have been always so, but especially so at that time when, throughout the entire world, there was as yet no Church which, by the intervention of the prayers of the faithful, might have tempered the deserved punishments of the world and the just judgment of God by begging for His mercy. Therefore, those things also which are regarded as evils by men, of whatever kind they are, were more severe without doubt, as will be proven in the order in which they already have been begun.

The Mithridatic War or, to speak more truly, the disasters of the Mithridatic War, involving many provinces at the same time, was drawn out and extended for forty years. For in the six hundred and sixty-second year[4] after the founding of the City, in which also the First Civil War began, blazing forth, moreover, in the consulship of Cicero and Antony, to make use of the words of the greatest of all poets, 'the city was almost consumed by barbaric poison.'[5] But in this period, thirty years are discovered for carrying on the war. Moreover, why forty years are mentioned by many is not easy to explain.

---

4 Reading of text is not clear.
5 Lucan 1.337.

(2) So Mithridates, the king of Pontus and Armenia, after
he tried to deprive Nicomedes, the king of Bithynia and friend
of the Roman people, of his kingdom, and was warned by the
Senate that, if he should attempt this, war would have to be
carried on against him by the Roman people, becoming enraged, immediately invaded Cappadocia and after driving the
king, Ariobarzanes, out, lay waste the entire province by fire
and sword. Then he brought a like slaughter upon Bithynia.
He afflicted Paphlagonia with a similar destruction after driving out the kings, Pylaemenes and Nicomedes. Afterwards,
when he had come to Ephesus, he ordered by a cruel edict that
whatever Roman citizens were found throughout all Asia
should be slaughtered on a single day. And this took place.
The great number of Roman citizens who were killed at that
time cannot by any means be either set forth or comprehended,
nor the mourning that took place throughout the many provinces, nor the groaning that occurred on the part alike of
those being killed and those killing, when individuals were
forced either to betray innocent guests and friends or themselves run the risk of receiving the punishment meant for their
guests. Archelaus also, a general of Mithridates, was sent ahead
into Achaia with one hundred and twenty thousand infantry
and cavalry, and gained possession of Athens and all Greece,
partly by force and partly by surrender. Sulla, to whom the
Mithridatic War fell by lot after he had completed his consulship, besieged Archelaus for a long time at Piraeus, the port
of Athens fortified by a sevenfold wall, and he captured the
city of Athens itself by storm. Later, he engaged Archelaus in
a pitched battle. One hundred and ten thousand of the army
of Archelaus are reported to have been killed, scarcely ten
thousand to have survived.[6] When Mithridates learned of the
disaster, he sent seventy thousand picked men from Asia to the
aid of Archelaus. In a second battle,[7] fifty thousand of these

---

6 This battle was fought near Chaeronea in Boeotia, 86 B.C.
7 This battle, which lasted two days, was fought near Orchomenos.

were killed, and in this battle Diogenes, the son of Archelaus,[8] was cruelly put to death. In a third battle, all the troops that Archelaus had were wiped out. For twenty thousand of his soldiers, when, after being driven into a swamp,[9] they implored the mercy of Sulla, were killed by the insatiable wrath of the victor, and a like number in addition were forced into the river[10] and slaughtered, and the remainder of the wretched soldiers were killed at random. Furthermore, Mithridates in Asia had it in mind to kill the leaders of the most famous cities and to confiscate their goods. When he had already killed a thousand six hundred, the Ephesians, fearing this as an example, threw out his garrison and blocked the gates. The people of Smyrna, Sardis, Colophon, and Tralles did likewise. Mithridates, becoming alarmed, concluded a treaty of peace with Sulla through his general, Archelaus. Meanwhile, Fimbria, an accomplice of the Marian criminals, the most daring man of all, killed Flaccus at Nicomedia, the consul to whom he had gone as a legate. As soon as he had gained possession of the army, he drove the son of Mithridates out of Asia to Miletopolis, and he attacked the quarters of the king and drove him from Pergamum, and, following him as he fled, besieged him at Pitane. And he surely would have captured him, if L. Lucullus had placed the good of the state above civil discords and had he been willing to press him by blocking his way to the sea with the fleet. Then Fimbria, becoming angry at the people of Ilium, through whom he seemed to have been repulsed in their zeal for the party of Sulla by the barring of their gates, completely destroyed the city of Ilium itself, that foster mother of Rome, by fire and sword. But Sulla rebuilt it immediately. This same Fimbria, when he was besieged at Thyatira by Sulla's army, driven by

---

8 Orosius follows Eutropius 5.6 here. He was the stepson, not the son, as is assumed here.

9 The marshes of Lake Copais, now drained, which in the early days covered most of the west plain of Boeotia.

10 The Cephissus or Cephisos River in Phocis and Boeotia, now *Cephisso, Gaurio,* or *Gerios,* which flows into Lake Copais.

desperation was killed in the temple of Aesculapius by his own hand. Fannius and Magius, fugitives from the army of Fimbria, joined with Mithridates. At the urging of these two, Mithridates made a treaty with Sertorius through legates who had been sent into Spain. Sertorius sent M. Marius to him for the purpose of confirming the treaty. The king, Mithridates, kept him in his company, and soon he made him a general in place of Archelaus, who had betaken himself with his wife and children to Sulla. Marius and Eumachus, generals who had been sent by Mithridates against Lucullus, after quickly gathering a large army met with P. Rutilius near Chalcedon and killed him, together with the largest part of his army. Lucullus surrounded Mithridates with a trench while he was besieging the Cyziceni and compelled him to endure what they had suffered, and to the Cyziceni themselves he sent a messenger from among the soldiers who was an expert swimmer to tell them to be of good cheer. This messenger, supported by two inflated bladders and himself holding a stick in the middle and propelling himself by his feet, covered a distance of seven miles. Mithridates, suffering from want, ordered part of his troops to equip themselves with arms and depart for home. Lucullus captured this entire force and destroyed it. He is reported to have killed more than fifteen thousand men at that time. At that time, also, Fannius, who had joined with Mithridates, and Metrophanes, the royal praetor, being conquered by Mamercus, took to flight with two thousand cavalry into Moesia, and digressing from there into Malonia, into the hills and fields, fell upon the Inarimi. In that place, not only did the mountains look scorched and the rocks darkened by a kind of soot, but also the fields, wretched in appearance by their burnt soil for a distance of fifty miles without a sign of either fire or crater, lay covered with a deep layer of decaying ash. Also in three places hot chasms were visible which the Greeks call freaks of nature. The soldiers, after wandering for a long time among these, at last were freed of unexpected dangers and secretly came to the king's camp. Deiotarus, the king of the Gallo-Greeks, killed the prefects of the king in battle.

Meanwhile, Mithridates was blockaded at Cyzicus for the same length of time as that which occupied his own blockade, and he pressed his army into great want and disease. For he is reported to have lost more than three hundred thousand men from hunger and disease in the one siege. He himself with a few men siezed a ship and fled secretly from the camp. Lucullus, without losing a soldier, was an eyewitness to the enemy's disaster and won a novel kind of victory. Presently, attacking Marius, he conquered him and put him to flight. In this battle, more than eleven thousand of the troops of Marius are reported to have been killed.[11] Later, Lucullus met with the same Marius in a naval battle and either sunk or captured thirty-two of the royal ships and many transports.[12] Many of those whom Sulla had proscribed were killed in that battle. On the next day, Marius was dragged from a cave where he was hiding and paid the penalty deserved by his hostile intentions. Moreover, in the same campaign, Lucullus laid waste to Apamia, and at the foot of Mount Olympus, after storming and capturing Prusa, a very well fortified city, he ravaged it. Mithridates, as he was sailing against Byzantium with his fleet in battle array, was caught by a storm and lost eighty beaked ships. He himself, when his ship was battered and sinking, leaped aboard a *myoparo* belonging to Seleucus, a pirate, the pirate himself giving him aid. From here he arrived at Sinope and later Amisus with great difficulty.

(3) In the same year at Rome, Catiline was accused of incest, which it was argued he had committed with Fabia, a Vestal Virgin. Supported by the favor of Catulus, he escaped.

Lucullus had laid siege to Sinope with a view to taking it by storm. Seleucus, the arch-pirate, and Cleochares, the eunuch, who were in charge of its defense, after pillaging and burning it, abandoned it. Lucullus, disturbed by the slaughter

---

11 In crossing the Aesepus and Granicus rivers.
12 Not far from Lemnos, near a barren island.

within the ranks of the wretched enemy, in short order extinguished the fire which had been set to it. Thus, the wretched city alternately was destroyed by its enemies, and allies by whom it should have been defended, and was saved by those who ought to have destroyed it. Now M. Lucullus, who had succeeded Curio in Macedonia, received in surrender the entire nation of the Bessi whom he had attacked in war.

At the same time, Metellus, the praetor of Sicily, when he discovered that Sicily had been ruined by the very disgraceful praetorship of C. Verres, while Pyrganion, the arch-pirate, who, after defeating the Roman fleet had gained possession of the port of Syracuse, was lacerating it with nefarious plunderings and slaughters, quickly crushed the man in a naval and land battle and forced him to depart from Sicily. Besides, Lucullus crossed the Euphrates and the Tigris, and at the city of Tigranocerta[13] met Mithridates and Tigranes with a very small number of his own men and killed a large number of the enemy. Thirty thousand men are reported to have been killed in that battle. Tigranes barely escaped, accompanied by one hundred and fifty horsemen, after having thrown away his diadem and tiara lest he be recognized. At that time, envoys came as suppliants to Lucullus from almost the entire East. With winter close at hand, Lucullus went back through Armenia into Mesopotamia, and stormed and captured Nisibis, a city famous at that time in these parts.

(4) During these same days, pirates were scattered over all the seas, not only intercepting supply ships, but also laying waste to islands and provinces, and they were greatly increased in number by those who joined them because of the existing impunity for their crimes and by their eagerness for booty. These pirates, after the great devastation, indeed, which they had carried on by land and sea, were crushed by Cn. Pompey with remarkable speed.

---

13 A city in Armenia, in Arzanene; later renamed Martyropolis; its exact location is unknown. The battle was fought in 69 B.C.

At the same time, Metellus devastated the island of Crete for two years and, after a long war, overcame it and reduced it under his power, and he exchanged the laws of Minos for those of the Romans.

Later Pompey, the successor of Lucullus, in Lesser Armenia near Mount Dastarcum, surrounded the king's camp with a siege. The king made a sally with all his troops in the night, and then also decided to repel his pursuers by battle. Pompey prepared to follow them as they fled. Thus battle was joined in the night.[14] At that time, the moon had arisen at their backs. The royal troops, judging the nearness of the enemy by the length of their shadow, cast all their missiles in vain. The Romans, as it were, unharmed, later made an attack and without trouble conquered them. For of the royal army, forty thousand were killed or captured; of the Romans, a thousand were wounded, but barely forty were killed. The king, in the midst of the commotion of battle, slipped away in flight, and aided also by the benefit of a dim night escaped; and abandoned by all his friends, philosophers, historians, poets, and doctors, alone leading his horse over unfrequented paths and trembling at all the noises of the night, he made his way to a certain stronghold and thence pushed forward into Armenia. Pompey, intending to follow the king between the two rivers which rose from one mountain but different caverns, that is, the Euphrates and the Araxes, founded the city of Nicopolis for the aged people, the camp followers, and the sick who wished to stay there. He granted pardon to Tigranes when he entreated him. The army of Orodes,[15] king of the Albanians, and his prefects[16] he defeated in battle three times. Later, he was happy to receive letters from Orodes and gifts for the restoration of peace with the Albanians. He routed Artoces, the king of Iberia, in battle and received all Iberia

---

14 Known as the battle of Nicopolis, 66 B.C.
15 Called Oroeses by some Greek writers.
16 Pompey's army, after being divided, was quartered in separate camps, 66 B.C.

in surrender. Then, when he had reorganized and pacified Armenia, the Colchians, Cappadocia, and Syria, moving on from Pontus into Parthia to Ecbatana, the capital city of the Parthian kingdom, he arrived there on the fifteenth day.

(5) While Mithridates was celebrating the rites of Ceres in the Bosporus, so great an earthquake suddenly arose that great damage to the cities and the fields is said to have followed from it. At the same time, Castor, the prefect of Mithridates who was in command of Phanagorium, after slaying the king's friends, occupied the citadel and turned over the four sons of Mithridates to the Roman garrison. Mithridates, roused in his ire, blazed forth into crimes. For he killed many of his friends at the time, including his son, Exipodra, when already he had slaughtered Machares in another parricide. Pharnaces, another son of his, terrified by what had happened to his brothers, won over to his side the army sent to attack him, and presently led it against his father. Mithridates, when from the highest point in the wall he had begged his son in vain and saw him to be inexorable, as he was about to die is said to have exclaimed: 'Since Pharnaces orders me to meet my death, I beg you, gods of my native land, if you exist, that he himself may someday hear these words from his children.' And straightway going down to his wives, concubines, and daughters, he gave them all poison. When he himself was the last to drain this poison, and yet on account of the antidotes with which he had often obstructed his vitals against the poisonous juices, he could not be killed by the poison, and when he walked about to no purpose, if in some way at last the infused death driven thereby might run through the veins of his body, he summoned a Gallic soldier who was then running through a break in the wall and offered him his throat. Such an end of life did Mithridates have, and the man left us a most forceful argument for his way of thinking, the most superstitious man of all, as it is said, seventy-two years of age, always accompanied by philosophers and by men most skillful in the arts.

'If you exist,' he said, 'gods of my native land.' Thus that
man, by long worship and long investigation, had come to feel
that these gods who were thought to exist did not exist. A
king of much experience and ripe in age did not understand
that there was a true God to whose knowledge one does not
come except by listening to Him with faith. But that these
gods were false he had perceived by the light of reason itself,
conceding in some measure to custom and to some extent to
his own mentality. 'If you exist, O gods,' he says, thereby
meaning: 'O, feeling that there is above man, a power more
powerful than man himself, and moved by the necessity of
praying, I commend to him my earnestness and make apologies
for my ignorance. I invoke a God who exists, while I meet
with one who is not.' Thus we must consider with sorrow
and anxiety of what punishment or of what judgment are
they worthy who, contrary to a command of truth already
divulged and made public, follow and worship those gods
about whom already even they were able to doubt at that
time when they were able to know no divinity other than these
same gods. Nevertheless, I present a brief consideration. What
was the nature of the times in those days over the entire East
when, for forty years, the wretched nations were ground down
by the successive devastations of such great generals, when
every city in the midst of such combats was inevitably endangered, destined to inflame another enemy with what it
had temporarily tempered the first, presently about to suffer
that as a disaster which it had had as a temporary remedy;
when the fearful legations from different provinces, in the
midst of succeeding Roman generals and Mithridates who was
harsher than his reputation, were bringing to each, according
as the fortunes of war favored each, uncertain excuses exag-
gerating the dangers which they were trying to cure? For
what Pompey, indeed the most moderate person among the
Romans, immediately did throughout most of the regions
of the East, when the Mithridatic War was ended, I shall set
forth briefly.

(6) In the six hundred and eighty-ninth year after the
founding of the City, and in the consulship of M. Tullius
Cicero and C. Antonius, Pompey, when the news of the death
of Mithridates was received, invading Syria Coele, and Phoenicia, first overcame the Ituraei and the Arabians, and captured their city which they call Petra. Then he sent Gabinius
with an army against the Jews and against their city, Jerusalem, over whom Aristobulus, after the expulsion of his brother,
Hyrcanus, ruled as king, the first to succeed to this office after
the priesthood. Pompey himself immediately followed and
he was received in the city by the fathers, but, being driven
back by the people from the wall of the temple, he directed
his attention to its capture by storm. This temple, fortified
not only by the nature of the locale, but also by a great wall
and a very large ditch, although he forced legion after legion
to succeed one another day and night without rest, was barely
captured in the third month.[17] Thirteen thousand Jews are
reported to have been killed there, and the rest of the multitude entrusted themselves to the Romans. Pompey ordered
the walls of the city to be overturned and leveled with the
ground and, after he had executed a considerable number of
the leaders of the Jews, he restored Hyrcanus to the priesthood
and led Aristobulus to Rome as a captive. Pompey himself,
before the assembly of the Roman people, narrated the story
of his having waged this war in the East against twenty-two
kings.

Meanwhile, the conspiracy of Catiline against his fatherland
broke out and was betrayed at this same time, but in Etruria
it was extinguished by a civil war. In Rome, the accomplices
in the conspiracy were put to death. But since Cicero carried
on the events of this history and Sallust described them, well
known to all, it is enough that the events be restricted by us
to a brief account. A rebellion also was stirred up among the
Peligni by the Marcelli, father and son, and was betrayed by

---

17 63 B.C.

L. Vettius, and when the conspiracy of Catiline was detected it was crushed, as if cut off at the roots. Punishment was exacted in two places, among the Peligni by Bibulus, and among the Bruttii by Cicero.

(7) In the six hundred and ninety-third year after the founding of the City and in the consulship of C. Caesar and L. Bibulus, three provinces, Gallia Transalpina, Cisalpina, and Illyricum, together with seven legions, were granted by the Vatinian Law to Caesar for a period of five years; later the Senate added Gallia Comata.

This story Suetonius Tranquillus has unfolded most fully, important portions of which we have excerpted.

A certain Orgetorix, the chief of the Helvetii, stirred up the minds of the Helvetii to arms with the hope of invading all the Gauls. This was the bravest tribe of all the Gauls, especially for the reason that they were in almost perpetual warfare with the Germans, from whom they were separated only by the Rhine River. When he was seized and forced to kill himself, the rest of the nobles were unable to check the people once their minds had been made up for booty. These, when the conspiracy had been organized and the day set, after burning their villages and homes, lest there should arise any hopeful desire of returning home, set out. When Caesar had taken his stand before them at the Rhone River, in a great and difficult war,[18] he twice conquered and, after conquering them, forced them to surrender. Of these, when they first set out, the entire number of Helvetii, Tulingi, Latobrigi, Rauraci, and Boii, including both sexes, amounted to about one hundred and fifty thousand persons. Of these, forty-seven thousand fell in battle, the rest were sent back to their own territories.

Later, Caesar won a victory among the Sequani against King Ariovistus[19] who was stirring up and winning over to

18 58 B.C., near Bibracte.
19 58 B.C., exact location is in doubt. Cf. T. Rice Holmes, *Caesar's Conquest of Gaul,* (Oxford, 1911) , pp. 636-657.

himself an incredible number of German troops, with whom he boasted that he had subjugated all the peoples of the Gauls, when Caesar's army, terrified by the number and courage of the Germans, had refused battle. Ariovistus, seizing a skiff and crossing the Rhine, escaped into Germany, but his two wives and the same number of daughters were captured. Now in the army of Ariovistus were the Harudes, Marcomanni, Triboci, Vangiones, Nemetes, Sedusii,[20] and Suebi. A battle took place, very severe on account of the phalanx of the Germans, which, with their battle line drawn closely together and their shields interlocked over their heads, safe from all sides, they had prepared for breaking the attack of the Roman battle line. After some Roman soldiers, distinguished for their agility and daring, leaped upon the overspread *testudo* and tore away the shields, one by one as if they were scales, and pierced the bare shoulders of the enemy from above, caught unawares and without a covering, the enemy, terrified by this new danger of death, broke up the terrifying formation. Then, turning into flight for fifty miles, they were killed in a manner that could not be satisfied, and the number of Germans present in the battle or the number killed could not be conjectured.

After all this, the tribe of the Belgae, which represents a third part of the Gauls, rose in rebellion against Caesar. Their forces were distributed as follows: The Bellovaci, who seemed to excel the rest in number and bravery, had sixty thousand picked troops; the Suessiones, fifty thousand from twelve towns; the Nervii, whose ferocity was so publicly known that never up to that time did they permit merchants to bring into their presence wine and other saleable goods by which pleasure might be introduced and bring a numbness to their courage, likewise, had fifty thousand. The Atrebates and Ambiani also had ten thousand; the Morini, twenty-five thousand; the Menapii, nine thousand; the Caleti, ten thousand; the Velocasses and Veromandui, each ten thousand; the Aduatuci,

---

20 The text reads Eduses and not Sedusii.

eighteen thousand; and the Condrusi, Eburones, Caerosi, and Paemani, who were called by one name, Germans, forty thousand. Thus they were reported to have been two hundred and seventy-two thousand picked soldiers. When these suddenly rushed out of the forest, Caesar's army was thrown into a panic and forced into flight, losing a great many of its men. Finally, under the encouragement of its leader, the Roman army stood its ground and, attacking the victors, slew them almost to the last man.[21]

(8) So when Caesar, after accomplishing great deeds in Gaul, decided to proceed into Italy, he sent Galba with the twelfth legion against the Veragri and Seduni. When he had settled in a village of the Veragri which was called Octodurus, for the sake of spending the winter there, and had assigned to the inhabitants the middle part of the town which was separated by a rapid stream, he noticed one day that they had departed in the night and occupied a neighboring hill. For the Veragri, holding in contempt the small number of Romans, hardly a half a legion, thought that booty, of its own accord and without any trouble, would come into their hands, and they had invited their neighbors to share in the slaughter and booty. When Galba was thus terrified and surrounded by the immediate dangers, and was in doubt as to a definite plan in the midst of varying opinions, the Gauls, suddenly pouring down the slope of the mountain, surrounded the unfinished camp and with rocks and darts overwhelmed the defenders stationed here and there along the ramparts. And when now the camp was broken into, on the advice of Pacuvius, the primipilar, and of Volusenus, the tribune, all the Romans burst forth from the gates and, attacking the enemy while off guard, first threw them into a panic and, then, turning them into flight, mercilessly slaughtered them. Now more than thirty thousand barbarians are reported to have been killed at that time.

---

21 57 B.C. Consult T. Rice Holmes, *op. cit.*, pp. 671-677.

Thus Caesar, when he thought that all the Gallic tribes had been pacified, was drawn back to a new and very great war. For while P. Crassus, a young man, was spending the winter by the Ocean among the Andicavi, the Veneti, and the other neighboring peoples, he suddenly formed a conspiracy and bound the Roman legates, indicating that they would return them to the Romans if they themselves should receive back their own hostages. As allies for that war, they received the Osismi, Lexovii, Namnetes, Ambivariti, Morini, Diablintes, and the Menapii; they asked for assistance also from Britain. When Caesar was informed by Crassus about the rebellion of tribes which had previously surrendered, although he realized how great the difficulty of entering upon a war was, yet thinking that an affair of so great importance ought not to be neglected lest the freedom to dare might be relaxed for the others by an example of this kind, and so having advanced to attack the enemy in a land battle in vain, for the enemy through the marshes flooded by the Ocean and through inaccessible retreats were protected by the safety furnished by the contour of the land, he ordered warships to be built on the Liger River,[22] by way of which they were floated down to the Ocean, and as soon as they were seen by the enemy, immediately two hundred and twenty ships made ready by the enemy and fitted out with every kind of armament, proceeded from their harbor[23] and took a position opposite the Romans. To Brutus, when he saw that a naval battle was on very unequal terms because the ships of the barbarians, joined by beams of solid oak and with hulls made tough by very strong holds like rocks, beat back the blows of the beaks of the opposing ships, the following was his first means of assistance. He prepared very sharp hooks fastened not firmly to poles but attached by ropes, with which, when there was need, they could catch hold

---

22 A river forming the boundary between Gallia Lugdunensis and Aquitania, now the *Loire*.
23 The mouth of the Auray River.

of the rigging from a distance and, by withdrawing the shafts and pulling in the hook by the cord, cut it down. When these contrivances were quickly made ready, he ordered his men to tear down the sailyards and the tackle of the ships of the enemy. Thus, with the sailyards crashed down, many of the ships were immediately rendered motionless as if they had been captured. Some, terrified by this danger, unfurled the sails where the wind was blowing and tried to escape, but, when presently they were abandoned by the wind, they became a laughing stock to the Romans. And so after all the ships had been set on fire and those Gauls who had engaged in battle had been killed, all the rest gave themselves up. But Caesar, chiefly because of the wrong done his ambassadors, and that he might imprint upon a people easily swayed to every proposal the mark of a terrible example, after he had killed all their chiefs with tortures, sold the rest into slavery. At the same time, Titurius Sabinus made a sortie and destroyed with incredible slaughter the Aulerci, Eburovices, and Lexovii,[24] who had killed their own leaders because they were unwilling to be responsible for renewing the war. But Publius Crassus, on arriving in Aquitania, was met with a battle. For the Sontiates, with a large force of cavalry and strong infantry troops, attacked the Romans and threw them into grave confusion for a long time; later, when they were conquered[25] and forced into the town of the Sontiates[26] and were besieged, since they saw that they were being overcome, they gave over their arms and were received in surrender. The Aquitani, alarmed by the slaughter, gathered an army from all sides. They also summoned assistance from Hither Spain. As commanders for the war, they appointed especially those who had served with Sertorius. While all these were preparing a siege for Crassus, he crushed and destroyed them in their own

---

24 Lexovii or Lexobii in Gallia Lugdunensis at the mouth of the Sequana; hence the name of the modern *Lisieux;* 56 B.C.

25 Near the source of the River Ciron.

26 Now the town of *Sos.*

camp.[27] For of the Aquitani and Cantabri, fifty thousand of whom at that time had come as auxiliaries, thirty-eight thousand are reported to have been killed. The Germans,[28] who had crossed the Rhine with immense forces and were preparing to bring all the Gauls under their subjection, were attacked by Caesar and utterly destroyed. It is reported that their number was about four hundred and forty thousand.

(9) Then Caesar constructed a bridge and crossed into Germany; he freed the Sugambri and Ubii from a siege, and by his coming terrified all Germany and the very largest and fiercest tribe, the Suebi, who, according to the report of many, had a hundred cantons and districts. Presently, he withdrew into Gaul after breaking down the bridge. From here he came to the Morini, from whom the crossing into Britain is very close and very short. After preparing about eighty transports and swift ships, he set sail[29] for Britain. Here, he was first reduced to weariness in a severe battle; then, caught by a disastrous storm, he lost part of his fleet,[30] no small number of soldiers, and almost all his cavalry. Returning to Gaul, he released his legions into winter quarters and ordered six hundred ships of both kinds to be built. With these, early in the spring, he was transported to Britain, and while he himself was proceeding against the enemy with the army, the ships riding at anchor were caught by a storm and, being either smashed against one another or dashed to pieces on the sands, were destroyed. Of these ships, forty were wrecked and the rest were repaired with great difficulty. In the first meeting with the Britons, Caesar's cavalry was defeated and there Labienus,[31] the tribune, was killed. In the second battle, with

---

27 56 B.C.

28 The Germans, i.e., the Usipetes and Tencteri. The exact place of the battle is uncertain.

29 August 25, 55 B.C., at Portus Itius (Iccius), now *Wissant* or *Witsand*, a few miles east of Cape Grisnez.

30 The reference here is probably to the cavalry transports which arrived some days later than the main body of troops.

31 Not Labienus but Quintus Laberius Durus.

great risk to his own men, he overcame the Britons and turned them into flight. From here he proceeded to the Thames River which, they say, is fordable at only one place. On the further bank of this river, under the leadership of Cassivellaunus, a large number of the enemy had taken their stand and had equipped almost the entire ford under the water with very sharp stakes. When this was detected and avoided by the Romans, the barbarians, being unable to endure the attack of the legions, hid themselves in the forest, whence by frequent sallies they often seriously harrassed the Romans. Meanwhile, the very powerful city of the Trinobantes and their leader, Mandubracius, after giving forty hostages, gave themselves over to Caesar. Several other cities, following this example, entered an alliance with the Romans, and, with these same people pointing the way, Caesar finally, with a severe battle, captured the town of Cassivellaunus which was situated between two marshes and protected by the overhead covering of the forest and was well filled with supplies of all kinds.

(10) Then Caesar, after he had returned from Britain into Gaul and had sent his legions into winter quarters, was beset and afflicted with the sudden uprisings of war from all sides. For, indeed, Ambiorix, forming a conspiracy with the Eburones and Aduatuci and inspired by the advice of the Treveri, laid an ambush for the legates, Cotta and Sabinus, together with their entire legion in the territory of the Eburones and utterly annihilated them.[32] Ambiorix, elated by this victory, quickly assembled the Aduatuci and the Nervii and many others for battle and hastened to Cicero, the legate, who at that time was in charge of the legion in winter quarters. The number of the enemy can be gathered from this incident, namely, since they were taught by Roman prisoners that in a siege of a camp a rampart should be built around it and since they had no farming instruments, by cutting the ground with their swords and carrying it away in their military cloaks,

---

32 In 54 B.C. at Aduatuca, between Maestricht and Louvain, modern *Tongres*.

within scarcely three hours they had made a rampart ten feet
high and a ditch fifteen feet wide over a distance of fifteen
miles in circumference. Besides, they erected twenty towers of
remarkable height. And when now the faltering wedge for-
mations of the enemy were fighting for seven days and nights
and a very strong wind suddenly arose, they hurled hot tiles
with their slings into the camp and threw darts aflame from
the heat and presently aglow from the fire which had been
started. When this had taken place, the breeze, pressing
violently through the straw thatch, fanned the fire which was
already spread about. But not even so did the Romans, although they were overwhelmed from all sides, yield to wounds,
hardships, long watches, hunger, and fire. Finally, a message
was given to Caesar that one legion had been wiped out and
that a second one was almost destroyed. When Caesar approached with two legions, the enemy abandoned the siege
and all, with their troops joined, rushed out to meet him.
Caesar by design hid himself in a very small camp, and he
ordered his cavalry which he had sent ahead to feign flight,
in order that this might induce the enemy, in their contempt
for him, to cross the intervening valley which appeared to him
to be dangerous. As the enemy approached, he also ordered
the gates to be barricaded. When the Gauls saw this, as if
they had already conquered, they turned about in order to
surround the rampart from without. Caesar suddenly poured
forth his army, all prepared, from every gate and, turning
them into flight, crushed them with very great slaughter. Now
there is said at that time to have been sixty thousand, of which
a few escaped through impassable swamps. Indutiomarus, the
chief of the Treveri, who had a large number of armed men,
on being assured of the accord of all Gaul, decided to destroy
the camp of Labienus and the legion over which he was in
command, something which he thought easy to do, and, then,
joining forces with the Eburones and the Nervii, to proceed
to overwhelm Caesar. Labienus, with all the trickery of which
he was capable, pretended that he was afraid and so with a

sudden sally crushed Indutiomarus who was rather careless
as he wandered in front of the rampart with his troops casting
insults. The remaining attempts of the Gauls were checked by
this victory of Labienus, and Caesar, for the remaining part
of the winter, was a little more peaceful. But Caesar, realizing
that greater troubles of war still existed for him, especially
since, with most of his army lost and the others seriously
wounded, he did not seem able even to withhold, not to say
check, an attack by the Gauls, asked Cn. Pompey, the proconsul, to enroll legions for him and send them to his aid.
And so before the winter was over, three legions came into his
camp. Therefore, Caesar, before the troops of the enemy
should come together, at the beginning of spring prepared
to attack the terrified enemy and to crush them while scattered
within their own territories. So, first of all, he ravaged the
territory of the Nervii, which was very rich and which he
permitted his army to plunder. Then, he attacked the Menapii
on three fronts, who seemed very well protected by immense
marshes and most impenetrable forests and, after inflicting
great slaughter on them in general, he received the remainder
in surrender as suppliants. Labienus, in a later battle, killed
all the troops of the Treveri, enticing them into battle by
trickery before they could join with the Germans who were
coming to their aid, and he immediately captured their city.
Caesar, wishing to avenge the death of his legates, Sabinus
and Cotta, after he learned that Ambiorix and the Eburones,
who had destroyed the legion, had taken refuge in the Arduenna Forest (this forest is the largest in all Gaul and extends
from the banks of the Rhine and the territories of the Treveri
up to the Nervii and in length spreads out for more than fifty
miles), calculating that the affair would be of very great
danger to his men if they, ignorant of the terrain, should be
dispersed and meet up with an enemy very well acquainted
with the territory, invited all Gaul by messengers to seek, according to their own pleasure, the plunder hidden in the Arduenna
Forest and ravage it. When this was done, with the Gauls

dying on all sides, he avenged the very great injuries done to the Romans without the risk of a single Roman. So by this very safe manner of conquering, Caesar returned to Italy without anxiety.

(11) So after Caesar had returned to Italy, Gaul again formed a conspiracy, and many peoples came together in it. Their leader was Vercingetorix, on whose advice all the Gauls immediately of their own accord set fire to their cities. The first city that was burned by its own people was Biturigo. Then the Gauls made an attack on Caesar, who, by forced marches through the province of Narbo, had returned secretly to his army. Caesar then shut off by siege a town by the name of Cenabum.[33] This was besieged for a long time, and finally, after heavy losses by the Romans, on a rainy day when the *agmenta* and thongs of the enemies' war machines slackened, by bringing towers into action, it was captured and destroyed. Forty thousand men are reported to have been involved there. Of these, eighty with difficulty slipped away and went to the nearest camp of the Gauls. Besides, the Arverni and other neighbors, (even the Aedui were won over to their cause) fought against Caesar in many battles. When the enemy wearied by fighting had withdrawn into a certain fortress, the soldiers eager for booty were intent on storming the town, although Caesar debated the matter in vain because of the unfavorableness of the terrain. So Caesar being hard pressed, with the enemy attacking from above, after losing a large part of his army, was overcome and fled. While these things were going on at Alesia, Vercingetorix, whom all with unanimous consent had preferred as king, persuaded everyone in all Gaul capable of bearing arms to be ready for service in war. For he said this was a war from which either perpetual liberty or everlasting slavery or death would result for all. And so, apart from that countless number which he had brought together before, about eight thousand horsemen and two hun-

---

33 Now *Orléans*.

dred and fifty thousand infantrymen were gathered. Then, the
Romans and the Gauls occupied two hills opposite each other.
From these positions, battling with frequent sorties and with
varying results, the Romans finally conquered, thanks to the
special bravery of the German horsemen whom, as long-stand-
ing friends, they had summoned to their aid. On another
day, Vercingetorix called all together who had escaped by
flight and said that he in good faith had been the author of
the plan for defending their freedom and for breaking the
treaty, and that now he was prepared for their decision,
whether they should all give themselves over to death at the
hands of the Romans or whether they would give himself
alone in the place of all. And so the Gauls made known their
wish, which, out of shame, they had concealed for a long time;
as if they had made the decision on the advice of the king,
immediately begging pardon for themselves, they gave him
over alone as the author of the great crime. The Bellovaci,
in the opinion of the Gauls themselves, were held braver than
all the other Gallic tribes. These, under the leadership of
Correus, renewed the war and took into their alliance for
taking up the war the Ambiani, the Aulerci, Caleti, Velocasses,
and the Atrebates, and they occupied a position surrounded
and protected on all sides by marshes and, when the battle
was joined, they slew a large band of the Remi who were
auxiliaries of the Romans. Then, when they themselves had
occupied a favorable position, well suited for ambushes, and
when the Romans learned of this and, drawn up and arranged
for battle, had come to the place of ambush, joining battle
they surrounded the Gauls as they fled by the same fortifications as those by which they had been enclosed, and killed
all to a man. Then Correus, disparaging either flight or
surrender, forced the Romans, intent on capturing him alive,
to put him out of the way by killing him. So when Caesar
thought that all Gaul had been pacified and would not dare to
aspire to any revolutions, he dismissed his legions into winter
quarters, but he himself laid waste the territory of Ambiorix,

who had stirred up so many wars, with a horrible slaughter of the inhabitants. But C. Caninius,[34] the legate, came upon a war among the Pictones, where a large number of the enemy surrounded the legion while encumbered on the journey and reduced it to the last extremity. But Fabius, the legate, on receiving a letter from Caninius, proceeded against the Pictones, and there, being informed by captives about the nature of the locale, he rushed upon the unsuspecting enemy and, while carrying on great slaughter, took away a great deal of plunder. Then, after he had given Caninius a sign of his arrival, Caninius suddenly rushed out from all parts of the camp and threw himself with his men upon the enemy. Thus, when Fabius pressed the attack on one side and Caninius on the other, in a very great and long battle, a countless number of Gallic troops were slaughtered. Then Fabius set out against the Carnutes, for he knew that Domnacus, a very old leader and instigator of the whole rebellion, had escaped from that battle, and, if he should join with the Aremorican peoples, he would again set very great upheavals in motion in Gaul. But while these tribes were still in trepidation over the newness of his tactics, by marvelous courage and swiftness, Fabius overcame them. Meanwhile, Draptes and also Lycterius, when they saw that Caninius and his legions were present in their territories, collecting troops from all sides, occupied Uxellodunum.[35] This town was located on the highest peak of a mountain and was surrounded on two sides by precipitous slopes and a river of considerable size, then, made secure by a very large spring in the middle of the slope and safe by a very great supply of grain within, it looked with contempt at the futile maneuvers of the enemy afar off. Caninius, as he was able to do only by Roman foresight, enticed the two generals into the plain with the largest portion of their troops and in a very great battle overcame them. For when one of

---

34 Gaius Caninius Rebilus.
35 Uxellodunum, a town in Aquitaine, in the territory of the Cadurci, now *Capdenac.*

the two leaders had been killed, the other fled with a very few men; no one returned to the town. But to take this town by storm, there was need of Caesar. So when Caesar was informed of the situation, he hastened to the place and, viewing all things, saw that if he should endeavor to take the town by force, his army would be destroyed to the joy and ridicule of the enemy, that there was only one source of help, namely, if the enemy in any way whatsoever should be deprived of their water supply. But this also Caesar could not have accomplished, if the spring, which they used for drinking water, continued to pour forth from the middle of the side of the sloping mountain. Caesar ordered sheds to be moved as near as possible to the spring and a tower to be built. Immediately, a great gathering took place from the town. Since these fought without danger to themselves, the Romans, although they resisted stubbornly and made frequent advances, in spite of this were killed in great numbers. So a rampart was erected and a tower sixty feet high, the top of which could be on a level with the location of the spring, so that missiles could be thrown on the same level and the rolling rocks cast from above need not be feared. But the townsmen, on seeing that not only their flocks but also their more elderly people were dying of thirst, filled tubs with grease, pitch, and shingles and, then, having set them afire, sent them tumbling down the slope and they themselves pouring forth from the whole town followed closely behind. When Caesar, as his machines caught fire, saw that the battle was serious and dangerous for his men, ordered cohorts to go around the town swiftly and secretly and suddenly to raise a great shout from all sides. When this was done, the townsmen, becoming frightened and wishing to run back to the defense of the town, withdrew from the attack on the tower and the demolition of the rampart. But the Romans, who, to cut off the water courses of the spring, were extending the passages under the safe protection of the rampart, found the hidden channels of water and, by dividing them into many different streams, caused the spring to be weakened in itself and to be used up. The townspeople, with their spring dried up, were seized with ultimate desperation and effected a surrender. Caesar, moreover, cut off the hands of all who had borne arms and spared their lives, that posterity might have the punishment of the wicked made clearer. For an example of the punishment strongly set forth is able to check audacity, since the very presence of the wretched left alive acts as a reminder for those who know and causes those who do not know to investigate.

(12) Since the Gauls were exhausted and thoroughly subdued, Caesar with his legions returned in safety to Italy, fearing no revolutions on the part of the Gauls behind him, knowing with certainty that he had left very few who had the daring to revolt or, if they should revolt, were to be feared. I would like now to set before your eyes a Gaul, drained of blood and crushed after those extremely burning fevers and internal fires had scorched the very vitals that sustained her, how emaciated and how pale she was, how dejected and enervated she lay, and how she also feared the very activities of necessary business lest they bring back the same inroad of evils. For the Roman army rushed upon it with a sudden attack like a plague, stronger than a very strong body, which blazes up the more seriously the more patiently it is endured. Wretched Gaul panted when, at the point of a sword, she was forced to profess a promise of eternal slavery, with her hostages in addition torn from her; she panted, as I have said, for that sweetness of liberty well known to all and so delightful, as for a draught of cold water, and the more she realized that it was being taken from her, the more eagerly did she desire it. Hence, that presumption so frequent against the forbidden things: an ill-timed freedom seized her to defend her liberty and insatiably to regain that liberty which had been wrested from her, which seemed not to extinguish the naturally conceived pestilence but to increase it. Hence, the Roman was the more cunning plotter before battle; hence, the more dangerous in battle; hence, the more ruthless victor after battle;

hence, all things were growing worse for the controling of impatience; and hence, there was no longer any belief in remedies.
And so, if I were able to question this nation, about which we
are speaking, as to what she thinks of those times when she was
enduring these very difficulties, she would, as I think, reply
saying: 'That fever has rendered me so feeble and made me
so cold that even this present change, which has touched
almost all, has been unable to warm or to rouse me, and the
Romans have so turned me back that I cannot rise against the
Goths.' But not even Rome itself has avoided the disasters
which she has inflicted. The powers of the military leaders
and the force of the legions have for a long time been so
exercised and increased in every corner of the world that,
when they came into conflict, they conquered with injury to
Rome by whose danger they were conquered. For when
Caesar returned from Gaul as victor civil wars followed,
preceded by other very serious evils, the murder of Crassus
among the Parthians and the slaughter of his army.

(13) In the six hundred and ninety-seventh year after the
founding of the City, Crassus, a colleague of Pompey in the
consulship, obtained by lot the command against the Parthians.
A man of insatiable cupidity, when he heard of the riches
in the temple of Jerusalem which Pompey had left untouched,
he turned aside into Palestine and came to Jerusalem; he
passed through the temple whose riches he plundered. Then,
turning his route through Mesopotamia into Parthia, and,
wherever his road led, he requisitioned auxiliaries from allied
states and exacted tribute. As soon as he crossed the Euphrates,
straightway he met Vageses, who had been sent to him as a
legate by Orodes, king of the Parthians, and was vehemently
rebuked because, led by avarice, he had crossed the Euphrates
contrary to the treaty of Lucullus and Pompey. Therefore,
Vageses said that Crassus would before long be burdened with
Chinese iron rather than with Parthian gold. Thus, when the

Romans had come near Carrhae,[36] the Parthians, under the leadership of the prefects, Surenas and Silaces, rushing forward suddenly, overwhelmed the Romans with arrows. There many senators, and also some of consular and praetorian rank, fell. Also Crassus, the son of Crassus, a very distinguished youth, was killed in battle. Besides, four cohorts with the lieutenant, Vargunteius, were caught in the midst of open country and slain. Surenas, suddenly taking his cavalry, hastened to follow Crassus and surrounded him, and, while Crassus was asking in vain for a conference, he slew him, although he would have preferred to have carried him off alive. A few with the help of the night escaped and took refuge in Carrhae. When this disaster of the Romans became known, many provinces of the East would have withdrawn from the alliance and protection of the Roman people had not Cassius, gathering a few soldiers from their flight, with exceptional bravery, spirit, and moderation checked Syria which was becoming uneasy. He overcame Antiochus and his mighty forces in battle and killed him; he also drove off the Parthians, which had been sent by Orodes into Syria and were already marching into Antioch, and killed their leader, Osages.

(14) Thus, the status of Rome is constantly disturbed by alternating changes and is like the level of the Ocean, which is different every day, and is raised for seven days by increases growing less daily, and in the same number of days is drawn back by the natural loss and internal absorption. To begin with events that follow next, when a Roman army perished at the Rhone River before the conquering Cimbri and Tigurini, Rome felt herself to be in very narrow straits, and when the slaughter by the Cimbri was immediately halted, she became elated by her great successes, forgetful of her former failures. Then the Italic War and the slaughter by Sulla checked her boasting about her very recent good fortune. Furthermore, after this domestic and internal disaster, by

---

36 Carrhae or Carrae, a city of Mesopotamia, the Charain or Haran of Scriptures.

which she was almost disemboweled and devoured to the very marrow, in almost an equal space of time, it was not only restored but was also extended, when Lucullus subdued Asia, Pompey Spain, Caesar Gaul, and thus the Roman Empire was extended almost to the outermost boundaries of the earth. A very vast disaster now followed this very wide expansion. For among the Parthians, the Roman consul was killed and his army destroyed, and that most terrible civil war between Pompey and Caesar was started, and in the midst of all this Rome itself was swept by fire and consumed.

In the seven hundredth year after the founding of the City, it is uncertain whence the fire took form and attacked the largest part of the City, and it is said that never before had the City been swept and laid waste by so great a fire. For it has been handed down by tradition that fourteen sections of the City, together with the Iugarian section, were destroyed. From this point, the Civil War now begins, which had long been in preparation by great dissensions and movements.

(15) For Caesar, on returning as victor from Gaul, demanded that a second consulship be voted him while absent. This was denied by the consul, Marcellus, with Pompey's support; then it was decreed by the Senate that Caesar should not come into the City without first disbanding his army, and on the authority of the consul, Marcellus, Pompey was sent with the imperium to the legions which were near Luceria. Caesar betook himself to Ravenna. M. Antony and P. Cassius, tribunes of the people, interceding in Caesar's behalf and being opposed by the consul, Lentulus, were barred from the Curia and the Forum, and proceeded to Caesar accompanied at the same time by Curio and Caelius. Caesar, after he had crossed the Rubicon River and as soon as he had come to Ariminum, informed the five cohorts, which at that time were all he had, and with which, as Livy says, he was attacking the whole world, what it was necessary to do. Deploring the injuries done him, Caesar publicly stated that the cause of the Civil War was the restoration of the tribunes to the fatherland.

Then, through Antony, he received from Lucretius the seven cohorts which were tarrying at Sulmo, and the three legions which were tarrying with Domitius at Corfinium he transferred to his party. Pompey and all the Senate, being alarmed at the increasing forces of Caesar, driven from Italy, as it were, crossed over into Greece and selected Dyrrachium as the base for carrying on the war. Caesar went to Rome and, after breaking down the doors of the treasury, seized the money which had been refused him, and took away from the treasury four thousand one hundred and thirty-five pounds of gold and almost nine hundred thousand pounds of silver. From here he departed to his legions at Ariminum; then, crossing the Alps, went to Massilia, to storm which, because it had not received him, he left Trebonius with three legions, and hastened to the Spains, which L. Afranius, M. Petreius, and M. Varro, Pompey's generals, were holding with their legions. After overcoming Petreius and Afranius there in many battles, he made a pact with them and dismissed them. In Further Spain, moreover, he took two legions from M. Varro. His generals were likewise successful; that is, Curio drove Cato out of Sicily, Valerius ejected Cotta from Sardinia, and Varus expelled Tubero from Africa. Caesar, on returning to Massilia, which had been overcome by a siege, sacked it of everything, leaving to its inhabitants only their lives and freedom.

But Dolabella, of Caesar's party, was overcome in Illyricum by Octavius and Libo, and, deprived of his troops, fled to Antony. Basilus and Sallustius, each with the legions over which they were in command, likewise Antony, and also Hortensius, rushing with his fleet from the lowest part of the sea (i.e., the Etruscan Sea), all alike proceeded against Octavius and Libo and were conquered. When Antony, with fifteen cohorts, had given himself over to Octavius all were led over to Pompey by Libo. Curio crossed over from Sicily into Africa with an army; King Juba immediately received and slaughtered him together with all his troops. While Octavius was trying to take Salonae by storm, he lost almost all the troops that he was commanding. Caelius withdrew from Caesar and joined with Milo in exile, and both, with a band of slaves, tried to take Capua by storm and were killed. Bibulus, being overcome with shame at Corcyra because the enemy had made a laughingstock of the defenses which he had extended by the sea and the town, wore himself out from lack of food and long watches. Appius Claudius Censorinus, who at Pompey's order was guarding Greece, wished to test the good faith of the Pythian oracle which had already been discredited, for the prophetess, being forced by him to descend into the grotto, is said to have replied on being consulted about war: 'Roman, this war does not concern you; you will obtain the Coela of Euboea.' Now they call the Euboic Gulf Coela. So Appius departed, made unsure by the perplexing prophecy.

That consultor reminds me to consider something raised by our critics. They especially complain that their sacred rights have been forbidden them because of the Christian faith and they have been deprived of their rites and ceremonies and, especially on this account, because when the consultation of entrails and prophecies ceased, future disasters, since they could not be known, were not avoided. Why, then, long before the reign of Caesar and the birth of Christ, as their own authors bear witness, had the good faith of the Pythian oracle come to an end? Now, it had come to an end because it was despised. Furthermore, why was it despised, if not because it was false, or without foundation, or dubious? Therefore, wisely did the poet forewarn:

'They depart without advice and hate the seat of the Sibyl.'[37]

And let them not by chance consider it of little importance that the oracle was abolished out of contempt and became out of date, that is, both the divinity and its seat. It was that Pythian Apollo who, they say, when the great Pythian died, the author and chief of all divination, appeared as the heir of

---

37 Vergil, *Aeneid* 3.452.

the seat, the divination, and the name, and that he chose to render responses there where divination itself, along with the author, seemed to have originated; furthermore, throughout other parts of the world also with foaming mouths and mad discourse all the madness of maddened beings belches forth, to whom many of the kings of the world rushed as if to the living voice of a divinity to be consulted, to whom also the Romans often sent the richest gifts. And if this Pythian Apollo, with a slow infiltration of knowledge, is left with ill-repute and abandoned, what can be hoped for that is alive from a dead animal, what that is true from a mad woman? What, finally, 'when the Tuscan at the altars has blown his ivory pipe,'[38] after the intestines of a fat animal have been laid bare, will the oracle, eager for gain, not invent, if, as they themselves confess, Apollo leads one astray either by speaking obscurely or falsely? Therefore, let them endure with equanimity, although they are unwilling meanwhile to imitate us, that we, by a true judgment, prohibit that also which their forefathers by experience have been able to despise.

Meanwhile, many kings of the Orient joined Pompey at Dyrrachium with auxiliaries. When Caesar had arrived there, he vainly surrounded Pompey with a siege, blockading him on the land side with a ditch fifteen miles long, although the seas were open to him. Pompey overthrew a citadel near the sea which Marcellinus was guarding, and killed Caesar's garrison which was staying there. Caesar went forth to attack Torquatus and his one legion. Pompey, on learning of this danger to his allies, gathered all his troops at that point, against whom Caesar immediately turned, abandoning the siege. Torquatus, however, rushed forth immediately and attacked the rear guard. So Caesar's soldiers, terrified by the double danger, fled although Caesar himself in vain stood in their way. But Pompey, on the testimony also of Caesar, as victor called off his pursuing army. Four thousand of Caesar's

---

38 Cf. Vergil, *Georgics* 2.193.

soldiers, twenty-two centurions, and many Roman cavalry were killed in that battle. Then Caesar, by a forced march, proceeded through Epirus into Thessaly, and Pompey with a very large force followed and joined battle. And so a battle was drawn up on both sides. Pompey stationed eighty-eight cohorts in a triple arrangement. There were, moreover, forty thousand infantrymen and six hundred cavalry in the left wing; in the right wing five hundred, besides many kings, a great many senators and Roman knights, not to mention a large force of light-armed men. Caesar, likewise, arranged eighty cohorts in a triple line. He had less than thirty thousand infantrymen and a thousand horsemen. It was, indeed, a sight to bemoan, the concentrated Roman forces drawn up on the plains of Pharsalia for mutual slaughter, which, if harmony had reigned among them, no peoples and no kings could have endured. At the first encounter Pompey's cavalry, being driven back, left its left wing exposed. Then, when slaughter was carried on for a long time and the result was in doubt, and on one side Pompey, while urging his soldiers on, was saying, 'Spare the citizens' and yet not doing so, and Caesar, on the other side, was doing this: pressing his men on saying, 'Soldier, hit him in the face,' finally, all Pompey's army fled and his camp was plundered. There were slain in this battle fifteen thousand of Pompey's troops and thirty-three centurions. This was the outcome of the battle at Palaeopharsalus. Pompey, while fleeing, fell upon a merchant vessel at the mouth of the Peneus River and crossed into Asia. From here, by way of Cyprus, he went into Egypt, and there, as soon as he reached shore, by order of the youthful Ptolemy to gain the favor of the victorious Caesar, he was killed. Pompey's wife and children fled. The rest of Pompey's fleet was laid waste and all who were in it were slaughtered, and there also Pompey Bithynicus was killed. But Lentulus, a man of consular rank, was slain at Pelusium. Caesar, after arranging his affairs in Thessaly, went to Alexandria, and when the head and ring of Pompey were brought to him and he beheld them, he burst into tears, and when he had withdrawn into the royal palace, he was cheated by the custodians from receiving the money, for they had cunningly despoiled their own temples in order that they might show that the royal treasury was empty and that they might incite the people with hatred for Caesar. Furthermore, the royal commander, already stained with Pompey's blood, planned the death of Caesar also. For when ordered to disband the army, consisting of twenty thousand armed men, over which he was in command, he not only spurned the order, but even drew up his men in battle order. In the battle itself, the royal fleet, which by chance was drawn up on shore, was ordered to be burned. This flame, when it spread also to a part of the city, burned four hundred thousand books which happened to be stored in a building nearby, indeed, a special monument to the zeal and interest of our ancestors, who had gathered together so many and such great works of distinguished minds. Regarding this matter, although today there exist in temples book chests which we ourselves have seen, and, when these temples were plundered, these, we are told, were emptied by our own men in our time, which, indeed, is a true statement; nevertheless, it is believed more honorably that other books were collected to emulate the ancient interests in studies rather than that there was another library at that time which is believed to have existed in addition to the four hundred thousand volumes and for that reason to have escaped destruction. Caesar afterwards captured the island where Pharos is located. Achillas went there with the Gabinian soldiers. A great battle was joined there, and a great number of Caesar's troops fell, and also all the slayers of Pompey were killed. Caesar, being hard pressed by the force of the attacking enemy, boarded a light boat. Presently, when this boat was weighed down by the weight of those who followed aboard and sank, with one hand raised aloft in which he held the charts, he swam two hundred yards to a ship, and presently, when forced into a naval encounter, by great good luck either sank the royal fleet or captured it.

(16) Caesar gave a warning to the people of Alexandria, who were entreating in behalf of their king, that the king should endeavor to try friendship with the Romans rather than arms; but, as soon as he was free, he immediately entered upon war, and straightway he, together with his entire army, was destroyed. For twenty thousand men are reported to have been slain in that battle, and twelve thousand, together with seventy ships of war, to have surrendered; five hundred on the side of the victors are said to have fallen. The king himself, a youth, being received into a skiff so as to flee, when many others jumped on, was submerged and killed. His body, on being washed ashore, was recognized by the evidence of a golden lorica. Caesar, after sending this lorica on ahead to Alexandria, forced all the Alexandrians in their despair to surrender and gave the kingdom of Egypt over to Cleopatra. Then, overrunning Syria, he conquered Pharnaces in Pontus. Now after he had come to Rome, and having been made dictator and consul, he crossed into Africa, and at Thapsus[39] he fought with Juba and Scipio and killed a large number of men there. The camps of both were ravaged; sixty elephants were captured. Cato committed suicide at Utica; Juba offered his throat to an assassin after offering him a price; Petreius transfixed himself with the same sword; and Scipio, in a ship in which while hastening to flee to Spain he was forced by the wind to return to Africa, killed himself. On the same ship, T. Torquatus was also slain. Caesar ordered the grandchildren of Pompey the Great to be killed and, at the same time, Pompey's daughter, and with these Faustus Sulla, Afranius, and his son, Petreius. Then he entered the City with four triumphs, and, after setting the affairs of the restored Republic in order, he immediately proceeded into the Spains against the sons of Pompey, and on the seventeenth day after he had departed from the City he arrived at Saguntum, and immediately waged many battles with varying results against the two Pompeys, Labienus, and Attius Varus. The last battle was waged at the

---

39 Now *Baltah*. In April, 46 B.C.

Munda River,[40] where the fighting took place with such great forces and the slaughter was so great that even Caesar, when his own veterans were not ashamed to give ground, seeing his own battle line cut to pieces and forced back, planned to anticipate by death the future disgrace of being conquered, when suddenly the army of the Pompeys, turning into flight, withdrew. Indeed, this battle was fought on the day on which Pompey, the father, had fled from the City to wage war, and for four years this Civil War thundered incessantly over the whole earth. T. Labienus and Attius Varus were slain in battle. Gnaeus Pompey escaped with a hundred horsemen. His brother, Sextus Pompey, after hurriedly bringing together no small band of Lusitani, joining battle with Caesonius was conquered and killed while in flight. The city of Munda was captured with difficulty when Caesar stormed it with a tremendous loss of men.

(17) Caesar returned to Rome, where, while he was attempting to make minor changes in the form of the government of the Republic contrary to the precedents of the forefathers, on the instigation of Brutus and Cassius, also with the knowledge of most of the Senate, he was stabbed twenty-three times and died. It is said that there were more than sixty accomplices in this conspiracy. The two Brutuses, C. Cassius, and other accomplices, with drawn daggers, withdrew into the Capitol. There was long deliberation as to whether the Capitol, together with the authors of the murder, should be burned. Caesar's body was seized by the people, driven on by grief, and was cremated in the Forum on a fire made from pieces of the tribunal benches.

Rome reckoned the extent of her kingdom by her misfortunes and, turning to her own destruction, laid claim to every individual nation in which she had conquered. To Asia, Europe, and Africa, I do not say to the three parts of the world but to every corner of these three parts, she exhibited

---

40 A river in Lusitania, between the Tagus and the Douro, now *Mondego*. On March 17, 45 B.C.

her gladiators, and to her enemies who were enjoying the holiday, she introduced a spectacle of vengeance that was pitiful. And yet it did not suffice that the very causes of troubles, together with their authors, had been destroyed; the recurring seeds germinated in the same field to cause immediately a great increase of disasters for those who harvest them with great sweat; the victor of the Civil War was killed by his fellow citizens; battle lines of conspirators were brought together for the slaying of one man. Now it was certain that Caesar, shamefully destroyed, could have had many avengers, but most of the nobility was joined together in a single chain of crime in order that so much material of evil might not be supplied by the magnitude of the war, but that it might be diminished by the brevity of the punishment. It is related that the famous Medea once sowed the teeth of a slain serpent, from which a crop suitable to the seed, armed men, emerged from the land, and they immediately slew one another in combat. Indeed, the fabrications of the poets imagined this; but when Caesar was killed, how many fully armed armies did Rome bring forth from his ashes! How many great wars did she stir up as a proof of his pitiful fertility, not to be read by youths, but to be viewed by peoples! And yet the beginning of all these evils was pride, from it civil wars blazed forth, from it they again multiplied. So not an unjust slaughter is theirs who strove after it unjustly, if the rivalry for power is both carried on and punished through them and in them, until those who have declined a partnership in power learn to endure another's power, and when the supreme power of the whole empire is reduced to one man, all submit to a far different mode of life, so that all humbly strive to please and not insolently to offend. But for so healthy a doctrine of humility there was need of a master. Thus opportunely, when the affairs of Augustus Caesar had been arranged, the Lord Christ was born, who, although he was in the image of God, humbly took on the image of a servant, so that, finally, at that time the teaching of humility became more appropriate, when, indeed, throughout the whole world the punishment of pride might be a warning to all.

(18) In the seven hundred and tenth year after the founding of the City, after Julius Caesar had been killed, Octavianus, who, in accord with the will of his uncle, Julius Caesar, had assumed his inheritance and his name and, likewise, on later taking over control of affairs, was called Augustus, as soon as he arrived in Rome, still a young man, dedicated his genius to civil wars. For, to unfold an accumulation of evils briefly, he carried on five civil wars: at Mutina, Philippi, Perusia, Sicily, and Actium. Of these, two, the first and the last, he waged against M. Antony, the second against Brutus and Cassius, the third against L. Antony, and the fourth against Sextus Pompey, the son of Cn. Pompey. Antony, after being pronounced an enemy by the Senate, shut in D. Brutus with a siege at Mutina. The consuls, Hirtius and Pansa,[41] and with these Caesar, were sent to liberate Brutus and to overcome Antony. Pansa, who arrived first, was caught in an ambush, and in the midst of the slaughter of his own men was himself also seriously wounded by a javelin and a few days later died from this same wound. Hirtius, who was bringing aid to his colleague, with a frightful massacre destroyed the great army of Antony. Caesar thus far had been protecting the camp. In a second battle against Antony, great losses were suffered on both sides. Then, in that place, Hirtius, the consul, was killed; Antony was conquered and fled, and victory was won by Caesar, to whom D. Brutus confessed taking part in the conspiracy which resulted in the assassination of Julius Caesar and poured forth prayers of repentance. Dolabella killed Trebonius, one of Caesar's assassins, at Smyrna. The Senate pronounced Dolabella an enemy. Both armies of the slain consuls obeyed Caesar. Afterwards, D. Brutus was captured by the Sequani in Gaul and killed. And Basilus, likewise one of the assassins, was killed by the hands of his own slaves. At the intercession of Lepidus, Caesar received Antony in his

---

41 Aulus Hirtius and Gaius Vibius Pansa.

favor and as pledge of his renewed favor took Antony's
daughter in marriage. Then, when they had reached the City
and a rumor about future proscription arose, C. Thoranius, a
man of praetorian rank, without fear of any such thing, was
killed in his own home by an attack of the soldiers, and many
others were slain. And so that unlimited slaughter might not
be carried on more widely and without restraint, the names of
one hundred and thirty-two senators were posted on a public
list, first, at the order and in the name of Lepidus, then, of
Antony, and, thirdly, of Caesar. Antony on his list proscribed his
enemy, Tullius Cicero; there also he placed the name of his
uncle, L. Caesar, and what increases the excessiveness of the
crime, while his mother was still alive; and there Lepidus added
to the same group of the proscribed L. Paulus, his brother.
Later, there was added to the number of the proscribed thirty
Roman knights. For a long time, many and varied murders took
place, and the homes of the proscribed were ransacked of everything and destroyed. But Dolabella in Syria carried on many
battles with Cassius, and when he was conquered by him, Dolabella committed suicide. Brutus and Cassius, after gathering
great armies, joined forces at Athens and laid waste all Greece.
Cassius attacked the people of Rhodes by land and sea and
forced them to surrender, leaving them nothing but their lives.
So Caesar and Antony pursued Brutus and Cassius into Macedonia with the great machines of war, and forced them to
commit suicide; although very clearly that battle was brought
to a conclusion, not by bravery on the part of Antony, but
by the good fortune of Caesar. For Caesar, being ill at that
time, when he had decided to stay in the camp to get some
rest, at the urging and entreaty of his physician, who confessed
that he had been warned by a dream to lead Caesar out of the
camp on that day for his safety's sake, with difficulty set out
into the open and presently his camp was captured by
the enemy. But Caesar's soldiers, in turn, captured the camp
of Cassius. Thus Brutus and Cassius, driven to desperation,
planned to commit untimely suicide before the end of the

battle.[42] For Cassius offered his head to the executioners who had been summoned, and Brutus his side. But at Rome, Fulvia, the wife of Antony and the mother-in-law of Caesar, exercised her mastery like a woman. It is uncertain in this change from the rank of a consul to that of a king whether she is to be numbered as the last of a declining power or the first of a rising power, certainly she was insolent even toward those through whom she was placed in a position to be insolent. For she attacked even Caesar with insults, factional strife, and plots after he returned to Brundisium. On being repulsed by him, she withdrew into Greece to Antony. When Sextus Pompey found himself listed among the number of the proscribed, he turned to piracy and laid waste the entire coast of Italy with slaughter and rapine. By seizing Sicily and forestalling the shipment of provisions, he brought famine to Rome. Presently, the triumvirs, not to say usurpers, Lepidus, Caesar, and Antony, made peace with him. But when Pompey, contrary to the pact, took over fugitives, he was regarded as an enemy. Mena, a freedman of Pompey, with a fleet of sixty vessels deserted to Caesar and at Caesar's command was himself in command of the same fleet. He and Statilius Taurus carried on a naval battle against Menecrates, a Pompeian general. Then Caesar himself fought a very bloody naval battle against these same Pompeians, but he immediately lost almost all his victorious fleet in shipwreck at Scylaceum. Ventidius routed the Persians and the Parthians who were making inroads into Syria in three very great battles, and he killed their king, Pacorus, in battle, indeed, on the day on which Crassus had been killed by the Parthians. Antony, after barely capturing one fort, made peace with Antiochus, that he himself might seem to have brought so important an affair to a conclusion. He placed Ventidius over Syria and ordered him to make war on Antigonus, who, at that time by chance, had vanquished the Jews and, after capturing Jerusalem, had

---

42 The Battle of Philippi, 42 B.C.

plundered the temple and had given over the kingdom to
Herod. Ventidius was immediately victorious over Antigonus
and received him in surrender. Mena, the freedman, returned to Pompey with six ships and, after being kindly
received by him, set fire to Caesar's fleet, although Caesar had
lately lost another fleet in a second shipwreck. The same
Mena later, on being overcome by Agrippa in a naval battle,
went over to Caesar with six triremes. For a third time,
Caesar left this deserter alone, permitting him only his life.
Then Agrippa fought a naval battle against Demochares and
Pompey between Mylae and the Liparian Islands and he was
victorious; and there at that time he sank or captured thirty
vessels, shattering the remainder. Pompey fled to Messana.
Caesar, meanwhile, crossed over to Tauromenium,[43] and
Pompey defeated him by a sudden attack. When many of his
ships had been sunk and a great number of his soldiers had
been lost, Caesar fled into Italy. And allowing no delay to
intervene, he returned into Sicily. And there he met Lepidus
coming from Africa to meet him, and Lepidus, by terrorizing,
threatening, and displaying arrogance, made good his claim
to the greater number of the troops. After a few days, Agrippa,
by order of Caesar who with his army drawn up was watching
from the shore, met Pompey in a terrific naval battle and was
victorious. For he either sank or captured one hundred and
sixty-three ships. Pompey with seventeen ships barely eluded
him and escaped. Lepidus, puffed up with great arrogance
because of his twenty legions, after he plundered Messana,
having turned it over to his soldiers, twice spurned Caesar
himself as he came toward him, and ordered rather that spears
be hurled at him. Caesar avoided these attacks by wrapping
a cloak around his left arm. Then, spurring his horse, he
returned to his own men, and drawing up his army went
against Lepidus, and after killing a few men, forced most
of the legions of Lepidus to go over to his side. Lepidus

---

43 Tauromenium or Taurominium, a town in the eastern part of Sicily
between Messana and Catana, now *Taormina*.

finally realized where his pride was leading him and, laying aside his military cloak and putting on a dark grey garment, he became a suppliant of Caesar's and obtained his life and his property, although condemned to perpetual exile. Taurus, Caesar's prefect, received in allegiance almost all of Sicily which had been sorely tried and frightened by warfare. Forty-four legions at that time were under the command of the one Caesar. The soldiers, rather arrogant because of their numbers, stirred up commotions for receiving grants of land; but Caesar, a man of great courage, discharged twenty thousand soldiers from service, restored thirty thousand slaves to their masters, and crucified six thousand whose masters did not exist. When Caesar entered the City in triumph, it was decreed by the Senate that he should have tribunician power for life. During these days from a commercial inn across the Tiber, a spring of oil burst forth and flowed throughout the whole day in a very large stream.

(19) Now after Antony had crossed the Araxes,[44] surrounded on all sides by every kind of misfortune, he, finally with difficulty, returned to Antioch with a few men. For although when conquered[45] by the great numbers of cavalry and archers, he always escaped from all the battles which he attempted in great numbers, thereafter, handicapped by the unexplored and unknown localities of the region, he was reduced by very serious hunger to eating unspeakable foods; a great many of his soldiers gave themselves up to the enemy. Then he passed over into Greece and ordered Pompey, who, after being conquered by Caesar, was preparing an army for war, to come to him with a few men. Pompey, fleeing from Antony's generals, Titius[46] and Furnius, and being frequently

---

44 Araxes, a river in Armenia Major on the border of Media; now the *Aras*.

45 According to Plutarch, *Antony* 50, although he won many victories, he could not follow them up because of lack of cavalry.

46 Marcus Titius, Antony's quaestor in the Parthian expedition, 36 **B.C.**, who hunted down Sextus Pompeius in the next year and had him murdered at Miletus.

beaten in land and naval warfare, was captured and a little later killed. Caesar subjugated and conquered Illyricum, Pannonia, and part of Italy in battle; Antony captured Arta-banes,[47] the king of Armenia, by treachery and guile, and binding him with a silver chain, forced him to reveal the royal treasures, and when the city in which the king had revealed that the treasures were hidden was captured, he carried off a large quantity of gold and silver. Elated by this money, he ordered war to be declared against Caesar and for divorce proceedings to be begun against Octavia, the sister of Caesar, his wife, and he ordered Cleopatra to meet with him from Alexandria. He himself set out for Actium,[48] where he had stationed his fleet, and when he found that almost a third of his rowers had died of hunger, without any emotion he said: 'Let only the oars be saved, for there will be no lack of rowers, as long as Greece has men.' Caesar, with two hundred and thirty beaked ships, set out from Brundisium for Epirus. But Agrippa, who had been sent ahead by Caesar, captured many merchant ships loaded with grain and arms on their way from Egypt, Syria, and Asia to the aid of Antony, and passing through the Peloponnesian Gulf, captured the city of Mothona, defended by a very strong garrison of An-tony's. Then he captured Corcyra; pursuing the fugitives in a naval battle, he routed them and, after carrying out many very bloody actions, he went to Caesar. Antony, becoming alarmed at the desertion and hunger of his men, decided to hasten the war, and suddenly drawing up his troops proceeded to Caesar's camp and was conquered. On the third day after the battle, Antony moved his camp to Actium,[49] prepared to bring matters to an issue in a naval battle. Caesar had two hundred and thirty beaked ships and thirty without beaks,

---

47 i.e., Artavasdes I, on being invited to visit the camp of Antony, was seized by him in 34 B.C. Contrary to Roman custom, Antony spared his life, but later he was put to death by Cleopatra.
48 A promontory and town in Epirus on the Ambracian Gulf, now *La Punta.*
49 The battle took place in 31 B.C.

triremes equal to Liburnian ships in speed, and eight legions stationed on board the fleet, besides five praetorian cohorts. Antony's fleet consisted of one hundred and seventy ships; inferior in number they excelled in size, for in height they were ten feet above the sea. This battle at Actium was renowned and great. From the fifth hour until the seventh, most serious slaughter was inflicted on both sides with hope of conquering remaining uncertain; the remainder of the day and the following night inclined toward a victory for Caesar. Queen Cleopatra was the first to flee with sixty very swift vessels; Antony also, pulling down the standard of the praetorian ship, followed his wife as she fled. When presently daybreak came, Caesar completed his victory. Of the conquered, twelve thousand are reported to have fallen, six thousand were wounded, of whom a thousand died in spite of the care given them. Antony and Cleopatra decided to send the children born of their union, together with part of the royal treasure, on ahead to the Red Sea; they themselves, after disposing troops about the two horns of Egypt, Pelusium[50] and Paraetonium,[51] prepared a fleet and troops for a renewal of the battle. Caesar, who had been named imperator for the sixth time and consul for the fourth time, together with M. Licinius Crassus, went to Brundisium. There he divided his legions and arranged garrisons for the world. From here he set out for Syria and soon approached Pelusium, where he was welcomed by Antony's troops of their own accord. Meanwhile, Cornelius Gallus, sent on ahead by Caesar, received in allegiance the four legions which Antony had stationed at Cyrene as a garrison, and then, after first defeating Antony, he captured Paraetonium, the first city of Egypt from the side of Libya, and straightway he again defeated him at Pharos.[52]

---

50 An Egyptian city at the eastern mouth of the Nile, modern *Castle of Tineh.*

51 A seaport town in Northern Africa, between Egypt and the Syrtes, now *Marsa Labeit.*

52 An island near Alexandria in Egypt, where King Ptolemy Philadelphus built a famous lighthouse, now *Faro.*

Antony entered a cavalry battle against Caesar; in this also he was wretchedly conquered and fled. On the Kalends of August at dawn, when Antony was going down to the harbor to draw up his fleet, all his ships suddenly went over to Caesar, and when he was deprived of his only protection, in fear with a few companions, he withdrew to the royal palace. Then, as Caesar threatened and the city was in panic, Antony transfixed himself with a sword and was carried half dead to Cleopatra in a tomb in which Cleopatra had betaken herself determined to die. Since Cleopatra realized that she was being saved for the triumph, seeking death of her own free will, was found dead, bitten, it is believed, on the left arm by the fangs of a snake, although Caesar immediately summoned the Psylli, who are accustomed to withdraw and suck out the poison of snakes from men's wounds. Caesar, as victor, gained possession of Alexandria, by far the richest and greatest of all cities. For Rome was so increased in its wealth that, on account of the abundance of money, the prices of property and other saleable goods were fixed at double the amount that they had been hitherto. By Caesar's order the following were killed: the elder son of Antony and P. Canidius, indeed, always a most bitter enemy of Caesar's and even unfaithful to Antony, and Cassius Palmensis, the last victim to pay for the murder of his father, Caesar, and Q. Ovinius, chiefly for this ignominy, because most unfittingly he had not been ashamed, a senator of the Roman people, to supervise the queen's spinning and weaving. Then Caesar with his infantry went into Syria, and withdrew into Asia to winter quarters, and afterwards proceeded through Greece to Brundisium.

(20) In the seven hundred and twenty-fifth year after the founding of the City, when the emperor himself, Caesar Augustus, for the fifth time, and L. Apuleius were consuls, returning from the East as victor, on the sixth of January entered the City with a triple triumph and, then, for the first time, since all civil wars had been put to sleep and been ended, he himself closed the gates of Janus. On this day, Caesar was

first saluted as Augustus, which name had been held inviolate up to that time by all, and up to the present had not been presumed by other rulers, and declares that the supreme power to rule the world is lawful. From this same day, the highest power in the state began to be in one man and has remained so, which the Greeks call monarchy.

Furthermore, there is no believer, or even one who contradicts the faith, who does not know that this is the same day, namely, in the sixth of January, on which we observe the Epiphany, that is, the Apparition or the Manifestation of the Sacrament of the Lord. Neither reason nor the opportunity demand that we now speak more fully about this sacrament which we observe most faithfully, so that we seem neither to have left it to interested inquirers nor to have pressed it upon the indifferent. But it was proper to have recorded this event faithfully for this reason, that in every respect the Empire of Caesar might be proven to have been prepared for Christ's coming.

For when, in the first place, returning from Apollonia after his uncle, C. Caesar, had been murdered, Augustus entered the City, at about the third hour, though the sky was clear and cloudless, a circle in the appearance of a rainbow appeared around the orbit of the sun, as if to point out Augustus as the one and the most powerful man in this universe and the most renowned man in the world, in whose time He was to come who alone had made the sun itself and the whole world and was ruling them.

Then when, in the second place, Augustus, after receiving the legions of Pompey and Lepidus in Sicily, had restored thirty thousand slaves to their masters and independently had distributed forty-four legions in his Empire for the protection of the world, and, after entering the City with an ovation, had decreed that all the former debts of the Roman people should be remitted and the records of account books also be restored, in those very days, a most abundant spring of oil, as I expressed it above, flowed for a whole day from an inn. What

is more evident than that by this sign the future nativity of
Christ was declared in the time when Caesar was ruling the
whole world? For Christ is interpreted as 'anointed' in the
language of His people among whom and from whom He was
born. And so, when at that time in which the tribunician
power was decreed to Caesar forever a spring of oil flowed for
a whole day in Rome, signs in the heavens and prodigies on
earth revealed that under the principate of Caesar and under
the Roman Empire throughout a whole day, namely, throughout the duration of the entire Roman Empire, Christ and
from Him, Christians, that is, the Anointed One and from
Him, the anointed ones, would come forth in abundance and
without cessation from an inn—from the hospitable and boun-
tiful Church; that all slaves who, however, acknowledged their
master should be restored by Caesar, and the others who were
found without a master should be given over to death and
punishment; and that the debts of sins should be remitted
under Caesar in that City in which the oil had flowed spon-
taneously.

Then, thirdly, when he entered the City in triumph as
consul for the fifth time, on that very day which we have mentioned above, he himself had the gates of Janus closed for
the first time after two hundred years and assumed that most
famous name of Augustus. What can more faithfully and
truthfully be believed and recognized, when peace, name, and
day concur in such a manifestation, than that this man had
been predestined, indeed, by a hidden order of events for the
service of His preparation, who, on that day on which a little
later He was to be made manifest to the world, chose the
banner of peace, and assumed the name of power.

What happened on his fourth return, when, after com-
pleting the Cantabrian War and pacifying all nations, Caesar
sought the City again, will be set forth in better order to bear
witness to the faith which we practice.

(21) In the seven hundred and twenty-sixth year after the
founding of the City, when the emperor, Augustus Caesar,

was consul for the sixth time and M. Agrippa for the second time, Caesar realizing that little had been accomplished over two hundred years in Spain, since he allowed the Cantabri and the Astures, the two bravest peoples of Spain, to enjoy their own laws, opened the gates of Janus and himself proceeded with an army into the Spains. The territory of the Cantabri and Astures is a part of the province of Gallaecia, where the extended range of the Pyrenees Mountains leads to the north not far from the second ocean. These peoples, who were not only prepared to guard their own freedom but also dared to take away that of their neighbors, were devastating the lands of the Vaccaei, Turmogidi, and the Autrigones by incessant raids. So Caesar established a camp at Segisama,[53] embracing nearly all of Cantabria with three armies. After his army had been wearied in vain and often led into danger, Caesar finally ordered a fleet to be moved up from the Gulf of Aquitania through the Ocean, and troops to be disembarked while the enemy were off guard. Then, at last, the Cantabri joined in a mighty battle under the walls of Attica and on being overcome took refuge on Vinnius,[54] a mountain very well fortified by nature, and here they were almost completely annihilated by hunger caused by the siege. Then, the town of Racilium,[55] although it fought back with great might for a long time, was finally captured and destroyed. In addition, Antistius and Firmius, legates, in extensive and serious battles, subdued the outer parts of Gallaecia, which, located on the Ocean, are bounded by mountains and forests. For by means of a ditch fifteen miles long they surrounded and besieged the mountain, Medullius, which overhung the Minius River,[56] where a large number of men were protecting themselves. So when this tribe of men, rough and fierce by nature,

---

53 In the province of Tarraco.
54 Marked the boundary between Cantabria and Asturia.
55 In Hispania Tarraconensis, a town of the Cantabri.
56 A river in Lusitania, now the *Minho,* said to derive its name from the vermilion (*minium*) in its waters.

realized that it was unable to endure a siege and was unequal to sustaining a battle, through fear of slavery it plunged into suicide. For almost to a man they eagerly killed themselves by fire, sword, and poison. But the Astures, who had pitched camp at the Astura River, would have overcome the Romans by their strong strategy and forces had they not been betrayed and prevented. When they tried suddenly to crush the three legates with their legions divided into three camps in three equal columns, they were exposed by the betrayal of their own men. Later, when they had withdrawn from the war, Carisius overpowered these with no small loss on the side of the Romans also. A part of these Astures escaped from the battle and took refuge in Lancia.[57] And when the soldiers prepared to attack the city which had been encompassed by fire, the general, Carisius, persuaded his men to put an end to the fire and obtained a willing surrender from the barbarians. For he strove earnestly to leave the city intact and safe as a witness to his victory. Caesar brought back this reward for his Cantabrian victory: that he should order the gates of war to be closed fast. Thus, in those days, Janus was closed for the second time through Caesar, for the fourth time since the founding of the City.

After this, Claudius Drusus, the stepson of Caesar, was allotted Gaul and Raetia, and with his troops subdued the bravest tribes of Germany. For at that time, as if they were hastening to a day established for peace, all the tribes like waves were moved to try war or an agreement of peace, either to accept the conditions of peace if they were conquered, or to enjoy tranquil peace if they conquered. The Norici, Illyrii, Pannonii, Dalmatae, Moesi, Thraces, and the Daci Sarmatae, the largest and strongest peoples of Germany, were either overcome or checked by different generals or even shut off by the largest of rivers, the Rhine and the Danube. Drusus in Germany first conquered the Usipetes, and then the Tencteri

---

57 A city of Hispania Tarraconensis, now *Castro,* the chief city of the Lanceati, a tribe of the Astures.

and Chatti. He slaughtered the Marcomanni almost to a man. Afterwards, he overcame the bravest nations, to whom nature gave strength and practice experience in the use of this strength, namely, the Cherusci, Suebi, and Sugambri, all in one battle, but also a severe one for his men. The bravery and ferocity of these men can be judged from the fact that, if ever their women were enclosed in the midst of their carts by an advance of the Romans, and if their weapons or anything that their fury might use as a weapon failed them, dashing their little children on the ground, they would throw them into the faces of the enemy, in the individual slaughters of their children committing murder twice.

Then, also, in Africa, Cossus, a general of Caesar's, confined within a restricted territory the Musolani and Gaetuli who are accustomed to roam far and wide, and forced them through fear to keep away from Roman boundaries.

Meanwhile, legates of the Indians and Scythians, after crossing over the whole world, finally came upon Caesar at Tarraco, a city of Hither Spain, beyond which they could not have sought him, and they poured out upon him the story of the glory of Alexander the Great. Just as the legation of Spaniards and Gauls came to him in the middle of the East at Babylon with considerations of peace, so in Spain in the farthest West, eastern India and northern Scythia besought him suppliantly with tribute from their countries. After the Cantabrian War had been carried on for five years and all Spain, with relief from its weariness, had been turned back and restored to a state of lasting peace, Caesar returned to Rome.

In those days also Caesar fought many wars by himself and many through his generals and legates. Among others, Piso was sent against the Vindelici, and when these had been subdued, he went to Caesar at Lugdunum. Tiberius, the stepson of Caesar, with a very cruel slaughter destroyed the Pannonians who had risen in a new revolt. The same Tiberius immediately laid hold of the Germans in war, of whom as victor he carried off forty thousand captives. This very great and formidable war, indeed, was carried on by fifteen legions for three years, and since the Punic struggle, there had been almost no greater war, as Suetonius testifies.

Indeed, at this same time, Quintilius Varus, who treated conquered peoples with astounding haughtiness and avarice, together with three legions, was completely destroyed by the Germans who had rebelled. Caesar Augustus took this loss to the state so hard that, by the force of the grief, he again and again dashed his head against a wall and cried out: 'O, Quintilius Varus, give me back my legions.'

But Agrippa overcame the Bosporani and, recovering the Roman standards which they had once carried off under Mithridates, conquered them and forced them to surrender.

The Parthians, as if they were the cynosure of all eyes with the entire world, either conquered or pacified, and as if the entire strength of the Roman Empire were to be turned against themselves alone, for the consciousness of the former slaughter of Crassus to be avenged consumed them, of their own free will returned the standards to Caesar which they had taken away after killing Crassus, and, after giving royal hostages, merited a lasting treaty with humble supplication.

(22) So in the seven hundred and fifty-second year after the founding of the City, Caesar Augustus, when from the East to the West, from the North to the South, and over the entire circuit of the Ocean all nations were arranged in a single peace, then for the third time had the gates of Janus closed. These gates for almost twelve years from that time were bolted constantly in most complete silence and were even marked with rust itself, and they were never opened except in the last of the old age of Augustus when they were disturbed by the revolt of the Athenians and the unrest of the Dacians. So after closing the gates of Janus, striving to nourish and expand by peace the state which he had sought to obtain by war, he established many laws through which the human race by willing reverence might exercise the habit of discipline.

As a man, he shunned the title of 'lord.' For when, while he was watching a play, the following line was pronounced in the mime: 'A gracious and good lord indeed,' and all, as if it had been said of him, approved with loud shouting, immediately with a gesture and a look he checked the unseemly flattery and, on the following day, rebuked them with a very severe edict, and thereafter he did not permit himself to be called lord either by his children or grandchildren, either in earnest or in jest.

So at that time, that is, in that year in which, by the ordination of God, Caesar achieved the strongest and truest peace, Christ was born, upon whose coming that peace waited and at whose birth as men listened, the angels in exultation sang: 'Glory to God in the highest and on earth peace to men of good will.' At the same time, this man to whom universal supremacy was conceded, did not permit himself to be called 'lord of men,' rather dared not, when the true Lord of the whole human race was born among men. Also in this same year, when God deigned to be seen as man and actually to be man, Caesar, whom God had predestined for this great mystery, ordered that a census be taken of each province everywhere and that all men be enrolled. So at that time, Christ was born and was entered on the Roman census list as soon as he was born. This is the earliest and most famous public acknowledgment which marked Caesar as the first of all men and the Romans as lords of the world, a published list of all men entered individually, on which He Himself, who made all men, wished Himself to be found as man and enrolled among men. From the foundation of the world and from the beginning of the human race, an honor of this nature had absolutely never been granted in this manner, not even to Babylon or to Macedonia, not to mention any lesser kingdom. It is undoubtedly clear for the understanding of all, from their faith and investigation, that our Lord Jesus Christ brought forward this City to this pinnacle of power, prosperous and protected by His will; of this City, when he came, He especially wished to be called a Roman citizen by the declaration of the Roman census list.

Therefore, since we have arrived at that period in which the Lord Christ first enlightened this world by His coming and granted Caesar a most peaceful reign, I should also bring this sixth book to an end by the following concluding statement. The growing years of Christianity and, more than that, increasing in the midst of hands that would repress it, and what advancements have been made and are sharply criticized by those very ones to whom we are compelled to give these replies, all this I shall include in the seventh book, if, however, I shall be able with God's help. Since from the beginning I have not been silent as to the fact that men are sinners and that they are punished on account of their sins, now also I shall set forth what persecutions of Christians have been carried on and what retributions have followed, aside from the fact that all men are prone to sin and are accordingly punished individually.

BOOK SEVEN

UFFICIENT PROOFS, in my opinion, have been gathered, by which, without any of the secrets which belong to the few faithful,[1] it can be proven completely that the one and true God, whom the Christian religion preaches, made the world and its creatures when He so willed, and through many separate acts set the universe in order, although He was not recognized in many of these acts, and that He established it for one purpose, when He was revealed by one event,[2] and, at the same time, made clear His power and patience by proofs of various kinds. In this, indeed, I realize that the narrow-minded and the pessimistic are a little offended because such great patience is mingled with such great power. For if He was powerful enough, they say, to create the world, to establish the peace of the world, and to introduce in it worship and knowledge of Himself, what need was there of such great or, as they themselves feel, of so pernicious a patience, that, in the end, by the sins, disasters, and sufferings of men, conditions came about which could just as well have been produced in the beginning by the power of the God whom you preach? To these persons, indeed, I could truthfully reply that the human race was so created and established from the beginning that living under religion, with peace, and without toil, by the fruit of obedience it might merit eternal life, but having abused the goodness of the Creator who granted it freedom, it turned the gift of liberty

---

1 Probably a reference to a custom of the earliest periods of the Church according to which knowledge of some of the mysteries of Christian faith was not made known to the pagans or to those obtaining elementary instruction in the faith.
2 The Incarnation.

283

into arrogance and descended from contempt of God into forgetfulness of God; and that now the patience of God is just and just in either case, inasmuch as not even when held in contempt does He wholly destroy him to whom He wills to be merciful, and being powerful, as long as He wills, He permits him who despises Him to be afflicted with troubles; and then that it follows that He always justly furnishes guidance to him, however ignorant, to whom someday, when he repents, He will mercifully restore the means of his former grace. But since, although these arguments are presented very truthfully and strongly, they nevertheless require a faithful and obedient listener; moreover, my present audience (I shall see whether or not they will believe at some time) certainly at present does not believe, and I shall now bring forward rather quickly arguments which they themselves, although they are unwilling to approve them, cannot disapprove. So, insofar as pertains to our human comprehension, both of us, we and our opponents, live with reverence toward religion and with the acknowledgment and worship of a higher power, the nature of our belief alone being different, because it is our practice to confess that all things are from and through one God, and theirs to think of as many gods as there are things. If, they say, it was in God's power, whom you preach, to make the Roman Empire so large and eminent, why, then, did His patience stand in the way of it having been made so before? To these persons my response would be in the same terms: If it was within the power of the gods, whom you preach, to make the Roman Empire so large and eminent, why, then, did their patience stand in the way of it having been made so before? Or did the gods themselves not yet exist? Or did Rome herself not yet exist? Or were those gods not then worshiped? Or did Rome not yet seem capable of power? If the gods did not yet exist, their argument fails. For to what purpose do I discuss the delay of the gods, when I do not even discover their nature? But if the gods did exist, either their power, as my opponents themselves judge, or their patience was at fault; either their patience, if it existed, or their power, if it was lacking. Or, if it seems more likely that there were, indeed, gods at that time who could have advanced the Romans, but that the Romans had not yet come into existence who could rightly be advanced, we are seeking the author of things and the power, not workmanlike skill and knowledge. For we are concerned with great gods, as they think, not with most paltry artificers who lose their skill if material is lacking. For if it was always possible for those gods to have foreknown and to have willed, rather their foreknowledge even being assumed, because in the case of omnipotence to foreknow in the case of its own works is the same as to will, whatever was foreknown, to which the will assented, ought not to have been awaited but to have been created, especially since they say that that Jove of theirs was accustomed in jest to turn heaps of ants into tribes of men. But I do not think that we need consider further the practice of religious rites, because in the midst of continual sacrifices there was no end or respite from ceaseless disasters, except when Christ, the Savior of the world, shone upon us. Although I think that I have already shown sufficiently that the peace of the Roman Empire was foreordained for His coming, nevertheless, I shall try to supplement that with a few more arguments.

(2) At the beginning of the second book when I touched lightly upon the time of the founding of Rome, I consistently described many points of similarity between Babylon, a city of the Assyrians, at that time the first in the world, and Rome which today equally dominates the world. I pointed out that the former was the first and the latter the last empire; that the former gradually declined and the latter slowly gained strength; that the former lost its last king at the same time that the latter had its first; then, that the former was attacked and captured by Cyrus and, as it were, fell in death at the time when the latter, rising confidently after expelling the kings, began to enjoy the freedom of its own plans; and especially that when Rome was claiming her independence then,

too, the Jewish people, who were slaves under the kings at Babylon, regaining their freedom, returned to holy Jerusalem and, just as had been foretold by the prophets, rebuilt the temple of the Lord. Furthermore, I had said that between the Babylonian Empire which had arisen in the East, and the Roman Empire which arose in the West and was nourished by the heritage of the East, there intervened the Macedonian and African Empires, that is, that in the North and the South in brief intervals they played the roles of protector and guardian. I realize that no one has ever doubted that the Babylonian and Roman Empires are rightly called that of the East and that of the West. That the Macedonian Empire was in the North, not only its very geographical location, but also the altars of Alexander the Great which stand to this day at the foot of the Riphaean Mountains, teach us. Moreover, that Carthage surpassed all Africa and extended the boundaries of its empire, not only into Sicily, Sardinia, and other adjacent islands, but also into Spain, both the records of history and remains of cities show us. It has also been said that the two cities had stood for very much the same number of years, when Babylon was laid waste by the Medes and Rome was attacked by the Goths.

But now to these remarks I add the following, to make it clearer that God is the one ruler of all ages, kingdoms, and places. The Carthaginian Empire, from its founding until its overthrow, lasted a little more than seven hundred years, likewise, the Macedonian Empire, from Caranus[3] to Perses,[4] a little less than seven hundred; yet both were terminated by the number seven, by which all things are decided. Rome herself also, although she was continued to the coming of our Lord Jesus Christ with her Empire intact, nevertheless, she, too, had difficulty on meeting this number. For in the seven

---

3 According to legend, founded the Argive dynasty in Macedonia in the middle of the eighth century, B.C.

4 The last king of Macedon and the eldest son of Philip V. He was in constant conflict with the Romans from 171 to 168 B.C., and died a captive in Italy.

hundredth year of its foundation, a fire of uncertain origin destroyed fourteen of its districts, and, as Livy says, never was the City damaged by a greater conflagration, so much so that some years later Caesar Augustus contributed a large sum of money from the public treasury for the restoration of the buildings which had then been burned. I would be able also to show that twice this same number of years remained for Babylon, which, after more than fourteen hundred years, was finally captured by King Cyrus, did not a consideration of present circumstances forbid. I very gladly add this, that in the forty-third year of Ninus, the first of all the kings, although his father, Belus, is vaguely reported to have reigned first, in the reign of that Ninus, then, in the forty-third year after he ascended to the throne, that holy Abraham was born, to whom promises had been renewed, and from whose seed Christ was promised. Then, in the time of that first of all the emperors, Caesar Augustus, although his father, Caesar, was more a surveyor of the Empire than an emperor, so in the time of that Caesar, almost at the close of the forty-second year after he began to rule, Christ was born, who had been promised to Abraham in the rule of Ninus, the first king. Now He was born on the twenty-fifth of December, as soon as all the increase of the coming year begins. So it happened that, although Abraham was born in the forty-third year, the birth of Christ took place toward the end of the forty-second, so that He Himself was born, not in a part of the third year, but rather the third year was born in Him. With how great and how new and unusual blessings that year abounded, I think, is held sufficiently known without my setting them forth. In the whole world there was one peace among all, not because of the cessation of war, but because of their abolition; the twin gates of Janus were closed since the roots of war had been torn out and not repressed; that first and greatest census was taken, since in this one name of Caesar all the peoples of the great nations took oath, and at the same time, through the participation in the census, were made a part of one society.

(3) Thus, in the seven hundred and fifty-second year after the founding of the City, Christ was born, bringing the saving faith to the world, truly, the rock placed in the midst of things,[5] where whoever shall strike against Him shall be dashed to pieces; whoever shall believe in Him shall be saved; truly, a glowing fire which illumines him who follows Him and consumes him who attacks Him; He is Christ Himself, the Head of the Christians, the Savior of the good, the Punisher of the wicked, the Judge of all, who set a pattern in word and in deed for His followers, and, to teach them that they should be more patient in the persecutions which they would endure for eternal life, He began His own sufferings as soon as he appeared in the world, brought forth by the Virgin's travail. For as soon as the king of Judea, Herod, had learned of His birth, then, he determined to kill Him, and he, then, put many little ones to death while pursuing the One. Hence, there is a worthy punishment for the wicked who pursue their malicious ways; hence, insofar as the world exists tranquilly, it is so because of those who believe; insofar as it is perniciously disturbed, it is so as punishment for those who blaspheme, while the faithful Christians are free from anxiety through all events, who securely have the peace of eternal life, or advantageously so even in this world. This I shall show more readily by the very facts when I relate them in order. After the Redeemer of the world, the Lord Jesus Christ, came on earth and was enrolled in Caesar's census as a Roman citizen, while the gates of war, closed for twelve years, as I have said, were held together in tranquil peace, Caesar Augustus sent Gaius, his grandson, to govern the provinces of Egypt and Syria. As he was passing from Egypt by the boundaries of Palestine, as Suetonius Tranquillus relates,[6] he disdained worship at Jerusalem in the temple of God, at that time held holy and much frequented. When Augustus learned this through him, using poor judgment he

5 Cf. 1 Cor. 10.4.
6 Cf. his *Life of Augustus* 93.

praised him for having done wisely. So in the forty-eighth year of Caesar's rule, such a dreadful famine came upon the Romans that Caesar ordered the bands of gladiators, all foreigners, and also very large groups of slaves, with the exception of doctors and teachers, to be driven from the City. Thus, with the *princeps* sinning against the Holiness of God and the people seized by famine, the enormity of the offense is shown by the character of the punishment. Then, to use the words of Cornelius Tacitus: 'When Augustus was an old man, Janus was opened, while on the extreme borders of the earth new peoples were sought, often to advantage and sometimes with loss, and Janus remained so until the rule of Vespasian.' Thus far speaks Cornelius.[7] But when at that time the city of Jerusalem had been captured and overthrown, as the prophets foretold, and after the complete destruction of the Jewish people, Titus, who had been ordained by the judgment of God to avenge the blood of our Lord Jesus Christ, as victor, holding a triumph with his father, Vespasian, closed the temple of Janus. Thus, although the temple of Janus was opened in the last days of Caesar, nevertheless, for long periods of time thereafter there were no sounds of war, although the army was in readiness for action. The Lord Jesus Christ Himself, then, in the Gospels, when in those times the whole world was living in the greatest tranquillity and a single peace covered all peoples and He was asked by His disciples about the end of the coming times, among other things said this: 'You shall hear of wars and rumors of wars. Take care that you do not be alarmed, for these things must come to pass, but the end is not yet. For nation will rise against nation, and kingdom against kingdom; and there will be pestilences and famines and earthquakes in various places. But all those things are the beginnings of sorrows. Then they will deliver you up to tribulation, and will put you to death; and you will be hated by all nations for my name's sake.'[8]

---

7 Taken from one of the lost books of the *Histories* of Tacitus.
8 Cf. Matt. 24.6-9.

Moreover, Divine Providence, by teaching this, strengthened the believers by giving warning and confounded the unbelievers by His predicting.

(4) In the seven hundred and sixty-seventh year after the founding of the City, after the death of Augustus Caesar,[9] Tiberius Caesar assumed the power and remained in it for twenty-three years.[10] He, by himself, carried on no wars, nor even by his lieutenants any serious ones, except that in some places uprisings of peoples were foreseen and quickly crushed. Indeed, in the fourth year of his rule, Germanicus, the son of Drusus and the father of Caligula, had a triumph over the Germans, against whom he had been sent by Augustus in his old age. But Tiberius himself, during most of his regime, ruled the state with great and serious moderation, so much so that he wrote to certain governors who were trying to persuade him to increase the tribute of the provinces that 'it is the part of a good shepherd to shear his flock, not to flay it.' After the Lord Christ had suffered and had risen from the dead and had sent out His disciples to preach, Pilate, the governor of the province of Palestine, reported to the emperor, Tiberius, and to the Senate about the Passion and Resurrection of Christ, and the subsequent miracles which had been performed in public by Him Himself or were being performed in His name by His disciples, and about the fact that He was believed to be a god by the ever-increasing multitude in the faith. Tiberius, with an approval of great popularity, proposed to the Senate that Christ be held a god. The Senate, roused with indignation because the matter had not, according to custom, been first referred to it, in order that it itself might be the first to decide upon the acceptance of a cult, refused to deify Christ, and by an edict decided that Christians were to be banished from the City, especially because Sejanus, the prefect of Tiberius, was most obstinately opposed to the acceptance of this religion. Nevertheless, Tiberius by an edict

---

9 August 19, 14 A.D., at Nola.
10 A.D. 14 to 37.

threatened the accusers of the Christians with death. Then, gradually, that most laudable moderation of Tiberius Caesar changed to a desire to punish the Senate for its opposition, for the emperor had a passion to do whatever he wished, and from a most mild ruler, he burst forth as a most cruel beast. For he proscribed a great many senators and forced them to death; he had selected twenty noblemen to be his counselors; of these he left scarcely two unharmed and killed the rest on various grounds; he killed his prefect, Sejanus, as he was attempting a revolution; his sons, Drusus and Germanicus, of whom Drusus was his natural son and Germanicus adopted, he destroyed very evidently by poison; he killed the sons of Germanicus, his son by adoption. It is a horror and a shame to relate his deeds one by one; he grew violent with such madness of lust and cruelty that those who had hoped to be saved by Christ the King were punished by Caesar the King. But in the twelfth year of his reign, a strange and incredible destruction took place at the city of Fidenae.[11] While the people were watching a gladiatorial combat, the seats of the amphitheater collapsed and killed more than twenty thousand persons. This, indeed, was a worthy warning of so great a reproach, that at that time men had come together to view the deaths of men when God had willed to become man to procure the salvation of man. Then, in the seventeenth year of the same emperor, when the Lord Jesus Christ voluntarily gave Himself over to the Passion, but through the impiety of the Jews was apprehended and nailed to the cross, as a very great earthquake took place throughout the world, rocks upon mountains were split and a great many parts of the largest cities fell by this extraordinary violence. On the same day also, at the sixth hour of the day, the sun was entirely obscured and a loathsome night suddenly overshadowed the land, as it was said: 'An impious age feared eternal night.'[12]

---

11 A very ancient city of Latium, on the left bank of the Tiber, five miles from Rome, now *Castel Giubileo.*

12 Vergil, *Georgics* 1.468.

Moreover, it was quite clear that neither the moon nor the clouds stood in the way of the light of the sun, so that it is reported that on that day the moon, being fourteen days old, with the entire region of the heavens thrown in between, was farthest from the sight of the sun, and the stars throughout the entire sky shone, then, in the hours of the day or rather in that terrible night. To this, not only the authority of the Holy Gospels attest, but even some books of the Greeks. Until this day after the Passion of the Lord, whom the Jews persecuted insofar as was in their power, continuous slaughters of the Jews rumbled without cessation until, exhausted and dispersed, they disappeared. For Tiberius, under pretext of military service, relegated their youth to provinces of a rather unhealthy climate, and the remainder of the same race or those who followed similar rites, he forced from the City under the punishment of continuous slavery if they did not obey. Indeed, the many cities of Asia which had been destroyed by the earthquake mentioned above, he released from their tribute and rewarded from his own funds as well. This Tiberius died under ambiguous indications of poisoning.

(5) In the seven hundred and ninetieth year after the founding of the City, Gaius Caligula, the third emperor after Augustus, began to rule and he remained in power for not more than four full years,[13] of all men before him the most profligate and one who seemed truly worthy to be used for the punishment of the blaspheming Romans and the persecuting Jews. This man, to describe briefly the magnitude of his cruelty, is said to have exclaimed: 'Would that the Roman people had only a single neck!'[14] He also often complained about the condition of his times because they were marked by no public disasters.

O, blessed beginnings of Christian times! How you have prevailed in human affairs, so that even the cruelty of man

---

13 37 to 41.
14 Suetonius, *Gaius Caligula* 30.

was able rather to wish for disaster than to find it! Behold, hungry ferocity complains about the general tranquillity:

> Impious fury within;
> Sitting on cruel arms and bound behind
> its back with a hundred brazen knots,
> roars horribly with a bloody mouth.[15]

Rebellious slaves and fugitive gladiators terrorized Rome, overturned Italy, destroyed Sicily, an object of fear to almost the entire human race in the whole world. But in the days of salvation, that is, in Christian times, not even an inimical Caesar can break the peace. Caligula, with extensive and incredible preparation, setting out to find an enemy for his idle forces, passing through Germany and Gaul, stopped at the Ocean coast within sight of Britain. And when he had received in surrender Minocynobelinus, the son of the king of the Britons, who banished by his father was wandering with a few followers, since grounds for war were lacking, he returned to Rome. Moreover, in these same days, the Jews, who at that time were being harassed everywhere with deserved misfortunes because of Christ's Passion, when a riot had been stirred up at Alexandria and they were overcome with slaughter and driven from the city, sent, as a legate to Caesar to set forth their grievances, a certain Philo, indeed, an especially erudite man. But Caligula, most bitter toward all men and especially toward the Jews, spurning Philo's legation ordered all the sacred seats of the Jews, and especially that famous sanctuary in Jerusalem, to be profaned by pagan sacrifices and filled with statues and images, and that he be worshiped there as a god. But Pilate, the governor, who had passed the death sentence upon Christ, after he had been the object and the cause of a great many riots in Jerusalem, on being ordered to do this by Gaius was tormented with such anguish that he stabbed himself with his own hand and sought a lessening of his evils by a quick death. Gaius Caligula

---

15 Vergil, *Aeneid* 1.294-296.

also added this crime to his acts of lusts, that of, first, polluting and defiling his own sisters and, then, condemning them to exile. And later he ordered all exiles also to be killed. But he himself was killed by his own bodyguard. Two pamphlets were found in his secret papers, to one of which had been ascribed the title, *The Dagger*, to the other, *The Sword*.[16] Both contained the names of outstanding men of both orders, the senatorial and the equestrian, with notations of those destined for death. There was also found a large chest of various poisons, and when these later were thrown into the sea on the order of Claudius Caesar, the waters became infected and killed many fish, whose dead bodies the waves tossed up at random over the neighboring shores.

A truly strong mark of a merciful God is His manifestation of grace toward a people soon to become believers in part and the tempering of His wrath toward a people then obstinately unbelieving, so that how great a multitude of men escaped the death that had been prepared for them may be learned from the number of fish which had been killed and was known to all, and what such a mass of poison, skillfully used, could have done in the wretched City which, even when carelessly used, polluted the sea.

(6) In the seven hundred and ninety-fifth year after the founding of the City, Tiberius Claudius, the fourth after Augustus, obtained the throne and remained in it for fourteen years.[17] In the beginning of his rule, Peter, the apostle of the Lord Jesus Christ, came to Rome and taught the saving faith to all believers with words of faith and attested it by most mighty miracles. And henceforth, Christians began to be in Rome. Rome felt that this favor had been conferred upon her because of her faith. For when, after the murder of Caligula, the Senate and the consuls had passed many decrees about abolishing the Empire and restoring the state to its former status, and completely wiping out the entire

16 Suetonius, *Gaius Caligula* 49.
17 41 to 54.

family of the Caesars, Claudius, soon after he established his rule, making use of a great clemency hitherto unknown in Rome, lest vengeance should grow wild against so many of the nobility if it should once begin, erased those two days from memory in which, unfortunately, decrees and actions had been taken concerning the form of the state, and ratified a pardon for all that had been done and said at that time and approved complete oblivion for all this. Thus that renowned and famous amnesty of the Athenians, which, indeed, the Senate, on Cicero's recommendation, had tried to introduce in Rome when Julius Caesar was murdered, but which had become inoperative when Antony and Octavius broke forth in their attempts to avenge Caesar's death, this amnesty Claudius confirmed with voluntary clemency on the demand of no one, although he was stimulated with much sterner cause to execute the conspirators. There happened also at the same time a grand miracle of God's present grace, for Furius Camillus Scribonianus, the governor of Dalmatia, plotted a civil war and won over many of the strongest legions to break their allegiance. Thus, on the day set for their coming together from all sides to the new emperor, their eagles could not be adorned nor the standards in any way pulled up and moved. The army, aroused by such a great and so unusual a true miracle and turned into repentance, abandoned Scribonianus, and immediately, on the fifth day thereafter, killed him and bound itself by the oath of its former military service. It is well known that nothing more regrettable or more harmful has ever happened to the City of Rome than civil wars. And so let anyone deny that this rising tyranny and that threatening civil war was divinely checked on account of the coming of the Apostle Peter, and tender shoots, as it were, of Christians, still a few in number, breaking forth to proclaim their holy faith. Who could furnish a similar example as a proof of the suppression of civil wars in past times?

Claudius, in the fourth year of his reign, desiring to show himself a useful leader of the state, looked for a war everywhere and victory from whatever source. So he directed an expedition into Britain, which seemed to be stirred up to rebellion on account of deserters who were not readmitted to their homeland. He crossed over into the island which no one had dared approach before Julius Caesar or after him, and there, to speak with the words of Suetonius Tranquillus: 'Without any battle or shedding of blood, within a very few days he received the greatest part of the island in surrender.'[18] The Orcades islands also, which lie beyond Britain in the Ocean, he added to the Roman Empire and, in the sixth month after he had set forth, he returned to Rome.

Let anyone who so pleases today make comparisons regarding this one island, period with period, war with war, Caesar with Caesar. For I say nothing about the outcome, since in this case it was a most fortunate victory, in that case a most bitter disaster. So, finally, let Rome realize that she had part of her good fortune formerly through His hidden providence in carrying on her undertakings, and by accepting this recognition she enjoys the fullest success, insofar as, on the other hand, she is not corrupted by the obstacles of her blasphemies.

In the same year of the reign of this emperor, a most serious famine took place throughout Syria which the prophets also had foretold; but Helena, the queen of the Adiabeni, a convert to the faith of Christ, ministered most generously to the needs of the Christians in Jerusalem by importing grain from Egypt.

In the fifth year of his reign, an island,[19] extending over a space of thirty stadia, emerged from the deep between Thera and Therasia.

In the seventh year of his reign, under Cumanus, the procurator of Judea, so great an insurrection broke out in Jerusalem in the days of the Passover that, when the people were

---

18 Suetonius, *Claudius* 17.
19 Thia or Mikra Kamméni in the Aegean Sea near Crete. The event occurred in 46 and is mentioned by several writers.

pressed together in the passage of the gates, thirty thousand Jews are reported to have been crushed to death and suffocated by the congestion.

In the ninth year of the same reign, Josephus reports that the Jews were expelled from the City by Claudius. But Suetonius convinces me more who speaks in the following manner: 'Claudius expelled the Jews from Rome, who were constantly stirring up revolutions because of their ill-feeling toward Christ.'[20] But it is by no means discernible whether he ordered the Jews to be checked and repressed because they were stirring up revolutions against Christ, or because he wished the Christians also to be expelled at the same time as those of a related religion.

But in the following year, so great a famine took place at Rome that the emperor, in the middle of the Forum, was taunted with reproaches by the people and most disgracefully pelted with pieces of bread; he escaped the fury of the excited people by fleeing with difficulty through a secret passage into the Palace.

Moreover, a short time later, he killed thirty-five senators and also three hundred Roman knights on very slight grounds; but he himself died from manifest indications of poisoning.

(7) In the eight hundred and eighth year after the founding of the City, Nero Caesar, the fifth after Augustus, took possession of the principate and remained in it for almost fourteen years.[21] In all vices and crimes, he was the follower of his uncle, rather he surpassed him. There was no form of vice that he did not practice—wantonness, lust, extravagances, avarice, and cruelty. Indeed, roused by wantonness and visiting almost all the theaters of Italy and Greece, even dressing himself disgracefully in every mode of dress, he often seemed to himself to outdo heralds, musicians, actors, and charioteers. Furthermore, he was driven by such great lusts that he is reported to have restrained himself not even from mother or

---

20 Suetonius, *Claudius* 25.
21 54 to 68.

sister or any blood relationship; he took a man for a wife,
and he himself was received by a man as a wife. Indeed, he
was of such unbridled extravagance that he fished with nets
of gold which were drawn up by purple cords, and he bathed
in cold and hot perfumes. It is also handed down that he
never made a journey with less than a thousand carriages.
Finally, he made a fire of the City of Rome as a spectacle for
his pleasure; for six days and seven nights the blazing City
caused astonishment to his royal eyes; the warehouses built
of square stone and those large tenements of old which the
scurrying flames could not reach, he crushed with huge machines, prepared once for foreign wars, and then set on fire,
while the unfortunate plebeians were forced into the shelter
of monuments and tombs. He himself, while viewing this
from the high tower of Maecenas[22] and while joyful over the
beauty of the flames, as it is said, in the costume of an actor
of tragedy, declaimed the Iliad. Moreover, of such rash avarice
was he that after this burning of the City, which Augustus
had boasted that he had rendered marble instead of brick, he
permitted no one to approach the remains of his own property; he himself took away whatever by any chance had survived the blaze; he also ordered that ten million sesterces be
appropriated annually by the Senate for his own expenses; he
deprived a great many senators of their property for no existing cause; in one day he completely wiped out the property
of all the merchants, even inflicting torture upon them also.
Moreover, he was so roused with cruel madness that he killed
the greater part of the Senate, and almost annihilated the
equestrian order. And he did not even refrain from parricides;
without hesitation, he destroyed mother, brother, sister, wife,
and all his other relatives and kinsmen. He increased this mass
of crime by his daring impiety against God. For he was the
first at Rome to torture and inflict the penalty of death upon

---

22 Maecenas had an extensive property on the Esquiline Hill, including a
magnificent house, gardens, and tower, which he bequeathed to Augustus.

Christians, and he ordered them throughout all the provinces to be afflicted with like persecution; and in his attempt to wipe out the very name, he killed the most blessed apostles of Christ, Peter and Paul, one by the cross and the other by the sword. Soon slaughters arising from all sides oppressed wretched Rome in rapid succession. For the following autumn, so great a pestilence fell upon the City that thirty thousand funerals were entered in the register of Libitina. Then, a disaster immediately fell in Britain, when two of the principal towns[23] were destroyed with great slaughter and death to Roman citizens and allies. Furthermore, in the East, when the great provinces of Armenia were lost, Roman legions were sent under the Parthian yoke, and Syria was retained with difficulty. In Asia, three cities, that is, Laodicia, Hierapolis, and Colossae, were destroyed by an earthquake. Indeed, when Nero learned that Galba had been proclaimed emperor in Spain by the army, he completely collapsed in courage and hope. When he was performing incredible evils to disturb, rather to destroy the state, he was pronounced a public enemy by the Senate, and fleeing more ignominiously, he killed himself four miles from the City, and in him the entire family of the Caesars came to an end.

(8) In the eight hundred and twenty-fourth year after the founding of the City, Galba took over full power of emperor in Spain. As soon as he learned of Nero's death, he went to Rome,[24] and he offended all by his avarice, cruelty, and laziness; he adopted as his son and successor Piso, a highborn and industrious young man, with whom in the seventh month of their reign he was slain by Otho.

Rome atoned for the recent harms done the Christian religion by the slaughter of her rulers and by the civil wars which broke out, and those standards of the legions, which at the coming of the Apostle Peter into the City were held fast by divine intervention and could by no means be pulled

23 Camulodunum and Verulanium.
24 He ruled from June 9, 68 to January 15, 69, when he was killed.

up to incite civil war that was being planned by Scribonianus, when Peter was killed in the City and Christians were racked by a diversity of punishments, were loosened in every part of the world. For Galba immediately had risen in revolt and, as soon as he was overcome, Otho seized imperial power and arose immediately in Rome, Vitellius in Germany, and Vespasian in Syria, all at the same time. Let them who take offense at Christian times, by all means acknowledge, even though unwillingly, both the power and mercy of God; how quickly the fires of such great wars were stirred up and repressed, whereas before, for the slightest causes, great and long-lasting disasters sprang up, and now the mighty crashes of the greatest evils resounding from all sides are suppressed with very little difficulty. For the Church, although harassed by persecution, was already in Rome to make supplication to Christ, the Judge of all, even for her enemies and persecutors. So when Otho, after Galba and Piso had been killed in Rome, had made his way to the throne in the midst of tumults and bloodshed, and as soon as he had learned that Vitellius had been made emperor by the German legions, first, causing a civil war with three minor battles, that is, in one in the Alps, in another around Placentia, and in a third near a place which they call Castores, and had met with the Vitellian generals and come off the victor, and when, in a fourth battle at Bedriacum,[25] he noticed that his men were being conquered in the third month after he had begun to rule,[26] he killed himself. Vitellius came to Rome as victor, where, after he had carried on many cruel and vile things, and also by his incredible gluttony brought disgrace on the life of human beings, after he learned about Vespasian, at first having attempted to abdicate but afterwards having been encouraged by certain persons, forced Sabinus, the brother of Vespasian, who suspected no trouble, together with other

---

25 Bedriacum, also Bebriacum and Betriacum, a village in Cisalpine Gaul, between Verona and Cremona, now *Cividale.*
26 Otho ruled from January 15, 69 to April 25, 69.

Flavians to take refuge in the Capitol, and setting fire to the temple, in the midst of flames and falling walls, gave all over into one death and tomb. Later, being deserted by his army which defected to the side of Vespasian and being frightened as the enemy were now approaching, after he had thrust himself in a small storeroom next to the Palace, being dragged forth most scandalously, he was led naked along the Sacred Way and was conducted to the Forum as bystanders threw dung into his face. In the eighth month after he had assumed the throne,[27] at the Germonian Steps he was tortured to death by the countless pricks of tiny stabs and was then dragged away by a hook and thrown into the Tiber and was deprived even of the usual burial. Moreover, in many nefarious ways, the soldiers of Vespasian for many days vented their fury on the Senate and Roman people with indiscriminate slaughter.

(9) In the eight hundred and twenty-fifth year after the founding of the City, after that indeed brief but troubled period of illegal attempts to sieze the throne, a calm serenity returned under the leadership of Vespasian.[28] For to pick up what I said a little above, the Jews, after the Passion of Christ, being completely destitute of the grace of God and, when they were beset by all evils on all sides, being led astray by certain oracular responses on Mount Carmel[29] which predicted that leaders coming out of Judea would take possession of things, and applying the prediction to themselves, broke out in rebellion and, annihilating the Roman garrisons, they also put to flight the governor of Syria who was bringing reinforcements and, after first capturing his standard, slaughtered his troops. Vespasian, being sent against these by Nero, had Titus, his elder son, among his lieutenants; for he brought with him into Syria many strong legions. And so when, after

---

27 Vitellius ruled from January 3, 69 to December 21, 69.
28 69 to 79.
29 Cf. Tacitus, *Histories* 2.78, according to which it is the site of an oracle. It is best known as a mountain sacred throughout Jewish history as a place of prayer.

capturing many of their towns, he had enclosed the Jews in the city of Jerusalem chiefly because they had gathered there on account of a feast day,[30] on learning of the death of Nero, at the urging of many kings and generals, especially on the advice of Joseph, a leader of the Jews, who, when captured and put in chains, very confidently had said, as Suetonius[31] relates, that he would immediately be released by the same person who imprisoned him, namely, the emperor, he seized the power, and leaving his son, Titus, in camp to take care of the siege of Jerusalem, proceeded through Alexandria to Rome; but on learning of the murder of Vitellius, he stopped for a short time at Alexandria. Titus, however, pressing the Jews with a heavy and long siege, making use of engines and all kinds of military machines, finally, not without much bloodshed among his own men, broke through the walls of the city. But to capture the inner fortification of the temple, which a large number of priests and chief men enclosed therein were guarding, there was need of a greater force and more time. Yet when he saw that this was reduced within his power, because of the nature and antiquity of the construction, he deliberated a long time as to whether he should set it on fire as a source of incitement to the enemy or whether he should save it as a proof of his victory. Since the Church of God was flourishing very abundantly throughout the whole world, this, in the judgment of God, was to be removed as something exhausted and empty and as fit for no good to anyone. So Titus, pronounced imperator by the army, set fire to the temple in Jerusalem and destroyed it, which, from the first day of its foundation until the last day of its overthrow, had lasted for one thousand one hundred and two years. He leveled all the walls of the city with the ground. Cornelius and Suetonius relate that six hundred thousand Jews were killed in this war. But Joseph, the Jew, who was in charge of the war at that time and who had found forgive-

---

30 The day of the Passover.
31 Cf. Suetonius, *Vespasian* 5.

ness and favor with Vespasian by predicting his accession to the throne, writes that eleven hundred thousand had perished by the sword and by famine and that the remainder of the Jews, driven by various conditions, were dispersed throughout the whole world. The number of these is said to have been about ninety thousand. Vespasian and Titus, the emperors, entered the City celebrating a magnificent triumph over the Jews. This was a fair sight and one hitherto unknown to all mortals among the three hundred and twenty triumphs which had taken place from the founding of the City until that time, namely, father and son riding in one triumphal chariot, bringing back a most glorious victory over those who had offended the Father and the Son. These emperors, since all wars and rebellions at home and abroad had been repressed, immediately proclaimed peace for the whole world and decreed that double-faced Janus be confined by the bolting of the gates for the sixth time since the founding of the City. For rightly was the same honor paid to the avenging of the Lord's Passion as had been bestowed upon His Nativity. Then, at that time, the Roman state without any confusions of wars extended itself immensely, for Achaia, Lycia, Rhodes, Byzantium, Samos, Thrace, Cilicia,[32] and Commagene, being reduced to provinces, obeyed the judges and laws of the Romans.

Moreover, in the ninth year of this emperor's reign, three cities of Cyprus were crushed by an earthquake and there was a great pestilence at Rome. And Vespasian, in his country estate among the Sabines, died from dysentery in the ninth year of his principate.

In the three hundred and twenty-eighth year after the founding of the City, Titus, the eighth emperor after Augustus, if Otho and Vitellius are excluded, reigned for two years.[33]

---

32 Orosius apparently has taken this list from Eutropius, who, in turn, took it from some version of Suetonius. The form 'Trachiam' appears in this list. This would indicate Cilicia Trachea, the mountainous part of Cilicia.

33 79 to 81.

There was such tranquillity under his rule that the blood of
no one at all was shed in the administration of the state. Yet,
at this time, a great many public buildings were burned by a
fire which broke out suddenly at Rome. They also say that
the top of Mount Bebius then blew off and poured forth great
fires and, by its torrents of flames, destroyed the neighboring
territory with its cities and people. Titus, to the great sorrow
of all, succumbed to disease in the same country estate in
which his father had died.

(10) In the eight hundred and thirtieth year after the
founding of the City, Domitian, the ninth emperor after
Augustus, succeeded his brother, Titus, to the throne. For
fifteen years this emperor passed, little by little, through all
kinds of crimes until he dared, by issuing edicts of most cruel
persecution everywhere, to uproot the Church of Christ most
firmly established in the whole world. He fell into such a condition of pride that he ordered himself to be called Lord and
God, and to be so described and worshiped. Because both of
envy and greed, he killed the most noble men of the Senate;
some publicly, others he drove into exile and there ordered
them to be butchered. Whatever could be thought of by an
intemperate lust he did. He erected many buildings in the
City after the property of the Roman people had been destroyed. Through his legates, he carried on war against the
Germans and Dacians with like destruction to the state, while
he himself in the City tore to pieces the Senate and the people,
and the enemy abroad crushed with continuous slaughter his
badly directed army. I would like to describe at length the
great battles between Diurpaneus,[34] the king of the Dacians,
and the general, Fuscus,[35] and the great losses to the Romans,
but Cornelius Tacitus, who has composed this story with the

---

[34] During the years of 81 to 96. This king is called Decebalus by some,
including Dion Cassius. He was hunted down and avoided capture by
suicide in 106.

[35] Cornelius Fuscus was entrusted with the conduct of the war against
the Dacians. He crossed the Danube and penetrated into Dacia (86 or
87), but met with a disastrous defeat and lost his life.

greatest care, has said that Sallustius Crispus[36] and a great many other writers had approved keeping silent regarding the numbers slain and that he himself had adopted the very same policy. But Domitian, elated by the most distorted form of vanity, held a triumph nominally over the enemy who had been overcome, but actually over the loss of his legions. This same emperor, crazed by his pride because of which he wished to be worshiped as a god, was the first emperor after Nero to order a persecution against the Christians to be carried on. Also at this time, the most blessed Apostle John was banished to the island of Patmos. Also among the Jews, an order was given that the race of David be searched out and killed by cruel tortures and bloody inquisitions, since the holy prophets were both hated and believed, as if some day there would be One from the seed of David who could acquire the throne. Yet directly, Domitian was cruelly killed in the Palace by those in his own home, and his body was carried out on a common bier by corpse bearers and buried most ignominiously.

(11) In the eight hundred and forty-sixth year after the founding of the City, although Eutropius[37] wrote that this was the eight hundred and fiftieth, Nerva, a very old man, was made the tenth emperor[38] after Augustus by Petronius, the praetorian prefect, and by the eunuch, Parthenius, the murderer of Domitian, and he adopted Trajan as his own successor, through whom, indeed by divine foresight, he took care of the afflicted state. Nerva, in his first edict, recalled all the exiles. Thus the Apostle John, being freed by this general amnesty, returned to Ephesus. Nerva, after a year of ruling had passed, was afflicted with a disease and died.

---

36 Gaius Sallustius Crispus, 86-34 B.C., the famous historian of the late Republic.

37 Cf. Eutropius, *Breviarium historiae Romanae* 8.1. Beginning with Romulus, he reached the Sullan Civil War in book 5, Caesar's death in book 6, and covered the Empire to Jovian's death (A.D. 364) in books 7-10.

38 96 to 98.

(12) In the eight hundred and forty-seventh year after the founding of the City, Trajan, a Spaniard by birth, took over the helm of state as Nerva's successor, the eleventh emperor after Augustus, and held it for nineteen years.[39] He took over the insignia of power in Agrippina, a city of Gaul. Then, he restored Germany across the Rhine to its former status; he subdued many tribes beyond the Rhine; moreover, the districts located beyond the Euphrates and the Tigris, he made into provinces; and he occupied Seleucia, Ctesiphon, and Babylon. In persecuting the Christians, the third emperor to do so after Nero, surely, he made an error in judgment when he ordered the Christians found anywhere to be forced to sacrifice to idols and, if they refused, to be killed, and when many were killed, warned by a report of Pliny the Younger, who had been appointed persecutor, together with other judges, that these people, beyond their profession of Christ and their respectable meetings, were doing nothing contrary to the law, and that, indeed, by their confidence in a harmless confession death seemed to no one of them serious and a matter of dread, he immediately tempered his edict by milder rescripts. However, the Golden House at Rome, built by Nero at a great expenditure of private and public funds, suddenly blazed up in fire, so that it was understood that the persecution, though started by another, was punished most severely on the buildings of him by whom it was first started and on the very author of it. Four cities of Asia, Elaea, Myrina, Pitane, and Cyme, and in Greece, the two cities of the Opuntii and the Oriti were laid low by an earthquake; three cities of Galatia were ruined by the same earthquake; the Pantheon at Rome was struck by lightning and burned; an earthquake in Antioch ruined almost the entire city. Then, all at once, the Jews in different parts of the world, as if enraged with madness, burst forth in an incredible revolution. For throughout all Libya, they carried on most violent wars against the

---

39 98 to 117.

inhabitants, and Libya was, then, so forsaken by the killing of the cultivators of the soil that, unless Hadrian afterwards had not gathered colonists from without and brought them there, the land would have remained completely destitute and without an inhabitant. Indeed, they threw into confusion all Egypt, Cyrene, and the Thebaid with bloody seditions. But in Alexandria, in a pitched battle, they were conquered and crushed. In Mesopotamia also, when they rebelled, by order of the emperor, war was introduced against them. And thus many thousands of them were destroyed in a vast slaughter. Indeed, they did destroy Salamis, a city of Cyprus, after killing all the inhabitants. Trajan, as some report, died of dysentery at Seleucia, a city of Isauria.

(13) In the eight hundred and sixty-seventh year of the City, Hadrian, the nephew of Trajan on his mother's side, became the twelfth emperor after Augustus and ruled for twenty-one years.[40] He, being a learned man, instructed in the Christian religion from books composed by Quadratus,[41] a disciple of the Apostles, by Aristides[42] of Athens, a man full of faith and wisdom, and by Serenus Granius, the legate, through a letter addressed to Minucius Fundanus, proconsul of Asia, gave orders that no one was permitted to condemn Christians without the presentation and proof of a crime. He, likewise, in the Senate was immediately called Father of His Country and his wife was called Augusta, contrary to the practice of the forefathers. Hadrian governed the state by very just laws. He carried on a war against the Sauromatae and conquered them. Indeed, he overcame the Jews in a final slaughter, who were disturbed by the disorders of their own crimes and were laying waste the province of Palestine, once their own, and thus avenging the Christians whom the Jews,

---

40 117 to 138.
41 Quadratus, the author of an apology presented to Hadrian in 124, received this title from Eusebius in his *Chronicle*.
42 Aristides of Athens, another well-known apologist for the Christians of the second century.

under the leadership of Cochebas, were torturing because they would not join them against the Romans; and he gave orders that no Jew should be permitted to enter Jerusalem, that the city be open only to Christians; and he restored the city to high prosperity by rebuilding the walls, giving orders that it be called Aelia after his own first name.

(14) In the eight hundred and eighty-eighth year after the founding of the City, Antoninus, with the surname Pius, was made the thirteenth emperor after Augustus; with his sons Aurelius and Lucius, he governed the state for nearly twenty-three years[43] so peacefully and scrupulously that properly he was called 'Pius' and the 'Father of His Country.' Now in his time, Valentinus, the heresiarch,[44] and Cerdo,[45] the teacher of Marcion, came to Rome. But the philosopher, Justin,[46] gave Antoninus his book composed in defense of the Christian religion and made him well disposed toward the Christian people. Antoninus was taken ill at the twelfth milestone from the City and died.

(15) In the nine hundred and eleventh year after the founding of the City, Marcus Antoninus Verus,[47] the fourteenth emperor after Augustus, together with his brother, Aurelius Commodus[48] took over the throne and remained in it for nineteen years. These were the first to protect the state with equal authority. Then, they carried on war against the Parthians with admirable bravery and success. Annius An-

---

43 138 to 161.
44 Valentinus, the Gnostic, founder and leader of a group in the time of Hadrian.
45 Cerdo, a Syrian Gnostic who probably came to Rome in 135, is little known. His disciple, Marcion, was very well known and influential in the second century.
46 Justin the Martyr, the most important of the Greek apologists of the second century and one of the noblest personalities of early Christian literature. The reference here is probably to the first of his two apologies written about 148.
47 Marcus Aurelius Antoninus Augustus, 161 to 180; emperor together with Lucius Verus from 161 to 169, together with Commodus from 177 to 180.
48 Known as Lucius Verus.

toninus Verus proceeded into this battle. For Vologesus, the king of the Parthians, with a severe attack was laying waste to Armenia, Cappadocia, and Syria. But Antoninus, having accomplished great exploits with his very energetic generals, captured Seleucia, a city of Assyria located on the Hydaspes River with four hundred thousand inhabitants, and with his brother celebrated the Parthian victory by a double triumph and, not long afterward, while he was seated in a carriage with his brother, he died, choking to death from an attack of a disease which the Greeks call apoplexy.

After his death, Marcus Antoninus alone ruled the state. But in the days of the Parthian War, severe persecutions of Christians on his order broke out for the fourth time since Nero in Asia and in Gaul, and many of the saints received the martyr's crown. A plague which broke out over many provinces followed, and so laid waste all Italy that everywhere country estates, fields, and towns were left without a cultivator and inhabitant and gave way to ruins and forests. Indeed, it is reported that the Roman army and all the legions stationed far and wide in winter quarters were so used up that the war against the Marcomanni, which broke out immediately, could not have been carried on without a new levy of troops which Marcus Antoninus held continuously at Carnuntium[49] for three years. That this war, indeed, was managed by the providence of God is made very evident, not only by many proofs, but especially by a letter of that very grave and discreet emperor. For when the tribes, barbarous by their cruelty and innumerable in number, that is, the Marcomanni, the Quadi, the Vandals, the Sarmatians, the Suebi, and almost all the Germans, had risen in rebellion, and the Roman army had advanced up to the territory of the Quadi and were surrounded by the enemy, it would have sustained more immediate danger from thirst on account of the scarcity of water than from the enemy; and when certain

---

49 Carnuntium, an old Celtic town of Upper Pannonia on the Danube, now near *Haimburg*.

soldiers proceeded to call upon the name of Christ, which they did suddenly and publicly, giving forth their souls in prayer with great constancy of faith, so great a force of rain was poured forth that it most abundantly refreshed the Romans without doing them any harm, and forced the barbarians who were terrified by frequent strokes of lightning, especially since a great many of them were killed, into flight. The Romans, attacking the enemy in the rear and slaughtering them to a man with a small number of raw recruits but with the most powerful aid of Christ, brought back a most glorious victory, one superior to those known in the past. A letter of the emperor, Antoninus, is also said by some authors to exist today in which he acknowledges that, through the invocation of the name of Christ by the Christian soldiers, the thirst of the army was relieved and the victory granted. The same Antoninus took his son, Commodus, with him into the government;[50] he also, throughout all the provinces, remitted the unpaid tribute of the past and he ordered that all the incriminating evidence of business with the imperial government be gathered together in the Forum and burned, and he tempered the rather severe laws by new enactments. Finally, while he was in Pannonia, he died of a sudden malady.

(16) In the nine hundred and thirtieth year after the founding of the City, Lucius Antoninus Commodus, the fifteenth emperor after Augustus, succeeded his father on the throne and remained on it for thirteen years.[51] He carried on a successful war against the Germans. But being completely depraved by disgraceful excesses and obscenities, he very often even fought in jest with the arms of gladiators, and in the arena he frequently opposed wild beasts. He also killed a great many senators, especially those whom he noticed were of pre-eminent birth and ability. Punishment for the City followed upon the sins of the ruler. For the Capitol was struck by lightning. The conflagration caused by this, in its

---

50 177 to 180.
51 180 to 192.

ravenous course, burned the library which had been established by the care and zeal of his ancestors, and other buildings
located nearby. Then another fire which arose later in Rome
leveled to the ground the temple of Vesta, the Palace, and a
very large part of the City. Commodus, who incommoded all[52]
and while alive was judged an enemy of the human race, is
said to have perished by strangulation in the home of Vestili-
anus. After this man, the elderly Helvius Pertinax was made
emperor by the Senate, the sixteenth after Augustus. He, in
the sixth month after he had begun to rule,[53] was killed in
the Palace through the conniving of Julianus, one skilled in
the law. After Pertinax had been killed, Julianus took over the
power,[54] but later at the Mulvian Bridge, he was overcome in
a civil war by Severus and was put to death in the seventh
month after he had begun to rule. Thus, between Pertinax
and Julianus one year was taken up.

(17) In the nine hundred and forty-fourth year after the
founding of the City, Severus, an African by birth from
Tripolis, from the town of Leptis, who wished to be called
Pertinax after the name of the emperor whose murder he had
avenged, gained the vacant throne, the seventeenth emperor
after Augustus, and held the power for eighteen years.[55] He,
cruel by nature and continually harassed by wars, ruled the
state very strongly indeed, but very laboriously. At Cyzicus,[56]
he conquered and killed Pescennius Niger,[57] who had aspired
to a tyranny in Egypt and Syria. He checked the Jews and the
Samaritans with the sword when they tried to rebel. He over-

---

52 The pun in Latin is *cunctis incommodus.*

53 From January 1 to March 28, 193.

54 From March 28 to June 1, 193.

55 From 193 to 211.

56 A city, celebrated in ancient times in Mysia, located on an island or
peninsula of the same name in the Propontis.

57 Pescennius Niger Justus, consul in 190 and next year governor of
Syria, where after the murder of Pertinax, he was proclaimed emperor
by his legions. Pretender from May, 193 to November, 194. He was
not present at the battle of Cyzicus, but was later captured and killed.

came the Parthians, the Arabians, and the Adiabeni. He afflicted the Christians with the fifth persecution after Nero, and a great many saints received the crown of martyrdom throughout the different provinces. Heavenly vengeance was immediately enacted and followed this wicked presumption of Severus against the Christians and the Church of God. For straightway Severus was seized, or rather brought back from Syria into Gaul for a third civil war, since he had already carried on one in Rome against Julianus,[58] another in Syria against Pescennius, and Clodius Albinus, an ally in the killing of Pertinax who had made himself Caesar in Gaul,[59] was already stirring up a third, in which war much Roman blood was shed on both sides. Now Albinus was overcome at Lugdunum and killed. Severus, the victor, was drawn back to the provinces of Britain by the revolt of almost all of his allies. Here, after great and serious battles had been continuously fought, he thought that the part of the island which had been received in surrender should be separated by a wall from the other tribes still unsubdued. And so he constructed a large ditch and a very strong wall, fortified at frequent intervals by towers, for a hundred and thirty-two miles from sea to sea. And there in the town of York, he died of a disease. He left two sons, Bassianus and Geta, one of whom, Geta, was judged a public enemy and perished; Bassianus, who assumed the name of Antoninus, took possession of the throne.

(18) In the nine hundred and sixty-second year after the founding of the City, Aurelius Antoninus Bassianus, known likewise as Caracalla, the eighteenth ruler after Augustus, took

---

58 Didius Julianus, emperor in 193, whose life is written by Spartianus, obtained the throne by bribing the praetorians.

59 April, 193. A native of Hadrumentum in Africa, belonged to a noble family. After Niger's death, while governor of Britain, he was proclaimed by Septimius a public enemy. In reply, Albinus was made Augustus by his army and in 196 A.D., he crossed into Gaul, hoping in vain to secure the support of the German legions before moving against Rome. He was killed in battle at Lugdunum on February 19, 197.

over the power and remained in it for almost seven years.[60] In his life, he was harsher than his father and more unrestrained than all men in his lust, for he even married his stepmother, Julia. While carrying on war against the Parthians, he was surrounded between Edessa and Carrhae and killed.

After him, Ophilus Macrinus, who was the praetorian prefect, became the nineteenth emperor after Augustus. With the aid of his son, Diadumenus, he seized the power but, when a year had passed, he was immediately killed in a revolt of the soldiers at Archelais.[61]

In the nine hundred and seventieth year after the founding of the City, Marcus Aurelius Antoninus, the twentieth ruler after Augustus, took over the power and held it for four years.[62] This emperor, a priest of the temple of Heliogabalus, left no memory of himself except one notorious for its defilements, crimes, and every obscenity. Moreover, when an uprising of the soldiers took place, he was killed at Rome together with his mother.

In the nine hundred and seventy-fourth year after the founding of the City, Aurelius Alexander[63] was made the twenty-first emperor after Augustus by the will of the Senate and the soldiers, and for thirteen years he had a worthy reputation for justice. His mother, Mamea, a Christian, arranged to receive instruction from the presbyter, Origen.[64] Now Alexander immediately made an expedition against the Persians and victoriously overcame Xerxes, their king, in a very great battle. Making use of Ulpian as his assistant, he exhibited

---

60 211 to 217. Co-emperor with Severus from 198 to 211; with Geta, 211 to 212.
61 217 to 218. A city of Cappadocia on the Halys River.
62 218 to 222. Better known as Heliogabalus or Elagabalus. His real name was Bassianus. The praetorians were bribed to kill Heliogabalus and his mother in 222.
63 222 to 235. Better known as Severus Alexander.
64 Renowned Christian theologian and teacher, 185 or 186 A.D. to 254 or 255.

the greatest self-restraint in administering the state but, in a revolt of the soldiers at Mainz, he was killed.

(19) In the nine hundred and eighty-seventh year after the founding of the City, Maximinus[65] was made the twenty-second emperor after Augustus, not by the Senate, but by the army, when he had waged a successful war in Germany. He carried into effect a persecution against the Christians, the sixth from the time of Nero. But immediately, that is, in the third year after he began to rule, he was killed by Pupienus at Aquileia. This put an end to the persecution as well as to his life. He instituted the persecution chiefly because of the Christian family of Alexander, whom he succeeded, and his mother, Mamea, and directed it against the priests and the clergy and, in particular, on account of Origen, the presbyter.

In the nine hundred and ninety-first year after the founding of the City, Gordian[66] was made the twenty-third emperor after Augustus, and he remained in power for six years. Now Pupienus, the murderer of Maximinus, and his brother, Balbinus, who had usurped the power,[67] were presently killed in the Palace. Gordian, still a boy, when he was about to set out for the East to do battle with the Parthians, as Eutropius[68] writes, opened the gates of Janus. I do not recall that any historian has written whether anyone after Vespasian and Titus closed them, although Cornelius Tacitus hands down that they were opened a year later by Vespasian himself. So Gordian, after successfully waging great battles against the Parthians, was treacherously killed by his own men not far from Circessus on the Euphrates.

(20) In the nine hundred and ninety-seventh year after the founding of the City, Philip, being made the twenty-fourth emperor after Augustus, shared the throne with his son,

---

65 235 to 238.
66 Gordian III, 238 to 244. Saluted as emperor by the praetorians at the age of 13.
67 From early March to the middle of June, 238.
68 Cf. his *Breviarium historiae Romanae* 9.2.

Philip,[69] and remained in it for seven years. He was the first of all the emperors to be a Christian and, after the third year of his rule, the thousandth year after the founding of Rome was fulfilled. Thus the most majestic of all past years, this anniversary year was celebrated with magnificent games by a Christian emperor. There is no doubt but that Philip obtained the favor of such devotion as this for Christ and the Church, since no author shows that there was any procession to the Capitol nor any sacrifice of victims according to custom. Yet both were killed, although in different places, one in a mutiny of soldiers, the other through the treachery of Decius.

(21) In the one thousand and fourth year after the founding of the City, Decius, the instigator and represser of civil war, after the two Philips were killed, seized the power as the twenty-fifth emperor after Augustus and held it for three years.[70] He immediately, in which he showed that he had killed Philip on account of this, sent out deadly edicts for the persecution and killing of Christians, the seventh persecution after the time of Nero, and he sent a great many saints from their crosses to receive crowns from Christ. And he appointed his own son as Caesar, with whom he was immediately killed in the very midst of the barbarians.

In the one thousand seventh year after the founding of the City, Gallus Hostilianus seized the throne as the twenty-sixth emperor after Augustus, and with difficulty held it for two years with his son, Volusianus.[71] Vengeance for the violation of the Christian name spread out and, where the edicts of Decius for the destruction of churches circulated, to those places a pestilence of incredible diseases extended. Almost no Roman province, no city, no house existed, which was not seized by that general pestilence and laid bare. Gallus and Volusianus, famous for this plague alone, were killed while carrying on a civil war against Aemilianus who was eager for

69 244 to 249; jointly with his son from 247 to 249.
70 249 to 251.
71 251 to 253.

a revolution. Aemilianus, however, was destroyed in the third month after entering upon his usurpation.[72]

(22) In the one thousand and tenth year after the founding of the City, two emperors in the twenty-seventh place after Augustus were established: Valerian being called Augustus by the army in Raetia, and Gallienus being made Caesar by the Senate at Rome;[73] and Gallienus unhappily remained in power for fifteen years, while the human race had little relief from an unusually continuous and severe pestilence. Wickedness, easily forgetful, called forth its own punishment. For impiety, while it is conscious of the scourge when beaten, becoming callous is not conscious of him by whom it is scourged. To pass over earlier persecutions, when the persecution of the Christians was inflicted by Decius, a great pestilence harassed the entire Roman Empire. Injustice deceived itself, being cheated to its own destruction by the poor judgment that the pestilence was of common occurrence and that the death which resulted from the diseases was a natural end and not a punishment. Again, therefore, and in a short time, they provoked the anger of God by their wicked actions and were about to receive a blow which they were forced to remember for a long time. For Valerian, as soon as he had seized the power, ordered the Christians to be forced by tortures into idolatry, the eighth emperor after Nero to do so. When they refused, he ordered them to be killed, and the blood of saints was shed throughout the length and breadth of the Roman Empire. Valerian, the author of the abominable edict, the emperor of the Roman people, being immediately captured by Sapor, the king of the Persians, grew old among the Persians in most humiliating slavery, for he was condemned to this menial service as long as he lived, namely, always by bending on the ground to raise the king as he was about to mount his horse, not by his hand, but by his back. And Gallienus, indeed, being terrified by such an evident judgment of God and moved by the wretched

---

72 From June to September, 253.
73 Valerian, 253 to 260; Gallienus with Valerian, 253 to 260, alone to 268.

example of his colleague, restored peace to the churches with anxious reparation. But the captivity of one wicked person, although perpetual and abominable beyond measure, did not compensate for the measure of the injury and vengeance against so many thousands of tortures of the saints, and the blood of the just cried out to God asking that it be vindicated in the same land where it had been shed. For not on the author alone of the order was punishment in a righteous judgment demanded, but it was just that also the performers of the judgment, the informers, the accusers, the spectators, and the judges, finally, all who assented to this most unjust cruelty even by tacit consent, for God knows all secrets, the largest part of whom were scattered through the provinces, be struck by the same blow of vengeance. Suddenly, from all sides by the will of God, the nations located on the boundaries of the Empire and left there for this purpose are loosed and, with the reins relaxed, rushed into the territory of the Romans. The Germans, making their way over the Alps, through Raetia and all Italy, came as far as Ravenna; the Alemanni ranging through the Gauls crossed even into Italy; Greece, Macedonia, Pontus, and Asia were destroyed by an influx of Goths; indeed, Dacia beyond the Danube was lost forever; the Quadi and the Sarmatians ravaged the Pannonian provinces; the further Germans, after stripping Spain, took possession of it; the Parthians seized Mesopotamia and devastated Syria. There still exist, throughout the different provinces in the ruins of great cities, small and poverty stricken settlements, preserving signs of their misfortunes and indications of their names, among which also in Spain we point out Tarraco as a consolation for our recent misery. And lest by chance anything of the Roman body be free from this mangling, tyrants conspired within, civil wars sprang up, a great deal of Roman blood was shed as the Romans and the barbarians vented their rage, but soon the wrath of God turned to pity, and the appearance of a vengeance begun was considered greater than a punishment in full measure. So Ingenuus, who had assumed the imperial purple, was the first to be killed at Mursa.[74] Postumus[75] in Gaul usurped the rule, indeed, to the great advantage of the state, for over a period of ten years, employing great bravery and moderation, he both expelled the dominating enemy and restored the lost provinces to their former condition; but he was killed in a mutiny of the soldiers. Aemilian, when he was attempting a revolution at Mainz, was overcome. After the death of Postumus, Marius seized the supreme power there, but was immediately killed. Then Victorinus[76] was made emperor by the Gauls on their own initiative, and a little later was killed. Tetricus,[77] who at that time administered the office of governor of Aquitania, succeeded him. He endured many mutinies on the part of the soldiers. But in the East, Odenathus gathered a band of peasants and overcame and repulsed the Persians, defended Syria, recovered Mesopotamia, and the Syrian peasants with their leader, Odenathus, went as far as Ctesiphon. But Gallienus, when he had abandoned the state and was indulging his lusts at Milan, was killed.

(23) In the one thousand and twenty-fifth year after the founding of the City, Claudius,[78] as the twenty-eighth emperor, assumed the power by the will of the Senate and straightway attacked and, with incredible slaughter, annihilated the Goths who for fifteen years had been laying waste Illyria and Macedonia. A golden shield was decreed him in the Senate House and in the Capitol a statue equally golden, but immediately, before he had fulfilled two years in power, he was seized by a disease and perished at Sirmium.

When Claudius died, Quintillus,[79] his brother, was elected emperor by the army, a man, indeed, of unparalleled self-

---

74 A city in Lower Pannonia, now *Esgek*.
75 Postumus, Marcus Cassianus Latinus, from between December 10, 258, and January 28, 259, to December 10, 268.
76 268 to 270.
77 270 to 273.
78 Claudius II, 268 to 270.
79 About two months in 270.

restraint and the only emperor to be preferred to his brother; he was killed on the seventeenth day of his rule.

In the one thousand and twenty-seventh year after the founding of the City, Aurelian, the twenty-ninth emperor, took over the power and held it for five years and six months,[80] a man of extraordinary ability in the affairs of war. Taking up an expedition on the Danube, he overcame the Goths in extensive battles and established Roman rule within its former boundaries. Then, turning to the East, he reduced Zenobia, who, when her husband, Odenathus, was slain, was taking the recovered province of Syria to herself, under his power by the fear of battle rather than by battle. Without difficulty, he overcame Tetricus, who in Gaul was not at all equal to controling the mutinies of his own soldiers and wrote: 'Snatch me from these evils, O thou who are unconquered,'[81] and thereby became the betrayer of his own army. Thus, as the reconqueror of the East and of the North, he held a triumph in great glory. He surrounded the City of Rome with stronger walls. Finally, when he was issuing a decree for the carrying on of a persecution against the Christians, the ninth after Nero, lightning struck in front of him to the great consternation of the bystanders, and not long afterward he was killed while on a journey.

(24) In the one thousand and thirty-second year after the founding of the City, Tacitus,[82] the thirtieth emperor gained the power, and in the sixth month of his reign was killed in the Pontus. After him, Florian, suffering a like fate in his reign, was killed precisely in the third month[83] at Tarsus.

In the one thousand and thirty-third year after the founding of the City, Probus, the thirty-first emperor, obtained the throne and held it for six years and four months.[84] He finally

---

80 March, 270 to August, 275.
81 Vergil *Aeneid,* **6.365.**
82 Marcus Claudius Tacitus; emperor from autumn, 275 to early April, 276.
83 Two months and twenty days, from April to July, 276.
84 276 to 282.

freed the Gallic provinces completely, which had been occupied
for so long by the barbarians, after destroying the enemy in
many serious battles. Then, he carried on two civil wars with
much shedding of blood: one in the East where he overthrew
and captured Saturninus who was enjoying a tyranny; the
other at Agrippina where he overcame and killed Proculus and
Bonosus in great battles. He himself, however, at Sirmium in
an iron-covered tower was killed in a mutiny of his soldiers.

In the one thousand and thirty-ninth year after the founding of the City, Carus of Narbo took up the power as the thirty-
second emperor and held it for two years.[85] When he had
made his sons, Carinus and Numerian, colleagues[86] in his rule,
and after he had captured two very famous cities, Coche and
Ctesiphon, in a war against the Parthians, in a camp upon the
Tigris he was struck by lightning and killed. Numerian, who
had been with his father, was treacherously killed, while re-
treating, by his father-in-law, Aper.

(25) In the one thousand and forty-first year after the
founding of the City, Diocletian was chosen as the thirty-third
emperor by the army and was emperor for twenty years,[87] and
as soon as he had full power he immediately, with his own
hand, killed Aper, the murderer of Numerian. Then, in a
very difficult battle, stubbornly contested, he overcame Carinus,
whom Carus had left as Caesar in Dalmatia where he was
living a profligate life. Later, when Amandus and Aelianus
had gathered together a band of peasants who were called
Bacaudae, and had stirred up ruinous revolts, he appointed
Maximianus, surnamed Herculius, as Caesar and sent him into
the Gallic provinces. He, by his military bravery, easily
brought to order the inexperienced and confused band of
peasants. Then, a certain Carausius, indeed low of birth but
quick in counsel and action, when being placed in charge of
the defense of the Ocean's shores, which at that time the

---

85 282 to 283.
86 Carinus from 283 to 285; Numerian from 283 to 284.
87 284 to 305.

Franks and Saxons were infesting, did more to harm than to advance the good of the state, arousing suspicion by restoring no part of the booty recovered from the pirates to its owners, but appropriating it for himself alone, for by deliberate neglect he permitted the enemy themselves to invade the territory; wherefore, when ordered by Maximianus to be killed, he seized the purple and occupied the British provinces. Thus, throughout the confines of the Roman Empire, the roars of sudden strife sounded, Carausius leading a rebellion in the British provinces and Achilleus in Egypt, while the Quinquegentiani disturbed Africa, and Narseus also, king of the Persians, pressed the East with war; Diocletian, being disturbed by this danger, made Herculius Maximianus Augustus[88] instead of Caesar, and he appointed Constantius and Galerius Maximianus as Caesars.[89] Constantius took to wife Theodora, the stepdaughter of Herculius Maximianus, by whom he had six sons, brothers of Constantinus. Carausius, after Britain had been claimed and very strongly held by him for seven years,[90] was finally treacherously killed by Allectus, his comrade. Then Allectus held the island which he had snatched from Carausius for three years. Asclepiodotus, the praetorian prefect, overcame him and took over Britain after ten years.[91] Now Constantius Caesar, when in a first battle his army was overcome by the Alemanni, himself barely escaped; but in a second battle, a very successful victory followed, for within a few hours sixty thousand Alemanni are reported to have been slain. But Maximianus Augustus in Africa subdued the Quinquegentiani. Furthermore, Diocletian, having besieged Achilleus at Alexandria for eight months, captured and killed him. But employing no moderation in his victory, he gave Alexandria over to plunder and defiled all Egypt with proscriptions and massacres. Besides, Galerius Maximianus, after he had

---

88 286.
89 293.
90 286 to 293.
91 293 to 296.

fought Narseus in two battles, in a third battle somewhere between Callinicus and Carrhae, met Narseus and was conquered, and after losing his troops fled to Diocletian. He was received by him very arrogantly, so that he is reported, though clad in purple, to have been made to run before his carriage, but he used this insult as whetstone to valor, as a result of which, after the rust of royal pride had rubbed off, he developed a sharpness of mind. Thus he brought troops together from all sides throughout Illyricum and Moesia and, hurriedly turning against the enemy, he overcame Narseus by his great strategy and forces. With the Persian troops annihilated and Narseus himself turned into flight, he entered Narseus' camp, captured his wives, sisters, and children, seized an immense amount of Persian treasure, and led away a great many Persian noblemen. Returning to Mesopotamia, he was received by Diocletian with the highest honor. Later, there was strenuous fighting by these same generals against the Carpi and the Basternae. Then, they conquered the Sarmatians, of whom a very large number of captives were distributed throughout the garrisons of the Roman frontiers.

Meanwhile, Diocletian in the East and Maximianus Herculius in the West ordered churches to be laid waste and Christians to be persecuted and put to death, the tenth persecution after Nero. This persecution was almost of longer duration and more cruel than all that had gone before, for it was carried on without cessation for ten years with the burning of churches, the proscription of the innocent, and the slaughter of martyrs. An earthquake followed in Syria, as a result of which, as buildings collapsed everywhere, many thousands of people were crushed in Tyre and Sidon. In the second year of the persecution, Diocletian demanded of the unwilling Maximianus that they both at the same time lay aside the purple and power and, after substituting younger men in the government, that they themselves grow old in private leisure. And so on the appointed day, they at the same time laid aside the power of government and all the trappings, Diocletian at Nicomedia and Maximianus at Milan.[92]

The Augusti, Galerius and Constantius, were the first to divide the Roman Empire into two parts. Galerius Maximianus took Illyricum, Asia, and the East; Constantius Italy, Africa, and the Gallic provinces, but Constantius, an extremely mild tempered man, being satisfied with Gaul (and Spain) alone, gave over the other districts to Galerius. Galerius chose two Caesars: Maximinus,[93] whom he established in the East, and Severus, to whom he turned over Italy, he himself remaining in Illyricum. But Constantius Augustus, a very calm man and skilled in government affairs, met death in Britain. He left Constantine, a son born of his concubine, Helena, as the elected emperor.

(26) In the one thousand and sixty-first year after the founding of the City, as the thirty-fourth emperor, he took over the helm of the Empire from his father, Constantius, who had held it most happily for thirty-one years.[94]

Suddenly, there is a convergence upon me and dancing in certain measured steps: 'Aha!' they say, 'at last you have come into our trap, O long awaited one. Here we were awaiting you to overrun your mark; here we catch you in your fall; here we hold you in your confusion. Until now we have been patient with you as you, in a manner, artificially and cleverly fitted in the accidental changes of the times with the vengeances exacted for Christians. And sometimes, indeed, being moved by the apparent truths set forth, inasmuch as we are men ignorant of the secrets of God, we turned pale with fear, but now our Maximianus has cleared away the entire stage setting of your play and has shone forth as the unshakable prop of our ancient religion. For ten years your churches have been overthrown, as even you confess; Christians

---

92 This took place on May 1, 305.
93 Maximinus, Gaius Galerius Valerius, surname *Daia* or *Daza,* and Severus, Flavius Valerius.
94 306 to 337.

over the whole world have been wracked with tortures and wiped out by deaths. We possess your own testimony that no earlier persecution ever was so severe or so long lasting. And yet behold, in the midst of the blessings of those most tranquil times, the blessings of the very emperors who accomplished them, there was an unusual happiness; there was no famine at home, no pestilence; no war abroad except voluntary, by which their forces could be exercised not endangered; furthermore, there was a condition of affairs hitherto unknown to the human race: the enduring association of many rulers at the same time and a great harmony and a joint power now looking to the common good which never took place before. Then also, something that never came to the notice of the human race before, for those very great emperors and persecutors laid aside their office and took on a life of rest as private citizens, which men judge the most blessed and highest good of life, and this the authors of persecution then assumed as a reward at a time when a persecution was stirred up and, in the middle of its course, was raging in the whole world. Or do you claim that this blessing also took place in those times as a punishment and do you strive to frighten us on this ground also?'

To these persons, I would humbly reply that, girded with the highest regard for piety, I am advising them of the truth and not frightening them with falsehoods. The Church of Christ has suffered ten persecutions from Nero to Maximianus. Nine vengeances, as I have called them, as they themselves do not deny, calamities, immediately followed. I do not make an issue of the expression, whether they seemed to have been merited vengeances or fortuitous changes, but they were, according to my testimony and theirs, calamities. Regarding the tenth persecution, these wretchedly blind people think that there is some uncertainty, since they do not see that it was the more serious for them according as it was less perceived. For the impious man is beaten and does not feel it. When this has been explained, because of the very facts of the case, they will confess, although unwillingly, that those wounds exist as the result of a very severe punishment for the Maximian persecution, because of which even now they grieve and grieve so much that they even cry out and drive us to cry out in return that we are becoming anxious as to how we may silence them.

(27) In the first book, it was set forth by us that Pompeius Trogus and Cornelius Tacitus recalled, not in detail as our Moses did, a faithful and complete source as even my critics themselves admit, that the Egyptians and their king, when they called the people of God, eager and ready to serve their God, back to the clay and straw to restrain them in their devotion, were harassed by ten very grievous plagues. Then overcome by their misfortunes, they not only forced them in their haste, but even loaded them down with their own gold and silver vessels. Later, forgetful of the lessons of the plagues, also in their hatred for a foreign religion, while they eagerly pursued the innocent, being finally overwhelmed in the Red Sea, they were completely destroyed. This I now relate and declare, although perchance not accepted on faith, yet to be proven by its results, because these events took place as an example for us. Both people serve the one God; both people have the one cause. The synagogue of the Israelites was subject to the Egyptians; the Church of the Christians was subject to the Romans. The Egyptians carried on persecutions; the Romans also carried on persecutions. In the former case, ten refusals were sent to Moses; in the latter, ten edicts were directed against Christ; in the one case, various plagues struck the Egyptians; in the latter, various calamities struck the Romans. In order to make a comparison between the two series of plagues, insofar, however, as the different forms can be compared, in the one case, the reproach caused blood everywhere to rise from the wells or to flow in the rivers. Here, in the Empire, the first slaughter caused the blood of the dying to exist everywhere, either corrupted by disease in the City or gushing forth from wars in the world. There, in Egypt, the

second plague discloses that the frogs, croaking and hopping in the temples, were almost the cause of starvation and exile for the inhabitants. Here, in Rome, under Domitian, the second punishment similarly disclosed that almost all the Roman citizens were forced into poverty and dispersed in exile by the wicked and unbridled running about on the part of his henchmen and soldiers. There, in Egypt, the third hardship included sciniphes, namely, very small and ferocious flies, which, often in midsummer hovering in swarms over filthy places and buzzing around, are accustomed to settle down and lodge themselves in men's hair and in the bristly hair of cattle with a stinging bite. Here, in the Roman Empire, the third plague, under Trajan, stirred up the Jews, who, although formerly dispersed everywhere and as quiet as if they did not exist, suddenly all of them, aroused in the heat of anger, vented their wrath in the whole world against the very people among whom they were living, not to mention the extensive destruction of many large cities which, at the same time, frequent earthquakes had overthrown. There, in Egypt, during the fourth plague, there were the dog flies, truly the offspring of putrefaction and the mothers of worms. Here, in the Roman Empire, likewise, in the fourth plague, under Marcus Antoninus, a pestilence spread over a great many provinces, also all of Italy including the City of Rome, and the Roman army, scattered along the distant frontiers in various winter quarters being loosed in death, was given over to putrefaction and worms. There, in Egypt, a fifth chastisement was fulfilled in the sudden destruction of flocks and beasts of burden. Here, in Rome, similarly in a fifth vengeance under the persecutor, Severus, the very vitals and mainstay of the state, that is, the people of the provinces and the military legions, were diminished by very frequent civil wars. There, in Egypt, a sixth distress brought on running sores and festering ulcers. Here, in Rome, likewise, there was a sixth punishment which took place after the persecution of Maximinus, who had ordered that the bishops and priests especially, that is, the primates of the churches, passing over the common people, be slaughtered; seething anger and hatred breathed forth frequently, not by the slaughter of the common people, but by the wounding and killing of the chief and powerful men. There, in Egypt, a seventh plague is reckoned, a shower of hail caused by the condensation of the air, which brought destruction to human beings, beasts, and crops. Here, in Rome, likewise, under Gallus and Volusianus who had succeeded the persecutor, Decius, who had met his death early, a seventh plague arose from the poisoning of the air. This pestilence throughout all the confines of the Roman Empire, from the east into the west, not only gave over to death almost the entire human race, but also 'poisoned the lakes and infected the grass.'[95] There, locusts stirring up from everywhere caused the eighth affliction for Egypt, seizing, tearing, and covering everything. Here, similarly, nations stirred up on all sides, which had destroyed all the provinces by slaughter and fire, brought on the eighth affliction, looking for the overthrow of the Roman world. There, in Egypt, the ninth upheaval consisted of long-lasting thick shadows, almost possible to be grasped, threatening more harm than it actually caused; here, in Rome, likewise, there was a ninth retribution when, during a frightful gale, a terribly distressing thunderbolt struck at the very feet of Aurelian who was directing the persecution, showing, when such a vengeance was being exacted, what power so great an avenger has, were He not both kind and patient. And yet within six months of that time, three successive emperors, that is, Aurelian, Tacitus, and Florian, for various reasons were killed. There, finally, in Egypt, the tenth plague, which was also the last of all, was the killing of the sons who were given birth to first; here, in Rome, the tenth, that is, the last punishment of all, was the destruction of the idols which, made originally, they especially loved.

---

95 Cf. Vergil, *Georgics* 3.481.

There, in Egypt, the king felt, tried, and feared the power of God, and so permitted the people of God to go free; here, in Rome, the king felt, tried, and believed in the power of God, and so permitted the people of God to be free. There, in Egypt, never afterwards were the people of God brought into slavery; here, in Rome, never afterwards were the people of God forced into idolatry. There, the precious vessels of the Egyptians were given over to the Hebrews; here, the chief temples of the pagans gave way to churches of Christians. Certainly, as I have said, I think that this ought to be pointed out, that just as when the Egyptians tried to pursue the Hebrews, who after these ten plagues were dismissed, eternal destruction through an overwhelming sea crushed them, so, too, at some future time a persecution by the Gentiles awaits us as we journey in freedom, until we cross the Red Sea, that is, the fire of judgment, with our Lord Jesus Christ Himself as our Caesar and judge. But those, to whom is transferred the role of the Egyptians, the power having been permitted them temporarily by the authority of God, showing their anger will persecute the Christians with the most serious tortures; yet all those same enemies of Christ with their king, Antichrist, being caught in the lake of eternal fire, which, because of the great darkness that intervenes, is entered upon while it is not seen, will receive the lot of perpetual damnation to burn with everlasting torments.

(28) So, as I have said, on the death of Constantius in Britain, Constantine was proclaimed emperor, the first Christian among the emperors with the exception of Philip, who seemed to me to have been established as a Christian emperor for only a very few years for this purpose alone, that the thousandth year of the founding of Rome might be dedicated to Christ rather than to idols. Now from Constantine to the present day, all the emperors have been Christians with the exception of Julian, whose destructive life was cut off, as it is said, while he was planning wicked deeds. This is the slow but certain punishment of the pagans; for this reason, the

sane rave; for this reason, though not hurt, they are goaded
by the sting of conscience; for this reason, though laughing,
they groan; for this reason, though living, they fail; for this
reason, they are secretly tortured whom no one persecutes;
for this reason, very few have remained who have never been
punished by any persecutor. But I shall bring out what an end
awaited those persecutors at that time as a result of whose
impunity they try not only to boast, but also to give insults.

While Constantine was most actively attending to the welfare of the state in the Gallic provinces, the soldiers of the
praetorian guard in Rome proclaimed Maxentius,[96] the son
of Herculius, who was idling his time away in Lucania,
Augustus. Maximianus Herculius, now a private citizen instead of an Augustus and still a public persecutor, tempted
by his son's opportunity, who had thrown aside the power,
attempted to seize the power of a usurper.[97] Galerius Augustus sent Severus Caesar with an army to Rome against Maxentius. When Severus was besieging the City, being treacherously deserted and betrayed by his own soldiers and while in
flight from the scene, he was killed at Ravenna. Herculius
Maximianus, a persecutor and formerly Augustus but now
a usurper, trying to despoil his son, already established in the
seat of government, of his garb and royal authority, became
frightened by the open insults and riotings of the soldiers,
and proceeded into Gaul, that joining with Constantine he
might, by like treachery, take away the power. Being detected
by his daughter and betrayed, then turned into flight, he was
seized and killed at Marseilles.[98] Furthermore, when Severus
was killed, Galerius made Licinius[99] emperor. And when he
himself had augmented the persecution ordered by Diocletian
and Maximianus by more dreadful edicts, and after he had
drained the provinces for ten years of every kind of man, his

---

96 307 to 312.
97 February, 307.
98 310.
99 308.

chest rotted within and his vital organs decayed. When, beyond
the horror of human misery he even vomited worms and his
physicians, being unable any longer to endure the stench,
were being put to death by his frequent orders, he was rebuked by a physician assuming courage out of despair, saying
that his punishment was the anger of God and so he could
not be cured by physicians. He then sent edicts far and wide
and recalled the Christians from their exiles. He himself,
however, unable to endure his torment, took his own life by
violence. So the state at that time came under the rule of
four new princes, Constantine and Maxentius, the sons of the
Augusti, and Licinius and Maximinus, self-made men. Constantine bestowed peace upon the churches after they had
been harassed by persecutors for ten years. The civil war
broke out between Constantine and Maxentius. Maxentius,
becoming exhausted again and again by many battles, was
finally conquered at the Mulvian Bridge and killed. Maximinus, the instigator of the persecution of the Christians
and its most cruel executor, died at Tarsus while he was
organizing a civil war against Licinius. Licinius, roused by
a sudden madness, ordered all Christians to be expelled from
his palace. Presently, a war raged between Licinius himself
and Constantine. But Constantine first conquered Licinius,
his sister's husband, in Pannonia, and then crushed him at
Cibalae,[100] and after gaining possession of all Greece, when
Licinius attempted to rise again by frequent battles on land
and sea, he finally overcame him and forced him to surrender;
but roused by the example of Maximianus Herculius, his
father-in-law, that he might not again take on the purple
when it was laid aside, to the ruin of the state, he ordered
him as a private citizen to be killed. Although all the agents
of that abominable persecution had now been put out of
existence, this man, also a persecutor to the full extent of his
power, was visited with a worthy punishment. The sons of

---

100 In Lower Pannonia.

Constantine, Crispus and Constantine, and the young Licinius, the son of Licinius Augustus and the nephew of Constantine by his sister, were proclaimed Caesars.

At this time, Arius, a priest of the city of Alexandria, going astray from the truth of the Catholic faith, established a dogma destructful to many. As soon as he became famous, or rather infamous, at Alexandria among his generally confused followers and his censurers, he was expelled from the Church by Alexander, at that time bishop of that same city. And when he also incited into sedition the men whom he had led astray into error, an assembly of three hundred and eighteen bishops was held at Nicaea, a city of Bithynia, by whom the Arian doctrine, being very clearly detected as destructful and wretched, was publicly exposed and condemned. But in the midst of these events, there were unknown reasons why the emperor, Constantine, turned the sword of vengeance and the punishment destined for the impious against even his close relatives. For he killed his own son, Crispus, and his sister's son, Licinius. He also subdued many nations in various battles. He was the first or the only one of the Roman rulers to found a city after his own name. This city, Constantinople, alone free of idols, in a very short time after its founding by a Christian emperor was raised to such a point that it alone could worthily be equal to Rome in beauty and power, which had been raised to her position after so many centuries and miseries. Then, for the first time, Constantine reversed the situation by a just and pious order, for by an edict he ordered that the temples of the pagans be closed without the killing of anyone. Soon he destroyed the strongest and most prosperous nations of the Goths in the very heart of the barbarian territory, that is, in the region of the Sarmations. He crushed a certain Calocaerus in Cyprus who was striving for a revolution. On his thirtieth anniversary as emperor, he appointed Dalmatius Caesar. And while he was preparing for war against the Persians, he died in his official residence near Nicomedia, leaving the state in very good order for his sons.

(29) In the one thousand and ninety-second year after the founding of the City, Constantius,[101] the thirty-fifth emperor, together with his brothers, Constantine[102] and Constans,[103] took over the power and held it for twenty-four years. Also among the successors of Constantine, there was Dalmatius Caesar, the son of his brother, but he was immediately ensnared by a faction of soldiers. Meanwhile, the ever-malignant struggle of the devil against the true God, which, from the beginning of the world down to the present day, has been disturbing the uncertain hearts of men away from the true path of religious faith by spreading clouds of error, after it ceased to persecute the Church of Christ with idolatrous zeal when the Christian emperors turned their sovereign power to better things, discovered another scheme by which to harass the Church of Christ through these same Christian emperors. Thus Arius, the author of a new heresy, and his disciples had ready access and an easy way to an intimate acquaintance with the emperor, Constantius. Constantius was persuaded to believe that there are certain gradations in God, and he, who had departed from the error of idolatry by the main door, was led back into its bosom by a side entrance, as it were, when he sought gods in God. So his power, when ridiculed, was armed with a perverted zeal and, under the name of religious devotion, the force of a persecution was stirred up. There was contention about the choice of a new name, that the churches should belong to the Arians rather than to the Catholics. There followed a terrible earthquake which leveled a great many cities of the East with the ground. Constantine, the second, while he was pursuing his brother, Constans, in war, offering himself to dangers with reckless petulance, was killed by his brother's generals. Constans fought nine battles with little success against the Persians and Sapor, who had laid waste to Mesopotamia. Finally, being forced to make an

---

101 Constantius II, 337-361.
102 Constantine II, 337-340.
103 Constans, 337-350.

attack in the night because of the mutiny and impudence of his soldiers, besides being conquered, he lost a victory which had been almost won. Afterwards, when he had given himself over to intolerable vices and by oppressing the provincials was gaining the favor of the soldiers, he was treacherously killed by Magnentius in a town called Helena in the vicinity of Spain. For Magnentius seized the power at Augustodunum, which he immediately extended over Gaul, Africa, and Italy.[104] In Illyricum, the soldiers chose as their emperor the aged Vetranio, a man simple of nature and agreeable to all, but who had never received the first rudiments of an education. When the aged emperor, at times against his will, was studying the alphabet and the syllables of words, he was ordered by Constantius, who at that time was preparing for war against Magnentius, afire with a feeling of revenge for his brother, to lay aside the power; giving up the purple together with his studies, and content with a life of leisure, he dismissed the palace and school at the same time. Nepotian, the son of Constantine's sister, relying on a band of gladiators, then seized the power at Rome. He, then, since he was wicked and on this account hateful to all, was overcome by the generals of Magnentius. There followed that horrible battle between Constantius and Magnentius, fought at the city of Mursa, in which the great loss of Roman forces did harm even to posterity. However, Magnentius, although conquered, escaped, and not much later killed himself by his own hand at Lugdunum. Decentius, also his brother, whom he had appointed Caesar over the Gauls, ended his life with the noose at Senones. Constantius immediately appointed Gallus, the son of his paternal uncle, Caesar, whom, again shortly after he appointed him, he killed since he acted cruelly and tyrannically. Silvanus also, eager for a revolution throughout the Gauls, he had quickly surrounded and crushed. So, after killing Silvanus, he created Julianus, his cousin on his father's side, the brother

104 350-353.

of Gallus, Caesar and sent him to Gaul; and thus Julianus Caesar very actively restored to their former condition the Gallic provinces which had been overturned and crushed by the enemy; with a small force he routed a great multitude of the Alemanni, and he pushed back the Germans across the Rhine. Elated by these successes, he usurped the dignity of Augustus and, presently, making his way through Italy and Illyricum, he deprived Constantius, who was occupied with battles against the Parthians, of a part of his dominion. On learning of the treachery of Julianus, while returning to civil war after abandoning his campaign against the Parthians, he died on the road between Cilicia and Cappadocia. Thus he, who had torn asunder the peace and the unity of the Catholic faith, arming Christians against Christians in civil war, so to speak, dismembered the Church, and spent, used, and expended the entire period of his restless reign and the very troublesome period of his life in civil wars stirred up even by his kinsmen and relatives.

(30) In the one thousand one hundred and sixteenth year after the founding of the City, Julianus, formerly Caesar, afterwards, however, seized the power as the thirty-sixth emperor after Augustus and held the supreme power alone for a year and eight months.[105] Attacking the Christian religion by cunning rather than by force, he strove to rouse men by honors to deny the faith of Christ and take up the worship of idols, rather than by inflicting tortures. But in a public edict, he ordered that no Christian should be a professor for the teaching of liberal studies. However, as we have learned from our elders, almost all everywhere respected the conditions of the order and preferred to give up their positions rather than their faith. Moreover, Julianus, when he was preparing war against the Parthians and he was taking with him to destined destruction Roman forces brought together from all sides, vowed the blood of Christians to his gods, intending to

---

105 From November 3, 361 to June 26, 363.

persecute the churches openly if he should be able to win a victory. Indeed, he ordered an amphitheater to be constructed at Jerusalem, in which on his return from the Parthians he might offer the bishops, monks, and all the saints of the locality to beasts deliberately made more ferocious and might view them being torn apart. Thus, after he moved his camp from Ctesiphon, being led into the desert by a treacherous traitor, when his army began to perish from the force of thirst, the heat of the sun, and especially when affected by the difficulty of marching through the sands, the emperor, anxious because of the danger of the situation as he wandered rather carelessly over the wastes of the desert, was struck by a lance of a cavalryman of the enemy whom he met and died. Thus, the merciful God ended these evil plans by the death of their evil author.

(31) In the one thousand one hundred and seventeenth year after the founding of the City, Jovian, in a very critical state of affairs, was made the thirty-seventh emperor by the army, and when, being caught in an unfavorable locality and being surrounded by the enemy, he possessed no chance to escape, he made a treaty with Sapor, the king of the Persians, although, as some think, little worthy yet quite necessary. For, that he might free the Roman army, safe and sound, not only from an attack of the enemy, but also from the dangers of the locality, he conceded the town of Nisibis and part of Upper Mesopotamia to the Persians. Then, while he was making his way through Galatia on his return to Illyricum, when he had withdrawn into a newly built bedchamber to rest, being overcome and suffocated by the heat of hot coals and the dampness of the walls recently smeared with plaster, he finally ended his life in the eighth month after he had begun to rule.[106]

(32) In the one thousand one hundred and eighteenth year from the founding of the City, Valentinian was made the thirty-eighth emperor at Nicaea by the consent of the soldiers,

---

106 From June 27, 363 to February 16, 364.

and he remained in this office for eleven years.[107]   Although as a Christian, without damage to his faith, he had performed military service under Julian Augustus as tribune of the *scutarii,* on being ordered by that sacrilegious emperor either to sacrifice to idols or to withdraw from the service, knowing as a man of faith that the judgments of God were more severe and His promises better, he departed of his own accord.   So after a slight intervention of time, after Julianus had been killed and presently Jovian had died, he who for the name of Christ had lost the tribuneship, as a reward from Christ received the power in the place of his own persecutor.   He afterwards made his brother, Valens, a sharer in the power,[108] and he later killed the usurper, Procopius, and many of his followers.   An earthquake, which took place throughout the whole world, so agitated and drove out the sea, that, when the sea was driven back over the neighboring level territory, many cities on the islands are reported to have been struck, to have collapsed, and to have perished.   Valens, being baptized and converted by the bishop, Eudoxius, a supporter of Arian doctrine, fell into that most violent heresy, but for a long time he concealed his wicked intention to persecute and he did not mingle his power with his wish, inasmuch as he was checked by the authority of his brother.   For in his regard, it was observed how much force the emperor could exercise in avenging the faith, who as a soldier had had such great firmness in retaining it.

In the third year of the rule of these emperors, Gratian, the son of Valentinian, was made emperor.[109]   In the same year, in the land of the Atrebates, real wool mixed with rain fell down from the clouds.

Furthermore, Athanaric, king of the Goths, persecuting the Christians in his own nation most cruelly, elevated many

---

107 364 to 375. He shared the office of emperor part of the time with
　　Valens and Gratian.
108 364. Valens ruled until 378.
109 367. Gratian ruled until 383.

barbarians, who were put to death because of their faith, to the crown of martyrdom; many of these, however, took refuge in the land of the Romans, not fearful as if seeking refuge with enemies, but full of confidence that they were going among brothers, by reason of their acknowledgement of Christ.

Valentinian, in the very territory of the Franks, crushed the Saxons, a tribe feared for its bravery and agility and located in pathless swamps on the shores of the Ocean, while they were planning a dangerous raid in great force against Roman possessions. The Burgundians, a new name for a new enemy, who, according to report, numbered more than eighty thousand armed men, settled on the bank of the Rhine. They, when the interior of Germany had once been subjected by Drusus and Tiberius, the adopted sons of Caesar, being dispersed in different camps, came together to form a great nation and so even took their names from their work, because their frequent dwelling places, established along the frontier in which they assumed possession and settled, are commonly called *burgi* and bear witness today that they are a very strong and destructive nation. Although by the providence of God they have all now become Christians, accepting the Catholic faith and our clergy whom they obey, they live kindly, gentle, and harmless lives, not, as it were, with the Gauls as their subjects, but really as their Christian brothers.

Now in the eleventh year of his rule, Valentinian, when the Sarmatians had overrun the Pannonian provinces and were laying them waste, while preparing a war against them at the town of Brigitio,[110] was choked by a sudden gush of blood, which in Greek is called apoplexy, and died.

After him, his son, Gratian, held the power in the West, while Valens, the uncle of the latter, was established in the regions of the East; he also made his brother, Valentinian, still very young, a partner in the power.[111]

---

110 In Lower Pannonia.
111 375.

(33) In the one thousand one hundred and twenty-eighth year after the founding of the City, Valens, the thirty-ninth emperor, held the power for four years after the death of Valentinian, who alone had been able to make him blush when he acted wickedly. Immediately, as if with the unbridled boldness of freedom, he made a law that monks, that is, Christians, who, laying aside the various activities of secular affairs were devoting themselves solely to the work of faith, should be forced into military service. At that time, a large number of monks filled and inhabited the vast solitudes of Egypt and the stretches of sands which had been known because of human contact with their dryness, sterility, and the large number of very dangerous snakes. To this place, tribunes and soldiers were sent to drag away the saints and true soldiers of God under another form of persecution. Many bands of saints were killed there. Moreover, let my very decision to remain silent suffice as an adequate indication of what actions were taken everywhere throughout the provinces by these and similar orders against the Catholic churches and the peoples of the right faith.

Meanwhile, in parts of Africa, Firmus, having stirred up the Moorish tribes and established himself as king, laid waste Africa and Mauretania; Caesarea, a very famous city of Mauretania, he captured by treachery, and after filling it with fire and slaughter, gave it over to the barbarians for plunder. Then Count Theodosius, the father of the Theodosius who later became emperor, being sent by Valentinian, crushed the Moorish tribes which had spread out in many battles, and forced Firmus himself, depressed and defeated, to take his own life. Afterwards, when, with a most experienced foresight, he had rendered all Africa and Mauretania better than they had been before, with envy creeping in and stimulating the action, he was condemned to death. At Carthage, he preferred to be baptized for the remission of his sins, and after he had attained the sacrament of Christ which he had sought, and after a glorious life in this world, also secure regarding his eternal life, he, of his own accord, offered his neck to the executioner.

The emperor, Gratian, meanwhile, still a youth, on perceiving the countless number of enemies pouring into Roman territory, relying on the power of Christ, set himself against the enemy with a very unequal number of soldiers and, immediately, at Argentaria, a Gallic town, completed a most formidable war with incredible good fortune. For more than thirty thousand Alemanni are reported to have been killed with very little loss to the Romans.

Now, in the thirteenth year of the reign of Valens, that is, a short time after Valens had carried on the destruction of the churches and the slaughter of the saints throughout the entire East, that root of our miseries all at once sent up very abundant shoots. For the race of Huns, shut off for a long time by inaccessible mountains, stirred up by a sudden rage burst out against the Goths and drove them in widespread disorder from their old homes. The Goths, fleeing across the Danube, were received by Valens without the negotiation of any treaty and they did not even give over their arms to the Romans, by which trust could be placed in the barbarians with greater safety. Then, on account of the intolerable avarice of the general, Maximus, driven by famine and injuries to rise in rebellion, they conquered the army of Valens and poured forth over all Thrace, mingling everything with slaughter, fire, and rapine. Valens, when, as he came out of Antioch, he was being dragged to his doom in an unfortunate war, stimulated by a late repentance for a very great sin, ordered the recall from exile of the bishops and other holy persons.

Thus, in the fifteenth year of his rule, Valens fought that lamentable war in Thrace with the Goths, who were then very well equipped with strong training and an abundance of resources. As soon as the squadrons of Roman cavalry were thrown into confusion by the sudden attack of the Goths, they left the companies of infantrymen without protection. Then the legions of infantry, becoming surrounded on all sides by the enemy's cavalry and, when first overwhelmed by showers of arrows and then mad with fear they were driven over devious paths, being completely cut to pieces by the swords and lances of those who were pursuing them, perished. The emperor himself, when wounded by an arrow and turned into flight he was carried to a house on a small farm and was concealed there, was caught by the pursuing enemy and was consumed by the fire that was set to the house, and, that the testimony of his punishment and of divine wrath might be a terrible example to posterity, he was even deprived of a common burial.

Let the wretched and stubborn heathen take consolation in this alone, that in Christian times and under Christian rulers such great disasters coming together at once overburdened the neck of the state already oppressed: the ruin of the provinces, the destruction of the army, and the burning of the emperor. This, indeed, contributes much to our grief, and it is the more wretched as it is new. But what does this profit for the consolation of the pagans, who plainly perceive that among these the persecutor of the churches also was punished. The one God handed down one faith and diffused one Church over the world. This Church He beholds; this Church He loves; this Church He defends. By whatever name anyone cloaks himself, if he be not associated with her, he is an alien, and, if he attacks her, he is an enemy. Let the heathen console themselves, insofar as they wish, in the punishment of the Jews and the heretics, but only let them confess that there is one God and that He is no respecter of persons as is especially proven by the destruction of Valens. Formerly, the Goths through legates had petitioned suppliantly that there might be sent them bishops from whom to learn the rule of the Christian faith. The emperor, Valens, with fatal perverseness, sent teachers of the Arian doctrine. The Goths clung to the basic teachings of the first faith which they had received. And so, by the just judgment of God, the very men burned him alive who, because of him, will also burn when dead for the vice of error.

(34) In the one thousand one hundred and thirty-second year after the founding of the City, Gratian, the fortieth ruler after Augustus, held the power for six years after the death of Valens,[112] although before this he had ruled for some time together with his uncle, Valens, and his brother, Valentinian. When he saw the afflicted and almost ruined condition of the state, with the same foresight with which Nerva had selected Trajan, a Spaniard, through whom the state was restored, he himself selected Theodosius, likewise a Spaniard, and invested him with the people at Sirmium for the necessary task of reestablishing the state, and he placed him in command of the East and likewise of Thrace,[113] in this case with better judgment, since in all the virtues of human life Theodosius was Trajan's equal and, in loyalty to the faith and in reverence for religion, he surpassed him beyond any comparison, for the one was a persecutor of the Church and the latter its propagator. Thus, Trajan was not blessed with even one son of his own, in whom he might rejoice as a successor, but the glorious descendants of Theodosius have ruled over the East and the West for successive generations down to the present day. Thus, Theodosius believed that the state which had been afflicted by the wrath of God was to be restored by His mercy; placing all his trust in the help of Christ, he attacked without hesitation the Scythian tribes, very mighty and feared by all our forebears and avoided even by Alexander the Great, as Pompeius and Cornelius testify, yet now, with the Roman army non-existent, very well equipped with Roman horses and arms, these, that is, the Alans, Huns, and Goths, he attacked and overcame in many great battles. He entered the city of Constantinople as a victor and that he might not exhaust the small band of Roman troops by constantly making war, he struck a treaty with Athanaric, the king of the Goths. Athanaric, however, as soon as he came to Constantinople, died. All the tribes of the Goths, with their king dead and

112 Until August 25, 383.
113 379.

beholding the bravery and kindness of Theodosius, gave themselves over to Roman rule. At this time also, the Persians
who, after Julian had been killed and other emperors frequently defeated, and now also with Valens driven into flight,
were belching forth their satisfaction for their most recent
victory with foul insults, of their own accord sent delegates
to Theodosius in Constantinople and suppliantly asked for
peace; and then a treaty was made which the entire East has
enjoyed very quietly to the present time. Meanwhile, when
Theodosius, after subjugating the barbarian tribes in the East,
had finally freed the Thracian provinces from the enemy and
had made his son, Arcadius, a sharer in his power, Maximus,
an energetic man, indeed, and honorable and worthy of the
throne had he not arrived at it by usurpation contrary to his
oath of allegiance, was made emperor by the army in Britain,
almost against his will,[114] and crossed over into Gaul where he
treacherously surrounded and killed Gratian Augustus who
was terrified by the sudden attack and was planning to cross
into Italy, and he expelled Gratian's brother, Valentinian
Augustus, from Italy. Valentinian, fleeing to the East, was
received by Theodosius with paternal devotion and presently
was even restored to power.

(35) In the one thousand one hundred and thirty-eighth
year after the founding of the City, Theodosius, the forty-first
emperor, after Gratian had been killed by Maximus, obtained
power over the Roman world and remained in it for eleven
years,[115] after he had already reigned in parts of the East for
six years during the lifetime of Gratian. So for just and necessary reasons, since, of his two royal brothers, the blood of one
who had been killed demanded vengeance and the wretchedness of the other who was in exile begged for restoration to
power, Theodosius placed his hope in God and hurled himself
against the usurper, Maximus, superior to him in faith alone,
for he was far inferior in every comparison of warlike equip-

114 383.
115 Until 395.

ment. Maximus had settled at Aquileia to be a spectator of his own victory. Andragathius, his count, was in charge of the administration of the entire war. When he had fortified extraordinarily all the approaches by way of the Alps and the rivers with very large numbers of troops and, strategically, which counted for more than large numbers of troops, by the ineffable judgment of God, while he prepared to catch the enemy off guard and to crush them by a naval expedition, of his own accord he abandoned the very passes which he had obstructed. Thus Theodosius, without being observed, not to say opposed, crossed the undefended Alps and, unexpectedly arriving at Aquileia, without treachery and without a contest surrounded, captured, and killed that great enemy, Maximus, a cruel man and one who also exacted from the very savage German tribes tribute and taxes by the terror of his name alone. Valentinian, after receiving the imperium, gained control of Italy. Count Andragathius, on learning of the death of Maximus, cast himself headlong from his ship into the waters and drowned. Theodosius, under the guidance of God, gained a bloodless victory. Behold how, under Christian rulers and in Christian times, civil wars, when they cannot be avoided, are concluded. The victory was arrived at, the city was broken through, and the usurper was captured. And this is a small part of the story. Behold, elsewhere a hostile army was conquered and the count of the usurper, more cruel than the usurper himself, was driven to his death; so many ambushes were broken up and avoided, and so many preparations were rendered of no avail. And yet no one employed trickery; no one arranged a line of battle; finally, no one, if the expression may be used, drew a sword from the scabbard. A most terrible war was accomplished even to victory without bloodshed and, on the occasion of the victory, with the death of two persons. And lest anyone think that this took place by chance, that the power of God, by which all things are dispensed and judged, by bringing forth its proof, may force the minds of the objectors either into confusion or belief, I mention a matter unknown to all and yet known to all. After this war, in which Maximus was killed, surely many civil and foreign wars have followed Theodosius and his son, Honorius, up to the present day, and yet almost all up to our own time have subsided with the fruit of a simple and holy victory at the cost of very little or no blood at all.

So Valentinian the Younger, being restored to his kingdom, on the destruction of Maximus and his son, Victor,[116] whom Maximus had left among the Gauls as emperor, himself passed over into Gaul, where, while he was living in peace in a quiet country, he was strangled at Vienne, as the reports say, through the treachery of his count, Arbogastes, and, that he might be thought to have planned death for himself voluntarily, he was hanged by a rope. Soon after Augustus Valentinian died, Arbogastes had the audacity to make Eugenius[117] a usurper and chose the man in order to place upon him the title of emperor. He himself a barbarian, intending to manage the government, outstanding in courage, wisdom, bravery, boldness, and power, gathered from all sides innumerable unconquered forces, either from the Roman garrisons or the barbarian auxiliaries, relying in the one case on his power, and in the other on his relationship. There is no need to expatiate on history known to very many, even as spectators, which those who have viewed it know better than I. There is strong proof in both instances that Theodosius always came off the victor through the power of God, not trust in man; in the one case, when Arbogastes, at that time while he was loyal to Theodosius, himself very weak, captured Maximus supported by so many troops, and when against the same Theodosius he abounded in forces gathered from the Gauls and the Franks, relying also especially on the worship of idols, he, nevertheless, succumbed with great ease. Eugenius and Arbogastes had made ready their lines in battle array on the plains and had occupied the narrow slopes of the Alps and

---

116 Flavius Victor, 384 to 388.
117 From May, 392 to September 6, 394.

the inescapable passes by cleverly sending ahead ambushing parties; although they were unequal in number and strength, yet by their strategy alone they were victors. Indeed, Theodosius, taking a position on the highest point of the Alps without food and sleep, realizing that he had been deserted by his own men, but not realizing that he had been surrounded by enemies, with his body spread upon the ground and with his mind fixed on heaven, he prayed alone to the one Lord Christ who is all powerful. Then, after he had passed a sleepless night in continuous prayer and after he had left pools of tears which he had paid as the price for heavenly assistance, he with confidence took up arms alone, realizing that he was not alone. With the sign of the cross he gave the signal for battle and, destined to be victorious, he plunged into battle, even though no one followed. The first way to safety was in the person of Arbitio, a count of the hostile party. When he had caught the unsuspecting emperor by laying an ambush about him, turning to revere the presence of Augustus, not only did he free him from danger, but he also drew up a defense for him. But when they had come to contiguous places for joining battle, immediately a great and indescribable whirlwind blew into the faces of the enemy. The darts of our men, which were shot and carried through the air and were borne through the great void farther than any man could throw, were almost never allowed to fall before striking a mark. And furthermore, the unceasing whirlwind struck the faces and breasts of the enemy, now heavily dashing their shields together and taking their breath when it pressed them closely together; and now tearing their shields violently away, it left them unprotected, and now holding their shields together tightly, it drove them back; the weapons also which they themselves had hurled strongly were caught by the backward force of the wind and, when driven back, transfixed the unfortunate throwers themselves. The fear of human conscience looked to its own good, for, as soon as a small band of their own men was routed, the army of the enemy surrendered to the victorious Theodosius;

Eugenius was captured and killed; Arbogastes destroyed himself by his own hand. So here, also, a civil war was extinguished by the blood of two men, not to mention those ten thousand Goths sent ahead by Theodosius whom Arbogastes is reported to have destroyed completely. To have lost these was surely a gain and their defeat a victory. I do not taunt our detractors. Let them set forth a single war, from the time when the City was first founded, which was undertaken with such a pious necessity, accomplished with such divine felicity, settled with such compassionate kindness, in which the battle did not exact heavy slaughter and the victory bloody revenge, and perhaps I shall concede that these seem to have been granted to the faith of a Christian general, although I am not concerned about this testimony, since one of them, an outstanding poet, indeed, but a most stubborn pagan, has borne witness both to God and man in the following verses,[118] saying:

> O thou much beloved by God! For thee the sky does battle,
> And the winds banded together come at the call of the trumpet.

Thus it is indicated from heaven between the party that placed hope humbly even without the aid of men on God alone, and the party that most arrogantly trusted in its own strength and in idols.

Theodosius, after organizing and tranquilizing the state, died while he was in Milan.

(36) In the one thousand one hundred and forty-ninth year after the founding of the City, Arcadius Augustus, whose son, Theodosius, now rules the East, and Honorius Augustus, his brother, on whom the state relies, in the forty-second place among emperors began to occupy the power, only in separate capitals.[119] Arcadius lived for twelve years after the death of

---

118 Claudian, *Panegyric on the Third Consulship of the Emperor Honorius* 96-98.

119 In the West, Honorius, 395-423; in the East, Arcadius, 395-408.

his father, and he handed down the supreme power on his death to Theodosius, his son, who was still very young.

Meanwhile, Count Gildo, who in the beginning of his brother's reign was in charge of Africa, as soon as he learned that Theodosius had died, as some say, moved by a kind of envy he tried to join Africa to the districts of the Eastern Empire, or, as another opinion has it, he did this thinking that there would be very little hope for the youthful rulers. He thought so especially since, except for these, hardly anyone before left in power as a youth had reached the maturity of full manhood, and they are found almost alone whom, on account of the father's eminent faith and his own, separated and forsaken, the protection of Christ had advanced, and so he dared to claim for himself Africa which had been detached from its allegiance to the state, content rather with pagan licentiousness than inspired with an ambition for royal affectation. His brother was Mascezel, who, abhorring the revolutionary undertakings of his brother, Gildo, left his two sons with the troops in Africa and returned to Italy. Gildo, holding the absence of his brother and the presence of the latter's two sons as matters of suspicion, treacherously entrapped the young men and killed them. Mascezel, his brother, was sent to pursue him in war as an enemy, the recent grief for his own bereavement giving assurance that he would be a fitting person in the service of the state. So Mascezel, already realizing from Theodosius how much in most desperate situations the prayer of man obtains from the mercy of God through faith in Christ, approached the island of Capraria, whence he took with him some holy servants of God who were moved by his prayers. Continuing with these in prayers, fasting, and the singing of psalms day and night, he won a victory without war and vengeance without slaughter. The name of the river is Ardalio, which flows between the cities of Theveste and Ammedera, where, with a small force, that is, with five thousand soldiers, as it is said, against seventy thousand of the enemy, he measured out a camp, since, after the intervention of a delay, he

wished to leave his position and cross through the passes of the
narrow valley that lay ahead. As night came on, he seemed
to see in a dream blessed Ambrose, bishop of Milan, who had
died a short time before, making a sign with his hand and
striking the ground three times, saying these words: 'Here,
here, here.' He wisely inferred that this signified, by the
worthiness of him who made the announcement, assurance of
victory, the place by the word spoken, the day by the number.
He accordingly held his ground and, at last on the third day,
after keeping vigil through the night in prayer and singing,
proceeded from the very mysteries of the heavenly sacraments
against the enemy who had surrounded him. When he hurled
at those who were the first to come to meet him pious words
of peace, he struck with his sword the arms of a soldier who
was stirring up a battle and forced him, weak because of the
wound, to lower the banner to the ground. At this sight, the
remaining cohorts, thinking that the front ranks were already
surrendering, turning their standards about, gave themselves
over to Mascezel. The barbarians, of whom Gildo had led a
great number into battle, being abandoned by the desertion
of the soldiers, fled in different directions. Gildo himself,
seizing a ship, attempted to escape and, after he had been
driven out to sea and then was forced back to Africa, perished
some days later by strangulation. In telling such great miracles,
we would run the risk, as it were, of presuming to lie impudently, did not the testimony of those who were present
anticipate our words thus far. No plots were concocted; there
was no corruption; seventy thousand of the enemy were overcome almost without a battle; he who was conquered fled
temporarily, lest the victor in his rage dare more; Gildo was
carried away to a different place, that his brother might not
know that he was killed, by whose killing he was avenged.
The same Mascezel, indeed, elated by the insolence that comes
from success and neglecting the companionship of the holy
men, with whom formerly by fighting for God he had been
victorious, even had the boldness to desecrate a church and

did not hesitate to drag certain men from it. Punishment followed him who committed the sacrilege. For while the same ones survived and exulted, whom he had dragged from the church for punishment, after some time, he himself alone was punished and in himself alone he proved that divine judgment ever keeps watch for a twofold purpose, since when he placed his hope in it, he was assisted, and when he contemned it, he was killed.

(37) Meanwhile, when the care of his children and the management of his two courts had been entrusted by the emperor, Theodosius the Elder, in the hands of very powerful individuals, that is, Rufinus over the palace of the East, and Stilicho over the power in the West, what each one did, or what he tried to do, the result in each case has shown, since the one, seeking royal dignity for himself, and the other, for his son, in order that in a sudden unheaval of events the necessity of the state might cover his criminal ambition, brought in the barbarian tribes and the other favored it. I keep silent about King Alaric and the Goths who were often defeated, often surrounded, and always released. I keep silent about those unfortunate affairs at Pollentia, when the highest command in the war was committed to a barbarian and pagan general, that is, Saul, because of whose wickedness the most solemn days and holy Eastertide were profaned and the enemy, who were withdrawing on account of religious scruples, were forced to fight, for indeed, as the judgment of God showed the power of His favor and the demands of His vengeance, we[120] conquered in fighting and in conquering we were conquered. I keep silent about the frequent internecine struggles between the barbarians themselves, when two divisions of the Goths, and then the Alans and Huns, devastated one another in various massacres. Radagaisus, the most savage by far of all former and present enemies, in a sudden attack spread over all Italy. For it is said that among his people there were more than two hundred thousand Goths. This man, in addition to

---

120 i.e., the Romans.

this incredible number of followers and his indomitable courage, was a pagan and a Scythian, who, as is customary with such barbarian peoples, had vowed to offer to his gods the blood of the entire Roman race. Therefore, when this man threatened the defenses of Rome, all the pagans in the City rushed together, saying that the enemy was powerful, not only, indeed, because of the size of his forces, but especially because of the assistance of the gods; moreover, that on this account the City was forsaken and would soon perish since it had abandoned the gods and the sacred rites. Everywhere there was much complaining, and immediately there arose discussions about renewing and celebrating the sacrifices; blasphemies raged in the whole City; the name of Christ was publicly weighed down with reproaches as if a curse upon the times. And so by the ineffable judgment of God, it happened that—since in a mixed population the pious are due grace and the impious punishment, and the enemy should be permitted to chastise the entirely stubborn and refractory City with scourges severer than usual, yet not be permitted to destroy all indiscriminately in unrestrained slaughter—at that time two peoples of the Goths, with two of their very powerful kings, ran wild through the Roman provinces. One of these kings was a Christian and more like a Roman, and, as the fact has shown, a man, through fear of God, restrained in slaughter; the other, a pagan, barbarian, and truly a Scythian, who loved not glory or booty so much as in his insatiable cruelty he loved slaughter for its own sake, and this man, already received in the bosom of Italy, from nearby was causing Rome to shake and tremble with fear. Thus, if the power of vengeance were permitted this man, whom the Romans thought should be feared especially on this account, because he invited the favor of the gods by the offering of sacrifices, more unrestrained slaughter would have burst forth without the benefit of a reform and the last error would have grown to be worse than the first, for if the pagans had fallen into the hands of a pagan and an idolater, not only would the remaining pagans undoubtedly

have been persuaded to restore the worship of idols, but the
Christians also would have been dangerously confused, since
the latter would be terrified by the warning and the former
encouraged by the precedents. Therefore, God, the just
steward of the human race, wished that the pagan enemy
perish and permitted the Christian enemy to prevail, in order
that the pagan and blaspheming Romans might be thrown
into confusion by the ruination of the one and punished by
the admission of the other, especially since the continence of
the emperor, Honorius, so remarkable in a king, and his most
holy faith merited divine mercy in no small measure. Indeed,
against that most cruel enemy, Radagaisus, it was granted that
the minds of other enemies with their forces be inclined to
give us aid. Uldin and Sarus, leaders of the Huns and of the
Goths, were on hand to aid the Romans; but God did not
allow the fact of His power to seem to be the valor of men,
and especially of the enemy. He forced Radagaisus, struck
with divine terror, into the mountains of Fiesole, and, according to those who set the number as low as possible, he encircled his two hundred thousand men without leadership and
food on a rough and dry mountain ridge with fear pressing
upon them from all sides, and the battle lines, to which a
little while before Italy seemed confining, he crowded upon
one small peak in the hope of finding a place to hide. Why
should I delay with many words? No army was drawn up for
battle; no fury and no fear presented the uncertainties of
battle; no slaughter was done; no blood was shed; and finally,
that which is usually considered ground for felicitation, the
losses of battle were compensated by a victorious outcome.
While our men were eating, drinking, and carousing, the
enemy, so numerous and so cruel, were weakened by hunger,
thirst, and exhaustion. This was of little consequence, if the
Romans did not know that he was captured and overcome
whom the Romans feared, and if they did not perceive that
idolater, whose sacrifices they feared more than his weapons,
overcome without a battle, and if they did not despise him

bound under the yoke and in chains. Therefore, King Radagaisus by himself, taking hope for escape, secretly deserted
his men and fell among our men, by whom he was captured,
held for a little while, and killed. Moreover, so great a number
of Gothic captives is said to have been made that, in the
manner of the cheapest cattle, they were sold in droves at
random for an *aureus* apiece. But God did not allow anything
to survive of this people, for immediately, when all who were
bought died, what their wicked buyers disgracefully did not
spend in buying, they mercifully spent for their burial. Therefore, ungrateful Rome, who, just as she now felt the indirect
mercy of God, not that her audacious idolatry be pardoned,
but that it might be checked, was soon, on account of the
pious remembrance of the saints, both living and dead, about
to suffer the wrath of God, but not in full. If by chance in
her confusion she should repent and through experience learn
faith, she was spared for a short space of time from the attack
of Alaric, a hostile king but a Christian.

(38) Meanwhile, Count Stilicho, sprung from the Vandals,
an unwarlike, greedy, treacherous, and crafty race, thinking it
of little consequence that he ruled under the emperor, struggled
in every way, as it is generally reported, to place in power
his son, Eucherius, who, already from boyhood and in private
life, had been planning the persecution of Christians. Therefore, when Alaric and the entire Gothic nation begged for
peace and suppliantly and simply for some place in which to
settle, supporting them by a secret treaty but publicly denying
them an opportunity of making either war or peace, he reserved them to wear down and terrify the state. Furthermore,
other nations, irresistible by reasons of numbers and strength,
by which now the provinces of the Gauls and the Spains were
being pressed, that is, the Alans, Suebi, and Vandals, as well
as the Burgundians driven by the same movement, were urged
to take up arms of their own accord, and, when once the fear
of the Roman name was removed, were stirred up. Meanwhile,
Stilicho wished to batter the banks of the Rhine and to strike

against the Gauls, hoping, in his wretchedness in this dangerous situation, that he could snatch the power away from his
son-in-law for his son, and that the barbarian peoples could be
as easily checked as they were aroused. And so, when this
character of such great crimes was made clear to the emperor,
Honorius, and to the Roman army, the army was very justly
aroused and killed Stilicho, who, that he might clothe one
boy with the purple, gave the blood of the entire human race;
Eucherius was killed, who, to win the favor of the pagans,
threatened to mark the beginnings of his reign by restoring
the pagan temples by overthrowing the churches; and a few
accomplices were also punished for their enormous plots. Thus,
with very little difficulty and with the punishment of a few,
the churches of Christ, together with the religious emperor,
were both freed and avenged. So, after such a great increase
in blasphemies as this and no repentance, that final and long-
impending punishment reached the City.

(39) Alaric was on hand, and he besieged, confused, and
broke into fearful Rome, but after having first given the order
that if any should take refuge in the holy places, especially in
the basilicas of the holy Apostles Peter and Paul, they should
permit these, in particular, although they were eager for
plunder, to remain unharmed and unmolested and then, insofar as they could, should refrain from shedding blood. It
happened also, by which it might be proven that the storming
of the City took place because of the wrath of God rather than
because of the bravery of the enemy, that the blessed Innocent, the bishop of the City of Rome, even as the just Lot
was withdrawn from Sodom, was, by the hidden providence
of God, at Ravenna at that time and did not see the destruction of the sinful people. While the barbarians were rushing
hither and thither through the City, one of the Goths, a powerful person and a Christian, by chance found in a church
building a virgin, advanced in years, dedicated to God, and
when he asked her respectfully for gold and silver, she, with
faithful firmness, replied that she had a great deal in her

possession and would presently bring it forth, and she did so,
and when she perceived that the barbarian was astonished
by the riches which were displayed, by the quantity, weight,
and beauty, although he did not know their nature, the virgin
of Christ said to the barbarian: 'These are the sacred vessels
of the Apostle Peter. Presume, if you dare; you will answer
for the deed. For my part, since I cannot protect them, I dare
not hold them.' Now the barbarian, stirred to religious awe
by the fear of God and by the faith of the virgin, reported
these matters by messenger to Alaric, who immediately ordered
that all the vessels, just as they were, be brought back to the
basilica of the Apostle, and that the virgin also, and with her
all Christians who might join her, be brought to the same
place under escort. This building, as they say, was far from
the sacred places and with half the City in between. And so,
to the great wonder of all, the gold and silver vessels, distributed one to each individual and raised above their heads,
were carried openly; the pious procession was guarded on all
sides for their protection by drawn swords; a hymn to God
was sung publicly with Romans and barbarians joining in;
in the sacking of the City, the trumpet of salvation sounded
far and wide, and invited and struck all, even those lying in
hidden places; from all sides they came together to the vessels
of Peter, the vessels of Christ; a great many, even pagans,
mingled with the Christians in profession, although not in
faith; and in this way they escaped temporarily that they
might become more confused; the more thickly the Romans
in their flight came together, the more eagerly the barbarians
surrounded them as their defenders. O sacred and ineffable
discernment of divine judgment! O that holy and saving river,
which, rising at a small house, while it flows in its blessed
channel to the seats of the saints, brings wandering and endangered souls to the bosom of salvation by its pious capacity!
O that glorious trumpet of Christian warfare, which, inviting
all in general to life by its very sweet tone, leaves those whom
it has not stirred up in their disobedience to salvation, for

death without an excuse! This mystery, which consisted in the transferring of vessels, in the singing of hymns, and in the escorting of the people, was, I think, like a large sieve, through which from the congregation of the Roman people, as from a great mass of grain, through all the openings of the hiding places from the entire circuit of the City, the living grain flowed forth, moved either by the occasion or by truth; but all who believed in the present salvation were received from the granary of the Lord's preparation, but the others, like dung and straw, already judged for their very unbelief and disobedience, were left for extinction and burning. Who can ponder these things with complete wonder? Who can proclaim them with worthy praise?

On the third day after the barbarians had entered the City, they departed of their own accord, after burning a number of the buildings, to be sure, but not so many, indeed, as an accident had caused in the seven hundredth year after the founding of the City. For if I review the conflagration exhibited among the spectacles of her own emperor, Nero, without a doubt this fire, which the anger of the conqueror brought on, would never bear comparison with that which was enkindled by the wantonness of the prince. Nor do I need, moreover, to recall the Gauls in a comparison of this kind, who directly, over a period of almost a year, held possession of the exhausted ashes of the burned and conquered City. And lest anyone perchance doubt that this was permitted the enemy for the chastisement of the proud, wanton, and blasphemous City, at the same time, the most famous sites of the City were destroyed by lightning, sites which could not be set on fire by the enemy.

(40) Thus, in the one thousand one hundred and sixty-fourth year after the founding of the City, an attack was made upon the City by Alaric; although the memory of this event is fresh, nevertheless, if anyone sees the multitude of the Roman people themselves and hears their talk, he will think that nothing took place, as even they themselves confess, unless by chance he is informed by the ruins of the fire still

remaining. In this attack, Placidia, the daughter of the princely Theodosius and sister of the emperors, Arcadius and Honorius, was captured and taken to wife by Athaulfus, a kinsman of Alaric's, as if, by divine decree, Rome had given her as a hostage and special pledge; thus, by her marriage with this most powerful barbarian king, she was of great benefit to the state.

Meanwhile, two years before the attack on Rome, the nations which, as I have said, were stirred up by Stilicho, that is, the Alans, Suebi, Vandals, and many others with these, overwhelmed the Franks, crossed the Rhine, and invaded Gaul, and with a forward rush reached as far as the Pyrenees, by the interjection of which they were temporarily repulsed and were poured back over the surrounding provinces. While these were running wild over the Gauls, in Britain, Gratian, a citizen of this island, was made a usurper and was killed. In his place, Constantine,[121] a man of the lowest military rank, on account of the hope alone which came from his name and without any merit for courage, was elected. He, as soon as he had entered upon his office, crossed over into the Gallic provinces. There, tricked again and again by the unreliable treaties of the barbarians, he was very harmful to the state. He sent magistrates into the Spains and, when the provinces received them obediently, two brothers, young, noble, and wealthy, Didymus and Verinianus, tried not only to seize the power of the usurper against the usurper, but to protect themselves and their country for the just emperor against the usurper and the barbarians. This was clear from the very order of events. For no one seizes unlawful power unless, after swiftly maturing his plans, he attacks secretly and publicly arms it, and his success rests on his being seen with the diadem and purple in his possession before he is found out. However, these men, spending a very long time merely in gathering their slaves from their own estates and supporting them out of their private incomes, and in no wise concealing their purpose, proceeded to the passes of the Pyrenees without disturbing anyone.

121 Constantine III, 407 to September, 411.

Against these, Constantine sent into the Spanish provinces his son, Constans, who, sad to say, had from a monk been made a Caesar, and, together with him, certain barbarians who, having once been received as allies and drawn into military service, were called *Honoriaci*. The first stroke of misfortune in the Spanish provinces came from these. For, after the brothers had been killed, who with their private forces were trying to protect the Pyrenaean Alps, these barbarians, as a reward for their victory, were given permission, first, to plunder in the plains of Pallantia; then, after the faithful and effective peasant guard had been removed, they were entrusted with the care of the mountains mentioned above and their passes. Therefore, the *Honoriaci*, being imbued with plunder and attracted by its abundance, in order that their crimes might be the more unpunished and that there might be greater freedom for their crimes, after betraying their watch over the Pyrenees and leaving the passes open, let into the Spanish provinces all the nations which were wandering over the Gauls and they themselves joined them. After they had engaged for some time in extensive and bloody raids and after grave devastation of property and people, regarding which they themselves are in no way repentant, dividing their holdings by drawing lots, they settled down in the possessions which they hold to this day.

(41) There would be a great opportunity now for me to speak about such things, did not, according to all men, in the mind of each and everyone a secret conscience speak. The Spains have been invaded; slaughters and devastations have been endured; indeed, it is nothing new, for during those two years when the sword of the enemy raged, they endured from the barbarians what for two hundred years they had once suffered at the hands of the Romans, what also under Gallienus, the emperor, they had experienced for almost twelve years when the Germans ravaged them. Yet who does not confess, if he knows himself, his acts, or even his thoughts, and fears the judgments of God, that he has endured all justly or

even sustained little? Since these things are so, nevertheless, the mercy of God, with the same compassion with which He had long ago made the prediction, brought it about that, according to His Gospel in which He constantly gave the warning: 'When they shall persecute in one city, flee into another,' whoever wished to go out and to depart, should enjoy the barbarians themselves as mercenaries, helpers, and defenders. At that time, they themselves offered this of their own accord; and they, who after killing everybody could have carried off everything, demanded a very small fee as a reward for their services and for the transportation of burdens. And this, indeed, was done by a great many. But those who were stubborn and did not believe in God's Gospel, or who were doubly stubborn if they had not even listened to it, and did not give way to God's wrath, were justly caught and overwhelmed by God's exceeding anger. And yet, soon after this, also the barbarians, detesting their swords, turned to their ploughs and now cherish the Romans as comrades and friends, so that now there may be found among them certain Romans who prefer poverty with freedom among the barbarians than paying tribute with anxiety among the Romans. And yet, if the barbarians had been admitted into the territory of the Romans for this reason alone, because, in general, throughout the East and the West the churches of Christ were replete with Huns, Suebi, Vandals, and Burgundians, and with innumerable and different peoples of believers, the mercy of God would seem to be worthy of praise and to be extolled, since, even if with our own weakening, so many peoples would be receiving a knowledge of the truth which, surely, they could never have discovered except with this opportunity. For what loss is it to the Christian who is eager for eternal life to be taken away from this world at any time and by whatever means? Moreover, what gain is it to the pagan in the midst of Christians, obdurate against the faith, if he protracts his day a little longer, since he, whose conversion is despaired of, is destined to die?

And since the judgments of God are ineffable, all of which we cannot know nor can we explain those which we do know, I shall explain briefly that those who know justly sustain the reproach of God our Judge, in whatever way it may take place, and those who do not know also justly sustain it.

(42) In the one thousand one hundred and sixty-fifth year after the founding of the City, the emperor, Honorius, seeing that nothing could be accomplished against the barbarians with so many usurpers opposed to him, ordered that the usurpers themselves be destroyed first. To Constantius, the Count, was entrusted the highest command in this war. The state, then, at last realized what advantage it received in finally having a Roman general and to what extent it had endured destruction over the long periods of subjection to the barbarian counts. So the Count Constantius proceeded with his army into Gaul and, at the city of Arles, besieged, captured, and killed the emperor, Constantine.

From this point on, to mention the succession of usurpers as briefly as possible, Constans, the son of Constantine, was killed at Vienne by his count, Gerontius, a worthless rather than a good man, and in his place was established a certain Maximus. But Gerontius himself was killed by his own soldiers. Maximus, divested of the purple and deserted by the soldiers of Gaul, who were transferred to Africa and then re-called to Italy, is now a needy exile among the barbarians in Spain. Later Jovinus, a man of very high rank in Gaul, fell as soon as he attained the place of a usurper. Sebastian, his brother, chose this alone, to die as a usurper for, as soon as he was elected, he was slain. What shall I say about the most unfortunate Attalus, to whom it was an honor to be slain among usurpers, and a gain to die? Alaric, who made, unmade, remade, and again unmade[122] his emperor, doing all this almost more quickly than it takes to tell it, laughed at the farce and viewed the comedy of the imperium. Nor is it to

---

122 The Latin reads: *facto, infecto, refecto, ac defecto.*

be wondered at that this wretched man was rightly ridiculed
for this pomp, when his shadowy consul, Tertullus, dared to
say in the Senate House: 'I shall speak to you, conscript fathers,
as consul and pontifex, of which offices I hold one and hope
for the other,' seeking hope from him who had no hope, and
surely accursed because he had placed his hope in man. So
Attalus, as it were, an empty figure of the imperium, was
taken with the Goths into the Spains, whence, departing in a
ship of uncertain destination, he was captured at sea, brought
to Count Constantius, and then displayed to the emperor,
Honorius. Although his hand was cut off, he was allowed to
live. Meanwhile, Heraclian, who had been made count of
Africa when the same Attalus[123] was carrying on his shadow
of a rule and who defended Africa strenuously against the
magistrates sent by him, obtained the consulship. Elated with
pride at this, he chose as his son-in-law, Sabinus, his chamber-
lain, a man keen of mind and full of enterprise, and one
worthy of being called wise if he had devoted the powers of
his mind to quiet studies. Heraclian supported him when he
exhibited certain dangerous suspicions, and Heraclian himself,
after holding up the African supply of grain for some time
contrary to law, finally hastened to Rome with a tremendous
fleet, quite incredible, indeed, in our times. For he is said to
have had at that time three thousand seven hundred ships,
a number which the histories tell us not even Xerxes, that
famous king of the Persians, or Alexander the Great or any
other king had. As soon as he disembarked on the shore with
his army of soldiers, on his way to the City, terrified in an
encounter with Count Marinus and turned into flight, seizing
a ship, he returned alone to Carthage and there he was immediately killed by a band of soldiers. Sabinus, his son-in-law,
fled to Constantinople, whence some time later he was brought
back and condemned to exile.

Honorius, the emperor, as I have said, was worthy of the
victory over this entire series of manifest usurpers or dis-

---

123 Priscus Attalus, 409-415.

obedient generals because of his high religious feeling and success; Count Constantius overcame them by industry and quickness. I say 'was worthy,' indeed, because in those days, on the order of Honorius and with the aid of Constantius, peace and unity were restored to the Catholic Church throughout all Africa, and the Body of Christ, which we are, was made whole by the closing of the schism, the execution of the blessed command being entrusted to the tribune, Marcellinus, a man especially prudent and industrious, and a most eager follower of all good studies. Count Marinus, stimulated by jealousy or corrupted by gold, killed him at Carthage. He, being immediately recalled from Africa and made a private citizen, was dismissed for punishment or to the penitence of his own conscience.

(43) In the one thousand one hundred and sixty-eighth year after the founding of the City, Count Constantius, while he was at Arles, a city in Gaul, by his vigorous action in carrying out things, drove the Goths out of Narbonne and forced them to depart into Spain, especially by forbidding and cutting off all passage of ships and the importation of foreign merchandise. At that time, King Athaulf ruled the Gothic peoples; he, after the invasion of the City and the death of Alaric, took Placidia, the captive sister of the emperor, as I have said, to wife and succeeded Alaric on the throne. He, as it has often been said and has been proven finally by his death, a very zealous seeker after peace, preferred to fight faithfully for the emperor, Honorius, and to employ the Gothic forces to defend the Roman state. For I myself also heard a man of Narbo, of renowned military service under Theodosius, also religious, prudent, and serious, relating at Bethlehem, a town in Palestine, to the most blessed priest, Jerome, that he was a very close friend of Athaulf at Narbo, and that he often learned from him under oath what he was accustomed to say when he was in good spirits, health, and temper: that he, at first, was ardently eager to blot out the Roman name and to make the entire Roman Empire that of the Goths alone, and

to call it and to make it, to use a popular expression, *Gothia* instead of *Romania,* and that he, Athaulf, become what Caesar Augustus had once been. When, however, he discovered from long experience that the Goths, by reason of their unbridled barbarism, could not by any means obey laws, nor should the laws of the state be abrogated without which the state is not a state, he chose to seek for himself the glory of completely restoring and increasing the Roman name by the forces of the Goths, and to be held by posterity as the author of the restoration of Rome, since he had been unable to be its transformer. For this reason, he strove to refrain from war; for this reason, to be eager for peace, being influenced in all the works of good government, especially by the persuasion and advice of his wife, Placidia, a woman, indeed, of a very keen mind and very good religiously. While he was very zealously occupied in seeking and offering this very peace, he was killed in the city of Barcelona in Spain by the treachery, as it is said, of his own men.

After him, Segeric was declared king by the Goths and, although he, too, was inclined toward peace by the judgment of God, nevertheless, was killed by his own men.

Then, Wallia succeeded to the throne, having been chosen by the Goths to break the peace; having been ordained by God for this purpose, to establish the peace. This man, then—being greatly terrified by the judgment of God, because when in the year before a large band of Goths equipped with arms and ships tried to cross into Africa, being caught in a storm within twelve miles of the Strait of Gades, they had perished in a miserable death; mindful also of that disaster under Alaric when, as the Goths tried to cross into Sicily, they were wretchedly shipwrecked in the sight of their own and drowned —arranged a very favorable peace with the emperor, Honorius, giving hostages of the higgest rank; he returned Placidia, whom he had held in the highest honor and respect while with him, to her brother; and for the security of Rome, he faced danger to himself by fighting against the other tribes that had settled throughout the Spains and conquered them for the Romans. However, the other kings of the Alans, the Vandals, and the Suebi had made the same kind of an agreement with us, sending the following message to the emperor, Honorius: 'Be at peace with us all, and receive hostages of all; we are in conflict with one another; we perish to the loss of one another; we conquer for you, but with immortal gain for your state, if we should both perish.' Who would have believed these things had not the facts proven them? Thus, we now learn daily, by frequent and trustworthy messages, that in the the Spains wars are being carried on among the barbarian tribes and that slaughter is taking place on both sides; and they say, especially, that Wallia, the king of the Goths, is intent on concluding a peace. As a result of this, I would, in any way whatever, permit Christian times to be blamed freely, if, from the founding of the world to the present, any equally fortunate period can be pointed out. We have made manifest, I think, and are showing almost no more by words than by my finger the countless wars which have been stilled, the many usurpers who have been destroyed, and the very savage peoples who have been checked, confined, incorporated, and annihilated with a minimum loss of blood, no struggle, and almost without any slaughter. It is left now for our detractors to repent of their deeds and to blush at the truth, and to believe, fear, love, and follow the only true God who is all powerful, all of whose deeds they have learned to be good, even those which they think are evil.

I have set forth, with Christ's help, according to your bidding, most blessed father Augustine, the desires and punishments of sinful men, the struggles of the world and the judgments of God, from the beginning of the world down to the present day, that is, during five thousand six hundred and eighteen years, as briefly and as simply as I could, but separating Christian times, because of the greater presence of Christ's grace, from the former confusion of unbelief. So now I enjoy the certain and only reward of my obedience, which

I ought to have desired; but as for the quality of my books, you who bade me write them shall see; if you publish them, they shall be approved by you; if you destroy them, they shall be condemned by you.

INDICES

GENERAL INDEX

(This index is confined mainly to names and events.)

Fidenae, 64, 291; Fidenates, 49, 64

Fiesole Mountains, 351

Fimbria, C. Flavius, 216, 234, 235

fire: consumed Rome, 258; from heaven, 76; hail mixed with, 30; of judgment, 328; outbreaks of, 4; serious devastation by, 144

Firmius, legate of Augustus, 277

Firmus, 338

Flacci, two, 195

Flaccus, *see* Fulvius, Valerius

flagitiis, 4 n.

flamines, 211

Flamininus, *see* Quintius

Flaminius, consul (223 B.C.), 148, 151

Flaminius, praetor, 164

Flamma, *see* Calpurnius

Flavians, 301

Flavius, leader of Roman Party, 154 n.

flood (s), 4, 21, 25, 28

Florian, 319, 327

Florus, xx, 179 n.

Formiae, city, 127

Fortunatae, 8

Fortune, temple of, 62 n.

Forum: Carthage, 133; Holitorium, 206; Rome, 48, 76, 126, 127, 144, 206, 212, 215, 216, 218, 258, 265, 297, 301, 310

Franks, 321, 337, 344, 356

Fraortes, 39

Fraucus, general of Marsi, 210

Freising, Otto of, xx

frogs in Egypt, 326

Fucinus, Lake, 210

fugitives, 173, 190

Fulvia, wife of M. Antony and mother-in-law of Caesar, 269

Fulvius, proconsul, 155, 157

Fulvius Centumalus, Cn., consul (229 B.C.), 147; (211 B.C.), 155

Fulvius Flaccus, Cn., praetor, 154

Fulvius Flaccus, M., consul (125 B.C.), 192, 194, 195

Fulvius Flaccus, M., consul (264 B.C.), 135 n.

Fulvius, M., praetor, 163, 164

Fulvius Flaccus, Q., consul (224 B.C.), 148; praetor, Hither Spain, 166; proconsul, 157

Fulvius Flaccus, Ser., consul (135 B.C.), 185; (133 B.C.), 190

Fulvius Nobilior, M., consul (189 B.C.), 164

Fulvius Nobilior, Ser., consul (255 B.C.), 139

Furius, tribune, 206, 207

Furius Camillus Scribonianus, governor of Dalmatia, 295, 300

Furius Pacilus, C., consul (251 B.C.), 141

Furius Purpurio, L. (not Fulvius), praetor, 162; consul (196 B.C.), 163

Furmius, legate, 277

Furnius, general of Antony, 271

INDEX OF HOLY SCRIPTURE

(References to scripture are indicated, first, by the passage in question and, second, by the book and chapter in which they occur.)

THE FATHERS OF THE CHURCH SERIES

(A series of approximately 100 volumes when completed)

418